Rock Gardens
Through the Year

Karl Foerster
Edited by Kenneth A. Beckett

Macdonald Orbis

The author Prof. Dr. h. c. Karl Foerster died in November 1970
Seventh edition revised by Bernhard Röllich

A Macdonald Orbis Book

© 1981 Neumann Verlag, Leipzig · Radebeul

© 1987 English translation Macdonald & Co (Publishers) Ltd

First published in Great Britain in 1987
by Macdonald & Co (Publishers) Ltd
London & Sydney

A member of BPCC plc

British Library Cataloguing in Publication Data

Foerster, Karl
    Rock gardens through the year.
    1. Rock plants
    I. Title
    635.9'672 SB 459

    ISBN 0-356-14442-9

Printed in the German Democratic Republic

Macdonald & Co (Publishers) Ltd
Greater London House
Hampstead Road
London NW1 7 QX

Contents

Introduction

This latest edition of my gardening and plant book has been made more attractive by the addition of a large number of colour and black and white illustrations and also more comprehensive by the inclusion of a great many new plants and descriptions in the text and lists. Less familiar plants are now included, amongst them many "long-players".

Once again the re-editing has been made possible by the untiring and never-failing support of my wife, who has played an important part in the successful outcome of my work.

One of the reasons books are written is that one has an urge to communicate with a wider audience than that provided by social interchange or a live audience. Books answer that deep need to find a response, to share in the desires and achievements of one's fellow gardeners and to make a contribution to the pleasure they derive from gardening.

More important, however, is the desire to do a good job, in small things as in large, and to receive critical acclaim.

This book deals not only with rock-garden perennials but also includes smaller bulbs and corms which are long-lasting and hardy. Some grasses are also included together with dwarf ferns and finally a wide range of miniature shrubs. Someone planning to plant a rock garden with small annuals and bedding plants will need to look elsewhere.

This book is not limited entirely to rock gardens, but sees them rather as an important aspect of the whole art of the country garden, the delightful counterpart to the formal garden. As well as on the rock garden itself, there are areas around larger rocks and shrubs where the rocks merge into the surrounding garden which call for many of the taller wild plants. Many of these are in fact plants native to the "mountain meadow" and will often be found in the wild, adjacent to rocky slopes.

Nor is it possible to omit the realm of water-side and water-plants, for both types are usually planted among or near rocks.

I have set myself an enormous, one might say an impossible, task even within the limits imposed by a book of this kind. It is intended as a practical handbook, a purpose which I hope it will fulfil. I feel that a book devoted to small perennials and closely related dwarf and wild plants is especially relevant today, as there are an increasing number of smaller gardens to be stocked and replenished in a way which will bring lasting pleasure.

Great emphasis is placed on the native habitats of each plant, in what localities and amongst which plants they grow naturally, for it is only by knowing the properties which a plant derives from its native soil that we can appreciate its future requirements.

In describing the plants with which, in their habitats, they grow in close proximity, I have restricted myself to those which are relevant to our gardens. No garden plant should ever be left in isolation without other plants around it. The fascinating contrasts and similarities which plants exhibit can be used repeatedly to great effect.

For the most part I have chosen not to rely on a totally alphabetical listing but have preferred to arrange plants in groups which flower at similar times of the year, an approach which I hope will prove more useful to the amateur gardener. This is one aspect that other books on rock gardens have neglected in favour of other aspects which lie beyond the scope of this present work. Thus, anyone who wants to know all there is to know about rock gardens would be well advised to consult other books in addition to this one. In some cases plants are arranged by size to distinguish between larger and dwarf varieties.

In my lists I have attempted to provide anyone planning a rock garden with new ideas and to offer advice based on years of experience with plants—how long, for example, would it take to discover from personal experience which small perennials continue to produce strong and lasting flowers well beyond the first appearance of their blossoms. Yet this important property of the best garden plants is often overlooked. There are a surprising number of plants to be seen in almost every garden which are really hardly worth growing, especially where space is limited, mainly because their period of attractiveness is so very short. Some indeed, are invasive and are capable of swamping a small rock garden. Perhaps the best—or worst—example is the ubiquitous snow in summer, *Cerastium tomentosum*. *Campanula rapunculoides*, the creeping bell flower, is another attractive scourge, and the small cypress spurge *Euphorbia cyparissias* knows no bounds in a light soil.

Why cover large areas of the garden with these less worthy plants when there are so many which can bring interest and beauty?

Not only do these small, delicate-looking perennial plants, which take up so little of the garden, draw closer the far-flung corners of the world; with the changing of the seasons they help change our concept of time. These small plants are more than "representatives" of their various homelands, for they also give us a new awareness of the vast, incomprehensible time spans in which our lives are played out. Here we find time spans both short and long—days, weeks, years—blossoming with unforeseen experiences. Time spans which have been unnaturally compressed are unfolded, exposed to the light. A year contains a host of separate moments and who knows it better than the gardener!

Many beginners find the Latin names which belong to all plants difficult to remember and see little point in their use. They are, however, completely international and allow us to enjoy browsing through nursery catalogues in any language which uses our letters. Also they have a meaning, commemorating famous plant collectors, not only easily remembered English ones, such as *Rhododendron forrestii* after George Forrest, but also many from Europe and Russia—Pylzow, for example, for whom *Geranium pylzovianum* was named. With such names everyone can remember great botanists and explorers from the past. What gardener should ever forget those intrepid explorers of the American Middle West, Lewis and Clark, in whose honour we have *Lewisia* and *Clarkia*. The many place-names too help to put the plants in their homes. Who does not grow something named *chinensis*, *nipponica* (Nippon = Japan) or *carpatica* (from the Carpathians). *Plena* of course means double, *nana*, small and so on; in fact a study of plant names opens a whole field of interest. How, after all, could a plant from high in Tibet be expected to have an English "common name"?

Now a few general comments about planting times, of which more can be found in the section "Planting Times and Methods for Various Rock-garden Plants". The uncertainty of beginners, and often of experienced gardeners, over planting times is one of the reasons why some gardeners rarely try anything new.

The chances of success are about the same regardless of whether one plants in autumn or spring, although one has a slightly greater chance of success by planting early in autumn, rather than late in spring. The exceptions to this are the bulbs and corms which should be planted between the beginning of August and November.

Many gardeners can't be bothered with putting in new plants in late summer and autumn. They forget how many years and how many autumns a single plant can last and blossom and how many times these plants will give them pleasure the following spring. If one fails to take advantage of the long peaceful autumn months as a suitable time for planting, one is likely to panic in the spring over whether it is now too late for planting, whether the plants are now too large, whether one can still plant roses or gentians in late April, etc.

Such concerns are not justified at all over the dwarf plants included in this book, but fortunately the horticultural trade takes human weakness into account and tends to increase stocks of rockery plants in containers, since they can tolerate this much better than many other bedding plants. If one uses well prepared potted plants one can now plant for the rock-garden at almost any time of the year, though times of summer drought are still best avoided.

Potsdam-Bornim   Karl Foerster
Summer 1962

The History
of Rock Gardens
and Their Place in
Natural and Architectural
Garden Design

Until a mere two hundred years ago, the great gardening traditions of Europe and of the Orient developed in their own ways without any contact. In the West the style of the flower gardens was mainly a formal one with paths, beds and steps laid out with mathematical precision. The fact that the garden designers were frequently also the architects of the houses and palaces they were intended to complement meant that gardens were often treated as outdoor extensions of the house design. These great formal gardens and landscapes persisted longest in mainland Europe, particularly in France, where a number of gardens laid out at the end of the seventeenth century by le Nôtre still survive.

In the East, in China and Japan, plants also played a very secondary role in garden design, the rocks themselves, their lay-out and positioning being fundamental. To European eyes, their placing, though far from being haphazard, was much more naturalistic. The aim, however, was to create a satisfying composition without necessarily adding any plants.

In the early eighteenth century the concept of the picturesque landscape was developed in England. This was based upon what were thought to be the perfect landscapes of classical times and it was this return to informality which, coupled with a growing knowledge of the naturalistic styles of the Far East, led to the development of rock gardens.

The nineteenth century saw an enormous influx of plants from all corners of the world and for a while all thoughts of style and informality seemed lost under a brilliant array of bedding plants and the use of colour for its own sake.

With this century came the marriage of all the earlier styles to give us the richness of garden design with which we are familiar today.

We are learning how the formality of the geometric house-garden can be made more picturesque with the addition of new plants, both cultivated and wild, within a setting of formal stone-terraces and walls, pools, canals or lakes. Other areas of the same garden will be given over to the natural style, often strikingly highlighted by the introduction of foreign flowers which share the delicate beauty of the wild flower and harmonize with the local flora.

What role do rocks play in the garden? What task is performed by the huge numbers of perennials, of mainly dwarf form, that we know as rock-garden plants?

Most natural rocks have the sculptural and artistic beauty, sometimes even the grandeur, of the rocky mountain landscape and form a wonderful backdrop for the flowers of the rock garden.

The role of stone in the garden is and will remain an incredibly rich one. Stone offers a framework for the best in garden design, a practical means, while enhancing the plants themselves, of dealing with variations in height. It can serve both as a solid and attractive pathway beneath our feet and protection from the eroding and softening effects of time.

The crowning glory of stone in the garden lies in the area of statuary, but the fascination of stone is equally present in natural rocks, which achieve their fullest effect within the garden setting, and offer future generations a link with the mysteries of the past.

People are at work everywhere and in every conceivable manner trying to salvage the life of the past from unchanging stone. Why should their garden gates be closed to it? Gardens should increasingly reflect the natural world and seek for new ways to develop and recreate it. Is it not true that nature consists to a large degree of mountains and rocks and that one of nature's dramas is the struggle between plant life and the unyielding stone upon which it grows?

Perhaps it is because of its traditional demand upon stone, an expensive medium in most areas, that rock gardens have failed to achieve universal popularity. Criticism of rockeries on the basis of the unattractiveness of so many designs should be treated in the same way as the suggestion that we should stop building houses in stone because there are so many ugly ones.

It is unthinkable that in the future we will not take advantage of the beautiful effects made possible by stone and its relationship with plants, space and light.

Today, there still exist in China ancient rock gardens, carefully arranged with blocks of stone forming natural towers, and sparsely planted with twisted ancient trees within decorated temple walls. Let us not however talk of imitating the Chinese in the area of garden design, but let us rather appreciate their exploratory work and be receptive to their ideas. This leads us to the surprising treasure house of the traditional Japanese garden. In the gardens of Japan, and of England too if one knows where to look, gardeners unfamiliar with stone and rock will be amazed at the variety of moods and effects which they can achieve.

The English, with their love of travel and of home, their passion for the Alps and the Far East, seem the obvious pioneers of the rock garden in Europe. The island people of Japan, with their beautiful volcanic landscape and coastline, would seem to have been faced with no alternative to the rock garden, through which they could take advantage of vast quantities of volcanic rock and rich plant life.

The art of the Japanese natural garden relies essentially upon rocks, even if only few in number, cleverly arranged to fit in with the existing natural features, such as sinkage from earthquakes or a narrow dried-up stream-bed meandering through ancient moss-covered rocks on which stone urns are placed. Small shrubs grow in lonely isolation, old-established plants which have survived many adversities. A bottomless chasm in time opens up, hieroglyphics can be found on the rocks, the sandy banks of the small stream-bed are covered with moss that is well cared for, even brushed, the sand between the rocks is freshly strewn from time to time; no one walks on it, there are stepping stones for that.

We must follow our own traditions of art and nature in our strivings towards enrichment or perfection while remaining receptive to outside influences. Conversely, we should not simply adopt foreign ways and opinions but adapt them to fit within our own traditions.

Architectural or formal rockwork should stand out in the garden more than natural rock gardens, which should generally form part of a larger natural garden. This is not to say that a smaller garden could not provide space for a fine example in the natural style, but it is certainly not so easy to create within a small, fenced or bounded area.

The natural rock garden should as far as possible form a natural outcrop amongst specially selected shrubs and plants. There are many ways of using stone in the form of paved paths or stepping stones—often a partly buried large rock will be sufficient—to lead into other parts of the garden and to link them with the actual rock garden. But such links are by no means essential. As I have already said, one must rid oneself of the mistaken idea that most alpine plants can only be used to full effect in some kind of rock garden. This misconception causes gardeners a lot of worry, robs them of their courage and stifles their imagination. There is a whole host of small perennials which will be quite at home in a rock-free natural or formal garden. Of course there are a few species which really only look right amongst rocks. I hope these remarks may lead to greater freedom of thought on the subject of rock gardens.

Rock gardens for many years have been developing from their small, timid beginnings. They began with small stalactite gardens where alpine plants were grown in carefully prepared soils and slowly spread beyond the alpines with their short spring flowering time. Today one can speak of a universal art of rock gardening extending throughout the course of the whole year.

Today we use small perennials which grow wild in all parts of the world so that there is scarcely a month of the year when the garden need be empty of blossom. Added to these are the specially cultivated varieties or cultivars.

From woods and mountains, from the edges of fields, from steppes, beaches, heaths, dunes and moors, from nurseries, plantations and botanical gardens come hosts of plants which, over the years, will grow well in our gardens without any trouble and without any time-consuming preparation of the soil. Many of them are only suitable for wild gardens, a good number are more suited to the formal rock or water garden. There are of course others which, correctly planted, will suit both the formal and the natural garden and which for this very reason are extremely popular.

A series of symbols included after each type of plant is intended to guide beginners over the particular requirements of each plant.

With the widely contrasting varieties of rock-garden plant now available there is always the danger of using the wrong plants in combination, but this danger is offset by the pleasure of discovering successful new combinations, of choosing toning or contrasting colour schemes in a variety of different ways to suit the requirements of the plot or the plants themselves. The wide variety of rockery plants also allows the gardener to plan for the changing seasons and to ensure that his rock garden will be a blaze of colour throughout the year.

Several colour regulations apply in the rock garden which do not in the rest of the garden. Here shape and form are more important than in a normal garden which is why I have distinguished between rates of growth for many plant types, dividing them into three groups. It is essential to avoid any part of the rock garden becoming overgrown, particularly if you are including coniferous shrubs. These important aspects of colour and growth rate are fully covered in my lists. Besides space and form, time is an important measuring-stick in the rock garden. Our small rockery plants, firmly rooted within the rhythms of the year, produce beautiful, long-lasting flowers, enabling us to fill our gardens with colour even during those in-between seasons when most gardens are bare of blossom.

In the last few weeks of autumn when the crocuses are still in bud there are many plants just coming into bloom, banishing the old belief that these weeks are times of decline and decay in the garden. Some bulbs will be poking through even in mid-winter. These flowers give us hope once more and rekindle our expectations.

Nowhere else but in the rock garden can such a short space of time and such a small area produce such magically picturesque effects, effects which will continue throughout the seasons. Many plants seem to flourish well with little attention, but things can go wrong. The effect of the rock garden is achieved initially by utilizing vertical space, by positioning your plants carefully on the layered ground to produce gradation of height. Everywhere small plants and rocks should lead the eye to ever larger ones.

A feeling for the needs of plants is built up over many years and plants we have come to love lead us to others. Every corner of the rock garden is full of possibilities. One square foot allows room for two or three plants which will delight us more with each succeeding year.

It has taken me many years to become familiar with the flowering times and individual requirements of the 200 species and forms of perennials and rock plants which are included in my lists; and still the number increases.

Every few years one looks back with astonishment, not only at the developments in and additions to the world of rock-garden plants, but also at one's own deep involvement in these developments. Most other areas of gardening are long established and much celebrated, but the delights of the rock garden are a relatively recent discovery.

The rock garden with its nooks and crannies and elevations brings not only a new depth to the garden where once there was only flatness, but a new dimension to time and to the seasons.

It is difficult to particularize all the benefits which accrue from the rock garden, but in general terms it gives a unique insight into the joy that gardening can provide, and a special element of that joy is experienced by experts and beginners alike through a whole host of miniature plants.

The rock garden is a haven for a multitude of horticultural treasures, small plants whose beauty and, particularly in the case of dwarf shrubs, whose powers of endurance we can only wonder at, for there is an endless variety of alpine plants always ready to carry us to ever greater heights of pleasure.

Countries of Origin of Hardy, Perennial Rock-garden Plants

The maps in the second half of this book showing the distribution of the most common perennials grown in our rock gardens will remove at a stroke the veil of ignorance and prejudice which clouds the vision of many gardeners and nature-lovers who, for the most part, remain blind to the vast number of countries from which our rock-garden plants originate. They have wrongly come to be primarily regarded as "alpine plants, mountain flora which adapt well to the garden situation".

In fact, there is a wide range of plants from the furthest corners and heights of the world's surface, which are able to survive and flourish even in city gardens.

These small plants have made gardening easier and more flexible than ever before for people from all walks of life. Through them we can establish new ties with far-flung corners of the world, with the Kamchatka Peninsula, Tierra del Fuego, Tibet or the shores of Hudson Bay. Montezuma's Aztec kingdom and the "Roof of the World" now provide our everyday world with apparently frail yet remarkably tough plants; countries more often associated with wild beasts of prey provide a wealth of plants which are now finding permanent homes in the small rock gardens of our great industrial cities.

Mediterranean plants, such as the Apennine anemone or the Dalmatian crocus, are now established favourites in our gardens. Few gardeners realize that many of our more familiar plants come from countries far away, while many plants from much nearer home are surprisingly unfamiliar. Many countries go unre-cognized for the contribution they make to our flower gardens throughout the year, for gardeners often fail to realize to what extent they rely on plants of Mediterranean origin.

One is continually amazed by the distances travelled by long-familiar flowers which we have come to regard as uniquely our own. A light pink variety of lily of the valley blooms in Siberia, the purple loosestrife of our local streams is now found naturalized in Australia, buttercups grow in Greenland. Wild marsh irises can be found as far afield as Africa, while foxgloves tower above the surprised traveller in the woods of Scandinavia.

The range of completely new plants from every part of the world which can happily adapt to our gardens seems to be inexhaustible.

How do all these plants reach us? In the twentieth century plant migration is still in its infancy, but those forces which allow plants to travel and migrate are more evident and more effective now than at any time in the past.

Wind, water, animals and vehicles, travellers and explorers, scientists and naturalists, monks and missionaries, collectors of rare or medicinal plants, nurseries, gardeners and seed-handlers, plantations and forestry, botanical gardens, flower-shows and public gardens, gardening books and magazines—all have played an important part; but by no means the least is the individual gardener who passes a plant over the fence to his neighbour.

Equal attention should be given in the garden to native and to foreign plants. We need to establish a sense of relationship with our own native plants while welcoming those beautiful strangers that are capable of surviving and flourishing in our gardens.

The timid and unaware gardener who shrinks from experimenting with glorious foreign plants may tell you that you are mad to try Chinese rock medlars in your garden, yet he does not consider himself mad when every single day he eats foods from the four corners of the world.

It all amounts to the ways in which we use the world-wide plant kingdom in our gardens. Our ultimate aim should be to bring them together in such a way that they create a harmonious and aesthetically pleasing effect.

Suggested Designs and Lay-outs for Rock Gardens

Preparation of site and choice of rocks

Inexpensive ways of obtaining the required quantity of soil

Three of the best but least exploited sources of soil are: soil excavated for the foundations of new buildings, which is normally thrown away rather than being put to use for landscaping purposes; soil excavated for a pool or pond alongside the site of the rockery; and soil removed when laying out sunken paths which, in addition to their many other advantages, produce a surprising amount of earth. I should also mention the soil produced when digging out sunken seating areas enclosed by sloping banks, small terraces or low walls. These form a charming feature of any garden and also produce an astonishing amount of earth. For more on sunken seating areas see page 19.

There are many gardeners who are prejudiced against garden pools, and to them I would suggest digging a hollow as if for a pool and then using it for some other purpose, such as a sunken "valley" or a seating area. Several times I have successfully planted such areas with low-growing field flowers. This gave the impression of a small tract of marshland, although the soil was not at all wet. Only a few stepping stones across the hollow are needed to complete the effect.

Preparing the soil for rock gardens

The preparation of soil for rock gardens is essentially the same as for flower-beds, differing only in that if the soil is very water retentive it should be placed over a layer of gravel, pebbles or rubble to assist drainage. With a light, very dry soil the opposite approach is necessary, with a layer of loam preventing water from draining away too quickly. This need not be friable loam; ordinary loam will serve the same purpose equally well. Heavy soils can be made lighter before planting by adding sand, peat, compost or manure. Light soils will bind better if you add friable loam and old manure, old peat and fairly heavy compost or old root-free pasture soil.

Choice and positioning of rocks

Avoid dull-coloured rocks where at all possible since these can look really miserable, especially in wet weather, whereas bright slabs of stone will give the opposite effect in sunny areas such as seating areas or patios—rather like the choice of a white tablecloth for meals. The most common mistake of all is to choose rocks that are too small; it is far better to use fewer, larger, more impressive rocks, the same being true of dressed slabs of stone.

Any natural stone or rock has its own rules which determine the best position for it in the rock garden, each possessing inbuilt advantages and disadvantages for any individual site. Rocks do not always have to be placed flat, half-covered in soil. You can stand the occasional rock on end and plant around it accordingly, taking care to avoid the danger of an unattractive spiky effect. Rocks placed too low to the ground will soon be overgrown by the plants.

There are two essential guidelines to be kept in mind: rocks at higher elevations should project higher from the soil, while rocks in hollows and crannies should be placed flatter. They should also be grouped in such a way as to avoid any sloping areas of soil. This is done by making terraces of earth supported by rocks or stone walls and incorporating pockets where plants can be positioned to hang down over the wall. The area at the base of the wall is ideal for plants that need extra protection and moisture.

I have often found the evening to be the best time for planning and positioning rocks and earth to the fullest effect.

An extremely useful feature is the inclusion of stepping stones or natural stone steps which allow comfortable access to any part of the rock garden without having to stand on the soil. Alternatively you may prefer a continuous path climbing up through the garden and forking around any steep elevation. On occasions I have used a path of this kind to great effect, with the earth above and below supported with lumps of granite, and paved quite simply with smaller pieces of stone. It only needs a little imagination to create a highly pleasing impression. The pleasure to be obtained from imitating wild natural features on a small scale and from incorporating miniaturized works of man, such as sunken roads or a mountain pass, is so great in itself that in laying out the rocks and earth one tends to overlook the next and finest stage—that of planting. This is a task which reveals to the full our dormant knowledge of stone and moss, mountain and valley, wild plants and natural forms. Proportion is everything and once you have mastered this you have established a wonderful bridge between the small-scale and the large. Few other areas of garden design can bring us so closely in touch with the earth's varying surfaces, and over the years all the different areas of the rock garden develop in their attractiveness as they become more richly covered with vegetation.

When constructing stone walls it is essential from the outset to prevent them being slowly pushed forward with time, either through insufficient distribution of weight at the back or through too shallow foundations below ground level.

When positioning rocks you must also bear in mind the great variations in the microclimate you are creating, remembering that shade is just as important as full sun.

In constructing as many horizontal, water-retaining pockets of earth or terraced beds as possible one must pay equal attention to the banks between them, supporting them as diversely and attractively as possible, since this also seems to please the roots of plants.

Many plants rely for their effect upon the varied and sympathetic placing of rocks in combination with the manifold magical effects of space, light and shadow. Vertical planes can be used to create beauty of quite a new kind, and here we still have much to learn.

To ensure durability and rigidity all terraces and masonry, all cemented or dry-stone walls must be solidly constructed of fairly large pieces or slabs of stone, incorporating sufficient pockets for subsequent planting. Depending on the height of the wall, the backward slope should be between 20 and 30 cm per metre height (8 to 12 in per yard height). Planting pockets should be filled with loam. Walls built at the correct angle will be less likely to give way under the extra pressure of the earth during heavy rain. Make sure that you can reach diagonally down into any planting pockets, for this will make filling with earth and planting easier.

Use areas at the base of supporting walls or rocks and at the edges of paths or lawns for plants that require extra moisture or protection, but bear in mind that you will have to take some steps to prevent them being walked on or encroached upon by the lawn. I usually protect these planted areas with a length of flat stone slabs laid flush with the ground about 20 cm (8 in) from the base of the wall or rocks. If they are really flush with the lawn you will have no difficulty mowing over the edges. Planting along the base of the wall also heightens the impression of irregularity, for you can use many plants to grow down over the wall, planting the lowest level most thickly, with the density thinning out at the higher levels. Allowing the lawn to grow right up to the wall, where it is difficult to cut, is a mistake that one comes across repeatedly.

In the case of stones and rocks surrounding pools and ponds one often finds large, tall stones projecting far into the water while flatter stones are restricted to the banks. Here we should take a lesson from our fellow-gardeners in the East, where the experience of many centuries should not be overlooked.

Any type of stone we choose may offer the same charms of colour and shape as any other, but some are better suited to a specific purpose. Some stone is best revealed in its natural form in a wild garden, whereas another can only be fully appreciated when quarried and dressed. We need to look at both the garden and the house when making our choice. The choice of the right stone for a particular garden is of prime importance and you will need to use both your eye and your intuition to understand the many unknown qualities of stone. The most effective key to unlocking the secrets of the stone are the plants which grow around it. Many seem to have sprouted from the stone itself or to be closely related to it.

This does not mean of course that one must restrict oneself to only one type of stone in the garden. While this is essential in an area of natural rock garden, many gardens provide a range of possibilities for using different stones in different areas where there will be no clash of style. In nature stones of different colours are occasionally found in close proximity, as is the case with the red and grey marbles of the Berchtesgaden Alps.

Architectural rock gardens provide an instance where different types of stone can be used in close proximity to great decorative advantage.

Suitable lay-outs for rock gardens

Basic differences in planting natural and formal rock gardens

Totally different factors govern the planting, positioning and choice of plants in a natural rock garden from those pertaining to an architectural, formal rock garden.

The natural rock garden is entirely governed by the laws of natural growth and placement of soil, stone and plants. These laws, which restrict our freedom of choice with regard to the lie of the soil, the arrangement of rocks and the choice and positioning of plants, are very different from those governing the formal rock garden, which allow far more room for movement. Here we are free to explore decorative effects with a host of cultivated noble plants, but even so we should not lose sight of the simple wild plants from which they were developed. If we take decorative effect too far and disregard the basic rules of garden design, we can expect only disappointment as the magic spell is broken; so we must tread with care the way between daring and caution. For instance, in a water garden for a formal rock garden it is quite acceptable to use garden varieties of iris which in a natural water garden would have to be replaced by wild varieties.

Alternative to a dividing fence

If your neighbour is in agreement, a dividing fence can be replaced with a bank of earth of similar height. The steep or terraced sides will offer room for a wide variety of small plants. For increased height lavender bushes or a row of *Pinus mugo* ssp. *pumilio* can be planted along the top of the bank, or you might prefer a hardy privet, or any low growing evergreen shrub. *Berberis* is a useful genus here.

Winding sunken paths

These offer the classic means of planting a whole range of shade-loving plants and ferns and most of the plants that flower in early spring. A winding sunken path is ideal, for along its meanderings through natural banks and terraces plants and rocks come into their own, particularly moss-covered rocks whose mossy covering will increase in these shady corners.

Generally, steep banks of earth which allow rain water to run off can be avoided or reduced by constructing light, flat terraces. The effects of space gained by only slight differences in height can be astonishing.

Under a pergola

This is a futuristic motif for rock gardens. Small side slopes can be made into flat terraces. The term pergola is not used here to mean the usual narrow stretch of trellis-work, but a wider covered walk, with benches, with height variations in the trellis-work and with indentations in the side walls which appear as open doors to the outside. The side terraces need neither run in straight lines nor all at the same height. They should recede in places, come forward in others and vary in height. In short, the pergola can be made into a model of good garden design. At one point the trellis could widen out to surround a round sunny area enclosing a water garden and seats. Alternatively, you could construct a stone flower-bed for hardy exotic plants such as early and late flowering yucca surrounded by flowering cacti intermingled with *Sempervivum* (houseleek) rosettes and blue flesh-leaved *Sedum* (stonecrop) and a sprinkling of any other plants you may fancy, such as *Perovskia atriplicifolia*, or *Asphodeline lutea* with their blue-green leaves and tall yellow flowers. (See small succulent gardens, p. 72).

Steps

Steps offer one of the best situations for rock gardens, be they formal or natural, straight or winding. When laying out steps make sure the treads are wide enough for comfortable use. Depending on the lie of the land you may find that the ground needs to be raised only on one side of the steps while the other is left rather lower. Supporting the banks at either side with undressed stone, preferably the same stone that forms the slabs for the steps, provides a wonderful setting for any rock-garden plants which need to be seen at close range. Where the sides are quite high you might consider combining a rock garden at the base with a natural garden without rocks higher up the slope. If you are laying out sunken steps you will have to dig out a lot of soil, but this can be spread over existing flower beds or shrubberies without noticeably increasing their height.

Sunken seating area surrounded by terraced rock garden

As protection from the wind or in the interests of privacy many gardeners like to replace flower-beds near the house with a small sunken area surrounded by two low rock-garden terraces rising to the level of the rest of the garden. By digging one area deeper still, you can include a small pool and water garden. It is by no means essential to construct stone terraces, the sides can quite easily be left as banks of earth planted with *Sedum* (stonecrop). It is often a good idea to place a sunken area of this kind in front of a summer house. With a few flat steps leading up to it the summer house will provide a good view of this small area with its terraced rock gardens.

Crazy-paving

Crazy-paving can form a charming rock-garden motif, with single stones or groups of stones removed to leave space for planting dwarf shrubs or perennials. These paved gardens have become so popular that many gardeners give over most of the garden to them or construct wide paths edged with small groups of plants.

The colour contrast between the plants and the toning or contrasting stone is incomparable, particularly if blue-green foliage is used to contrast with a reddish stone. As the rain slowly dries on the stone between plants fresh from the spring rain one cannot fail to experience the joy of the changing seasons and of rebirth.

Layered slabs

A small rock garden of layered stone slabs has its own peculiar charm; yellowy grey slabs of travertine, for example, planted with evergreen dwarf shrubs and perennials, or red sandstone planted with bluish-green foliage plants and blue-green dwarf conifers. The slabs are arranged like overlapping coins in an irregular fashion, framed at the edges by a regular strip of border stones. In constructing the garden you can imitate the strata of natural rock formations with a few higher sections, but for the most part the garden should be fairly flat and rather stylized. In either case the stratified effect is charming. The individual stones should not be too flat, but should show natural irregularities with the flat dressed surface not too smooth. The garden will be full of places where the soil is revealed for planting. If you pack loam and old manure between the layers you will be able to plant the cracks between them and the roots will eventually grow down between the stones into the soil below.

Existing slopes

A lot can be done with small slopes and mounds which have previously been dead areas, havens for weeds. They can be made to rise gently in waves, transformed into flat terraces or used for a sunken path or steps leading to a sunken seating area. Alternatively you can emphasize the height difference with a pool and waterfall. When dealing with these areas it is essential at all costs to avoid steep banks of earth, putting in their place stone walls supporting horizontal beds. Should this prove impossible you will have to choose your plants for the bank very carefully.

Longer slopes should be made to rise in a series of humps and hollows. The humps should be covered with rocks, small shrubs and taller rock-garden plants, while the hollows are restricted to low-growing foliage plants.

Every small, neglected incline can be transformed into a source of pleasure. Dealing with a small incline has turned many a rock gardener into a rock-garden fanatic.

Steeper inclines and slopes

These seem to have been specially created for transforming into formal terraced gardens or natural rock gardens, and nothing will add greater beauty to your garden. In constructing a walled garden be careful not to repeat the old mistake of building the supporting walls too upright but slope them gently backwards. This will prevent soil being washed down the wall during rain or watering, which can spoil the attractiveness of an upright wall. At various places on the wall you can set stones to project slightly to allow the planting of flowering plants on its face. Combine this with bringing the wall itself forward at the corners and in the centre, and you can vary the effect through shadow as well as through colour tones in the plants and stone.

If you want to keep the walls as low as possible to bring out the effect of the terraced beds to the full, you can still break up the wall area by the addition of raised platforms for tubs.

If you prefer not to use stone you can turn a slope into a wild garden and construct a flat winding path up the slope.

These methods do not apply only to very large gardens, but can also, under the right conditions, produce charming effects in even the smallest of gardens.

Natural garden area in the lawn

It is often possible to add interest to a long stretch of lawn laid out between straight paths by introducing an area of wild garden without rocks, especially where the lawn grows around trees. Many gardens have mature coniferous trees growing directly out of closely trimmed grass and, while the reasons for this are understandable, a golden opportunity is being missed. A small group of birch trees, for instance, can be turned into a wild garden by the addition of climbing plants like woodbine or clematis. Planted as a natural garden, the small group of birches no longer grows starkly out of the lawn and this shady area of conifers gives the mown lawn a feeling of warmth. Stylized natural gardens enclosed by formal stonework can also be used to break up large areas of lawn.

To create a natural garden around conifers, a flat lawn should be made to rise and fall gently so that the depressions can provide extra soil to raise the ground level immediately around the trees. Raising the level will transform a few individual trees into a uniform group. The raised area should then be planted with heather, gorse, juniper, tall grasses and ferns to give a similar effect to that of individual conifers growing on flat-topped hummocks in a dune landscape. Where necessary a narrow trench will prevent the lawn growing back amongst the new plants. To undulate the lawn in this way you will have to remove a number of flat turfs which can be replaced once the soil has been landscaped.

Allowing for the natural features of the site

Rock gardens in disused sand, gravel-pit or quarry

Old gravel-pits or quarries will sometimes make a veritable rock-garden paradise. The best way of making the pit completely accessible is by means of a gently spiralling path linking the centre of the pit with the top edge. This long spiralling path can be broken up and the planting opportunities increased by taking the path backwards or forwards and by laying out small terraces and steps. A pool could be included at the centre. Quarries are often extremely steep with inaccessible faces and it may require major work to make surfaces, pockets and clefts large enough to take sufficient soil for planting. Yet it is certainly true that with the necessary skill disused quarries can be turned into magnificent rock gardens. It must be better to turn old deserted gravel-pits and quarries of manageable size into attractive places than to let them become mere refuse dumps.

Rock garden between existing rocks in the garden

The number of gardens in Europe, from the South to the far North, which take the form of natural rock gardens is extremely large and is increasing all the time. If the rock is deep-lying and does not project sufficiently from the ground, it must be exposed to achieve its greatest effect. The remaining soil must be broken up to a good depth. If the rocks are very large, plant shrubs around them to lead the eye grad-

ually down to the smaller rock-garden plants. Sometimes larger, bizarre shrubs will be necessary to reduce large outcrops of rock to garden proportions. If the rocks are really over-sized it may be necessary to conceal them partially with earth if they are ever to look right with small plants. Once the rock has been broken down it only remains to make pockets of soil and to put in your plants.

An outcrop of larger separated rocks can be brought together by placing large stepping-stones and steps between them before planting them in a unifying way.

Straight rock-garden borders for perennial plants, grasses, ferns, bulbs and shrubs

Formal rock gardens which are particularly suitable for mountain resorts can grace many parts of the garden in the form of long, regular, metre-high beds which are effective despite their rather isolated air. These raised beds can border a path through a lawn. At the base where the stone terracing meets the lawn or the path, expose a narrow strip of soil which can be planted with perennials and surround it with a narrow line of flat stone slabs to make for ease of mowing. The slabs will prevent the lawn encroaching on the bed. Setting the stone walls at an angle will encourage the growth of plants along its base.

Strip gardens bordering or at an angle to flower-beds

Possible variations on perennial borders are much greater than one would think, and I believe that with improvements in plant quality a new era of perennial borders is about to begin. Where possible one should avoid a straight edge to borders, allowing it to curve in and out even though this may take away part of a path or lawn. In either case, straight or irregular perennial borders are highly effective and for many gardens this is the only way to include miniature perennials.

Sometimes it will be practical to separate these areas from the main flower beds by a footpath or line of slabs, or alternatively you may prefer to make them accessible by placing stepping stones supported by a few bricks at intervals through the border. I have occasionally divided long borders of this type at regular intervals into three spring, three summer and three autumn areas, so that some areas were in bloom throughout the year. On other occasions I have planted the whole border with aubrietia hybrids, dwarf irises, arabis (rock cress) and phlox interspersed with a few small grasses and dwarf conifers, again to great effect.

At the corners of borders, instead of planting perennials across the whole width of the bed you can include a strip of evergreen dwarf conifers, turning them into a miniature dwarf perennial garden. This is particularly effective in combination with the perennial border already described.

Dry stone walls

One of the more unusual ways of displaying small plants is to plant them in the cracks of a wall. The fact that they bloom and flourish in such unlikely surroundings shows their great powers of endurance.

In planting a wall there are several points to consider. Is the wall a supporting wall with the soil it supports reaching right to the top, or a dry wall free-standing on both sides? Is the climate dry or damp? In which direction does the wall face? The range of plants suitable for wall planting in moist climates is much larger than that for dry climates, and includes not only the plants designated with two sun symbols in the alphabetical lists, but also most of those shown with only one sun symbol. The direction of the wall also has a big influence on the choice of plants.

The earth along the top of a free-standing

wall should have a shallow furrow to allow for thorough watering of the earth between the stones two or three times a year. Both free-standing and supporting walls should include layers of earth between the stones and should be built with a slight backwards slant rather than upright. All these points are of fundamental importance if you are to achieve the right effect.

Even north-facing walls come into their own here and can produce amazing results. Few gardeners seem to be aware of the vast number of plants which can survive on a north-facing wall.

When constructing your walls work plenty of loam and well-rotted manure in amongst the stones; this will not only support your plants but also help to make the wall more solid. If such a commodity is unobtainable add a good fertilizer as you plant.

Water gardens

(This sections deals with the use of existing pools and streams or the construction of pools and streams in both natural and formal styles. Waterside and water plants are listed on pages 68 to 71).

The beauty of Japanese garden design reaches its peak in the water garden. Here water and earth, heights and depths, flat or vertical stones and plants are brought together in complete harmony. Although inspired by Japan, our garden design has taken a different course. The extraordinarily rich world of waterside plants both large and small which is now available has removed any echoes of Japan from our waterside and water gardens. There is no better way of showing off rock-garden plants than in harmony and contrast with water.

The combination of flowing water with larger rocks can produce a series of winding streams and small pools. The sides of the stream should be completely cleared of grass and weeds and the banks planted with plants typical of the natural waterside.

A narrow winding path can then be laid out to separate these streamside plants from nearby lawns or shrubberies. With both natural and formal streams and pools, waterside plants should grow as thickly as possible at the water's edge except, of course, where a paved area leads right up to the water. One sees so many pools with wide stone borders separating the plants from the water, or completely surrounded by lawn, neither of which produces a good effect. Border stones should be placed to extend a few inches over the water.

To protect the sides of the pool against ice damage the corners should slant downwards at an angle of about 120 degrees. It is usually a good idea to concrete the base of the pool and to leave it free of earth, placing all your water plants in the pool in pots. This has many advantages, not the least being that it keeps fast-spreading plants under control.

If you are including large water-lilies, they should not be in small pots but in containers about the size of a water-butt, whereas the dwarf water-lilies, described later, need tubs 30 to 40cm (12 to 16in) in height and diameter. For the larger varieties, rather than putting them in tubs, it is a good idea to make several large holes in the bottom of the pool and to fill them with earth. Even the large water-lilies need far less attention than their beauty would have one think. Marliac, one of the best-known growers of water-lilies, cultivated them exclusively in sawn-down rain-butts.

Before concreting the base of the pool it is important to lay a good layer of rubble and to pound it down well.

An alternative to the concrete pool is a pool constructed with polythene or butyl pond liners with "welded" seams. This method has been proved over many years, and I can testify from experience to its success. It is also suitable for large swimming pools and is even used for reservoirs. Its strength and durability is sufficient to allow one to ice-skate on the pool in winter. The pond-liner method has therefore brought great advances in the development of waterside and water gardens and made them a reality in even a small garden.

Larger architectural lay-outs with pool

Many people are averse to formal rock gardens in the grand style, despite their fondness for rock-garden plants. I can think of one garden which was extremely effective once the plants had developed, where the contrast between a rigid architectural framework and wild plants not usually associated with gardens was exploited to the full. I once visited this garden, which I had planted some years previously, on an afternoon when the owner was showing round a group of visitors. The question which the visitors, who were extremely interested in the concept of a wild garden such as this, returned to again and again was, "Did all these wild plants grow here naturally from seed or were they planted deliberately?" I was amazed at the interest shown by so many people, many of whom knew nothing of gardening, in this disciplined yet natural wild beauty. It was clear proof of the extent to which even a formal architectural rock garden of this type could awaken a love of rock-garden plants in people who were previously strangers to them.

Sunken rock gardens

A hedged-in area about the size of a normal room can provide much more space for plants if it is made into a sunken area with a regular path winding around it from top to bottom, descending one level at each corner and leading ultimately to a seat by a small pool where the ground is lowest. Space for rock-garden plants is provided in narrow terraces built one above the other and low, slightly slanting supporting walls. A small area of this kind makes an excellent early spring or late autumn garden in which, surrounded by plants and well-protected from the wind, you can enjoy any early or late sunshine. Alternatively, it can harbour a collection of small, long-flowering plants or be planted almost entirely with blue flowers with just a touch of contrasting colour. You can put seating all along the terraced path, using rocks to provide special planting places.

This rock-garden showcase can house a selection of the finest plants available. Here you can recreate springtime in the mountains, for you have the ideal situation for many varieties of saxifrage and primula, for snowbells and for many other mountain flowers.

Rock gardens for balconies, patios, roof gardens, courtyards, window-boxes, tubs, boxes, troughs and *jardinières*

All these methods of growing plants are still to some extent in their infancy although today we have made some progress and have gained sufficient knowledge of the appropriate plants to feel free to encourage more people to try them and to provide a home for these plants in even the smallest type of garden.

The number of plants which will grow long and well in fairly shallow containers and which are strong enough to resist the pressure of the frozen earth is quite extensive. These "doll-sized gardens" can be constructed with an iron framework which allows a second, smaller container to be suspended above the lower one, bringing the small plants closer to eye level. Small portable gardens like this can be used anywhere, for you can even choose plants that prefer shade. The range of small perennial plants is extensive. Very similar to these containers are window-boxes which are very easy to fix in place.

To grow small plants in balcony boxes it is best to use impregnated wood, although plastic is now very popular since plastic boxes last longer and are lighter. I have seen bulbs continuing to flower in city centres seven years after planting, for example dwarf tulips, small narcissi, hyacinths, snowdrops, *Chionodoxa*, *Scilla*, all growing in ordinary boxes.

In the case of small plants for balconies, there are many possibilities besides the usual boxes of flowering plants, and no one will regret experimenting with them. Twelve years ago I planted 15 cm (6 in) dwarf conifers in fairly shallow boxes and these have now grown to 50 cm (20 in). A wealth of experience with balcony plants still remains as yet unexplored!

Some roof gardens are capable of taking the weight of thick layers of soil even when soaked with water and there is no reason why you should not make an ordinary rock garden here, although to lessen the weight it is best to use volcanic rock. Other roof gardens are more suitable for large boxes with tubs and bowls. As the examples of such gardens in Florence and Rome clearly show, this can produce astonishing results, for both cities are roof-garden paradises. One can only marvel at the inventiveness of these southern roof gardeners, who achieve amazing results with their boxes of succulents. There are even shady cactus houses on some roofs. But even in the North similar possibilities are expanding. The work of modern plant breeders has turned many species, dahlias for instance, into excellent container specimens by producing bushier, shorter plants. With modern aids and modern plant material you can now achieve astonishing results with containers. Even today there are still some flat-dwellers who would love a garden of their own yet remain unaware of the possibilities. Our homes and cities offer far more opportunities for growing plants than anyone would believe. I have seen the back yard of a city house that was filled with the glowing colours of dahlias all growing in tubs.

To make it easier to grow perennials on balconies and patios a range of double tier boxes and tubs has recently been introduced. Obviously, nothing is intended here against the many bedding plants for balconies, although their sun and shade requirements are all too often overlooked. It is more a question of taking into account, on the balcony as in the garden, the alternation between resting periods and those of growth. For this purpose a second tier of boxes is arranged below the top layer. These boxes planted with bulbs can be stacked between planks of wood against the house wall once they have finished flowering and left to dry out from early summer to the beginning of September, when watering is resumed. Two to three good waterings will be enough to encourage root growth through the autumn. You can leave the boxes stacked until the early spring and then move them to wherever they are to flower.

Rock gardens and cemeteries

Large-leafed ivy often seems to offer the obvious solution here, but should be avoided for graves wherever possible. Small-leafed ivy fulfils the same purpose but is more delicate-looking and warm and has the advantage of withstanding severe frost. The number of evergreen deciduous and coniferous shrubs and plants suitable for both sunny and shady graves and requiring very little attention is almost endless. Small perennials include evergreen, long-flowering and perpetual plants while of the shrubs, dwarf conifers and dwarf evergreens are most suitable.

Planting Times and Methods for Rock-garden Plants

The main planting times and hence the time when most firms send out their bulbs and plants are spring, between the end of February and the end of May depending on the weather, and autumn, between the end of August and the end of November, again depending on the weather.

There are many factors concerning the condition of the soil, the plants and the weather besides those that I am able to include here, and when in doubt you would be well advised to consult an experienced gardener. The higher the moisture content of the air, the better nature can work. Occasionally, during the first and last two weeks of the planting periods I have indicated, there may be periods of intense heat or cold, but these will be shortlived and you can delay planting for a time until the weather is more favourable. In cooler climates, particularly in quite high mountain areas or in northern regions, spring planting times are likely to be much later. Weather conditions are different from year to year even in the weeks just before orders are delivered. If you are in doubt, leave it to the supplier to choose the correct time for planting. The increasingly common rearing of plants and shrubs in containers has served to spread planting times over the whole year.

Protective coverings for the first winter after planting must be removed early in the spring so that things newly planted do not suffocate or rot. You should bear in mind that evergreen plants, perennials or shrubs may need protection from the sun for some time longer. Even plants which have become firmly established

under cover will need some protection from frost in the first few days after you remove the protective cover.

When planting, you should always water immediately and thoroughly; this is particularly important with shrubs and plants supplied in pots. Watering should continue from time to time until the roots are firmly established, the frequency depending upon the moisture content of the soil and weather conditions. Thorough watering as winter comes on is one of the best ways of protecting against frost, particularly with shrubs.

Deciduous shrubs not supplied in pots should be thoroughly pruned before planting, usually cutting back about a third of the growth, and you should continue to prune them from time to time depending on their situation in the garden and their growth rate. However, there are plants—including *Hamamelis*, *Fothergilla*, *Acer* and *Magnolia*—which should never be pruned. Some inexperienced gardeners are reluctant to prune their shrubs at all, and if in doubt you should ask about pruning requirements when buying shrubs. There is not doubt that pruning encourages and speeds up new growth. It is important to avoid exposing plant roots to the air for longer than necessary, as sunlight and wind are poison to roots.

There are many instances where planting seems to be straightforward, but which nevertheless require special care. For all the countless conifers which become firmly established when planted in a good ball of earth, there are others, which in unusually hot spring weather may need frequent watering and protection with raffia matting against warm winds. When you consider that these shrubs will still be there for many springs to come, you will realize that it is worth making the effort to give them a good start in life.

In general all flowering bulbs should be planted at a depth three times their diameter; however, smaller bulbs should never be set deeper than 5 cm (2 in) and larger ones no deeper than 20 cm (8 in), slightly less in heavy soil. It is particularly important with lilies for the rooting soil to be loose and porous. A light sprinkling of fresh sand in the planting hole will help considerably. Some protection against cold is only necessary for late planting of bulbs and corms, but you will need to add some fertilizer to the soil both around and under the bulbs.

Planting shrubs, bedding plants and bulbs

Shrubs

Dwarf shrubs supplied in pots are usually planted in March, April, May or September to October, but if special circumstances require it they can be planted at other times of the year. For autumn and winter planting in cold areas, the earth should first be covered with manure or old loam held in place with small spruce branches or other sticks or twigs to keep out frost. There are many coniferous shrubs, however, that will not tolerate manure and for these it is better to use peat.

Shrubs supplied with bare roots are usually planted from March to the end of April, and by early May at the latest, or from mid-September through to late November. Even the hardiest of these will need the same protection as pot shrubs during the first winter. Nursery catalogues make it clear which varieties are available containerized and which only bareroot.

Bedding plants

Here again it is necessary to differentiate between plants in individual containers and those in boxes (flats) or just in a loose ball of soil. An increasing number of rock-garden plants can now be supplied in pots or similar containers, and these can be planted at any time of the year. These too should be protected with conifer branches in cold areas during the first winter after planting. Bare root plants should be put in from March to mid-May and from mid-August to mid-November.

With many plants, particularly dwarf varieties, planting from pots produces quicker growth. However, there is the danger of forgetting to loosen and spread the outer network of roots and this neglect can be particularly serious in dry soils. I once did an experiment with two potted *Sedum sieboldii*, loosening the roots of one but not the other. For four years the one I did not loosen looked very sorry for itself beside the abundant growth of the other.

Bulbs

Smaller spring-flowering bulbs should be planted from mid-August to the beginning of November. If you plant early they will require little protection during the first winter and no protection at all for following winters. With late planting, bedding the bulbs in damp sand will greatly speed up rooting. A thick covering of leaves over newly planted bulbs has one disadvantage in that it does not show up mice tracks, so it is better to use some material that can be lifted easily from time to time to check the state of the bulbs. Mice are much more likely to eat freshly planted bulbs than long-established ones and they seem to prefer garden crocuses to the earlier varieties. This is another reason why early planting is recommended whenever possible, but on occasions it is unavoidable that one will have to plant late. Tulips, daffodils and hyacinths can be planted as late as early December, for most varieties are amazingly indestructible.

Autumn-flowering bulbs: the glorious and long-flowering autumn crocuses, *Colchicum* and *Sternbergia*, one of the most beautiful groups of garden plants, should be planted in July and August but can be planted with good results even closer to their flowering time. The strength and endurance of these beautiful autumn flowers are quite extraordinary. In cold areas they may need to be covered for the first winter.

Rock-garden bulbs which flower at other times are dwarf varieties of tiger lily and other varieties suitable for rock gardens, such as *Lilium chalcedonicum*, *L. hansonii* and even *L. martagon* and its hybrids; these often produce better effects in a rock garden than in a flower-bed. They should be planted from October to the end of April. During mild winters they will need no protection. Many lily bulbs are ready for planting even earlier in the autumn, but most nurseries send them out slightly later. While on this subject I am reminded of the odd exception of the white Madonna lily, which is of course unsuitable for either rock or wild gardens, but whose best planting time is August.

Late summer is also the time to plant hardy gladioli, which look excellent in rock gardens and at the edge of a small pool. Like *Colchicum* and autumn crocus, these plants would be much more widely used were it not for their unusual planting time. (Yet some people must have birthdays even at this time of the year and these plants would make excellent presents.)

Cyclamen which flower in early and late autumn should be planted slightly later than those which flower in early spring, that is, not until the end of September.

Any spring, summer or autumn bulb can, of course, be grown in a pot and then planted with the soil from the pot at any convenient time.

When to plant

Shrubs

Dwarf deciduous shrubs with bare roots, such as *Hypericum*, *Potentilla*, lavender: mid-September to end of November, mid-March to beginning of May. Plant in open ground in winter. Protect as for evergreen shrubs.

Deciduous shrubs in containers, such as azaleas and magnolia: end August to end November, mid-March to mid-May. In winter plant in open ground or with protection from frost in cold areas. Protect surrounding soil as for evergreen shrubs.

Evergreen and dwarf deciduous shrubs in containers, such as rhododendron, azalea, *Andromeda*: end August to end October, mid-March to end May and, with a few exceptions, even later. In winter in open ground. Cover the surrounding ground for the first winter after autumn planting and protect the shrub against strong sun or frost with conifer branches, reeds or anything else that will provide shade from the onset of winter until about the end of March.

Dwarf conifers in containers such as dwarf cypresses, dwarf junipers, dwarf firs: can be planted at any time other than periods of heavy frost. After autumn planting protect for the first winter as for evergreen deciduous shrubs.

Bedding plants

Rock garden and leafy plants with bare roots, such as *Gypsophila*, cushion-leafed phlox, grasses: mid-August to mid-November, mid-March to mid-May. After autumn planting protect during first winter with light, well-ventilated covering.

Rock garden and leafy plants in pots or containers, such as *Aubrieta*, *Saxifraga*, *Campanula* (essential with these to remove the root covering): any time from mid-March to mid-November, except at times of extreme heat. In winter in open ground, with some exceptions. After late planting protect during first winter with light, well-ventilated covering. Protect around plants with leaves weighted down with old flower or grass cuttings. Evergreens do not need the extra leaf protection but should similarly be covered with a light, well-ventilated protection.

Bulbs

Large, spring-flowering bulbs, such as tulips, daffodils, hyacinths: mid-August to end of November. Planted even later in open ground they will flower later.

Small, spring-flowering bulbs, such as crocuses, *Eranthis*, snowdrops and *Scilla* mid-August to beginning of November or even later.

Small spring-flowering bulbs in containers: not only mid-August to beginning of November, but throughout winter in open ground and into the spring until just before flowering.

Large early summer and summer bulbs, such

as various lilies, *Galtonia candicans*: beginning of August to mid-May, depending on flowering time, except in heavy frost.

Lilies, most types and varieties: end September to end November in open ground and from March to mid-April (Madonna lilies in August).

Large early summer and summer bulbs in containers: at any time throughout the year, except in heavy frost.

Autumn-flowering bulbs, such as *Colchicum*, autumn crocuses, *Sternbergia*: preferably in July, but if necessary from beginning of August to end of October. Plant colchicums 20 cm (8 in) deep, autumn crocuses 10 cm (4 in).

Marsh plants

Marsh and similar plants to be planted in moist areas: beginning of April to beginning of October, but not during intense heat.

Water-lilies and water plants

Water-lilies and water plants: end April to mid-August when water temperature is sufficiently high to ensure growth. Winter protection for water-lilies is only necessary if the water is drained.

Times and methods for planting dry walls and rock clefts

The best time is March/April, except for bulbs and corms, which should be planted in autumn. The easiest method, of course, is to use plants in containers. Once again I must remind you to loosen any dense fibrous roots which may have become enmeshed inside their pot; failing to do so will hamper growth over many years, as my comparative experiments have shown.

Wherever there are gaps in the wall use a metal dibber to make slanting holes in the soil within the wall and remove some of the earth. Then press the roots with their surrounding earth into the hole. Add some good, loamy soil, press well in and water immediately before the hole is completely filled with earth. After planting it is often advisable to hammer in a few stones to fill in the opening in the wall.

When planting in warm weather hang a few conifer sprigs over the planting pocket and secure in place by banging a small piece of wood into the gap. Whenever possible you should plant at the same time that you build the wall or erect your rocks, but this is not always feasible. A more important aspect to pay attention to during building is to include layers of loamy soil and manure as you build. In cases of slow rooting, rare instances admittedly, you will need a thin stick to make slanting watering holes before further watering.

If you plant your wall with plants that generally require more moisture than a dry wall will provide, you can keep the soil moist by sinking vertical drainpipes into the soil at metre intervals, to be filled with water from time to time during dry weather. Plant growth will neatly cover the tops of the pipes.

Delayed planting

If for some reason rock-garden plants cannot be planted immediately, do not plant them temporarily in clumps, but separately so that each root has sufficient soil around it. Temporary planting followed by replanting will always have some detrimental effect on the plant. It is amazing how many gardeners and even retailers demand their money back for plants killed through replanting, as if they had died under normal handling, and nurseries are usually quite willing to recompense them, for they know that "the customer" has an amazing memory for such trivialities. Memory is an indestructible perennial, and no one has a better memory than the customer!

Tending your Rock Garden

Preliminary remarks

The more thought you put in to laying out the rock garden, the easier it will be to care for. The main thing here, as I have said, is to avoid steep banks of earth and to think about the biological requirements of each plant when planting. If your garden takes a lot of caring for then you can be sure that you have gone wrong somewhere with the basic design or planting. Plants which do not balance each other, where one outgrows the others, may have been planted too close to one another. You may have planted others too close to the roots of a shrub. The Japanese overcome this problem by burying a thin vertical stone slab in the earth to prevent roots spreading, while allowing them to take advantage of the shade provided by the shrub.

The pleasure of growing small plants is one that increases continually. The more I have to do with them, the more I realize what a rewarding pastime it is. These plants respond to correct care with rapid development, together with prolonged and repeated flowering, so that it becomes a pleasure rather than a chore to look after them.

One often hears gardeners complain that they have been unlucky with a particular plant. They fail to realize that luck plays no more of a part here than in any of the other things in which they have been "unlucky".

Opinions will of course differ on the amount of attention a plant requires and these differing opinions can never be fully resolved. But with more and more plants being specially developed for rock gardens, success without great labour is increasingly assured. In fact with good lay-out and careful choice of plants many tasks become unnecessary and those that remain are made much easier to cope with.

Watering

If the rock garden has been planned correctly, so that water has as little opportunity as possible of running off banks of earth, watering will be as easy and effective as with a normal flower-bed. The best way is to install a sprinkler which gives a fine spray. In addition to helping preserve the looseness of the soil, a fine spray has the advantage of being warmed slightly by the air. Many gardeners, however, prefer to water exclusively with a watering can and install a small pool to provide a source of warm water either at the foot of the rock garden or within it.

The less experienced the gardener, the more he tends to worry about watering, and he frequently adopts the technique of hoeing to break up the soil and watering very infrequently but very thoroughly. I should mention here that mature plants with well-established roots to which ordinary watering will not penetrate sufficiently can be thoroughly watered and will retain water better if you make a shallow depression around them. Older plants treated in this way will soon show a marked difference by producing richer, longer-lasting flowers. I have found this to be true, for example, of very old trailing campanulas or delphiniums. This tip is one you will not require often, but it is well worth knowing.

After a very dry autumn newly rooted evergreen plants should be watered thoroughly so that they start the winter with damp soil around the roots.

In discussing these various aspects of watering I may give the impression that more care is necessary than is in fact the case, providing of course that your rock garden is correctly laid out, positioned and planted.

Fertilizers

The best way to feed and provide additional nutrients for perennial plants is to cover the soil with rotted, earthy manure. This also has the surprising effect of keeping the soil moist.

Plants in walls and clefts of rocks will respond well to liquid manure applied after making downward slanting holes above the roots. Liquid feeds are now freely available from garden centres and have clear instructions on how they should be applied.

You should not use fertilizer in the rock garden after July, but up till then infrequent feeding of old plants of many rock-garden species will give them extra strength, a fact easily demonstrated by comparative tests.

Fresh or insufficiently rotted manure should not be used in the rock garden, nor should undiluted liquid manure. Manure that is ready for use is of course not particularly attractive, but you can improve the look of it by light raking. Where you have young plants in the garden do not bring the manure covering too close, for, as with raw peat, it may damage the plants. With well-established rock gardens which need feeding after several years it is best to lift any large leaves and tuck the manure beneath.

Weeding

The main thing here is to keep the rock garden free from perennial weeds which like to take root in the shelter of the rocks and to proliferate from there. Removing weeds before they have a chance to seed will reduce them considerably with time. Trouble with weeds is usually no more than a childhood illness which attacks the rock garden during the first year, usually, but not always, because there may be new weed sources which you can do nothing about.

Covering the ground with rocks, slabs or gravel remains a worthwhile method of keeping weeds away from your plants, while at the same time retaining the moisture of the soil. A common preventative measure is to cover the soil with solid green ground cover plants which can be bought cheaply in quantity. It is also a way of cutting costs. Here oases of flowering plants can be grown out of an inconspicuous, neutral carpet. Experience will show that many of these carpet plants give excellent protection against weeds, while others seem to trap them. Since I discovered the excellent way in which *Paronychia kapela* and the evergreen *Thymus villosus* keep the weeds at bay, I have used the pearlwort *(Sagina subulata)* less and less. Although measures of this kind make the rock garden easier to care for, it is still important to include sufficient steps and stepping stones. Stepping stones should be laid over bricks or pebbles so that they are at least 5 cm (2 in) above ground level, otherwise they will gradually become covered with soil and disappear.

Protecting small plants against cold

For their first winter after autumn planting small plants—but not bulbs which you planted earlier in the autumn—need protection against frost, and this is best done by spreading the ground with leaves held in place with netting or, more attractively, with conifer branches. This is only necessary in continental climates.

Newly planted evergreens, on the other hand, should not be covered with leaves but merely with conifer twigs or some other light and airy protection. You must allow them to get sufficient sun to survive the winter. Heavy shade will often damage them, whilst light shade may prevent flowering.

It cannot be too forcefully emphasized that for every rock-garden plant which fails to survive a severe winter, there are other species, subspecies and cultivars which will survive anything. Thus, in the case of the *Arabis caucasica*, which rarely survives a really severe winter, there are now other species available which retain their beauty both during and after an arctic winter.

Small bulbs planted rather late in autumn should be protected during the first winter by a covering of conifer twigs; this will not normally be necessary with tulips, hyacinths and large daffodils, though some protection may be a good idea in exposed places. When planting bulbs deep (12 to 15 cm/5 to 6 in), make sure the soil below is sufficiently nutritious.

Occasionally, albeit rarely, there may be severe frosts as early as October which will play havoc with delicate newly planted plants while having no effect upon well-established ones, so you should not delay in protecting your newly planted autumn plants against exceptional weather conditions.

Fallen leaves collecting in corners where *Aubrieta* hybrids, *Arabis* or other small evergreen perennials are growing, can be enough to kill them.

Primulas of the *juliae* groups are extremely hardy and will survive and flower well whatever the weather. For autumn planting, cover with conifer twigs. Although *Primula vulgaris* is evergreen, it should be protected with a light, firmly anchored covering of leaves in areas where arctic cold without snow seems likely. Freshly planted primulas are more sensitive to a thick covering of leaves than are well-established plants.

With well-established unprotected *Primula elatior* hybrids it is sometimes impossible to say whether they have been damaged by frost or by being left too long in the same place. When replanting older plants it is best to change the soil and to add some new plants. But they will continue to do extraordinarily well over many years. *Primula auricula* × *pubescens* and other evergreen alpine primulas are hardy and need no protection. *P. saxatilis*, *P. sieboldii*, *P. florindae* and *P. sikkimensis* also need no protection whatsoever. *P. rosea* 'Grandiflora' in light shade and a sufficiently moist soil will also survive unprotected. *P. denticulata* likes a covering of twigs but this is not essential. *P. japonica*, *P. beesiana*, *P. bulleyana*, *P.* × *bulleesiana*, *P. pulverulenta* and *P. burmanica* in continental climates are best protected every winter with conifer twigs. None of these plants will survive continually cold and wet winters.

Grasses should be planted in early spring so that the roots are well established before the onset of winter. It will usually do more harm than good to cover them as this usually produces fungi, especially in the evergreen *Carex* and *Festuca* types. Late-planted grasses will often not tolerate cold winters, and are particularly affected by alternating frost and mild weather.

Newly planted ferns or those of doubtful hardiness can be covered with dry leaves held in place with wire netting.

Planting Schemes for Flowering Throughout the Year with Relevant Plant Lists

General remarks on the rock garden through the year

(The lists group together plants that flower in a particular season) The "rock garden through the seasons"—this phrase not only sounds good but is entirely justified. I like to look upon a rock garden as the "second hand" of the seasonal clock. Here, despite the many changes attempted by horticulturalists, most plants still retain their natural flowering times. The modern rock garden will include both very early- and very late-flowering plants together with several winter flowerers.

The different effects produced by full sun and shade can be used to great effect here, especially in the early spring, and can be exploited by positioning a few plants of the same species on both the north and south sides of the same rock.

Flowering times are of course dependent upon the light and warmth requirements of each plant and thus the periods I have indicated are to some extent relative, being affected by climatic differences from one year to the next and equally by the position an individual plant occupies within the same rock garden. The main thing, however, is to know which plants flower together and this my lists indicate, even though the time may vary slightly from year to year.

In the realm of rock-garden plants the period of flowering is in itself a time of constant change, with flowers continually opening and closing and then the following day reappearing, often at a precise time, before disappearing completely and apparently for good—then suddenly, some time later, we are amazed by the start of a new, much longer period of flowering. I am thinking of the small, large-blossomed white evening primrose from North America *(Oenothera caespitosa)*, which suddenly, just before sunset, opens its beautifully shaped buds to reveal large, fragrant, funnel-shaped flowers, blossoming in the most unexpected places which are reached by its underground runners. Or the continual surprise when a blue flax *(Linum)* which has apparently finished flowering suddenly breaks forth into full bloom once more. What is it that suddenly causes the plant to reveal all its glory a second time: the weather, the time of day, or some unknown inner timeclock? After a long drought the blue clouds are suddenly back! The Missouri evening primrose with its large lemon-coloured flowers is another plant which obeys the fixed laws of its internal clock through early and late summer, presenting us with a liberal succession of new flowers one after the other.

Only those who have seen them at first hand can truly appreciate the changes wrought in the rock garden by succeeding hours, weeks and months.

A longer period of second flowering is in preparation throughout the summer as plants soak up the sun before blossoming in late summer with a beauty often far surpassing their first flowers. The garden is changing continually; everything is developing in unexpected counterpoint. What is all this leading up to? We cannot know. What beauty is brewing

1. *Helleborus niger* ssp. *macranthus* (text p. 197), will flower as early as January in a mild winter. The flowers of this subspecies can last well into March.

2. *Adonis amurensis* (text p. 152) always surprises us afresh in early spring, when it unfolds its vivid starry flowers.

3. Every year *Hamamelis japonica* brings pleasure, with its scented blossoms appearing in January and February.

1. *Galanthus elwesii* (text p. 116), flowers weeks before the snowdrop G. nivalis, which is very common in many gardens.
2. Everyone awaits with impatience the first flowers of *Galanthus nivalis* (text p. 116), the well-known snowdrop.
3. *Narcissus asturiensis*, is a real treasure of early spring. This lovely dwarf narcissus needs a rather sheltered situation.

4. Many plant-lovers are still unaware that some irises can bloom as early as late February. One of the most beautiful is the *Iris reticulata* hybrid 'Harmony', which flowers in mid-March.

1. *Anemone blanda* unfolds its conspicuous starry flowers in March. The best white sort is the large-flowered 'White Splendour'.

2. One of the most attractive cultivas is the 'Radar' hybrid.

3. *Eranthis hyemalis* (text p. 115) – Winter Aconites in full bloom are an irresistible lure to the first bees of early spring.

4. *Puschkinia scilloides* var. *libanotica*; the Lebanon or Striped Squill (text p. 119), is sometimes confused with *Scilla mischtschenkoana*.

5. *Crocus tomasinianus* (text p. 113) – an indispensable garden treasure. It seeds itself readily in any favourable position.

Right-hand page:
1. Of the American Dog's Tooth Violets, *Erythronium tuolumnense* (text p. 115), is one of the most suitable for the garden. Left alone, it readily increases.
2. The *Erythronium revolutum* hybrid 'White Beauty', with its large white petals and yellow base, will flower regularly every year.
3. One of the best-known Dog's Tooth Violets, *Erythronium dens-canis* (text p. 115), has several varieties. Those that increase the most readily are not necessarily the best-flowering ones.

1. The hybrid 'Large Yellow' is the most free-flowering and largest of the yellow crocuses.
2. The *Crocus vernus* variety 'Remembrance', is early-flowering and its colour goes well with 'Large Yellow' as both flower at the same time.

3. All *Crocus chrysanthus* cultivars are finely-veined on the three outer petals. On the pale yellow 'Marietta' these veins are light purplish-red.
4. *Crocus versicolor* 'Picturatus', with its distinctive veining, flowers extremely abundantly in the second half of March.

1. *Muscari armeniacum* 'Blue Spike' – a form with heavy double flowers, which produces no seeds.

2. *Chionodoxa luciliae* (text p. 111–2), seeds itself readily in a good position. Therefore this species should only be planted near strong-growing neighbours.
3. *Chionodoxa luciliae* 'Pink Giant', has large, pale pink flowers and only increases by offsets.
4. *Scilla sibirica* brings a highly desirable shining blue in spring (text p. 119). It spreads rapidly by seed and should be sited carefully.

1. *Narcissus cyclamineus*
(text p. 118) – a gem
among the dwarf nar-
cissi, which only pros-
pers in damp, slightly
acid soil.
2. *Corbularia bulbocodium,*
is a lovely plant that
goes very well with
blue grape hyacinths.
3. *Tulipa greigii* 'Red
Riding Hood' is one of
the most popular cul-
tivars at present. It
combines good growth
with resilience.

1. *Fritillaria imperialis* 'Lutea maxima', is strong-growing and long-lasting. It looks magnificent against a back-drop of dark shrubs.

2. *Fritillaria pallidiflora* (text p. 115–6) – a species from Central Asia with several pale yellow tulip-shaped flowers to each stem. It increases very slowly.

3. *Fritillaria meleagris*, the Snake's-head Fritillary (text p. 116), likes a good humus-rich soil. Its special charm lies in the colours and patterns on its flowers as they quiver in the breeze.

Left-hand page:

1. The magic of the fritillary reveals itself most of all when one looks closely into the flower.

2. The seed pods of *Fritillaria imperialis* (text p. 116), the Crown Imperial, begin to ripen as early as June and a few weeks later only an empty space reminds us of the pleasure they brought.

3. Clumps of *Fritillaria imperialis* such as this one can be very old. The plants in this group came from a free-flowering parent and have not been transplanted for fifteen years.

41

No rock garden should be without wild tulips. With enough sun and good drainage they will join other early spring flowers in bringing a blaze of colour to the garden.

1. The Lady Tulip *Tulipa clusiana* (text p. 120), needs dry summers if it is to survive.

2. *Tulipa clusiana var. chrysantha* (text p. 120) – the yellow Lady Tulip demands the same conditions.

3. *Tulipa maximowiczii* (text p. 121), flowers about ten days earlier than *T. linifolia* (text p. 120).

4. *Tulipa kaufmanniana* is known in various colours. The small-sized 'Ancilla' grows to only 15 cm (6 in). Its flower is red-coloured on the outside.

5. *Tulipa violacea* (text p. 120), comes in various shades. This is the 'Rosea' form.

1. *Tulipa kaufmanniana* 'César Franck' – an early variety, whose petals are carmine-red on the outside, with yellow edges.

2. *Tulipa kaufmanniana* (text p. 120) – a tulip no garden should be without.

3. *Tulipa praestans* (text p. 120) – an easily-grown Central Asian species that comes in a number of varieties.

4. *Tulipa batalinii* 'Bronze Charm' – a cross between *T. batalinii* and *T. linifolia*, varying in colour from bronze to apricot.

1. *Tulipa kaufmanniana* 'Shakespeare', is one of the smallest forms at only 15 cm (6 in). Recommended also for the richness of its flowers.

2. 'Stresa' – a hybrid of *Tulipa kaufmanniana*. *T. greigii* also belongs to this class of tulips.

3. The dwarf *Tulipa tarda* (text p. 120), will increase well in the right situation.

4. *Tulipa fosterana* 'Madame Lefeber' (also known as 'Red Emperor'), is a long-lasting species tulip for warm spots in the garden. This cinnabar-red shade needs to be used with discretion in the springtime.

1. *Fritillaria camtschatcensis*, the Black Sarana (text p. 116), will only survive in a cool, moist, slightly acid, well-drained soil and in slight shade – requirements very similar to many wild lilies.
2. *Hepatica nobilis*, our well-known Liverwort (text p. 200) – an indispensable spring treasure for semi-shade.
3. *Plagiorhegma dubium* (text p. 218) – a plant from the forests of the Far East.
4. *Cyclamen coum* ssp. *caucasicum* (text p. 114), varies considerably in the colour of its flowers and the pattern of its leaves. We can enjoy its flowers in early spring.

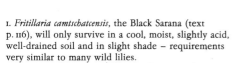

1. *Sanguinaria canadensis*, the Bloodroot (text p. 243) – a spring flower whose anemone-like blooms are unfortunately short-lived.

2. The double form *Sanguinaria canadensis* 'Plena' has an especially long flowering season. Unfortunately it is often difficult to obtain.

3. *Trillium sessile*, the Toad Trillium (text p. 119, 120), sometimes has strikingly-spotted leaves.

4. *Trillium grandiflorum* – a large-flowered Wake-Robin (text p. 119–20), the most handsome of the species and the readiest to proliferate. As with all trilliums, every part of the plant above ground comes in threes.

Right-hand page:
1. *Iris X warlsind* (text p. 117), is a hardy Juno iris hybrid that combines all the best characteristics of its parents *I. warleyensis* and *I. sindjarensis*. In recent times a number of colour variations have become available.

1. *Helleborus niger* var. *altifolius* (text p. 197), produces flowers for cutting as early as December, so this Christmas Rose is aptly named.

2. *Pulsatilla halleri* ssp. *slavica* (text p. 241–2), mingles furry buds with early flowers.

3. Who does not covet *Primula vulgaris* ssp. *sibthorpii* (text p. 221) for their garden?

4. *Primula vulgaris* (text p. 221–2) – a wild species that should be used more widely.

5. *Dodecatheon meadia* 'Hermes' – a long-lasting white-flowered Shooting Star.

behind such apparent stillness? (See list of perennials which blossom twice, p. 98f.)

Yet it is not only in the period of second flowering but also in the way they start to grow in spring that rock-garden plants seem to shake off the shackles of winter. Amidst the late winter snow and ice, autumn crocus and spring heather are suddenly in bloom, precursors of the spring. What can it be that we see putting up small brown-sheathed stalks from the wet soil at the beginning of Lent? An early *Narcissus bulbocodium* has appeared.

In autumn there are comparable pleasures. In October the spring faces of crocuses and gentians peep out at us from beneath moss-grown rocks, blooming amidst the scent of autumn violets and early Christmas roses while, even as late as that, butterflies flutter and bees buzz around them.

Even the magic of the low-lying rock garden which seems to take us back through time cannot be compared with the magic of spring in the mountains, which on the higher peaks extends into early summer and even into full summer, giving us the joy of springtime twice a year. With every stage one climbs one is taken slowly back into the spring.

The rock garden in early spring

Just as the jeweller sets his costly gems in gold pendants, chains or crowns, we need the natural or formal rock garden to bring together and display the boundless jewels of the early spring. When I began searching for species and varieties to create a long garden season, checking their staying powers and designing suitable sites for them in the garden, they lay scattered and little known. They were often grown in isolation in inappropriate garden situations and were frequently regarded as mere curiosities.

Botanical gardens tended to display their earliest flowering plants in any odd corner of their enormous grounds. My approach was to group together plants which blossom from the end of February to the end of April by dividing each month into two halves and demonstrating which plants belong together and show to best effect by being planted side by side. The idea of planting all these perennials, bulbs, dwarf shrubs, small shrubs, medium-sized shrubs, early-leafing and evergreen plants, grasses and ferns together in formal or natural stone terraces now has much wider currency.

Today early spring is a garden season which no true gardener fails to take advantage of, for he knows that the change from spring to summer, from summer to autumn and from autumn to winter can only be fully appreciated if the first changing weeks of the succeeding seasons are experience to the full.

The early spring garden is today an essential part of the gardener's year. That is why I am including the lists, but even those who already know about early spring flowers will have to keep a close eye on nurseries and gardens if they want to keep up to date, for every year there are new and exciting additions to the list of early-flowering plants.

In the rock garden one can find ways of tempting plants out of the ground even earlier than usual by choosing or constructing warm corners out of the wind, often so far in advance of their normal flowering time that this is just beginning as the flowers in the sheltered corners are beginning to fade. The pleasure to be found in this is catching and can lead to intense rivalry between one garden and the next. There are simply no words adequate to describe the pleasures of early spring with all its great variety.

(See the following list for precise details)

Late February

Herbaceous plants

Adonis amurensis
Helleborus abchasicus
– *niger* ssp. *macranthus*
– – 'Maximus'
– *odorus*
Petasites fragrans
Primula vulgaris ssp. *sibthorpii*
Saxifraga burserana 'Major'

Bulbs

Crocus angustifolius
– *biflorus*
– *imperati*

49

– *sieberi*
– *tomasinianus*
Cyclamen coum
– – 'Album'
Eranthis hyemalis
Galanthus elwesii
– *ikariae*
– – ssp. *latifolius*
– *nivalis*
Narcissus asturiensis

Flowering shrubs

Cornus officinalis, large shrub to small tree
Corylus avellana, large shrub
Daphne mezereum, dwarf shrub
– – 'Alba', dwarf shrub
Erica herbacea (syn. E.carnea) 'King George',
    dwarf shrub
Hamamelis japonica, medium to large shrub
– – 'Ruby Glow' ('Adonis')
– *mollis*, medium to large shrub
Jasminum nudiflorum, small shrub
Rhododendron dauricum, medium shrub
– *mucronulatum*, medium shrub
– × *praecox*, small shrub

Early March

Herbaceous plants

Adonis amurensis 'Pleniflora'
Helleborus hybrids, various varieties
Hepatica transsylvanica (syn. H.angulosa)
Primula vulgaris varieties
Pulmonaria rubra
Saxifraga × *apiculata*
– × *elisabethae*
– × *haagii*
– × *irwingii*
Viola odorata 'Augusta'

Bulbs

Anemone blanda, various colours
Bulbocodium vernum
Chionodoxa luciliae
Crocus chrysanthus varieties
– *etruscus*
– *flavus*

– *fleischeri*
– *korolkowii*
– × *stellaris*
– *tomasinianus* varieties
– *versicolor*
Cyclamen coum ssp. *caucasicum*
Eranthis cilicicus
Galanthus elwesii
– *plicatus*
Iris bakerana
– *danfordiae*
– *histrio* var. *aitabensis*
– *histrioides* 'Major'
– *reticulata* varieties
Leucojum vernum
– – ssp. *carpaticum*
Muscari azurea
– – 'Alba'
Scilla bifolia
– *mischtschenkoana* (syn. S.tubergeniana)

Early-leafing shrubs

Cornus mas, large shrub to small tree
Corylopsis pauciflora, dwarf shrub
Lonicera × *purpusii*, small shrub
Salix caprea, large shrub

Flowering shrubs

Abeliophyllum distichum, small shrub
Lonicera standishii, medium shrub
Prunus mandshurica, large shrub to small tree
Sorbaria sorbifolia, small shrub

Late March

Herbaceous plants

Adonis vernalis
Brunnera macrophylla
Draba aizoides
Helleborus lividus ssp. *corsicus*
– late hybrids
Iberis saxatilis
Lathyrus vernus
– – 'Alboroseus'
Primula denticulata, various colour forms
– *juliae*
– *juliae* hybrids

Pulsatilla halleri ssp. *slavica*
Saxifraga grisebachii
− × *arco-valleyi*
− × *rubella*
− × *suendermannii* 'Major'
− *marginata* var. *rocheliana*
Synthyris stellata
Viola odorata cultivars

Bulbs

Anemone nemorosa varieties
Corydalis solida 'Transsylvanica'
Crocus vernus early garden cultivars
Eranthis × *tubergenii*
Erythronium dens-canis early varieties
Iris bucharica
− *willmottiana*
Leucojum vernum
− − ssp. *carpaticum*
Muscari species and varieties
Narcissus cyclamineus
− × *johnstonii* ('Queen of Spain')
Scilla sibirica var. *taurica*
Tulipa kaufmanniana
− *kaufmanniana* hybrids

Flowering shrubs

Acer rubrum, tree
Cornus mas, large shrub
Rhododendron × *praecox*, small shrub
Salix aegyptiaca, large shrub
− *hastata* 'Wehrhahnii', small shrub

Early-leafing shrubs

Betula platyphylla, tree
Caragana arborescens, large shrub
Lonicera × *heckrotti*, climber
Malus baccata var. *mandshurica*, large shrub
Paeonia suffruticosa, small to medium shrub
Prunus padus var. *commutata*, large shrub
Ribes speciosum, medium shrub

Early April

Herbaceous plants

Alyssum montanum
Arabis caucasica

− *procurrens*
Bergenia species and varieties
Caltha palustris var. *alba*
Carex fraseri
− *montana*
− *morrowii* 'Variegata'
− *plantaginea*
Dentaria pentaphyllos (syn. Cardamine
  pentaphyllos)
Doronicum orientale cultivars
Draba species and cultivars
Iberis saxatilis
Omphalodes verna
− − 'Alba'
Podophyllum hexandrum 'Majus' (syn. P. emodi)
Primula juliae hybrids
− *marginata* and cultivars
− *rosea*
− − 'Grandiflora'
Pulmonaria angustifolia 'Azurea'
− *rubra*
− *saccharata* (syn. P. picta) 'Mrs Moon'
Pulsatilla vulgaris, various colours
Saxifraga juniperifolia ssp. *sancta*
Sesleria heufleriana
Soldanella montana
Uvularia grandiflora
Vinca minor in 3 colours
Viola gracilis 'Major'
− *odorata* 'The Czar'
− − 'Triumph'

Bulbs

Anemone apennina, various colours
− *ranunculoides*
Narcissus bulbocodium
Erythronium dens-canis late cultivars
Fritillaria imperialis and cultivars
− *meleagris* and cultivars
− *pallidiflora*
− *raddeana*
Hyacinthus orientalis cultivars
Iris aucheri (syn. I. sindjarensis)
− *sind-pers*
Muscari late cultivars
Narcissus cyclamineus hybrids
− × *incomparabilis* early cultivars
− *pseudonarcissus*
− 'King Alfred' and other early cultivars
Scilla sibirica cultivars

Trillium chloropetalum (syn. T.sessile var. californicum)
– *sessile*
– – 'Rubrum'
Tulipa (common, early garden tulip)
– *fosteriana* 'Red Emperor'
– *greigii* 'Aurea'
– *greigii* hybrids
– *turkestanica*

Early-leafing shrubs

Daphne blagayana, dwarf shrub
Magnolia stellata, medium shrub
Mahonia aquifolium 'Moseri', small shrub
Pieris floribunda, small shrub
– *japonica*, small shrub
Prunus cerasifera 'Atropurpurea', large shrub
– *padus*, usually large shrub
– *subhirtella*, large shrub
– *tenella*, small shrub
– – 'Alba', small shrub
– *triloba*, medium shrub
Rhododendron canadense, small shrub
– *kaempferi* hybrids
– *kurume* hybrids (hardy cultivars)
– *repens* hybrids, all early cultivars
Viburnum × *burkwoodii*, large shrub

Late April

Herbaceous plants

Ajuga species and cultivars
Alyssum saxatile cultivars
Androsace species and cultivars
Arabis caucasica 'Plena'
Arnebia pulchra (syn. A.echioides)
Aubrieta hybrids
Caltha palustris 'Multiplex'
Cardamine species and cultivars
Corydalis cava
– *cheilanthifolia*
– *lutea*
Doronicum columnae (syn. D.cordifolium)
Draba sibirica
Epimedium species and cultivars
Euphorbia polychroma (syn. E.epithymoides)
Gentiana acaulis hybrids
Hutchinsia alpina

Iris pumila 'Atroviolacea'
– – 'Caerulea'
Mertensia primuloides
Phlox subulata in various colours
Plagiorhegma dubium (Jeffersonia dubia)
Potentilla neumanniana (syn. P.tabernaemontani) 'Nana'
Primula auricula
– *elatior* hybrids in various colours
– × *pubescens* and old cultivars
Symphytum grandiflorum
Tiarella cordifolia
Veronica armena
Vitaliana primuliflora (syn. Douglasia vitaliana)
Waldsteinia geoides
– *ternata*

Bulbs

Anemone nemorosa late cultivars
– *ranunculoides* 'Plena'
Arum maculatum
Erythronium oregonum
– *evolutum* hybrid 'White Beauty'
– *tuolumnense*
Hyacinthus orientalis single and double late cultivars
Narcissus barrii (small narcissus) cultivars
– × *incomparabilis* forms
– *leedsii* (small-headed narcissus) forms
– × *medio-luteus* (syn. N. × poetaz) (tazetta narcissus) forms
– *pseudonarcissus* (trumpet narcissus) and cultivars
Puschkinia scilloides var. *libanotica*
Scilla hispanica early cultivars
Trillium grandiflorum
Tulipa biflora
– *hageri* 'Splendens'
– *montana* (syn. T.wilsoniana)
– *praestans*
– *tarda*

Flowering shrubs

Acer species, large shrub to tree
Amelanchier canadensis, large shrub
Berberis thunbergii, small shrub
Caragana pygmaea, small shrub
Chaenomeles hybrids, medium to large shrubs
– *japonica* var. *alpina*
Clematis alpina, climber

Cytisus × *kewensis*, dwarf shrub
– × *praecox*, medium shrub
– *purpureus*, dwarf shrub
Daphne cneorum 'Major', dwarf shrub
Deutzia gracilis, medium shrub
Exochorda 'The Bride', wide spreading shrub
Forsythia species and cultivars, medium to
    large shrub
Pyrus species, large shrub
Prunus × *blireana*, large shrub
– × – 'Moseri', large shrub
– *persica* cultivars, large shrub
Rhododendron impeditum cultivars
– *kurume* hybrids (late forms)
– *racemosum*, dwarf shrub
– – *repens* hybrids (late forms)
Ribes sanguineum 'Atrorubens', medium shrub
Viburnum carlesii, small to medium shrub
Wisteria sinensis, climber

The rock garden in spring

A mass of May flowers in full bloom in a rock
garden or around a pool reveals the beauty of
the season in an unforgettable way.

May

Herbaceous plants

Achillea, all small milfoils
Ajuga reptans
Androsace late forms
Anemone × *lesseri*
– *narcissiflora*
– *sylvestris*
Aquilegia species and cultivars
Arenaria species
Armeria maritima cultivars
Aster alpinus cultivars
– *tongolensis*
Buglossoides purpurocaerulea
Campanula cochleariifolia 'Miranda Bellardii'
– *portenschlagiana*
– – 'Birch Hybrid'
– *pulla*
Cardamine trifolia
Centaurea montana, various colours

Cerastium species
Convallaria majalis
Cypripedium calceolus
– – var. *pubescens*
Dianthus gratianopolitanus
– *microlepis*
– *plumarius*
Dicentra eximia
– – 'Alba'
Dodecatheon species
Doronicum columnae
Erodium species
Euphorbia myrsinites
Galium odoratum
Gentiana acaulis hybrids
– *dinarica*
Geum coccineum 'Borisii'
– × *heldreichii* 'Luteum'
– *rivale* 'Leonard'
Gypsophila repens
Haberlea rhodopensis
Hemerocallis early species and cultivars
Heuchera species and cultivars
× *Heucherella tiarelloides*
Iberis sempervirens
Iris germanica (dwarf bearded group)
– – (medium bearded) early cultivars
– *humilis*
Linum narbonense
– – 'Six Hills'
Lysimachia nummularia
– – 'Aurea'
Maianthemum bifolium
Matricaria oreades
Menyanthes trifoliata
Mertensia paniculata
Moehringia muscosa
Myosotis palustris (syn. M. scorpioides)
– *rehsteineri* (syn. M. caespitosa ssp.
    rehsteineri)
Paeonia mascula
– *mlokosewitschii*
– *peregrina*
– *tenuifolia*
– *wittmanniana*
Paradisea liliastrum
Phlox divaricata
– – 'Snow Carpet'
– *douglasii* hybrids
– *subulata* cultivars
Polemonium × *richardsonii*
Polygonatum commutatum

Polygonum sericeum
Potentilla aurea
− − ssp. *chrysocraspeda* (syn. P. ternata)
− *fragiformis*
− *pyrenaica*
Primula alpicola
− *frondosa*
− × *pubescens*
− *sieboldii* cultivars
Ramonda myconi, various colours
Ranunculus aconitifolius
− *acris* 'Multiplex'
− − 'Pleniflorus'
Salvia × *superba* 'May Night'
Saponaria caespitosa
Saxifraga arendisii hybrids
− *callosa* ssp. *callosa* (syn. S. lingulata)
  'Superba'
− *cotyledon* 'Pyramidalis'
− *muscoides* 'Findling'
− *paniculata* (syn. S. aizoon) cultivars
Sedum krajinae
Sisyrinchium angustifolium
Thalictrum aquilegifolium
Tiarella wherryi
Trollius small species and hybrids
Veronica austriaca ssp. *teucrium* (syn.
  V. teucrium)
− *prostrata*
Viola cornuta
− *labradorica*
− *sororia* (syn. V. papilionacea)

Bulbs

Allium cyaneum
− *karataviense*
− *moly*
− *neopolitanum*
Arum species
Camassia species and cultivars
Gladiolus byzantinus
Muscari late species and cultivars
Narcissus poeticus cultivars
Ornithogalum montanum
− *umbellatum*
Scilla hispanica cultivars
Tulipa sprengeri

Flowering shrubs

Berberis candidula, dwarf shrub
− *empetrifolia,* dwarf shrub
− × *stenophylla*
− *thunbergii* and cultivars
− *verruculosa,* dwarf shrub
Cotoneaster dammeri, dwarf shrub
− − var. *radicans,* dwarf shrub (mat-forming)
− *microphyllus,* dwarf shrub
Cytisus decumbens, dwarf shrub
Deutzia gracilis, small shrub
Exochorda racemosa, large shrub
Genista sylvestris var. *pungens* (syn.
  G. dalmatica), dwarf shrub
Helianthemum nummularium, dwarf shrub
Kalmia latifolia, dwarf shrub
Paeonia suffruticosa (syn. P. arborea) large shrub
Potentilla fruticosa early forms, dwarf to
  medium shrub
Rhododendron hippophaeoides, dwarf shrub
− *kaempferi* (syn. R. obtusum var. kaempferi),
  dwarf to small shrub
− *obtusum,* dwarf to small shrub
− *repens* hybrids
− *vaseyi,* small shrub
− *yedoense,* small to medium shrub
Rosa hugonis, large shrub
− *pimpinellifolia* and cultivars, small shrub
− *willmottiae,* large shrub
Zenobia pulverulenta, medium shrub

The rock garden in early summer

Early summer is quite different from both spring and summer. A sunny slope in the rock garden planted with early summer flowers is different in atmosphere from the same slope at any other time of the year. One would scarcely believe the hosts of wild flowers which can be included on one garden slope, where flowers make their home amidst fantastic ferns and shrubs, and soak up the afternoon sun. The early summer is also one of the times in the gardening year that blue plants reveal their varied tones. Larger flowers, such as delphiniums and white marguerites, throw off the restrictions of the formal flower-bed and add a touch of nobility to the wild rocky landscape.

Beginning of June to beginning of July

Herbaceous plants

Achillea ageratifolia
– taygetea hybrids
– tomentosa
Aethionema grandiflorum
Alyssum prostratum
– – 'Eburneum'
Antennaria dioica 'Rubra'
Anthemis marschalliana (syn. A.biebersteiniana)
Artemisia species
Aster × alpellus
– tongolensis cultivars
Astilbe, japonica early low-growing hybrids
– simplicifolia early hybrids
Astrantia carniolica
– major
Athamanta turbith ssp. haynaldii (syn. A.matthioli)
Campanula carpatica cultivars
– – var. turbinata cultivars
– cochleariifolia cultivars
– garganica cultivars
– glomerata 'Superba' and others
– persicifolia cultivars
– portenschlagiana
– – 'Birch Hybrid'
Cardamine trifolia
Carlina acaulis ssp. simplex (syn. C.acaulis var. caulescens)
– – – – 'Bronze'
Centaurea pulcherrima
Chrysanthemum maximum low-growing forms
Delphinium grandiflorum (blue and white)
– – hybrids (Belladonna group)
– – (Elatum group) low-growing cultivars
Dianthus carthusianorum
– cruentus
– deltoides
– microlepis
– pavonius (syn. D.neglectus)
– pinifolius
– plumarius
– spiculifolius
– strictus var. integer
Eryngium alpinum
Filipendula vulgaris
Gaillardia dwarf hybrids

Gentiana freyniana
– septemfida
– – var. lagodechiana
– – – – 'Doeringiana'
Geranium species and cultivars
Geum coccineum 'Borisii'
– – hybrid 'Georgenberg'
– montanum 'Olivanum'
Gillenia trifoliata
Globularia cordifolia
– trichosantha (plus later-flowering cultivars)
Gypsophila repens hybrid 'Rosy Veil'
Heuchera sanguinea 'Splendens'
– – hybrids and later-flowering cultivars
Hieracium × rubrum
Leontopodium species
Lewisia cotyledon hybrids
Lysimachia species
Marrubium supinum
Meconopsis betonicifolia
Meum athamanticum
Minuartia laricifolia
Nepeta species
Oenothera species
Origanum vulgare 'Compactum'
Oxalis adenophylla
Papaver alpinum
Patrinia triloba
Penstemon species
Phlox arendsii low-growing hybrids
Pimpinella saxifraga 'Rosea'
Polygonum affine 'Superbum'
– bistorta 'Superbum'
Potentilla atrosanguinea 'Gibson's Scarlet'
– nepalensis 'Miss Willmott'
– – 'Roxana'
– recta 'Warrenii'
Primula beesiana
– burmanica
– bulleyana
– florindae
– japonica cultivars
– sikkimensis
Prunella species and cultivars
Salvia × superba
Santolina species
Saponaria × olivana
Saxifraga cotyledon 'Pyramidalis'
Scabiosa caucasica cultivars
Scutellaria alpina
Sedum mid-season cultivars
Sempervivum species, hybrids and cultivars

Silene alpestris
Stachys byzantina (syn. S.olympica)
Thymus species and cultivars
Trollius chinensis 'Golden Queen'
– *pumilus*
Verbascum hybrids
Veronica prostrata
– *spicata*
Yucca filamentosa

Bulbs

Allium late species and cultivars
Gladiolus communis
Lilium bulbiferum ssp. *croceum*
– *cernuum*
– *hansonii* and hybrids
– *hollandicum* hybrids
– *martagon*, various colours
– *pardalinum*
– *pumilum*

Flowering shrubs

Bruckenthalia spiculifolia, dwarf shrub
Cotoneaster congestus, dwarf shrub
Dryas octopetala, dwarf shrub
Erica vagans cultivars, dwarf shrub
Fuchsia magellanica 'Gracilis', dwarf shrub
– – 'Riccartonii', dwarf shrub
Genista tinctoria 'Plena'
Helianthemum species and cultivars, dwarf shrub
Moltkia petraea, dwarf shrub
Spiraea japonica (*bumalda* hybrids), dwarf to small shrub

The rock garden in summer

The flowers that bloom in the main holiday period, from the beginning of July to mid-September, are much more widely seen and admired than those of any other season. Public gardens in the mountains, on moorland and at the coast, for example at hotels and resorts, can give an impressive idea of the plants that belong to a particular region and can provide ideas for gardeners working on a smaller scale. In private gardens, which often only receive attention at weekends, those plants with a long season are particularly valuable.

Whatever plants are grown from among the wealth of summer flowers available, it is important that they should have an adequate supply of water during dry spells. Even during a summer heatwave the rock garden should convey the freshness of the mountains.

Early July to late August

Herbaceous plants

Acantholimon glumaceum
Acanthus species
Adenophora species
Anaphalis triplinervis
Anemone vitifolia 'Robustissima'
Artemisia vallesiaca
Aster amellus 'Cassubicus' and other cultivars
– *ptarmicoides* 'Major'
– *sedifolius* 'Nanus'
– – 'Nanus Roseus'
Astilbe simplicifolia hybrids and late cultivars
Astragalus species
Campanula carpatica late cultivars
– – var. *turbinata*
– *pulla*
Coreopsis verticillata 'Grandiflora'
Deschampsia cespitosa cultivars
Dianthus carthusianorum
– *knappii*
– *sylvestris*
Eryngium planum
– × *zabelii* 'Violetta'
Gentiana asclepiadea
– *cruciata*
– – ssp. *phlogifolia*
– *dahurica*
– *septemfida*
Gypsophila repens hybrid 'Rosy Veil'
Hosta low-growing cultivars
Inula ensifolia 'Compacta'
Liatris elegans
Limonium small species
Linum flavum 'Compactum'
Morina longifolia
Opuntia species and varieties
Phuopsis stylosa 'Rubra'
Platycodon grandiflorus 'Apoyama'
– – 'Mariesii'
– – 'Mother of Pearl'

Potentilla atrosanguinea 'Gibson's Scarlet'
Rosularia chrysantha
Scutellaria baicalensis
Sedum summer-flowering groups
× *Solidaster luteus*
Stachys grandiflora 'Superba'
Veronica longifolia cultivars
– *spicata* ssp. *incana*

Bulbs

Allium late species and cultivars
Colchicum early species
Crocus early autumn group
Cyclamen purpurascens (syn. C. europaeum)
Scilla autumnalis

Flowering shrubs

Calluna vulgaris cultivars, dwarf shrub
Caryopteris × *clandonensis*, small shrub
Daboecia cantabrica cultivars, dwarf shrub
Hypericum patulum var. *henryi*, small shrub
Lavandula angustifolia, small shrub
Perovskia abrotanoides, small shrub

The rock garden in autumn

Autumn too has become a great season for the rock garden, and indeed, the flowers of this season are amongst the finest in the garden. They include the fading summer flowers as well as a strange resurrection of many spring flowers. The real autumn flowers include Michaelmas daisies, with their lilac, pink and white colourings, as well as dwarf berrying shrubs. The main colour in the autumn rock garden is provided by Japanese and Chinese anemones, the low-growing autumn gentian from western China and the many types and varieties of autumn crocus. The combination of autumn rock-garden plants with other beautiful October flowers and foliage can provide weeks of beauty quite unknown to our forefathers.

Early September to late October

Herbaceous plants

Anemone hupehensis 'Splendens'
Arum maculatum (attractive berries)
Aster amellus cultivars
– *dumosus* hybrids
– *linosyris*
Ceratostigma plumbaginoides
Chrysanthemum arcticum
Gentiana farreri
– *sino-ornata*
– – 'Praecox'
Helleborus niger 'Praecox'
Pennisetum alopecuroides (syn. P. compressum)
Saxifraga fortunei
– – 'Rubrifolia'
Sedum cauticolum
– – 'Robustum'
– *sieboldii*
Solidago late low-growing species and forms
Tricyrtis macropoda
Uniola latifolia
Viola odorata 'The Czar' second flowering

Bulbs

Colchicum species and cultivars
Crocus species and forms
Cyclamen hederifolium (syn. C. neapolitanum)
– – 'Album'
Sternbergia lutea

Flowering shrubs

Caryopteris incana
Lespedeza thunbergii, small to medium shrub
Perovskia atriplicifolia, small shrub

The rock garden in late autumn

November in the rock garden is first and foremost the month of the Christmas rose, but also a month when the double colchicums are still in flower. Primulas are in blossom again before their long winter sleep and glowing autumn leaves are flaming everywhere on the fresh evergreen carpet foliage. A November rock garden can give hours of unbelievable pleasure. The renowned sunshine of a mountain evening is brought down to the plains by a host of evergreen shrubs, now bursting with strength.

Nowadays, gardens can help even elderly people shake off the feeling of uselessness in their declining years by providing them with a continuing interest in life.

Early November to December

Herbaceous plants

Aster dumosus late hybrids
– *ericoides*
Chrysanthemum indicum late hybrids
Helleborus niger
– – 'Praecox'
– – var. *altifolius*
Saxifraga fortunei

Bulbs

Colchicum late species and cultivars
Crocus late species and cultivars

Flowering shrubs

Calluna vulgaris late autumn cultivars
Cornus mas, large shrub, attractive berries
Cotoneaster horizontalis, attractive berries
– other species with decorative berries
Daphne mezereum, attractive berries
Empetrum nigrum, attractive berries
– *atropurpureum,* attractive berries
Erica erigena 'Molten Silver' (syn.
   E. mediterranea)
Euonymus nanus, attractive berries
Helianthemum second flowering
Mahonia aquifolium 'Moseri', attractive leaves
Skimmia japonica, attractive berries
Vaccinium oxycoccos, attractive berries
– *vitis-idaea,* attractive berries
Viburnum farreri late autumn flowering, large shrub
– *opulus* 'Nanum', attractively coloured leaves

The rock garden in winter

Far from being a time of unrelieved bleakness, winter is a season in which a number of very valuable plants come into their own. The last of the autumn flowers may continue well into the winter months and in mild conditions or in warmer regions there will be a precocious blooming of spring flowers. In addition, the true flowers of winter are there to brighten the long dark months and numerous evergreens to provide a background of beautiful foliage.

Early November to late February

Herbaceous plants

Adonis amurensis
Chrysanthemum indicum hybrids, late and
   winter cultivars
– *koreanum* hybrid 'Innocence'
Helleborus abchasicus
– – hybrids
– *niger*
– – 'Maximus'
– – 'Praecox'
– – ssp. *altifolius*
– *lividus* ssp. *corsicus*
Primula vulgaris ssp. *sibthorpii*
Viola odorata 'Triumph', in sheltered warm areas of the rock garden—and many other plants from the early spring list, depending on the weather and their stage of development.

Bulbs

Crocus byzantinus
– *hyemalis*
– *laevigatus* var. *fontenayi*
– *longiflorus*
Cyclamen coum
Eranthis cilicica
– *hyemalis*
Galanthus elwesii
– *nivalis*
– – ssp. *cilicicus*
Narcissus asturiensis
Scilla mischtschenkoana (syn. S. tubergeniana)

Flowering shrubs

Chimonanthus praecox, small shrub
Corylus avellana, large shrub
Daphne mezereum, small shrub
Erica herbacea cultivars, dwarf shrub
Hamamelis japonica, medium to large shrub
– – 'Ruby Glow' ('Adonis'), large shrub
– – var. *flavo-purpurascens,* large shrub
– – var. *zuccariniana,* large shrub
– *mollis,* large shrub
– – 'Brevipetala', large shrub
Jasminum nudiflorum, medium shrub
Rhododendron dauricum, medium shrub
– *mucronulatum,* dwarf shrub
Viburnum farreri, medium shrub

Plant Lists
for Various Sites

The spring and summer rock and wild garden around deciduous trees

A very attractive alternative to more formal gardens is a small wild garden in which plants are associated with a few carefully arranged rocks. A small area around a clump of trees can be filled with spring woodland flowers, violets, woodruffs, lilies of the valley and primroses, and in summer with tall harebells, foxgloves and astilbes. A level sunken garden path should wind through the area between the occasional natural rock, partly sunk in the ground.

Herbaceous plants

Anemone sylvestris
Aquilegia vulgaris
Aruncus dioicus (syn. A. sylvestris)
Asarum europaeum
Astilbe simplicifolia hybrids
Buglossoides purpurocaerulea
Campanula tall species
Clematis species
Convallaria majalis
Corydalis species
Dictamnus albus
– – 'Albiflorus'
Digitalis grandiflora
– *purpurea* (die after flowering, but prolific seed dispersal)
Epimedium all species and cultivars
Galium odoratum

Geranium large species
Hacquetia epipactis
Hepatica nobilis, various colours
– *transsylvanica* (syn. H. angulosa)
Maianthemum bifolium
Melittis melissophyllum
Omphalodes verna 'Alba'
– – 'Grandiflora'
Paradisea liliastrum
Polemonium × *richardsonii,* various colours
Polygonum sericeum
Primula species and some cultivars
Pulmonaria species
Salvia × *superba*
Thalictrum aquilegifolium
Vinca minor cultivars
Viola odorata cultivars
Waldsteinia geoides
– *ternata*

Ferns

Athyrium filix-femina
Dryopteris austriaca (syn. D. dilatata)
– *carthusiana*
– *filix-mas*
– – 'Barnesii'
– *pseudo-mas*
– × *tavellii*
Gymnocarpium dryopteris
– *robertianum*
Osmunda regalis
– – var. *gracilis*
– – 'Purpurascens'
Phyllitis scolopendrium
Polypodium vulgare

Polystichum aculeatum
– setiferum

Grasses

Brachypodium sylvaticum
Calamagrostis × *acutiflora* 'Stricta'
Carex morrowii
– pendula
– sylvatica
– umbrosa
Deschampsia cespitosa cultivars
Luzula nivea
– sylvatica
– – 'Marginata'
Melica nutans
Molinia caerulea
– – ssp. *altissima*

Bulbs

Anemone apennina
– blanda
– nemorosa
– ranunculoides
Corydalis species
Crocus byzantinus
Cyclamen hederifolium (syn. *C.neapolitanum*)
– purpurascens
Eranthis species
Galanthus species and cultivars
Leucojum vernum
– – ssp. *carpaticum*
Lilium martagon
Ornithogalum species

Flowering shrubs

Clematis montana, climber
– viticella, climber
Cornus mas, large shrub
– officinalis, large shrub
Corylus avellana, large shrub
Crataegus laevigata, large shrub
– monogyna, large shrub
Daphne mezereum, small shrub
Euonymus europaeas, medium shrub
Hedera helix cultivars, dwarf shrub and climber
Laburnum alpinum, large shrub
Lonicera caprifolium 'Praecox', climber
– × tellmanniana, climber
Prunus padus, tree

Ribes alpinum, small to medium shrub
Rosa species, medium to large shrub
Sorbus, large shrubs only
Vaccinium myrtillus, dwarf shrub
– vitis-idaea, dwarf shrub
Viburnum species, small to large shrub

Coniferous and heather gardens

The plants used around existing or newly planted coniferous trees are closely akin to those of the heather or moorland garden. A garden of this kind offers the classic opportunity to display the treasures of moorland plants, with heather in flower continuously and broom flowering for months on end, amidst juniper bushes and wild roses. Laying out a heather garden of this kind is one of the most rewarding of garden activities. Flowering starts as early as January with the cultivars of the spring heath, *Erica herbacea*, and continues right through to October with the late-flowering *Calluna vulgaris*. Heathers which become too tall and spreading over the years can easily be cut back. It is essential to add peat, compost or moorland soil every few years.

The beauty of the unassuming heather garden is beyond compare. It can become a haven of peace enriched with incomparable colour tones.

Portuguese thyme, *Thymus villosus*, whose light bluish-green colouring fits so well here, makes an ideal evergreen basis for a heather garden. It will grow unchanged for decades, will not interfere with other plants and will keep down weeds, although couch grass will need to be removed as soon as it appears.

A number of beautiful flowering heathers have been excluded from my list because their flowers are too short-lived, but I have included a number of new discoveries. I should also mention here that all double callunas flower for more than twice as long as the single varieties.

Most junipers will not tolerate dense shade but some will grow well with a light cover of conifers and thin canopied trees such as birches. A beautiful effect can be achieved by positioning large rocks amidst groups of wild, tousled junipers and planting the edges with bush or rambling roses.

Herbaceous plants

Acaena species
Adonis vernalis
Ajuga reptans
Alyssum saxatile
Anaphalis triplinervis
Antennaria dioica 'Rubra'
Anthemis marschalliana (syn. *A. biebersteiniana*)
Anthyllis montana
Arabis procurrens
Armeria maritima
Artemisia vallesiaca
Aster alpinus
– *amellus* low-growing cultivars
– *dumosus* hybrids
– *tongolensis*
Athamanta turbith ssp. *haynaldii* (syn. *A. matthioli*)
Campanula carpatica cultivars
Carlina acaulis ssp. *simplex* (syn. C. *acaulis* var. caulescens)
– – – – 'Bronze'
Chrysanthemum arcticum
Dianthus gratianopolitanus 'Compactus Eydangeri' and others
– *carthusianorum*
– *cruentus*
– *deltoides*
– *spiculifolius*
– *sylvestris*
Digitalis grandiflora
– *purpurea* 'Excelsior Hybr.'
– – 'Gloxiniaeflora'
Geranium small species and cultivars
Globularia cordifolia
Gypsophila repens 'Rosy Veil'
Helianthemum species and cultivars
Hieracium × *rubrum*
Inula ensifolia 'Compacta'
Linum flavum 'Compactum'
– *narbonense*
Limonium, low-growing species
Nepeta × *faassenii*
– × – 'Superba'
Origanum vulgare 'Compactum'
Petrorhagia saxifraga
Potentilla aurea 'Plena'
Potentilla cinerea

– *neumanniana* (syn. P. tabernaemontani) 'Nana'
Salvia × *superba* 'May Night' and others
Saponaria ocymoides
Satureja montana 'Alba Compacta'
Scabiosa caucasica
Scutellaria alpina
Sedum album cultivars
– *hybridum*
– *reflexum*
– – 'Glaucum'
– *sexangulare*
– *spectabile* cultivars
– *spurium* cultivars
– *telephium* cultivars
Sempervivum species and forms
Thymus, all in basic list
Verbascum hybrids
Veronica low-growing and medium species and cultivars
Viola canina
– *odorata*

Dwarf shrubs

Andromeda polifolia
Arctostaphylos uva-ursi
Berberis × *stenophylla*
Betula nana
Calluna, all in dwarf shrub list
Chamaedaphne calyculata 'Nana'
Cotoneaster adpressus
Cytisus decumbens
– × *kewensis*
– *purpureus*
Empetrum nigrum
– *atropurpureum*
Erica herbacea (syn. E. carnea) cultivars in list
– *vagans* cultivars in list
Genista sylvestris var. *pungens*
– *tinctoria* 'Plena'
Juniperus sabina
Lavandula angustifolia
Picea dwarf cultivars in list
Pinus dwarf cultivars in list
Salix repens
Vaccinium vitis-idaea
Viburnum opulus 'Nanum'

Larger border shrubs

Acer monspessulanum, large shrub to small tree
– *palmatum*, small tree

Berberis gagnepainii, large shrub
– *thunbergii,* small shrub
– *vulgaris,* large shrub
– *wilsoniae,* small shrub
Betula pendula, tree
Clematis viticella, climber
Cornus mas, large shrub
– *officinalis,* large shrub
Cytisus × *praecox,* medium shrub
– × – 'Hollandia', medium shrub
Euonymus europaeus, medium shrub
Hippophae rhamnoides, medium shrub
Ilex aquifolium, large shrub
Juniperus communis, medium to large shrub
– – 'Hibernica' and other cultivars, medium
    to large shrub
Laburnum × *watereri,* tree
Larix leptolepis, tree
Lonicera caprifolium, climber
– *periclymenum,* climber
– *sempervirens,* climber
– × *tellmanniana,* climber
Picea abies, tree
Pinus nigra ssp. *nigra* (syn. P. nigra var.
    austriaca), tree
– *sylvestris,* tree
Prunus spinosa, large shrub
Ribes alpinum, medium shrub
Rosa canina, large shrub
– *hugonis,* large shrub
– *pimpinellifolia,* small shrub
– *willmottiae,* large shrub
Sorbus aucuparia saplings
Taxus species and cultivars
Viburnum opulus, large shrub

Ferns

Dryopteris filix-mas
Polypodium vulgare

Grasses

Bouteloua gracilis
Briza media
Calamagrostis × *acutiflora* 'Stricta'
– *varia*
Carex humilis
– *montana*
Deschampsia cespitosa
Eragrostis curvula
Festuca amethystina

– *cinerea*
– *tenuifolia*
– *valesiaca* 'Glaucantha'
Helictotrichon sempervirens
Koeleria glauca
Melica transsylvanica
Molinia caerulea
– – ssp. *altissima*
Panicum virgatum
Sesleria species
Stipa species

Large and small wild flowers and bulbs for shady areas

Ever richer and stronger colours from larger plants such as woody spiraeas, roses, rhododendrons, azaleas, astilbes, phlox and lupins, can be found in semi-shaded areas of the garden, but there are many corms and bulbs, such as some dahlias and almost all tulips, which are now adding fresh colour to these areas. A host of small herbaceous plants and smaller bulbs have recently appeared which provide a new range of flowering times, stretching from early spring to late autumn.

This is an area full of surprises. The problem of shady gardens has never been completely solved. Many flowering plants will flourish there against all expectation, suddenly bursting into wonderful blossom in semi- or full shade. The Cinderella of the garden has found her prince in the modern art of gardening which can turn every shady corner into a wealth of flowers. As more and more houses are built with small or medium-sized gardens it will become essential to try every means at our disposal to solve the problem of the shady garden, and here even the small herbaceous plant has an important part to play. Thousands of gardens are still full of unused semi-shady and shady areas which could become, year in and year out, a mass of unbelievable life and blossom. By the right choice of shrubs many of these could become ideal settings for small plants, with no great effort or expense, and they would require little attention in the future.

Besides areas in shadow thrown by shrubs,

there are areas of shade thrown by buildings or fences. These lie idle because the gardener is unaware of the possibilities of planting them with beautiful plants which thrive just as well in shade as in sun.

Stone in all its forms is a great help in protecting and framing small plants in shade and semi-shade, and showing off their beauty to the full. An astonishingly large part of the globe is covered with forest and woods, and these it was which produced the shade-loving flowers and most of the early spring flowers which blossom for as long as the wood remains cool and light; so a good way to deal with shady areas is to plant them as early spring gardens and, as summer approaches, to add woodland flowers, particularly those of the mountain forests, which flower in summer and autumn, and to surround them with woodland ferns and grasses.

In many light and weather conditions these new garden plants can create extraordinary effects of light, sky and sun, so transforming familiar corners that it seems as if our whole northern world has been transported across space to the unfamiliar, strongly-coloured Mediterranean. Even after these effects have faded, something of the magic still clings to the pergola, the rockery path and the pine clearing.

Our main concern here is not with the trees but with the woodland garden or shady rock garden which grows beneath them, so you should avoid allowing the branches to grow too thickly above the garden or the roots to come too close to the small plants. For it is not just a question of "shade" but of the great variations of shade or root growth which affect plant development.

The climate too has an effect. In cooler climates many plants will not survive too much shade, but this is balanced by their tolerance of the greater amount of air and ground moisture accompanying this type of climate.

In smaller garden areas one remedy can be to remove a small tree or lop off a few branches. Areas like this can be of great benefit to the housebound, providing a view through the window of early spring flowers, blue geraniums, spiraeas, blue-leaved plantain lilies *(Hosta)*, autumn anemones and ferns. Light-coloured sandstone slabs not only can make the whole garden accessible, but also can help bring out the beauty of the colours and shapes.

In an area of semi-shade, large and small ferns and grasses and other plants with decorative foliage play an important part, giving an impression of moisture and freshness even if the ground is quite dry. Small groups of flowering plants among them can produce astonishing effects, leading the eye quickly over the areas that are without flowers. Always putting flowers with other flowers is a form of gluttony. One should not ignore the many ornamental grasses, large and small garden ferns and other kinds of decorative foliage which provide a breathing space between the flowers, cover the soil with green, complement the early spring flowers and demonstrate the endless possibilities for breathing life even into apparently desolate and dull corners of the garden.

These dimly lit corners call out for rock or stone slabs to cover the soil and to create a sense of order, strength and light.

Do not assume that these remarks apply only to "large scale" projects. The methods can be adapted to any garden, however small. Everything is relative. The love of gardening can develop in a small garden just as well as in a large one.

Plants for partial and semi-shade

(many will also grow well in sun if the soil is moist)

Herbaceous plants

Aconitum × *arendsii*
– *carmichaelii* var. *wilsonii*
– *vulparia*
Actaea species and cultivars
Adonis amurensis
Ajuga reptans and cultivars
Alchemilla alpina
Aquilegia alpina 'Superba'
Arabis procurrens
Arnebia pulchra (syn. A. echioides)
Aruncus dioicus (syn. A. sylvestris)
Asarum europaeum

Aster divaricatus
Astilbe chinensis var. *pumila*
– taller hybrids
Astrantia major 'Rosea'
Azorella trifurcata
Bergenia species and cultivars
Brunnera macrophylla
Buglossoides purpurocaerulea
Campanula glomerata
– *lactiflora*
– *persicifolia*
– *portenschlagiana*
– *poscharskyana*
– *pulla*
– × *pulloides*
Cardamine species
Ceratostigma plumbaginoides
Chelone obliqua (limited use)
Chiastophyllum oppositifolium
Cimicifuga acerina
Clematis recta 'Grandiflora'
Codonopsis clematidea
Convallaria majalis
Cornus canadensis
Cortusa matthioli
Corydalis species
Cotula squalida
Cypripedium species
Dicentra species and cultivars
Dictamnus albus
Digitalis
Dodecatheon meadia
Doronicum species and cultivars
Epimedium species and cultivars
Euphorbia polychroma
Galium odoratum
Gentiana asclepiadea
– *cruciata*
Geranium macrorrhizum
Geum species and cultivars
Gillenia trifoliata
Haberlea rhodopensis
Hacquetia epipactis
Helleborus all species and hybrids
Hemerocallis species
Hepatica species and forms
Heuchera species and cultivars
Horminum pyrenaicum
Hosta all species and cultivars
Lathyrus vernus 'Alboroseus'
Lysimachia nummularia
Lythrum species and cultivars

Maianthemum bifolium
Meconopsis cambrica
Melittis melissophyllum
Mertensia species
Meum athamanticum
Mitella diphylla
Moehringia muscosa
Myosotis palustris
Omphalodes verna 'Grandiflora'
Oxalis acetosella
Patrinia triloba
Phuopsis stylosa
Phyteuma scheuchzeri
Plagiorhegma dubium
Platycodon grandiflorus cultivars
Pleione bulbocodioides var. *limprichtii*
Podophyllum hexandrum 'Majus' (syn. P.emodi)
Polemonium reptans 'Blue Pearl'
– × *richardsonii*
Polygonatum multiflorum
– *odoratum*
Polygonum affine
Primula, all except for Auricula group
Pulmonaria species and cultivars
Ramonda species
Sagina subulata
Sanguinaria canadensis
Saxifraga moss and shade species, hybrids and
    cultivars
– *fortunei*
Soldanella montana
Stachys grandiflora 'Superba'
Symphytum grandiflorum
Synthyris stellata
Thalictrum minus 'Adiantifolium'
Tiarella cordifolia
– *wherryi*
Tricyrtis hirta
– *macropoda*
Uvularia grandiflora
Vinca minor and forms
Viola odorata cultivars
– *sororia* (syn. V.papilionacea)
Waldsteinia species
Wulfenia carinthiaca

Grasses

Carex fraseri
– *morrowii* 'Variegata'
– *ornithopoda* 'Variegata'
– *plantaginea*

– *sylvatica*
– *umbrosa*
Deschampsia cespitosa and cultivars
Festuca scoparia
Luzula species and forms
Molinia caerulea
– – 'Variegata'
Sesleria heufleriana (limited use)

Ferns

all, with the exception of *Ceterach officinarum*
and *Thelypteroides palustris*

Bulbs

Allium neapolitanum
Anemone species
Arum species
Camassia species
Cnionodoxa species
Corydalis species
Crocus species (limited use)
– *byzantinus* (unrestricted use)
Cyclamen species
Eranthis species and hybrids
Erythronium species and cultivars
Fritillaria camtschatcensis
Galanthus species and forms
Hyacinthus orientalis (limited use)
Leucojum vernum
– – ssp. *carpaticum*
Muscari species and cultivars
Narcissus cyclamineus and hybrids (variable
   results)
Ornithogalum species (limited use)
Puschkinia scilloides
Scilla species and cultivars
Trillium species and cultivars

The dune garden

Near the decorative and functional seaside garden there is almost always space that can be devoted to a garden planted in natural style. Many steep hotel and resort gardens which have to battle continuously with the wind and the elements could easily be converted into small wild gardens for duneland plants while retaining their paths and seating areas. And even inland there are thousands of "sand gardens" or sandy tracts of land which were once duneland and which could be planted in a natural style with both large and small dune plants.

Which are the most attractive of the duneland plants? Undoubtedly the sea buckthorn *(Hippophae rhamnoides)* with its silver-green leaves and, when male and female are planted side by side, its mass of orange berries growing amidst steel-blue lyme grass *(Elymus glaucus)*, dwarf burnet roses *(Rosa pimpinella)*, low-growing prostrate broom (*Cytisus scoparius* ssp. *maritimus*) and sea thistle with heather growing between junipers and dwarf conifers, all interwoven with delicate grasses, blue fescues in particular. Great colour effects can be created simply with masses of dwarf creeping willows (*Salix repens* ssp. *argentea*) dotted with red and white sea thrift *(Armeria maritima)*, in whose grassy leaves gulls like to lay their eggs.

The most common duneland shrubs are sea buckthorn, alpine currant, wild rose and rowan. Blackthorn and dwarf conifers stand alongside honeysuckle, protecting and providing shade for many small duneland plants such as wood and dog violets. One can watch the gradual proliferation of duneland shrubs such as the sea buckthorn and blackthorn as they put out runners under the sand. Nor should we forget the rushes *(Juncus inflexus)* which are considered weeds in most countries.

All the plants I have named are child's play to grow, except for one or two which will only grow in specially chosen or prepared soil.

If you intend to plant a dry slope with cultivated duneland plants in the hope that it can then be left to its own devices as far as weeding goes, then naturally you should choose fast-spreading varieties. For small areas, however, it is a good idea to replace the lyme grass *(Elymus glaucus)* which spreads rapidly, with blue oat grass (*Helictotrichon sempervirens* syn. *Avena sempervirens*), which hardly spreads at all. You can have sea buckthorn growing out of the dune grass, remembering to include both male and female varieties. When sea buckthorn is planted it should be pruned back to about 20 cm (8 in), as should climbing roses. For larger areas, lyme grass can be replaced with the much more effective giant blue *Elymus giganteus*

'Glaucis', and this can also be used in smaller areas if, to prevent the roots from spreading, it is planted in a small pot sunk into the ground. If you want to include conifers, choose *Pinus mugo* in one of its varied shapes, or black pine *(Pinus negra)*. You can intermingle the creeping willow *(Salix repens)* with the burnet rose *(Rosa pimpinellifolia)*. For carpeting plants use sea thrift *(Armeria maritima)* in a new cultivar 'Düsseldorf Pride', which blooms more frequently, interspersed with the white 'Alba'. Suitable grasses include the blue fescues *(Festuca cinera, F. ovina, F. valesiaca* 'Glaucantha') and the tall *Festuca mairei*. The sea rush *(Juncus maritimus)* can be used to best effect in low-lying sections. For convenience you can replace sea thistle *Eryngium maritimum* with *Eryngium* × *zabelii* 'Violetta' or *Eryngium bourgatii*. To all these plants you can add the sea lavenders *(Limonium vulgare, L. latifolium* and *L. latifolium* 'Violetta'). As a backdrop to your garden you can use *Pinus mugo*, sea buckthorn and broom *(Cytisus scoparius)*.

There are also low-growing dwarf brooms such as *Cytisus decumbens*, the purple broom *(Cytisus purpureus)*, dyer's greenweed *(Genista tinctoria* 'Plena') and many others which are less suitable for rock or wild gardens, but which go well in a dune garden, being robust plants that thrive in any conditions. If you are tempted to start a dune garden, begin on a small scale and do not be put off by the great number of suitable plants, for you can include a good cross-section even in a small area. You need not necessarily restrict yourself to European dune-land plants. There are valuable plants from other coastal regions, not to mention mountain and moorland.

Laying out the garden with a miniature natural landscape helps to strengthen our ties with nature even where garden space is limited. Of course the size of the garden must determine the scale of your natural garden.

Herbaceous plants

Armeria maritima
Crambe cordifolia
– maritima
Eryngium bourgatii
– maritimum
– × zabelii 'Violetta'

Gypsophila species
Limonium latifolium
– vulgare
Ononis spinosa
Polygonatum commutatum
Veronica longifolia
Viola canina
– sororia (syn. V. papilionacea)
– – 'Immaculata'

Non-spreading grasses

Bouteloua gracilis
Carex morrowii
– – 'Variegata'
– pendula
Festuca amethystina
– cinerea
– mairei
– ovina
– valesiaca 'Glaucantha'
Helictotrichon sempervirens (syn. Avena sempervirens)
Juncus inflexus
Koeleria glauca

Spreading grasses

Elymus giganteus 'Glaucus'

Shrubs

Calluna vulgaris cultivars, dwarf shrub
Cytisus decumbens, dwarf shrub
– purpureus, dwarf shrub
Genista pilosa, dwarf shrub
– tinctoria 'Plena', dwarf shrub
Hippophae rhamnoides, large shrub
Juniperus communis, medium to large shrub
Lonicera caprifolium 'Praecox', climber
Pinus mugo ssp. *mugo*, medium to large shrub
– – ssp. pumilio
– nigra, tree
– pumila, large shrub
– sylvestris, and dwarf cultivars, shrub or tree
Prunus spinosa, medium shrub
Ribes alpinum, small shrub
Rosa canina, large shrub
– pimpinellifolia and cultivars, small shrub
– rubiginosa
– rugosa and cultivars
Salix repens, dwarf shrub
Vaccinium vitis-idaea, dwarf shrub

Waterside gardens, large and small

When planting a waterside garden it is important to realize that waterside vegetation does not require particularly wet soil. Our list takes this fact into account.

In a formal water or waterside garden you should include cultivated varieties, whereas a natural garden should not aim at a showy effect but should be limited to simple wild flowers.

Just as you should contrast flat and upright rocks in an informal rock garden, you should combine low-growing plants with a few taller types—for example *Lysimachia nummularia* with *Trollius* hybrids or *Tradescantia* × *Andersoniana* hybrids, hostas with taller grasses, irises with forget-me-nots, *Ligularia* × *hessei* with *Rodgersia*.

If you are planting the banks of a natural pond get rid of the fastspreading reeds which can soon produce an untidy look, and replace them with giant *Miscanthus floridulus* or the more graceful *M. sinensis* 'Gracillimus'. If the reeds are growing too thickly to allow for planting, one possible solution is to make a narrow, sunken water channel from the pond to a nearby area of lawn where it opens out into a sunken pool. You can then surround the new channel and pool with a waterside garden and plant true water plants in the stream and pool. Water plants are listed in the following section.

To plant the banks of a brook or stream, you should first clear the area of perennial weeds or grass. By adding rocks you can introduce a few twists and drops into a straight stream. If you lay out a path along the stream you create a clearly defined area between the two which can be cleared and planted and maybe include a few rocks to add variety.

Waterside plants

Small herbaceous plants

Astilbe chinensis 'Pumila'
Brunnera macrophylla
Caltha palustris
– – var. *alba*

Doronicum orientale
Hosta smaller species and cultivars
Lysimachia nummularia
Myosotis palustris
Primula denticulata
– *florindae*
– *japonica*
– *juliae* hybrids
– *rosea*
– *sikkimensis*

Bulbs

Gladiolus communis
– *palustris*

Medium to tall herbaceous waterside plants with no special moisture requirements

Astilbe arendsii hybrids
– *simplicifolia* hybrids
– *thunbergii* hybrids
Euphorbia palustris
Filipendula palmata
– *rubra* 'Venusta'
– *ulmaria*
Hemerocallis species, hybrids and cultivars
Hosta taller species and cultivars
Iris kaempferi cultivars
– *laevigata*
– *ochroleuca*
– *sanguinea*
– *sibirica*
Ligularia × *hessei*
Lysimachia punctata
Lythrum salicaria 'Rakete'
Rodgersia cultivars (semi-shade)
Thalictrum aquilegifolium
Tradescantia andersoniana hybrids
Trollius 'Goldquelle'
– 'Lemon Queen'
– *chinensis* 'Golden Queen' plus other cultivars

Grasses

non-spreading waterside types
Carex grayi
– *morrowii* 'Variegata'
– *muskingumensis*
– *pendula*
– *pseudocyperus*

Glyceria spectabilis 'Variegata' (slightly
   spreading)
Juncus inflexus
Miscanthus floridulus
– *sinensis* 'Gracillimus'
– – 'Silver Feather'
Sinarundinaria murielae
– *nitida*

Ferns

all larger types and varieties

Planting in water

If you plan to plant large water-lilies in an artificial pond you will either have to make the
pond deep (at least 70 cm, 30 in) or include
deeper planting holes in the base, whereas
dwarf water-lilies, which are no less impressive, require only 15 to 30 cm (6 to 12 in) of water
above the roots. They have one further advantage over the large lilies in that their leaves
cover a smaller area of water. They are usually
planted in pots, made stable by being surrounded with stones. In a sunny position they
will flower for five years before the soil needs
changing. If you plant larger lilies in pots you
will need much larger containers. A sawn off
rain butt would be about right. If you drain
your pool in winter you should protect the lilies with a thick covering of leaves and stand
the pots on the base of the pool. I have a pool
at home, thirty square metres in size and with
sides sloping at 120 degrees, in which both water and plants have remained in excellent condition for fifteen years without attention. Correct planting, as well as the addition of a
limited number of fish will keep the water clear
in a small pond, for both plants and fish contri-
bute to the pond's "recycling". Even a small
number of fish will keep the gnats at bay. Adding moorland soil will get rid of brown algae
which discolour the water quickly and perma-
nently.

All plants which spread are best planted in
pots, but you must not combine spreading and
non-spreading plants in the same container.
The soil should be rich in nutrients and, if possible, enriched with extra loam. You can buy
wide, shallow, willow baskets, which you line
with roofing felt and plant with miniature water landscapes. Perforated plastic pots serve the
same purpose and usually last longer, but make
sure they are of a neutral colour. You will need
at least 10 cm (4 in) of water above the soil.

It is a good idea to plant a few tall plants,
such as the flowering rush *(Butomus umbellatus)*
close to your water-lilies.

Plant forget-me-nots in fairly large tubs together with purple loosestrife or rushes,
through which the shoots of the long-flowering
forget-me-nots can rise up from the surface
while other stems flower flat in the water. If
you put them in too small a pot it will only be a
matter of months before these spreading plants
stop producing flowers, so you will need quite
large tubs. The beautiful loosestrife *Lythrum
virgatum* 'Rose Queen' will not survive planting
in water!

During the first year it is easy to overlook
the fact that many water plants spread, and not
to notice the danger until some time later when
they are already established in loose soil rather
than pots. You may suddenly find that they
have spread over an area of four square metres.
The common arrowhead *(Sagittaria sagittifolia)*
survives the winter in small corms and with the
spring suddenly appears in unexpected places,
but its growth can be easily restricted. Water
grasses will serve to show off your flowers both
on the bank and in the water.

Water plants

Measurements given refer to the average
   height of water above soil. S. = spreading, so
   best planted in containers.

Herbaceous plants

Acorus calamus 'Variegatus', sweet flag, up to
   10 cm (4 in), height 30 to 45 cm (12 to 18 in),
   May/June
Alisma plantago-aquatica, water plantain, 20 cm
   (8 in), height 1 m (3 ft), July/September
Butomus umbellatus, flowering rush, 20 to 40 cm
   (8 to 16 in), height 1.5 m (4½ ft), June/August

Calla palustris, bog arum, 5 to 15 cm (2 to 6 in), height 15 cm (6 in), June/July, S.

Caltha palustris, common marsh marigold, 0 to 5 cm (0 to 2 in), height 30 cm (12 in), April/May

Euphorbia palustris, water spurge, 5 to 30 cm (2 to 12 in), height 1 m (3 ft) or more, May/June

Hippuris vulgaris, mare's tail, 10 to 30 cm (4 to 12 in), height 30 cm (1 ft), June/August, S. (very invasive)

Hottonia palustris, water violet, 5 to 20 cm (2 to 8 in), height 15 cm (6 in), May/July, S.

Hydrocharis morsus-ranae, frogbite, up to 10 cm (4 in), floating, July/August

Iris kaempferi, Japanese iris, 5 to 10 cm (2 to 4 in), height 30 cm (1 ft). Many cultivars. Dry-plant from August. June/July

– *laevigata,* 5 to 10 cm (2 to 4 in), requires continuous moisture, height 30 cm (1 ft), many beautiful varieties

– *pseudocorus,* yellow flag, up to 10 cm (4 in), height 1 m (3 ft), June

– *versicolor,* 0 to 15 cm (0 to 6 in), height 1 m (3 ft), June

Lysichitum americanum, skunk cabbage, 5 to 15 cm (2 to 6 in), yellow, height 30 cm (1 ft) or more, April/May

– *camtschatcense* 5 to 15 cm (2 to 6 in), white, height 30 cm (1 ft) or more, May/June

Lythrum salicaria, purple loosestrife, up to 5 cm (2 in), height 90–120 cm (3–4 ft), June/August

Mentha aquatica, water mint, 1 cm (½ in), height 30 cm (1 ft), July/August, S.

Menyanthes trifoliata, Bog bean, bank and standing water, height 15 cm (6 in), May/June

Myosotis palustris, water forget-me-not, up to 5 cm (2 in), height 20 cm (8 in), May/October

Nuphar lutea, yellow water-lily, 40 to 70 cm (18 to 30 in), floating, June/August

Nymphaea hybrids, all floating, but watch for variations in water depth. All flower June/September

– – 'Aurora', 20 to 40 cm (8 to 16 in), coppery pink

– – 'Col. A. I. Welsh', 40 to 60 cm (16 to 24 in), sulphur yellow

– – 'Ellisana', bright red, 40 to 60 cm (16 to 24 in)

– – 'Escarboucle', carmine red, 40 to 60 cm (16 to 24 in)

– – 'James Brydon', crimson pink, 40 to 60 cm (16 to 24 in)

– – 'Laydekeri Lilacea', pink toning to carmine red, 20 to 40 cm (8 to 16 in)

– – 'Laydekeri Purpurata', deep carmine red, 20 to 40 cm (8 to 16 in)

– – 'Laydekeri Rosea', purply pink, 20 to 40 cm (8 to 16 in)

– – 'Marliacea Albida Rosea', delicate pink, 40 to 80 cm (16 to 36 in)

– – 'Marliacea Chromatella', light yellow, 40 to 80 cm (16 to 36 in) at least

– – 'Marliacea Colossea', flesh pink, 40 to 80 cm (16 to 24 in)

– – 'Maurice Laydeker', purple-red, up to 15 cm (6 in), dwarf variety

– – 'Murillo', red, 40 to 80 cm (16 to 36 in)

– – 'René Gerard', rose crimson, 80 to 100 cm (38 to 42 in)

– – 'Sioux', first yellow, developing later to copper pink, 20 to 80 cm (8 to 36 in)

– *odorata,* dark pink developing to light pink, 40 to 80 cm (16 to 36 in), June/September

– – 'Sulphurea', soft sulphur yellow, 20 to 40 cm (8 to 16 in), June/September

– *pygmaea* 'Alba' dwarf waterlily, white, only 5 to 15 cm (2 to 6 in), June/September

– *tuberosa,* scented waterlily, white, flowers stand above water line, some known varieties, June/September

Nymphoides peltata, fringed waterlily, yellow, 10 to 70 cm (4 to 36 in), floating, July/August, S.

Orontium aquaticum, Golden club, 10 to 30 cm (4 to 12 in), height 30 cm (1 ft), April/June

Ranunculus aquatilis, water crowfoot, 20 to 50 cm (8 to 20 in), flowering flat over the water, June/August

– *lingua,* great spearwort, 5 to 30 cm (2 to 12 in), height 60 to 120 cm (2 to 4 ft), June/August, S.

Sagittaria sagittifolia, common arrowhead, 15 to 30 cm (6 to 12 in), height 30 to 45 cm (1 to 1½ ft), June/July, S.

– – var. *leucopetala,* pure white flowers, 15 to 30 cm (6 to 12 in), height 30 to 45 cm (1 to 1½ ft), June/July, S.

Sparganium erectum, branched bur-reed, 30 cm (12 in), height 30 cm (1 ft) or more, June/July

Stratiotes aloides, water soldier, free-floating, 30 to 100 cm, (12 to 36 in), grows to around 15 cm, 6 in, July/August, S.

Trapa natans, water chestnut, beautiful rosettes of leaves, floating, 10 to 20 cm (4 to 8 in), June/August, S.

(Place in a wide, shallow container of earth—

almost at water-level—to allow young shoots, which sink in the autumn, to remain as far as possible within the container.)

Typha angustifolia, reedmace, 20 to 40 cm (8 to 16 in, height 3 m (3 to 9 ft) spadix 15 cm (6 in) long, July/August, S.

– *minima,* 10 to 20 cm (4 to 8 in), height almost 30 to 75 cm (1 to 2½ ft), spadix 5 to 10 cm (2 to 4 in) long, June/July, S.

Grasses

Carex grayi, up to 10 cm (4 in), height 60 to 90 cm (2 to 3 ft), June/August

– *lasiocarpa,* downy-fruited sedge, up to 15 cm (6 in), height 60 cm (2 ft) or more, May/June

– *pseudocyperus,* Cyperus sedge, 5 cm (2 in), height 90 to 120 cm (3 to 4 ft), June/July

Glyceria maxima 'Variegata', reed sweet grass, up to 20 cm (8 in), height 30–45 cm (12 to 18 in), July/August

Juncus inflexus, hard rush, 10 to 20 cm (4 to 8 in), height 30 cm (1 ft), June/August

Schoenoplectus lacustris, common bulrush, 5 to 50 cm (2 to 18 in), height 90 to 120 cm (3 to 4 ft), June/September, S.

– *tabernaemontani* 'Zebrinus', zebra club-rush, 5 to 30 cm, (2 to 12 in), height 30 cm (1 ft), June/July

Ferns

Thelypteris thelypteroides, marsh fern, 5 to 10 cm (2 to 4 in), height 90 cm (3 ft), S.

Extremely dry rock gardens

The realm of rock-garden plants includes a host of much-neglected plants which thrive in extremely dry conditions. A collection of these planted in the right conditions will produce astonishing harmonies and contrasts. They include most dwarf and small shrubs. Most plant-lovers and gardeners have no idea of the pleasure that they can derive from laying out a dry slope, for these dry plants combine great beauty with durability. For sandy, dry slopes it is important to distinguish between those plants which do well in a poor soil and those which like a dry, loose, nutritious soil, enriched with old, weed-free compost.

Dry rock garden

Herbaceous plants

Acaena species
Achillea species
Aethionema grandiflorum
Alyssum species
Anaphalis triplinervis
Androsace sarmentosa
Antennaria dioica 'Rubra'
Anthemis marschalliana (syn. A. biebersteiniana)
– *nobilis* 'Plena'
Arabis procurrens
Armeria species
Artemisia species
Asarum europaeum (shade)
Aster amellus cultivars
– *dumosus* hybrids
Athamanta turbith ssp. *haynaldii* (syn. A. matthioli)
Aubrieta hybrids
Bergenia species and cultivars
Buglossoides purpurocaerulea
Campanula carpatica cultivars
– *cochleariifolia* cultivars
– *portenschlagiana* cultivars
– *poscharskyana* cultivars
Carlina acaulis ssp. *simplex* (syn. C. acaulis var. caulescens)
– – – – 'Bronze'
Centaurea species
Cerastium species
Chrysanthemum arcticum and cultivars
Cirsium acaule
Coreopsis verticillata 'Grandiflora'
Corydalis lutea (shade)
– *ochroleuca* (shade)
Dianthus carthusianorum
– *doltoides* and cultivars
– *gratianopolitanus*
– *pinifolius*
– *plumarius* 'Blaureif'
Draba species
Epimedium species and cultivars (shade)
Eryngium species

Euphorbia most species
Geranium species and cultivars
Globularia cordifolia
Gypsophila species, hybrids and cultivars
Helianthum hybrids
– *nummularium*
Helleborus foetidus
Hieracium × *rubrum*
Iberis species and cultivars
Inula ensifolia 'Compacta'
Iris pumila
Jovibarba species
Leontopodium species and cultivars
Liatris species and cultivars
Limonium species
Linum flavum 'Compactum'
– *narbonense*
Meum athamanticum
Minuartia laricifolia
Nepeta species and cultivars
Oenothera species and cultivars
Onosma species
Opuntia species and varieties
Origanum vulgare
Orostachys spinosus
Paradisea liliastrum
Paronychia serpyllifolia
Petrorhagia saxifraga (syn. Tunica saxifraga, Kohlrauschia saxifraga)
Phuopsis stylosa 'Rubra' (syn. Crucianella stylosa)
Platycodon grandiflorus 'Mariesii'
Polygonum affine 'Superbum'
Potentilla species and cultivars
Prunella grandiflora and cultivars
– *incisa*
Salvia × *superba* cultivars
Satureja montana
– – 'Lilacina'
Saxifraga encrusted species and cultivars
Scutellaria alpina
– *baicalensis*
Sedum species and cultivars
Sempervivum species and cultivars
Silene maritima 'Weisskehlchen'
Solidago dwarf species and cultivars
× *Solidaster luteus*
Stachys byzantina (syn. S. olympica)
– – 'Silver Carpet'
Thymus species and cultivars
Verbascum species and cultivars
Veronica species and cultivars

Viola odorata cultivars (semi-shade)
Yucca filamentosa and cultivars

Grasses

Bouteloua gracilis
Carex grayi
– *montana*
Festuca amethystina
– *cinerea*
– *mairei*
– *ovina*
– *punctoria*
– *tenuifolia*
– *valesiaca* 'Glaucantha'
Helictotrichon sempervirens (syn. Avena sempervirens)
Koeleria glauca
Pennisetum alopecuroides (syn. Pennisetum compressum)

Dwarf conifer shrubs

All species and forms when well-rooted; prior to this, help rooting with a little water (see list p. 125 ff.).

Dwarf deciduous shrubs

Most species and cultivars when well-rooted; prior to this, help rooting with a little water (see list p. 121 ff.).

Hardy succulents and other hardy exotic plants

This section touches upon a charming new area of our rock gardens, although it is the main feature of many rock gardens in milder parts from the Mediterranean to the tropics. In fact the succulent rock garden is representative of the whole art of the rock garden in the southern hemisphere, and we too are now able to share some of its beauty in the form of winter-hardy succulents. These include winter-hardy cacti, spurges, *Sempervivum*, particularly the large rosette types, *Sedum*, *Orostachys* and *Yucca*. Rock gardens of this type can also include many bizarre northern plants and here you will have to use your imagination and knowledge of plants.

Succulent rock gardens are becoming continually more popular as more and more people are including them in their gardens. The succulent rock garden provides an opportunity to use many succulent house-plants out of doors during the summer, a practice which is already very popular in more southerly areas.

Gardeners who have already come to love winter-hardy perennials will find it easy to adapt to succulents, for there is little difference between the winter protection which both require. What strange colours are unfolded here, often disregarded by the rest of the world! What a wealth of plants ranging from simplicity to nobility! The succulents are the mainstay of rock gardeners in subtropical and tropical regions. They have attained enormous popularity in wide areas of South, North and Central America, where wild cacti are the main features of such gardens. They thrive in a most astonishing variety of situations, and I have no doubt that winter-hardy succulents are about to transform the face of our rock gardens.

A list of plants that I have successfully tried out follows below. Stone plays a particularly important part here. Limestone gives a rather strange effect; red sandstone, yellow travertine or volcanic rock are much more appropriate. You must choose a very sunny site, for these plants need to roast in the sun if they are to become hardy against frost. A site out of the wind is naturally best. *Opuntia* should be protected in winter with a few coniferous branches. So if you have a sunny, fairly dry spot where you want to try a succulent garden, you should lay down a layer of porous rubble and above this construct a low mound of soil, supported by a few rocks.

Succulent plants

Lewisia cotyledon hybrids
Opuntia hardy species and cultivars
Rosularia pallida
Sedum species and cultivars
Supervivum species, hybrids and cultivars
Umbilicus spinosus
Yucca filamentosa

Suitable partners
Herbaceous plants

Acantholimon species
Acanthus species
Artemisia species
Asphodeline species
Astragalus angustifolius
Chrysanthemum haradjanii
Eriophyllum lanatum
Eryngium species and cultivars
Euphorbia capitulata
– *myrsinites*
Marrubium supinum
Morina longifolia
Oenothera missouriensis
Origanum vulgare
Stachys byzantina (syn. S. olympica)
Thymus villosus

Bulbs

Allium (see bulb list p. 110)
Eremurus species and cultivars
Galtonia candicans (H2 hardiness)

Grasses

Bouteloua gracilis
Festuca amethystina
– *cinerea*
– *mairei*
– *ovina*
– *punctoria*
– *tenuifolia*
– *valesiaca* 'Glaucantha'
Helictrotrichon sempervirens

Dwarf shrubs

Caragana pygmaea
Caryopteris × *clandonensis*
Ephedra distachya var. *helvetica*
Genista radiata
– *sagittalis*
Helianthemum single cultivars
Lavandula angustifolia
Moltkia petraea
Perovskia atriplicifolia
Santolina chamaecyparissus
– *virens*

Colour Tones and Contrasts with Herbaceous Plants, Bulbs and Shrubs

What is the correct way of using the hosts of herbaceous plants? This is by far and away the most important question for rock gardeners. Herbaceous plants present new problems in which rocks have little part to play, except in their important role as stepping stones. This new wealth of plants lends itself to a variety of garden situations, one of the most obvious of being as a wide border to traditional flower-beds.

The new, bright colours invite startling combinations, but here these small plants can produce a number of problems.

The following sets of colour triads include the best examples of each individual colour from the whole range of small herbaceous plants, small bulbs, grasses, a few larger herbaceous plants and dwarf shrubs, and cover plants in flower from early spring right through to late autumn.

Any colour depends on the colours that surround it for its full effect, and colour triads will only work if the colours are chosen thoughtfully and with care. A few of the colours included here have been possible only after many years of hybridization.

The following colour triads can be varied to suit your own particular taste and to fit the situation and size of your garden:
Silver grey with pure blue and warm red,
White, orange and light to medium blue,
Blue-green, red-brown and yellow,
Pink, white and purple,
Bronze and boldly variegated plants with blue-grey grasses and *Dianthus*.

Colour triads

Silver grey with pure blue and warm red

Silver grey

Herbaceous plants (foliage)

Achillea serbica
– clavennae
– umbellata
Anaphalis triplinervis
Antennaria dioica 'Rubra'
Anthemis marschalliana (syn. A. biebersteiniana)
Artemisia nitida
– schmidtiana 'Nana'
Cerastium tomentosum var. *columnae*
Lavandula angustifolia
Leontopodium alpinum
Marrubium supinum
Potentilla argentea var. *calabra*
Saxifraga callosa ssp. *callosa* var. *australis* (syn. S. lingulata var. lantoscana)
– cochlearis
– cotyledon 'Pyramidalis'
– hostii
– paniculata
Sempervivum arachnoideum ssp. *tomentosum*
Stachys byzantina (syn. S. olympica)
– – 'Silver Carpet'
Veronica incana 'Argentea'

Pure blue

Herbaceous plants

Brunnera macrophylla
Buglossoides purpurocaerulea
Ceratostigma plumbaginoides
Delphinium 'Piccolo'
– 'Wendy'
– grandiflorum
Gentiana acaulis and hybrids
– cordifolia
– freyniana
– phlogifolia
– septemfida
– – var. lagodechiana 'Doeringiana'
Geranium meeboldii
Globularia species
Linum narbonense
Mertensia primuloides
– virginica
Myosotis palustris
Omphalodes verna 'Grandiflora'
Pulmonaria angustifolia 'Azurea'
Veronica austriaca ssp. teucrium 'Shirley Blue'
– – – – 'True Blue'
– prostrata 'Caerulea'

Bulbs

Allium cyaneum
Anemone nemorosa 'Royal Blue'
Chionodoxa luciliae
– sardensis
Crocus speciosus var. aitchisonii
– – 'Cassiope'
Iris histrioides 'Major'
– reticulata 'Blue Veil'
– – 'Cantab'
– – 'Harmony'
Muscari armeniacum 'Cantab'
– aurcheri
– azurea
– botryoides 'Heavenly Blue'
– racemosum
– – ssp. neglectum
Scilla bifolia
– hispanica 'Blue Queen'
– sibirica
– – 'Spring Beauty'

Dwarf shrubs

Moltkia petraea

Warm red

Herbaceous plants

Androsace carnea var. laggeri
Armeria maritima 'Düsseldorf Pride'
Dianthus cruentus
Geum coccineum
Helianthemum 'Firebrand'
– 'Rubin'
– 'Supreme'
Heuchera 'Firebird'
– 'Scintillation'
Potentilla atrosanguinea 'Gibson's Scarlet'
Primula elatior red hybrids
– rosea
Saxifraga arendsii 'Triumph'
Sedum cauticolum
– – 'Robustum'
– spurium 'Purple Carpet'

Bulbs

Tulipa red cultivars
– kaufmanniana hybrids, early and late pure
  red varieties
– praecox
– sprengeri

Dwarf shrubs

Fuchsia magellanica 'Riccartonii'
Rhododendron ferrugineum
– repens hybrids

White, orange and light to medium blue

White

Herbaceous plants

Achillea serbica
– clavennae

– *ptarmica* 'Nana Compacta'
– *umbellata*
Anaphalis triplinervis
Anemone narcissiflora
– *sylvestris*
Arabis procurrens
Armeria caespitosa 'Alba'
– *maritima* 'Alba'
Aster alpinus 'Albus'
Astilbe simplicifolia hybrids 'Irrlicht'
Athamanta turbith ssp. *haynaldii* (syn.
A. matthioli)
Campanula carpatica 'White Clips'
– – var. *turbinata* 'Alba'
– *cochleariifolia* 'Alba'
Cardamine trifolia
Chrysanthemum arcticum
Convallaria majalis
Delphinium grandiflorum 'Album'
Dianthus pinifolius
Dicentra eximia 'Alba'
Dodecatheon meadia 'Hermes'
Epimedium grandiflorum
– × *youngianum* 'Niveum'
Geranium dalmaticum 'Album'
– *sanguineum* 'Album'
Gypsophila repens 'Monstrosa'
Helleborus niger
– – var. *altifolius*
– – ssp. *macranthus*
– – 'Praecox'
Hepatica nobilis 'Alba'
– *transsylvanica* (syn. H. angulosa) 'Alba'
Heuchera hybrid 'Scintillation'
Heuchera sanguinea 'Alba'
Hutchinsia alpina
Iberia saxatilis
– *sempervirens*
Iris barbata 'Snow Cap' (dwarf bearded group)
Leontopodium
Matricaria oreades
Minuartia larifolia
Oenothera speciosa
Omphalodes verna 'Alba'
Phlox subulata 'May Snow'
× *arendsii* 'Susanne'
Primula denticulata 'Alba'
– *elatior* white hybrids
– *juliae* hybrids 'Snow White'
Ranunculus aconitifolius 'Plena'
Sagina subulata
Sanguinaria canadensis

– – 'Plena'
Satureja montana 'Alba Compacta'
Saxifraga arendsii hybrids 'Snow Carpet'
– *callosa* 'Superba'
– *cochlearis*
– *cotyledon* 'Pyramidalis'
– *muscoides* 'Findling'
– *paniculata* 'Altissima'
– *trifurcata*
Sedum album
– *spurium* 'Album Superbum'
Silene maritima 'Alba'
Tiarella cordifolia
– *wherryi*

Bulbs

Allium neapolitanum
– *odorum*
Anemone apennina 'Alba'
– *blanda* 'White Splendour'
– *nemorosa* 'Grandiflora'
– – 'Alba Plena'
Chionodoxa luciliae 'Alba'
Colchicum autumnale 'Album Plenum'
– *speciosum* 'Album'
Corydalis cava 'Alba'
Crocus biflorus 'White Lady' and other white
cultivars
– *fleischeri*
– *kotschyanus* 'Albus'
– *speciosus* 'Albus'
– *vernus* 'Blizzard'
– – 'King of the Whites'
– – 'L'Innocence'
Cyclamen coum 'Album'
– *hederifolium* (syn. C. neapolitanum) 'Album'
Erythronium dens-canis 'Album'
– – 'White Splendour'
Fritillaria meleagris 'Alba'
– – 'Aphrodite'
Galanthus caucasicus
– *elwesii*
– *ikariae*
– *nivalis*
– – 'Flore Pleno'
– – ssp. *cilicicus*
Hyacinthus orientalis 'L'Innocence'
Leucojum vernum
– – ssp. *carpaticum*
Muscari azurea 'Alba'
– *botryoides* 'Album'

Narcissus poeticus
Ornithogalum montanum
– *narbonense*
Scilla hispanica 'Alba'
– *sibirica* 'Alba'
Trillium grandiflorum
– *nivale*
Tulipa stellata
– *turkestanica*

Dwarf Shrubs

Calluna vulgaris 'Alba Plena'
Daphne blagayana
– *mezereum* 'Alba'
Deutzia gracilis
Erica herbacea (syn. E.carnea) 'Alba'
– *vagans* 'Alba'
– – 'Lyonesse'
Philadelphus lemoinei hybrid 'Manteau
  d'Hermine'
Rhododendron mucronatum
Spiraea decumbens

Orange

Herbaceous plants

Geum coccineum 'Borisii'
– × *heldreichii* 'Splendens'
Hieracium × *rubrum*
Potentilla aurea (syn. P.ternata)
– *nepalensis* 'Roxana'
Primula elatior orange hybrids

Bulbs

Corydalis solida 'Transsylvanica'
Fritillaria imperialis
Lilium pensylvanicum (syn. L.dahuricum)
Tulipa kaufmanniana 'Fritz Kreisler'
– – 'Orange Boy'

Dwarf shrubs

Chaenomeles japonica

Light to medium blue

Herbaceous plants

Aster dumosus hybrid 'Lady in Blue'
Aubrieta 'Lobelia'
Campanula carpatica 'Blue clips'
– *cochleariifolia* 'Miranda Bellardii'
Gentiana farreri
Iris germanica (dwarf bearded), 'Blue Denim'
– – 'Caerulea'
– – 'Ragusa'
Primula vulgaris 'Carulea'
Veronica prostrata 'Pallida'

Bulbs

Allium caeruleum
– *cyaneum*
Anemone apennina
– *nemorosa* 'Allenii'
– – 'Blue Beauty'
– – 'Celestial'
Crocus salzmannii
– *tomasinianus*
– *vernus* 'Queen of the Blues'
Hyacinthus orientalis 'Myosotis'
– – 'Queen of the Blues'
Iris reticulata 'Cantab'
Muscari azurea (syn. Hyacinthella azurea)
Scilla hispanica 'Myosotis'
– *mischtschenkoana* (syn. S.tubergeniana)

Blue-green, red-brown and yellow
Blue-green

Deciduous and coniferous foliage plants
Herbaceous plants

Acaena buchananii
Aethionema grandiflorum
Dianthus gratianopolitanus
– – 'Compactus Eydangeri'
Eryngium × *zabelii* 'Violetta'
Euphorbia myrsinites
Hosta sieboldiana 'Glauca'
Sedum anacampseros
– *cauticolum*
– *ewersii* 'Nanum'

– – var. *homophyllum*
– *forsteranum* ssp. *elegans*
– *sieboldii*
– *spectabile*

Grasses

Festuca cinerea
– *ovina*
– *valesiaca* 'Galucantha'
Helictotrichon sempervirens 'Pendula'

Bulbs

Allium karataviense

Dwarf shrubs

Juniperus horizontalis 'Glauca'
Picea abies 'Pumila Glauca'
– *pungens* 'Glauca Procumbens'

Red-brown

Deciduous foliage

Herbaceous plants

Ajuga reptans 'Purpurea'
– – 'Multicolor'
Sedum album 'Murale'
– *kamtschaticum* var. *middendorfianum*
– *spurium* 'Purple Carpet'
Sempervivum 'Alpha'
– 'Gamma'
– 'Metallicum Giganteum'
– 'Rubin'
– 'Zirkon'
– *marmoreum* 'Mahogany'
– *tectorum* 'Triste'

Dwarf shrubs

Berberis thunbergii 'Nana'

Yellow

Herbaceous plants

Achillea tomentosa

Adonis amurensis
– *vernalis*
Alyssum montanum
– *saxatile*
– – 'Citrinum'
– – 'Compactum'
Anthemis marschalliana (syn. A.biebersteiniana)
Coreopsis verticillata 'Grandiflora'
Corydalis lutea
Doronicum orientale 'Spring Beauty'
– – 'Miss Mason'
Draba aizoides
– *sibirica*
Eriophyllum lanatum (syn. E.caespitosum)
Euphorbia palustris
Geum 'Georgenberg'
– *montanum* 'Olivanum'
Helianthemum 'Jubilee'
– 'Golden Queen'
– 'Wisley Primrose'
Hypericum olympicum
Iris germanica (dwarf bearded group) 'Excelsa'
– – 'Lutea'
– – 'Path of Gold'
Inula ensifolia 'Compacta'
Linum flavum 'Compactum'
Lotus corniculatus 'Peniflorus'
Oenothera missouriensis
– *tetragona*
Potentilla aurea
– – 'Plena'
– *cinerea* (syn. P.arenaria)
– *fragiformis*
– *pyrenaica*
– *recta* 'Warrenii'
Primula Elatior yellow hybrids
– *florindae*
– *sikkimensis*
– *vulgaris*
Saxifraga × *apiculata*
– × *elisabethae*
– × *haagii*
– *juniperifolia* ssp. *sancta*
Sedum forsteranum ssp. *elegans*
– *kamtschaticum* 'Variegatum'
– – var. *middendorfianum*
– – – – 'Diffusum'
– *krajinae*
– *ochroleucum*
– *selskianum*
– *sexangulare*
Trollius species and hybrids

Bulbs

Allium flavum
Anemone ranunculoides
– – 'Plena'
– – 'Superba'
Corydalis bracteata
Crocus candidus var. subflavus
– chrysanthus
– – 'Cream Beauty'
– – 'E.P.Bowles'
– flavus
– – 'Dutch Yellow'
– – var. sulphureus 'Concolor'
– × stellaris
Eranthis cilicica
– hyemalis
– × tubergenii 'Glory'
– × – 'Guinea Gold'
Erythronium tuolumnense
Fritillaria aurea
– imperialis 'Lutea'
– pallidiflora
Hyacinthus orientalis 'City of Haarlem'
– – 'King of the Yellows'
– – 'Yellow Hammer'
Iris danfordiae

Dwarf shrubs

Cytisus decumbens
– × kewensis
Genista tinctoria 'Plena'
Hypericum hookeranum 'Hidcote'
Potentilla fruticosa 'Farreri'
– – 'Purdomii'

Pink, white and purple

Pink

Herbaceous plants

Aethionema grandiflorum
Androsace sarmentosa
Anemone hupehensis 'Praecox'
– – 'Splendens'
Antennaria dioica 'Rubra'
Arabis × arendsii 'Rosabella'
Armeria maritima 'Rosea Compacta'

Aster dumosus 'Judith'
– – 'Mrs Ralph Woods'
Astilbe 'Cologne'
– 'Europa'
Aubrieta hybrid 'Red Carpet'
Centaurea pulcherrima
Chrysanthemum arcticum 'Roseum'
Dianthus carthusianorum
– deltoides
– gratianopolitanus
– – 'Compactus Eydangeri'
– plumarius 'Altrosa'
Dicentra eximia
Dodecatheon meadia
Geranium sanguineum var. prostratum
Gypsophila repens 'Rosea'
– repens 'Rosy Veil'
Helianthemum 'Wisley Bridesmaid'
Hepatica nobilis 'Rosea'
Lathyrus vernus 'Albo-roseus'
Lychnis viscaria 'Plena'
Petrorhagia saxifraga (syn. Tunica saxifraga)
   'Rosette'
Phlox subulata 'Atropurpurea'
Platycodon grandiflorus 'Mother of pearl'
Primula elatior pink hybrids
– japonica 'Rosea'
– marginata 'Rosea'
– saxatilis
– vulgaris ssp. sibthorpii
Sedum album 'Murale'
– spurium 'Roseum Superbum'
– – 'Salmoneum'
Silene alpestris 'Heidi'
Thymus praecox
Veronica prostrata 'Rosea'
– spicata 'Erika'
– – 'Heidekind'

Bulbs

Allium narcissiflorum
– oreophilum
Anemone apennina 'Purpurea'
– blanda 'Charmer'
Chionodoxa luciliae 'Pink Giant'
Colchicum autumnale 'Plenum'
Cyclamen coum
– hederifolium (syn. C.neapolitanum)
– pseudibericum
– purpurascens
Erythronium dens-canis 'Pink Perfection'

– – 'Rose Beauty'
Hyacinthus orientalis 'Gertrude'
– – 'Pink Pearl'
– – 'Queen of the Pinks'
Scilla hispanica 'Rose Queen'
Tulipa kaufmanniana hybrids (pink varieties)

Dwarf shrubs

Calluna vulgaris 'H.E.Beale'
– – 'J.H.Hamilton'
Cytisus purpureus
Daphne cneorum 'Major'
– *mezereum*
Erica herbacea (syn. E. carnea)
Rhododendron Ghent hybrids (pink cultivars)
– *hirsutum*
– *mollis hybrids*
– *mucronulatum*
– *racemosum*

White

See list pages oo and oo

Purple

Herbaceous plants

Ajuga reptans 'Atropurpurea'
Aquilegia alpina 'Superba'
Aster × *alpellus* 'Triumph'
– *amellus* 'King George'
– – 'Empress'
– – 'Violet Queen'
– *dumosus* 'Dandy'
– – 'Jenny'
– – – *frikartii* 'Mönch'
– *tongolensis* 'Wendy'
Aubrieta hybrid 'Blue Emperor'
– – 'Dr Mules'
– – 'Tauricola'
Campanula carpatica 'Kobalt'
– *portenschlagiana*
– – 'Birch Hybrid'
– *poscharskyana* 'Stella'
– *pulla*
– × *pulloides*

Geranium walichianum 'Buxton's Blue'
Iris germanica (dwarf bearded group)
  'Atroviolacea'
Limonium latifolium 'Violetta'
Phlox subulata 'G.F.Wilson'
Phyteuma scheuchzeri
Polemonium × *richardsonii* 'Superbum'
Primula-juliae hybrid 'Märzfreude'
– *marginata*
– – 'Hyacinthina'
– × *wockei*
Prunella grandiflora 'Loveliness'
Pulsatilla halleri ssp. *slavica*
– *vulgaris*
Salvia × *superba*
– × – 'May Night'
Satureja montana 'Lilacina Compacta'
Scabiosa caucasica 'Moorheim Blue'
Scutellaria alpina
– *baicalensis*
– *scordifolia*
Veronica incana 'Argentea'
– *longifolia*
– – 'Foerster's Blue'
– *spicata*
– – 'Romiley Purple'
Vinca minor
– – 'Bowles Variety'
Viola cornuta 'Minor'
– *gracilis* 'Lord Nelson'
– *odorata* 'Triumph'

Bulbs

Anemone apennina
– *blanda* var. *scythinica*
– *nemorosa* 'Robinsoniana'
Crocus asturicus 'Atropurpureus'
– *imperati*
– *nudiflorus*
– *sieberi*
– *speciosus* 'Oxonian'
– – 'Pollux'
– *tomasinianus* 'Barr's Purple'
– – 'Whitewell Purple'
– *vernus* 'Blue Flag'
– – 'Purpureus Grandiflorus'
– – 'Remembrance'
– – 'Uncle Tom'
– – 'Zulu'
Hyacinthus orientalis 'Purple King'
Iris reticulata 'J.S.Dijt'

An easy-to-manage mixed arrangement of tulips, cushion-forming perennials, grasses and shrubs creates flowering features at different times of the year and invites us to linger.

1. A few bulbs in moist soil will produce a fine group of *Leucojum vernum*, the Spring Snowflake (text p. 118).
2. *Cyclamen coum* (text p. 114), is usually in flower by February.
3. *Bulbocodium vernum*, the Spring Bulbocodium (text p. 111), appears early in the year from March onwards, and has unique, red-violet flowers.

1. *Muscari latifolium*, a
deep-blue Grape Hya-
cinth, is one of the
most attractive early
spring flowers.

2. *Fritillaria meleagris*,
the Snake's-head Lily
(text p. 116), comes in
wine, violet and white
varieties.

3. *Ornithogalum umbella-
tum*, the Star of Bethle-
hem, will thrive in any
soil.

4. *Allium karataviense*
(text p. 110), is one of
the completely hardy
alliums.

1. *Pulsatilla vulgaris*, the
Common Pasque
Flower (text p. 242) –
one of the 'permanent
fixtures' of the rock
garden, which should
not be removed once
established.
2. *Pulsatilla vulgaris*
'Alba' – a white variety.
3. *Pulsatilla vulgaris*
'Rubra' – a striking red
variety that occupies a
noble place in this cul-
tivated group.
4. *Pulsatilla vulgaris* ssp.
grandis (text p. 242), is
unfortunately rarely
grown. The plants illus-
trated here were photo-
graphed in the wild.

1. *Arnebia pulchra*, the Prophet Flower (text p. 157), with its black-spotted yellow flowers, is one of the treasures of the garden.
2. *Geranium subcaulescens* 'Splendens' – a profusion of bright carmine-red flowers in summer.

3. *Lewisia* species were formerly regarded as difficult, but now the *Lewisia cotyledon* hybrids have firmly taken their place in many gardens. Given a shady, well-drained soil with gravel around their crowns, they will flower freely every year.

1. to 3. *Allium flavum*, the Yellow Onion (text p. 110), is best with other alliums such as *A. cirrhosum* (syn. *A. pulchellum*) (text p. 110). Both are similar in form but vary in colour. Plant them amidst moderately-sized, deep blue speedwell and suitable grasses. Rather apt to self-seed widely.

1. *Uvularia grandiflora* (text p. 273–4), surprises us with its blue-green clumps in April/May.

2. and 3. *Podophyllum hexandrum* 'Majus', produces pale pink cup-shaped flowers in May, which later develop into large bright red berries.
4. *Hacquetia epipactis* (text p. 195), with its yellow flowers, needs semi-shade in the garden as it does in the wild.

mpressive living pictures can be created at will in
he sink garden – as here with succulents – provided
hat due regard is paid to the needs of the plants that
re used.

and 2. Sink gardens allow many difficult treasures
) be grown in the tiniest space. They are easy to
ook at and easy to look after!

89

1. *Anemone blanda*, the Grecian Windflower (text p. 110), needs a warm sheltered position if it is to continue to thrive.

2. *Adonis vernalis*, the Yellow Adonis (text p. 152), is a plant of dry grasslands and in the garden requires a fairly well drained humus-rich soil and a sunny position.

3. *Adonis amurensis* (text p. 152), flowers weeks before the European adonis, *A. vernalis*.

1. *Tricyrtis macropoda* (text p. 273), does well in slight shade and is excellent with dwarf ferns and blue and white *Polemonium X richardsonii*.

2. *Synthyris stellata* (text p. 255), a beautiful North American woodland plant, bears lilac-blue, snapdragon-like flowers reliably early, from mid-March.

1. *Anemone sylvestris* (text p. 154–5), likes a lightly-shaded position and a humus-rich, chalky soil. Its fluffy seed-pods are also interesting.

2. *Primula denticulata* (text p. 222), comes in violet, white and red shades. The red form illustrated is a cultivated type which demonstrates the hybridist's skill.

3. *Primula elatior*, the Oxlip (text p. 223), blooms as soon as the snows melt. Regrettably it has tended to lose its place in the garden to the colourful primrose-cowslip hybrids.

4. *Waldsteinia geoides*, the Golden Barren Strawberry (text p. 278), forms long-lived thickets which will do well even in an unpromising situation.

1. *Primula marginata* (text p. 222–3) – an easy-growing primula from the Lake- and Cottian Alps. It has been widely used for cross-breeding.

2. *Primula X wockei* (text p. 223), is a product of *P. X arctotis* and *P. marginata*. It is free-flowering.

3. The white form of *Primula marginata* is still to be seen very seldom.

4. 'Marven' is still one of the best primula varieties *(P. X venusta X P. marginata)*.

5. Of all the *Primula marginata* varieties, 'Linda Pope' must surely be the best-known.

1. *Epimedium X versicolor* 'Sulphureum', has beautiful bronze shoots.
2. *Epimedium X youngianum* 'Niveum', with its snow-white flowers, is the longest-flowering of all the barrenworts.
3. *Epimedium pinnatum* ssp. *colchicum* (text p. 173) from the Caucasus, has deep yellow flowers. Sheltered from the winter sun it remains almost evergreen.
4. *Epimedium grandiflorum* (text p. 173), is the largest of the white-flowered species but is rather a spindly plant.

1. *Cornus canadensis*, the Canadian Dogwood (text p. 168), will form a thick carpet in the right conditions – shade and a cool, damp, acid, humus-rich soil.

3. *Anemone narcissiflora* (text p. 154) – a real mountain anemone which grows just as well in the garden. A good root-ball must first be established in a pot.

2. and 4. *Dentaria penta-phyllos* (text p. 169–70), likes chalky, humus-rich soil in a shady spot.

1. *Rhododendron ferrugineum* (text p. 127), photographed in the wild.
2. *Rhododendron kotschyi* (text p. 128), is one of the best-growing dwarf types for the rock garden. It is very common in the southern Carpathians.

3. Kurume rhododendron hybrids, have been bred in a wide range of colours.
4. *Rhododendron repens* hybrid 'Baden Baden' is still one of the most valuable varieties from this class. Its bell-shaped dark red flowers appear early in May, making it unsuitable for situations subject to late frosts.

Iris reticulata 'Pauline'
Muscari armeniacum
– *botryoides*
– *moschatum*
– *racemosum*
Scilla hispanica 'Sky Blue'

Dwarf shrubs

Lavandula angustifolia 'Hidcote Blue'
Perovskia atriplicifolia
Rhododendron impeditum

Coloured foliage contrasted with variegated

Herbaceous plants

Ajuga reptans 'Atropurpurea'
– – 'Multicolor'
– – 'Variegata'
Arabis caucasica 'Variegata'

Euphorbia polychroma (syn. E.epithymoides)
  (blossom)
Hosta fortunei 'Aurea'
– – 'Semperaurea'
– *sieboldiana* 'Aureomarginata'
Lysimachia nummularia 'Aurea'
Saxifraga umbrosa 'Aureopunctata'
Sedum kamtschaticum 'Variegatum'
– – var. *middendorfianum*
Vinca minor 'Variegata'

Grasses

Alopecurus pratensis 'Variegatus'
Arrhenatherum elatius ssp. *bulbosum*
  'Variegatum'
Carex morrowii 'Variegata'
– *ornithopoda* 'Variegata'
Glyceria maxima 'Variegata'
Luzula sylvatica 'Marginata'

Dwarf shrubs

Euonymus fortunei, var. *radicans* 'Variegata'

Long
and Twice-flowering
Plants of the Rock Garden

Most catalogues of rock-garden plants make special mention of the long-flowering plants and offer suggestions on other plants which can be successfully combined with them, for suppliers recognize the fact that it is these lists that tempt many beginners to make their first selection of rock-garden flowers. In addtition they advise on plants for areas where the longest possible flowering-time is desirable. The best effects can be achieved by combining different types of long-flowering plants. A knowledge of long-flowering plants is obviously helpful to the gardener who plants various seasonal areas in the rock garden, for there are many long-flowering plants which will extend the seasonal flowering times without taking up too much of the space to be devoted to plants of the particular season.

This list is based on an extensive period of observation, but I am sure that there are still many omissions, especially as new long-flowering plants appear on the market every year, with new additions appearing from the most unlikely sources. With cross-breeding, larger wild plants produce smaller varieties with equally long flowering times. Thus we now have the new, early-flowering, low-growing variety of sage, *Salvia* × *superba* 'May Night', the extremely low-growing *Gaillardia* hybrid 'Kobold', and the pink double-flowered Gypsophila 'Rosy Veil', to mention but a few.

'Long-players'

(Small herbaceous plants that flower for a long time or frequently)
Figures refer to months of flowering.
Achillea ptarmica 'Nana Compacta' 6/8
Aethionema grandiflorum 6/7
Anaphalis triplinervis 7/10
Anemone hupehensis 'Splendens' 8/10
Anthemis nobilis 'Plena' 6/9
Aster amellus 'Violet Queen' 9/10
Aubrieta hybrid 'Blue Emperor' 4/5
– 'Red Carpet', 4/6
Brunnera macrophylla 3/5
– – 'Langtrees' 3/5
Calluna double cultivars 7/9
Campanula cochleariifolia 'Miranda Bellardii' 6/8
– *portenschlagiana* 6/9
– – 'Birch Hybrid' 6/8
– *poscharskyana* 6/8
– – 'E. H. Frost' 6/9
– – 'Glandore' 6/8
– – 'Lisduggan' 6/8
– – 'Lynchmere' 6/8
– – 'Stella' 5/8
Carlina acaulis ssp. *simplex* 6/10
– – – – 'Bronze' 6/10
Chrysanthemum arcticum and cultivars, 9/10
Coreopsis verticillata 'Grandiflora' 7/9
Corydalis lutea 4/11
– *ochroleuca* 4/11
Dianthus carthusianorum 6/9
Dicentra eximia 5/7
– – 'Alba' 5/7
Dryas octopetala 5/7

– × *suendermannii* 5/7
Erica herbacea (syn. E.carnea) 'Alba' 3/5
– – 'Vivellii' 3/5
– – 'Winterbeauty' 12/4
– *vagans* 'Lyonesse' 7/8
– – 'MrsD.F.Maxwell' 8/9
– – 'StKeverne' 7/9
Erodium manescavii 6/9
– *petraeum* ssp. *glandulosum* (syn.
    E.macradenum) 6/8
Gaillardia 'Kobold' 7/9
Gentiana × *macaulayi* 'Wells Var.' 6/8
– *sino-ornata* 9/11
Geranium dalmaticum 'Album' 7/8
– *endressii* 7/8
– *farreri* 6/8
– *sanguineum* 'Album' 6/7
– – var. *prostratum* 6/7
– *subcaulescens* 'Splendens' 5/8
Geum coccineum 'Borisii' 5/9
– × *heldreichii* 'Splendens' 6/7
– – hybrids 6/8
Gypsophila repens 'Monstrosa' 5/9
– – 'Rosy Veil', with pruning 6/9
Helianthemum species and cultivars in basic list
    6/9
Helleborus niger 'Praecox' 10/12
– – ssp. *macranthus* 12/3
Heuchera, all species and cultivars in basic list
    6/8
Hieracium × *rubrum* 6/8
Hutchinsia alpina 5/6, also earlier
– – ssp. *auerswaldii* 4/6, also earlier
Knautia macedonia 7/9
Leontopodium alpinum 6/8
– *palibinianum* 6/7
– *souliei* 6/8
Limonium latifolium 'Violetta' 6/8

Linum flavum 'Compactum' 6/9
– *narbonense* 5/7
– *perenne* 6/9
Myosotis palustris 5/9
Nepeta × *faassenii* 6/10
– × 'Six Hills Giant' 6/9
Oenothera fruticosa 'Yellow River' 6/9
– *missouriensis* 6/10
– *tetragona* 'Fireworks' 6/8
Phuopsis stylosa 5/7
Polemonium × *richardsonii* 5/6 and 9
– × – 'Album' 5/6 and 9
– × – 'Superbum' 5/6 and 9
Polygonum affine 'Superbum' 6/10
– *amplexicaule* 6/10
Potentilla atrosanguinea 'Gibson's Scarlet' 7/9
– *nepalensis* 'Fire Flame' 6/8
– – 'Miss Willmott' 7/9
– – 'Roxana' 7/9
– *recta* 'Warrenii' 6/9
Prunella grandiflora 6/9
Scutellaria alpina 6/8
– – 'Alba' 6/8
– – 'Rosea' 6/8
– *baicalensis* 7/9
– *orientalis* var. *pinnatifida* 6/8
Sedum spurium 6/9
– *telephium* 9/10
Silene maritima 'Flore Plena' 6/8
Tiarella wherryi 5/6 and 8/9
Veronica spicata cultivars in basic list 6/7
Viola cornuta 'Boughton Blue' 5/9
– – 'Hansa' 5/9
– – 'W.H.Woodgate' 5/9
– *gracilis* 'Lord Nelson' 5/7
– – 'Major' 5/7
– *odorata* 'The Czar' 3/4 and 9/10

The Evergreen Rock Garden

In the rock garden, as in other parts of the garden, it is important to be familiar with evergreen foliage plants, ferns and grasses, dwarf deciduous and coniferous shrubs. They give great beauty to the winter garden and indeed well into the spring, and lose their good looks only after the heaviest frosts or after being covered with snow. Coniferous shrubs remain undamaged through the worst winter conditions, so if you choose several species and forms your garden will flourish even in winter.

The planting of rock gardens with a large number of small evergreen plants rather than large evergreen shrubs has now become popular with many gardeners and their gardens have an atmosphere of comfort and warmth even in the severest winters. With skill and courage even the smallest, the so-called miniature rock garden can be completely transformed.

The following list of easy-to-grow evergreen plants and dwarf shrubs, breaks new ground and results from years of observation of an enormous number of plants. All these, except in the most exceptional winter conditions, will withstand frost, snow and spring frosts.

I hope the list will serve to offer new suggestions to gardeners, both amateur and professional. Even in flat beds, without rocks, these plants will produce extremely beautiful effects at times when the garden usually has little to offer.

List of evergreens

Herbaceous plants

Acantholium glumaceum
Achillea serbica
– *umbellata*
Androsace sarmentosa
Antennaria dioica 'Rubra'
Arabis 'Rosabella'
– *procurrens*
Arenaria tetraquetra
Armeria all species
Asarum europaeum
Aubrieta hybrids
Azorella trifurcata
Campanula persicifolia ssp. *sessiliflora* (syn. C.grandis)
– *portenschlagiana*
Cyclamen hederifolium (syn. C.neapolitanum)
Dianthus gratianopolitanus
– – 'Compactus Eydangeri'
Draba aizoides
– *bruniifolia*
Geranium macrorrhizum
Globularia species
Haberlea rhodopensis
Helianthemum all species
Helleborus foetidus
Helleborus hybrids
– *lividus* ssp. *corsicus*
– *niger*
– – var. *altifolius*
– – 'Maximus'
– – 'Praecox'
Heuchera hybrids

– sanguinea 'Splendens'
× *Heucherella tiarelloides*
Hieracium × *rubrum*
Horminium pyrenaicum
Hutchinsia alpina ssp. *auerswaldii*
Iberis species
Matricaria oreades
Pachysandra terminalis
– – 'Green Carpet'
Paronychia serpyllifolia
Ramonda myconi
– nathaliae
Saxifraga species (except S.fortunei), hybrids
   and cultivars
Sedum album
– – 'Murale'
– divergens 'Atropurpureum'
– hybridum
– reflexum
– – 'Viride'
– sexangulare
– spathulifolium
– – 'Cape Blanco'
– – 'Purpureum'
Sempervivum species, hybrids and cultivars
Thymus serpyllum cultivars
– villosus
Wulfenia carinthiaca

Dwarf leafy shrubs

Arctostaphylos nevadensis
– uva-ursi
Berberis candidula
– empetrifolia
– hookeri
– × *stenophylla*
– verruculosa
Buxus microphylla
– sempervirens 'Globosa'
Calluna vulgaris and cultivars
Cotoneaster adpressus
– congestus
– conspicuus
– dammeri
– – var. *radicans*
– horizontalis var. *perpusillus*
– – 'Saxatilis'
– microphyllus
– var. *melanotrichus*
Cytisus species
Daphne blagayana

– × *burkwoodii*
– cneorum 'Major'
Dryas octopetala
– × *suendermannii*
Empetrum atropurpureum
– nigrum
Erica herbacea (syn. E.carnea) cultivars
– tetralix cultivars
– vagans cultivars
Euonymus fortunei 'Coloratus'
– – 'Gracilis'
– – 'Minimus'
– – var. *radicans*
– – *vegetus*
Gaultheria procumbens
Hedera helix 'Conglomerata'
– – 'Minima'
Helianthemum species, hybrids and cultivars
Hypericum calycinum
Iberis saxatilis
– sempervirens
Kalmia latifolia
Lavandula angustifolia
Ligustrum vulgare
Mahonia aquifolium 'Moseri'
Pachysandra terminalis
– – 'Green Carpet'
Polygala chamaebuxus
Potentilla fruticosa
Prunus laurocerasus 'Compactus'
Rhododendron (see List p. 127 ff.)
Vaccinium vitis-idaea

Small and medium-sized
evergreen grasses

Carex firma
– morrowii 'Variegata'
– pendula
– plantaginea
Festuca cinerea
– scoparia
– tenuifolia
– valesiaca 'Glaucantha'
Juncus inflexus (syn. J.glaucus)
Luzua sylvatica

Evergreen ferns

Asplenium ruta-muraria
– septentrionale
– trichomanes

Blechnum penna-marina
– *spicant*
Ceterach officinarum (limited use)
Polypodium interjectum 'Cornubiense'
– *vulgare*
Polystichum aculeatum
– *acrostichoides*
– *lonchitus*

Evergreens in shade

Phyllitis scolopendrium
Polystichum setiferum
– – 'Plumosum Densum'
– – 'Proliferum'
– – 'Wollastonii'
The dwarf conifers have a separate list (see p. 124 ff.)

The Fragrant Rock Garden

The numerous aromatic spots where many of the plants in this book grow wild stretch right around the globe. If one were to draw lines linking all the countries of origin of our small herbaceous plants, one would be amazed at the dense network covering the earth's surface.

Where these plants grow the air is full of wild scents, from the freshness of the mountains with their melting snows, the scent of woods and meadows, the tang of the seashore and moorland, the burnt-spice aroma of heath, maquis and steppe, the strange smell of rocky islands in the sun and the thousand other scents of a host of uninhabited places stretching from the mountains of the tropics to the polar ice-cap, from seashore to glacier.

Even for those of us who live in more civilized areas, the landscape and garden can offer a host of perfumes right through the year, giving us some idea of the fragrance which fills the air day and night in the areas where our rock garden plants originate.

The heavier the perfume, the more it becomes intermingled with all the wild perfumes which come with the changing weather and the passing hours.

List of perfumed rock-garden plants

Fl. = Blossom   Lv. = Leaves

Herbaceous plants

Achillea umbellata, Lv.

Aethionema grandiflorum, Fl.
Alyssum montanum, Fl.
– *saxatilis*, Fl.
Anthemis nobilis 'Plena', Lv.
Arabis caucasica, Fl.
Aster amellus, Fl.
Codonopsis clematidea, Fl.
Convallaria majalis, Fl.
– – 'Rosea', Fl.
Dianthus alpinus, Fl.
– *carthusianorum*, Fl.
– *cruentus*, Fl.
– *deltoides*, Fl.
– *gratianopolitanus*, Fl.
– *plumarius*, Fl.
– *sylvestris*, Fl.
– *superbus*, Fl.
Dictamnus albus, Fl.
Dodecatheon meadia, Fl.
Galium odoratum, Fl.
Geranium macrorrhizum, Lv.
Helleborus niger, Fl.
– *odorus*, Fl.
Hemerocallis citrina, Fl.
Hemerocallis hybrid, depending on parentage, Fl.
– *middendorffii*, Fl.
– *minor*, Fl.
Hosta plantaginea, Fl.
Iberis sempervirens, Fl.
Iris germanica (large bearded group), scent highly variable, Fl.
– – (medium bearded group), many varieties, Fl.
– – (dwarf bearded group), many varieties, Fl.

– humilis, Fl.
– pumila, Fl.
Melittis melissophyllum, Fl.
Nepeta × *faassenii*, Lv.
Nuphar lutea, Fl.
Nymphaea hybrids, Fl.
Oenothera missouriensis, Fl.
Origanum vulgare 'Compactum', Fl.
Paradisea liliastrum, Fl.
Petasites fragrans, Fl.
Phlox arendsii hybrids, Fl.
– divaricata, Fl.
Phuopsis stylosa, Fl. Lv.
Polemonium × *richardsonii*, Fl.
Primula auricula, Fl.
– beesiana, Fl.
– bulleyana, Fl.
– elatior hybrids, Fl.
– florindae, Fl.
– × pubescens, Fl.
– sikkimensis, Fl.
– vulgaris, Fl.
Salvia × *superba* var., Fl., Lv.
Santolina chamaecyparissus, Lv.
Satureja montana, Lv.
Thymus serpyllum, Lv.
Viola odorata, Fl.

Bulbs
(all Fl.)

Colchicum autumnale
– bornmuelleri
– hybrids, depending on parentage
Corbularia bulbocodium
Crocus flavus
– heuffelianus
– longiflorus
– medius
– vernus
Cyclamen purpurascens
Fritillaria imperialis
Galanthus nivalis
Hyacinthus orientalis
Iris danfordiae
– histrioides 'Major'
– reticulata
– reticulata hybrids
– xiphioides

Lilium hansonii
– hybrids, depending on parentage
　　(particularly *hansonii* hybrids)
– martagon
– pyrenaicum
– regale
Muscari comosum
– neglectum
– racemosum
Narcissus, very variable perfumes
Tulipa greigii
– tarda
Tulipa (garden tulips), very variable

Shrubs

Abeliphyllum distichum, Fl.
Calycanthus floridus, Fl.
Caryopteris × *clandonensis*, Fl.
– incana, Fl.
Chimonanthus praecox, Fl.
Chionanthus virginicus, Fl.
Corylopsis pauciflora, Fl.
Daphne blagayana, Fl.
– cneorum 'Major', Fl.
– mezereum, Fl.
Gaultheria procumbens, Lv.
Hamamelis mollis, Fl.
Ledum palustre, Lv.
Lonicera × *purpusii*, Fl.
Magnolia stellata, Fl.
Mahonia aquifolium 'Moseri', Fl.
Perovskia atriplicifolia, Lv.
Philadelphus lemoinei hybrids, Fl.
Rhododendron flavum, Fl.
– hirsutum, Fl.
– impeditum, Lv.
– prinophyllum (syn. Rh. roseum), Fl.
– vaseyi, Fl.
– yedoense var. *poukhanense*, Fl.
Rosa rubiginosa, Fl.
– spinosissima forms, Fl.
Skimmia japonica, Fl.
Viburnum × *bodnantense*, Fl.
– × burkwoodi, Fl.
– × carlcephalum, Fl.
– carlesii, Fl.
– farreri (syn. V. fragrans), Fl.

Grasses, Ferns, Bulbs and Shrubs for the Rock Garden with Lists of Plants

Grasses for shade and sun

As in the rest of the garden, small and medium sized grasses, sedges and rushes have up to now seldom been used in the rock garden, although they play such an important part in the alpine landscape, their seeds being carried up massive rock faces to settle in clefts—as *Carex firma* has done, for instance, on rock walls in the Alps. There are, however, many other ways in which grasses can be used in the rock garden. There are wood and steppe grasses, dune and moorland grasses as well as waterside grasses, all waiting to be included in rock and wild gardens and in and around the rock garden pool. Spreading grasses are excluded, for they are generally quite uncontrollable. The beautiful grasses with their charming colourings and their wild magic can help prevent the juxtaposition of unsuitable plants by paving the way from one to another.

Grasses produce very striking effects and many are quick-growing, so that it often becomes evident a few years after planting that one should have been more sparing in their use. They are also very useful for they can even keep nearby spreading plants in check; for instance, grasses planted nearby will keep the fast-spreading *Oenothera speciosa* or common bugle under control. Grasses also have an important role to play in shady spots. Some go well with ferns, others less well. Many flowering and foliage plants take on a completely new lease of life when combined with grasses.

The widespread hard rush, *Juncus inflexus*, can be planted in water with forget-me-nots, or on the bank between *Tradescantia andersoniana* hybrids, but it can also be used on higher ground to complement any possible combination of rock-garden plants. For many small grasses there is, however, no suitable place other than the rock garden, where they show off the plants to perfection. The charm added by one single example often becomes fully apparent only when we take it away.

In our gardens it is almost exclusively with the beauty of mown grass that we are familiar, which is or can be magical in itself, but mown grass tells nothing of the beauty of grass as it grows, just as short hair on a woman tells us little of the magic of long flowing locks. Looking after our hair has become an important part of our everyday lives and decorative grasses could come to be of equal importance to the garden.

In the heather garden with its subdued colourings, colourful grasses have a different purpose, providing delightful contrasts of colour and structure with the heather growing up to the rocks. What a beautiful sight it is when a steel-blue *Helictotrichon sempervirens* (Avena sempervirens) blue oat grass, pushes its way from under an old granite rock, its dewy leaves contrasting with the asters growing amidst silver grey heather, while Catsfoot, or mountain everlasting *Antennaria dioica*, weaves its grey braids. Here too the introduction of a few grasses bring encouraging results. They are indispensable for those making their first attempt at a natural garden. Flowering times for grasses extend from March to October, depending on genus. Many early spring grasses have almost black flowers, many mountain grasses have white flowers while others tend towards silver grey or pale yellow. Many flower only for a few weeks, others for months. Many flowers remain as dry stems which retain their linear beauty and delicate colouring for years.

The following lists are not exhaustive but offer many suggestions that you can use for both sunny and shady areas of the rock garden. The first numeral refers to the height of the blades of grass, the second to the flower stem.

A key to symbols and abbreviations used can be found on page ooo, as well as on the bookmark provided.

Low-growing grasses, sedges and rushes

(20 to 30 cm, 8 to 12 in)
All H1

Arrhenatherum elatius ssp. *bulbosum* 'Variegatum', a variegated false oat-grass, 30 to 50 cm (12 to 20 in), ○ ⋙ ⟡

Carex atrata, black sedge, 20 to 30 cm (8 to 12 in), ○ to ☀ △ ⊖

– *firma*, a dwarf sedge, 10 to 15 cm (4 to 6 in), ○ to ☀ ▯ ‡ ⸬

– *fraseri*, 25 to 40 cm (10 to 16 in), ◑ to ● ⊖ ≃ ▢ Y ⟡ ‡

– *montana*, mountain sedge, 20 to 30 cm (8 to 12 in), ○ to ○○ ⊕ ▢ ⋙ Y

– *ornithopoda* 'Variegata' variegated bird's-foot sedge, 15 to 20 cm (6 to 8 in), ◑ ≃ △ Y ⟡

Festuca alpina, Alpine fescue, 20 to 30 cm (8 to 12 in), ○ to ○○ ⊕ ≃ ⸬ △ ‡

– *amethystina*, 20 to 40 cm (8 to 16 in), ○ to ○○ ‖ △ ‡

– *eskia*, 30 cm (12 in), ○ to ○ ⊕ ≃ ‡

– *flagellifera*, brown hair-sedge, 20 to 40 cm (8 to 16 in), ☀ to ◑ ⸬ ⟡ ‡

– *glacialis*, 10 to 15 cm (4 to 6 in), ○ to ☀ ≃ ‖ ‡

– *glauca*, blue fescue, 25 cm (10 in), ○ to ○○ ⊕ ⸬ ‡

– *punctoria*, 15 to 20 cm (6 to 8 in), ○○○ ⊕ ⸬ △ ‡

– *scoparia*, 10 to 20 cm (4 to 8 in), ☀ ≃ ▢ ⸬ ‡

Hakonechloa macra 'Albo-aurea', 30 to 50 cm (12 to 20 in), ○ to ☀ ⸬ ▢ ⟡

– – 'Aureola' 30 to 50 cm (12 to 20 in), ○ to ☀ ⸬ ▢ ⟡

Juncus effusus 'Spiralis', spiralling soft rush, 30 to 35 cm (12 to 14 in), ○ to ◑ ⊖ ≌ ⋙

Koeleria glauca, a blue-green hair grass, 20 to 40 cm (8 to 16 in), ○ to ○○○ ‖

Luzula pilosa, hairy wood-rush, 15 to 30 cm (6 to 12 in), ◑ to ● ⊖ ≃ ▢ Y ‡

– *sylvatica*, greater wood-rush, 20 to 40 cm (8 to 16 in), ◑ to ● ⊖ ≃ ▢ Y ‡

– – 'Variegata', variegated wood rush

Melica ciliata, hairy melick, 30 to 60 cm (12 to 24 in), ◑ ⊕ ▢ Y

– *nutans*, mountain melick, 30 to 50 cm (12 to 20 in), ◑ to ● ⊕ ▢ Y

Poa alpina, Alpine meadow grass, 15 to 30 cm (6 to 12 in), ○ ≃ ‖

– *caesia*, blue meadow grass, 15 to 20 cm (6 to 8 in), ○ ≃ ‖ ▯ ⟡

Sesleria varia, blue moor grass, 20 to 40 cm (8 to 16 in), ○ to ○○○ ⊕ ‖ ‡

Medium-height grasses, sedges and rushes

(50 to 90 cm, 2 to 3 ft, produce excellent effects planted in isolation around the edge of the rock garden or with small herbaceous plants)
All H1

Achnatherum (Stipa) calamagrostis, 50 to 70 cm (20 to 28 in), ○ ⊥ ✕

Alopecurus pratensis 'Aurea', golden foxtail, 50 cm (20 in), ○ to ☀ ≃ ⸬ ⟡

Bouteloua gracilis, 30 to 50 cm (12 to 20 in), ○ to ○○○ ≃ ✕ ✿

Briza media, quaking grass, 30 to 50 cm (12 to 20 in), ○ to ○○ ✕ ✿

– *subaristata*, 30 to 60 cm (1 to 2 ft), ○ to ○○ ✕ ✿

Carex grayi, 60 to 80 cm (24 to 33 in), ○ to ◑ ≌ ⊔ ✕ ✿ ‡

– *morrowii* 'Evergold', a gold-striped sedge, 30 to 50 cm (12 to 20 in), ◑ to ● ≃ ▢ Y ⟡ ‡

Chrysopogon nutans, a gold bearded grass, 90 to 110 cm (36 to 40 in), ○ ≃ ⊥ ✕

Eriophorum latifolium broad-leaved cotton-grass, 30 to 60 cm (1 to 2 ft), ○ ⊖ ≌ ⊔ ⋙ ✕ ✿ ⚭

– *vaginatum*, hare's tail grass, 30 to 60 cm (1 to 2 ft), ○ ⊖ ≌ ⊔ ⋙ ✕ ✿ ⚭

Helictotrichon sempervirens (Avena candida), plus 'Pendula' variety, blue oat grass, 40 to 120 cm (18 to 48 in), ○ to ○○ ⊕ ⊥ ‡

Juncus inflexus, hard rush, 30 to 50 cm (12 to 20 in), ○ to ◐ ≃ ⊝ ◠ ⊥ ⊔ ∿ ‡

Luzula nivea, snowy wood rush, 30 to 50 cm (12 to 20 in), ◐ ≃ ⫶ Y ✂ ❦ ‡

Melica transsilvanica, 50 to 100 cm (20 to 40 in), ○ to ○○○ ⊕ ‖ ⊥ ✂ ❦

Molinia caerulea, plus varieties, purple moor grass, 40 to 80 cm (18 to 33 in), ○ to ◐ ⊝ ≃ ⊥ Y ⊔ ✂

Molinea caerulea ssp. *altissima,* giant purple moor grass, 60 to 180 cm (2 to 6 ft), ○ to ◐ ⊝ ≃ ⊥ Y ⊔ ✂

Panicum virgatum 'Rubrum', 60 to 90 cm (2 to 3 ft), ○ to ◐ ≃ ⫶ ✂ ❦

Pennisetum alopecuroides (Pennisetum compressum), 50 to 80 cm (20 to 33 in), ○ ≃ ◠ ⫶ ⊥ ⊔ ✂ ❦

– *orientale,* 50 to 80 cm (20 to 33 in), ○ ≃ ⫶ ⊥ ✂ ❦

Sesleria heufleriana, a green moor grass, 30 to 50 cm (12 to 20 in), ○ ≃ ⫶ ⊥ ✂ ‡

Spartina pectinata 'Aureo-Variegata', 120 cm (4 ft) and more, ○ to ○○ ⊥ ✂ ❦

Stipa barbata, 40 to 80 cm (18 to 33 in), ○ to ○○ ⊕ ⊥ ✂ ❦

– *capillata,* 80 to 130 cm (33 to 50 in), ○ to ○○ ⊕ ⊥

– *pennata,* feather grass, 30 to 80 cm (12 to 33 in), ○ to ○○ ⊕ ⊥ ✂ ❦

– *pulcherrima,* 50 to 100 cm (20 to 40 in), ○ to ○○ ⊕ ⊥ ✂ ❦

– *stenophylla,* 30 to 80 cm (12 to 33 in), ○ to ○○ ⊕ ⊥ ✂ ❦

Ferns for the rock garden

Rock gardens and particularly wild gardens are the natural habitat for ferns in cultivation. Here they come to life and combine well with herbaceous plants, shrubs and grasses. Here they shake off the associations they have in many peoples' minds with steamy jungles.

There are a host of ferns suitable for shady or semi-shady rock gardens, for the early spring garden or a garden under trees or along the banks of a stream. Ferns will also adapt to sunny spots providing the soil is moist, or can be kept moist. More and more species and varieties of ferns are making their home in sunny garden plots.

There are both small and very large ferns, some which will live in a dry rock cleft and others which will grow for years in water. Many ferns grow in northern and southern hemispheres but those from the North are generally best for our gardens. A few, however, such as *Blechnum penna-marina* from the Tierra del Fuego with its gorgeous, dark green ground cover, come from far off. There are upright and flat-growing forms, with colours ranging from silver-grey to emerald green and deep red, there are those which are sturdy or extremely delicate, all waiting to complement the other plants of the rock garden.

Anyone who ignores this great wealth of beauty, is leaving an unnecessary gap in his garden. Here a shady spot can produce unbelievable effects, especially with the inclusion of woodland flowers. The list of ferns which follows includes only the easy-to-grow species and forms of a wide range of small ferns.

Ferns in the garden give a whole new aspect to our relationship with plants. It is only with ferns that one can exploit a shady garden to the full and provide the right setting for many shady woodland flowers. In many inaccessible corners of the world, far from civilisation and the eyes of man the wild ferns live out their lives in silent solitude, echoes of ages past amidst the pulse of modern life. The way in which ferns have spread geographically is most impressive and full of surprises. We can only marvel at the way in which many ferns suitable for the garden have spread through the temperate zones of the northern and southern hemispheres, but equally suprising is the fact that many ferns are found only in very limited areas. Many ferns grow in both the subtropical and temperate zones, others have spread as far as the polar regions, while many others are native to tropical and subtropical zones. With the exception of a few established gardens, where ferns already play an important part, these noble plants are mostly newcomers to our gardens, but as more and more gardeners recognize their usefulness and indestructibility things should soon change.

The two lists that follow will offer all gardeners the opportunity to use ferns throughout the rock garden, for cracks in walls or clefts in rock or in combination with leafy and coniferous shrubs in shady or semi-shady areas.

Small ferns

(about 20 to 30 cm, 8 to 12 in)
H1 unless stated

Adiantum pedatum 'Minor', a dwarf maidenhair fern, 20 cm (8 in), ◐ ⊖ ▢ ⋙ Ⅴ ✕

– *venustum*, Venus's hair, 25 cm (10 in), ☀ to ●
⊖ ▢ ⋙ Ⅴ ✕ ♠ H2

Asplenium ruta-muraria, wall rue, 5 cm (2 in), ☀
⊕ ‖ ⚶

– *scolopendrium* 'Cristata' *(Phyllitis scolopendrium)*, 30 cm (12 in), plus all hart's tongue fern varieties, ☀ to ● ≃ ‖ Ⅴ ⊡ ⚶

– – 'Marginata', a variegated hart's tongue fern, 30 cm (12 in)

– – 'Undulata', a dwarf hart's tongue fern, 25 cm (10 in)

– *trichomanes*, maidenhair spleenwort, 15 cm (6 in), ☀ to ● ‖ ⚶

– *viride*, green spleenwort, 15 cm (6 in), ☀ to ●
⊕ ‖

Athyrium filix-femina, miniature lady fern, 30 cm (12 in), ◐ also ● ⊖ ≌ Ⅴ

– – – 'Minutissima', dwarf lady fern, 30 cm (12 in), ◐ also ● ⊖ ≌ Ⅴ

– *nipponicum* 'Pictum', Japanese painted fern, 45 cm (18 in), ◐ also ● ⊖ Ⅴ H2

Blechnum penna-marina, a hard fern from temperate southern hemispheres, 10 cm (4 in), ●
⊖ Ⅴ ⚶ H2

Ceterach officinarum, rusty-back fern, 10 cm (4 in), ☀ ⊕ ‖ ⊡ ♡ ⚶

Cystopteris fragilis, brittle bladder fern, 25 cm (10 in), ○ to ◐ ‖ Ⅴ

Gymnocarpium dryopteris, oak fern, 25 cm (10 in), ◐ to ● ⊖ ⋙ Ⅴ

– *robertianum*, limestone fern, 25 cm (10 in), ◐ to ● ⊕ ⋙ Ⅴ

Phegopteris connectilis, beech fern, 20 cm (8 in), ◐ to ● ≌ ⋙

Polypodium vulgare, common polypody, 20 cm (8 in), ● ≃ ‖ ⋙ Ⅴ ⚶

– *interjectum* 'Cornubiense', a feathery polypody, 30 cm (12 in), ☀ to ● ≃ ‖ ⋙ Ⅴ (⚶)

Polystichum lonchitis, holly fern, about 25 cm (10 in), ☀ to ● ≃ ‖ Ⅴ ⊡

Thelypteris decursiva-pinnata, an oak fern from East Asia, 40 cm (16 in), ◐ to ● ≃ ⋙ Ⅴ

Woodsia alpina, Alpine woodsia, 10 cm (4 in), ☀ ≃ ‖ ⊡

– *ilvensis*, oblong woodsia, 20 cm (8 in), ☀ ≃ ‖ ⊡

– *obtusa*, a larger Woodsia fern, 30 cm (12 in), ☀ ≃ ‖ ⊡

Medium-sized ferns

(50 to 90 cm, 2 to 3 ft)
All H1 unless stated

Adiantum pedatum, a hardy maidenhair fern, 60 cm (2 ft), ● ≃ ▢ ⋙ Ⅴ ✕

Asplenium scolopendrium, harts tongue fern, 40 to 50 cm (16 to 24 in)
Plus the following variety

– – 'Crispa', 40 cm (16 in), ☀ to ● ≃ ‖ Ⅴ ⊡ ⚶

Athyrium filix-femina, lady fern, about 40 cm (16 in)

All *Athyrium* varieties ◐ to ● ≃ Ⅴ ⊔

Athyrium filix-femina 'Fritzelliae', about 40 cm (16 in)

– – – 'Oligophlebium', 40 cm (16 in)

– – – 'Victoriae', 50 cm (20 in)

Blechnum spicant, hard fern, about 30 cm (12 in), ◐ to ● ⊖ ≃ ⚶

Cyrtomium falcatum, Japanese holly fern, 60 cm (2 ft), ◐ to ● ⊖ ≃ ⚶ H3

Cystopteris bulbifera, about 40 cm (16 in), ◐ to ● ⊖ ⋙ Ⅴ

Dryopteris erythrosora, 80 cm (30 in), ☀ to ● ≃ ⊥ Ⅴ ⊔

Onoclea sensibilis, sensitive fern, 40 cm (16 in), ◐ to ● ≌ Ⅴ ⊔ ⋙

Osmunda regalis var. *gracilis*, a dwarf royal fern, 60 cm (2 ft), ◐ to ● ≌ ⊥ Ⅴ ⊔ ⋙

Polystichum acrostichoides, 80 cm (30 in), ◐ to ● ≌ Ⅴ ✕

– *munitum*, 80 cm (30 in), ◐ to ● Ⅴ ≃

– *setiferum*, soft shield fern, up to about 60 cm (2 ft), ☀ to ● ≃ ⊥ Ⅴ

Thelypteris hexagonoptera, 30 cm (12 in), ◐ to ● ≃ ⋙ Ⅴ

– *thelypteroides*, marsh fern, up to 80 cm (30 in), ◐ ≌ ▢ ⋙ ⊔ ⋙

Hardy flowering bulbs and corms

In the area of bulbs we once again have to deal with two different types of plants, one of which produces richly-coloured flowers and is suited to the formal or architectural flower bed, while the other is more appropriate to the wild or rock garden.

The importance of bulbs for these peaceful areas of the garden—and their ability to bloom not only in spring and early spring but right throughout the year—is something which has happily long been recognized. Few gardens fail to make use of bulbous plants.

It will always be a matter of opinion as to whether a particular genus and its species have an over-cultivated appearance unsuited to wild or rock gardens, and more appropriately to our enquiries, to the natural rock garden. The fine line separating the suitable from the unsuitable often has to be drawn through the centre of a genus of plants. Thus there are undoubtedly a number of daffodil and tulip cultivars and also of hyacinths which are entirely suitable for the natural rock garden, whereas others look better in a formal setting. The distance separating the suitable from the highly unsuitable is often small and is always a matter of personal opinion and taste. It is not always the splendour of a particular plant which makes it unsuitable. Thus in an architectural terrace with beds and supporting walls planted in a natural style the noblest types of fritillaries will look right in early spring, whereas many types of garden tulips would destroy its whole character.

This book is full of hints on the importance of making such distinctions and deals with the increased possibilities offered by the architectural rock garden as against the natural rock garden.

The ways in which stone can show off plants in the garden are boundless. Stone is particularly important where bulbs are concerned in that the stone serves to protect them for the many months of the year when they remain invisible underground. This is particularly true of small bulbs which need to remain undisturbed.

So what surprises does the bulb kingdom hold in store for the rock and wild garden?

January and February: Snowdrops, winter aconites and earliest crocuses are opening.

March: In the wild garden the main month for crocuses, anemones and the earliest of all, the grape hyacinths, the aconites, *Eranthis*, early *Scilla* and *Chionodoxa*, *Bulbocodium vernum*, *Cyclamen*, later snowdrops, snowflakes, dogtooth *Erythronium*, with early irises, daffodils, hyacinths appearing in warm corners and the new March tulips.

April: April belongs to the hyacinths, many wild tulips both large and small, all possible wild daffodils, grape hyacinths, white, pale-blue and pink wood anemones and Apennine anemones, Aaron's rod, the dazzling or more modest fritillaries in white, red and yellow varieties, the early star of Bethlehem and the last of the late crocuses.

May: Wild tulips and daffodils are still in flower together with the wild and late grape hyacinths and the early *Allium* species.

June: In June dwarf *Lilium bulbiferum* and new early flowering hybrids appear in the rock garden. These may at first be rejected on the grounds that they are too showy, but remember that they originated in flowers of the mountain meadow. In June the last of the wild tulips are still in flower together with many *Allium* species. This is the month when growers begin sending out *Allium*. Few gardeners are aware that these plants flower from the end of April until September and that they come in a wide variety of sizes and shapes and in colours ranging from yellow, to violet, amethyst, deep red, blue and white. June is also the great month for lilies and irises.

July: Everything I have said about June applies to this month also. Of course the peaceful rock garden should not be turned into a blaze of colour, and there are plenty of quiet, subdued plants among those that flower in July. Yet we must also bear in mind the requirements of the "architectural rock garden", which allows much more opportunity for experimenting with more showy flowers. The winter hardy gladiolis are simple enough to suit any natural rock garden.

August: The end of August sees the first autumn crocuses and, earlier still in warm spots, montbretia in flower, while the lilies are still in bloom. Montbretia can look extremely "natural" in artificial waterside gardens. Early autumn crocuses should be combined with the alpine aster and any type of grass.

September/October are the main months for the autumn crocuses and colchicums and similar plants, such as *Sternbergia*. Autumn crocuses look well planted with low-growing asters, dwarf berrying shrubs, autumn-flowering *Sedum* and October saxifrages, with October Christmas roses, blue *Ceratostigma* and the many other small plants which have brought a whole new flowering season to the wild and rock garden. Already the earliest snowdrop, *Galanthus nivalis reginae-olgae*, is with us as a promise of spring.

Common bulbs and corms

H1 unless stated.

Allium · Onions and Leeks · Onion Family (Alliaceae)
○ to ○○○ ⊕ △ ⅄ ✂ ○

Early May

Allium aflatunense ❀
Around 15 to 50 cm (30 to 60 in), scarlet red to lilac coloured; northern Persia.

– *atropurpureum*
Around 60 to 75 cm (24 to 30 in), wine-red; SE Europe to Central Asia.

– *karataviense* ☾ ❀
About 20 cm (8 in) tall, whitish-grey tending to pale pink globular flowers; Alatau Mountains, Kazakhstan.

– *neapolitanum*
15 to 20 cm (6 to 8 in), drooping, highly scented flowers, pure white; Mediterranean area, grows wild in Austria in the southern Tirol.

Mid-season June

Allium caeruleum
60 cm (2 ft), deep cornflower-blue with colour sometimes varying slightly, good cutting-flowers; SE Europe to Siberia.

– *christophii* ❀
30 to 45 cm (12 to 18 in), bright amethyst globular flowers, good cutting-flower for drying, attractive growing amidst *Sedum*; Persia.

– *cyaneum* ‖ 🛢
15 cm (6 in), bright blue; west China.

– *kansuense* ‖ 🛢
Around 15 cm (6 in), blue or violet, drooping umbelliferous flowers; scree slopes of Kansu (west China).

– *moly* ◑
Around 20 cm (8 in), golden-yellow; southern Europe.

– *narcissiflorum* ○ to ☀ ‖ 🛢
Around 20 cm (8 in), large, bright rose, drooping bell-shaped flowers, a beautiful plant requiring careful handling; scree slopes of north Italian Alps.

– *oreophilum* (syn. A. ostrowskianum)
Around 15 cm (6 in), carmine pink; Turkestan.

– – 'Zwanenburg'
Useful improvement on the type plant with deep carmine-pink flowers.

Late July and August

Allium cirrhosum (syn. Allium polchellum) ‖ 🛢
Around 15 cm (6 in), similar to *Allium flavum* but violet or occasionally pink; lower alpine areas to southern Europe.

– – 'Album'
Snow-white, otherwise the same as the type plant.

– *flavum* ‖ 🛢
Sulphur-yellow, 20 to 25 cm (8 to 10 in); southern Europe.

– *rosenbachianum* ❀
Around 1 m (3 ft), rose-lilac, perfumed, flowers into early autumn, absolutely hardy and durable; Turkestan, N. Afghanistan.

Anemone · Anemones · Buttercup Family (Ranunculaceae)
◑ ≃ ⋙ ⅄ ✂ ○ H1

Flowering time: late February to March

Anemone blanda · Grecian Windflower ∧

About 8 cm (3 in), purple-blue; southern Bulgaria, Greece and Turkey.

– – 'Alba', white-flowered.

– – 'Atrocaerulea', dark violet.

– – 'Charmer', dark-rose variety, improved form of *A. blanda* 'Rosea'.

– – 'Radar', bright carmine red with white centre.

– – var. *scythinica*, opening white, outside petals light purple-blue; northern Kurdistan.

– – 'White Splendour', snow-white, long-flowering, large blossoms.

Flowering time: mid March to April

Anemone nemorosa · Wood Anemone ⋙
Our familiar native spring anemone, 15 cm (6 in).
– – 'Allenii', outside petals pale rose-lilac, opening white and lavender blue, large flowers.
– – 'Grandiflora', large flowers, pure white, quick-growing.
– – 'Leeds Variety', large-flowered, white, with overlapping perianth leaves.
– – 'Robinsoniana', lavender colour, highly unusual cup shape.
– – 'Royal Blue', deep blue, the only cultivar of this colour, but not yet very common.

Flowering time: mid April

Anemone × *lipsiensis* (A. ranunculoides × A. nemorosa) ⋙
Sulphur-yellow, large-flowered.
– *nemorosa* 'Alba Plena', double white, very late flowering.
– – 'Blue Bonnet', pale lavender-blue, opening toning to crimson.
– – 'Celestial', late pale-blue wood anemone.
– – 'Vestal', pure white, very large flowers, petaloid centre.
– *ranunculoides* · Yellow Wood Anemone ⋙
10 cm (4 in); native to Europe, Caucasus to Siberia.
– – 'Plena', double, smaller flowers than the species.
– – 'Superba', bronze-leaved yellow wood anemone, dark yellow, large flowers.

Flowering time: mid April to May

Anemone apennina · Blue Wood Anemone ⋙
15–20 cm (6–8 in); Apennines, southern Europe.
– – 'Alba', white, pale-blue outer petals.
– – 'Plena', double blue.
– – 'Purpurea', crimson-pink

Arum · Arum Family (Araceae)
◐ to ● ⊕ ≃ △ ⋎ ♘ ⚇

All flower April to May, producing red berries in autumn.
– *italicum* · Italian Arum H2
Larger than *A. maculatum*, up to 60 cm (2 ft), leaf buds form as early as autumn, so best in a sheltered site; spathe greenish-white inside, reddish along edges, leaves dark green, arrow-shaped, curling up in summer.
– – 'Marmoratum', leaves marbled, white-ribbed, otherwise like type plant.
– *maculatum* · Lords and Ladies, Cuckoo Pint H1
About 20 cm (8 in), native, hardy, spathe whitish green inside with reddish flecks, leaves sometimes spotted with black, reproduces by self-seeding.

Bulbocodium · Lily Family (Liliaceae)
○ to ○○ ≃ △ ⋎ H1

– *vernum* · Spring Bulbocodium
Pinkish-mauve, star-shaped, clustered, low on the ground, flowers similar to autumn crocus, likes damp soil, 5 cm (2 in), March/April; Pyrenees, Dobruja to southern Russian steppes.

Camassia · Camass Quamash · Lily Family (Liliaceae)
○ ≃ ⋎ ✕ H1

– *cusickii*
Up to 90 cm (3 ft), light blue panicles, up to hundred flowers, earliest flowering species; protect from summer winds; Oregon.
– *leichtlinii*
Flowers of this Camassia vary from white to cream, blue and violet, up to 60 cm (2 ft), most attractive of the species; California to British Columbia.
– *quamash* · Common Camass
Up to 90 cm (3 ft), blue, varying, also white; western United States (California, Utah to British Columbia).

Chionodoxa · Snow Glory · Lily Family (Liliaceae)
○ to ◐ ⋎ ✕ ○ H1

– *gigantea*
10 to 12 cm (4 to 5 in), large pale-blue flowers with small white centre, end March/beginning April; Anatolia.
– – 'Alba', snow-white flowers, otherwise like species.
– *luciliae* · Glory of the Snow

8 to 10 cm (3 to 4 in), bright blue with more pronounced white centre, fast-spreading, self-seeding; Turkey.
– – 'Alba', snow-white noble form.
– – 'Pink Giant', large, light-pink flowers, slow-spreading.

Colchicum · Autumn crocus · Lily family (Liliaceae)
○ to ○○ ⊕ ≈ Υ ✕ ◯ ῷ H₁

Flowering time: Early autumn (end August/mid September)

Colchicum autumnale · Meadow Saffron
Native autumn crocus of mountain meadows up to 1400 m (4500 ft), slow-spreading compared with *C. speciosum*, pinkish-mauve, without checkered design, earliest flowering sort.
– – 'Album', white, small-flowered.
– *bornmuelleri* (syn. C. speciosum bornmuelleri)
Pale lilac-pink, very large flowers, beautiful cup shape; Asia Minor.
– *byzantinum*
Pale pinkish-mauve, richly flowering; Turkey.
– – hybrid 'Autumn Queen', early form, deep purplish-violet, white centre.
– – – 'Princess Astrid', another early cultivar, light pinkish-violet.
– *neapolitanum*
Lilac-pink with white ground, profuse flowers; Italy.

Flowering time: late autumn (mid September/end October and into November)

Colchicum agrippinum
Purple blossoms checkered white, small flowers; origin unknown, possibly Asia Minor.
– *autumnale* 'Alba Plenum'
Snow-white double autumn crocus, slow-spreading.
– – 'Plenum', thick petalled double cultivar, lilac pink, long but very late flowering, slow-spreading.
– *byzantinum* var. *cilicicum*
Purple petunia colour, darker than *C. byzantinum*, perfumed; Turkey.
– – hybrid 'Conquest', dark purple, checkered, late.
– – – 'Lilac Wonder', pale lilac, very slightly checkered, richly flowering.

– – – 'The Giant', light mauve, white-throated, slightly checkered, very late.
– – – 'Violet Queen', petals more pointed, red-purple with white chequering.
– – – 'Waterlily', warm lilac-pink, double, large-flowered, late.
– *sibthorpii*
Light mauve, sprinkled with checkered pattern, large-blossomed; southern Bulgaria, northern Greece.
– *speciosum*
Varying from deep purple, lighter throat, larger flowers; Caucasus.
– – 'Album', pure-white, delightful with grasses.

Corydalis · Fumitory Family (Fumariaceae)
◑ to ● ⊕ ≈ Υ ◯ ῷ H₁

Flowering time: early March/April

Corydalis angustifolia
An early spring corydalis, about 15 cm (6 in), white; Caucasus to northern Iran.
– *bracteata*
About 10 cm (4 in), pale yellow; Altai.
– *densiflora*
A pink dwarf corydalis, 15 cm (6 in); Italy to western Asia.
– *pumila* (syn. C. decipiens)
A purplish-pink dwarf corydalis, only 8 cm (3 in); northern to eastern Europe and parts of Central Europe.
– *solida*
Purple, some with white, 20 cm (8 in), self-seeding, native to much of Europe.
– – 'Transsylvanica', beautiful cultivated variety with orange-red flowers.

Flowering time: April/May

Corydalis cashmeriana
7.5 to 20 cm (3 to 9 in), sky blue flowers, best in peaty soil; Kashmir to Bhutan.
– *caucasica*
Reddish-purple, 15 cm (6 in); Caucasus.
– *cava*
Reddish, also white, 15 cm (6 in); native to southern and Central Europe.
– *pauciflora*
Pink to bluish-mauve, 8 cm (3 in); Alaska, also East Asia.

Crocus · Iris Family (Iridaceae)
○ to ◑ ⊕ ≃ Υ ○ ♉ Hɪ

Flowering time: end February/early March, all about 8 cm (3 in)

Crocus angustifolius (syn. C. susianus) · Cloth of Gold Crocus
  Brilliant golden yellow with outer featherings of bronze; Crimea, south-west Russia.
– *balansae*
  Brilliant golden orange; western Asia Minor.
– *biflorus*
  White to brown with lilac veining; Italy, south-east Europe, Asia Minor.
– – var. *weldenii*
  Pure white, greyish-blue toning outside.
– *etruscus*
  Outside reddish-yellow, inside pale lilac varying; western Italy.
– *fleischeri*
  White, purple feathering at throat; Asia Minor.
– *heuffelianus*
  Transparent violet with darker cross-veining; Carpathians and foothills.
– *imperati*
  Opening lilac, outside veined in brownish yellow and purple; southern Italy. Very early.
– *sieberi*
  A dwarf crocus, light blue with golden yellow throat; Greece.
– – 'Hubert Edelsten', extremely beautiful form, deep purple colour, each petal with band of white.
– *tomasinianus*
  Pale mauve, spreads abundantly; Dalmatia to central Bulgaria.
– – 'Barr's Purple', large lilac flowers.
– – 'Whitewell Purple', rich bluish-purple, impressive yet delicate, as easy to propagate as the species.

Flowering time: mid to late March

Crocus ancyrensis
  Deep golden yellow, orange-red stigma; Asia Minor.
– *candidus* var. *subflavus*
  Amber yellow, bronze shading outside; Asia Minor.
– *chrysanthus*
  The species is yellow, but with many beautiful cultivars in various colours and featherings; Bulgaria, Greece, Asia Minor.
– – 'Advance', opening yellow, outer petals violet.
– – 'Blue Bird', opening white, outer petals greyish-blue.
– – 'Blue Peter', light-blue opening, outer petals warm purple-blue.
– – 'Cream Beauty', deep cream.
– – 'E. P. Bowles', deep yellow, outside petals feathered with purple.
– – 'Lady Killer', white opening, outer petals purple edged in white.
– – 'Snow Bunting', opening white, outer petals with dark lilac feathering.
– – 'Zwanenburg Bronze', golden yellow, outer petals shading to dark bronze.
– *flavus* (syn. C.aureus) · Dutch Yellow Crocus
  Deep golden-yellow; Balkans, west Turkey.
– – 'Dutch Yellow', the familiar large yellow spring crocus. Forms no seeds. (of hybrid origin).
– × *stellaris*
  Opening orange, outer petals with narrow black stripes, less spreading than C. flavus, a hybrid of unknown origin.
– *vernus* × *tomasinianus* 'Vanguard'
  Opening light mauvish-blue, outer petals silver-grey, blossoms at same time as 'Dutch Yellow'.
– *versicolor* 'Picturatus'
  Flowers late March, white, with distinct purple veining

Flowering time: end March/early and mid April, large-flowered garden varieties of *Crocus vernus*

Early
  'Early Perfection', violet blue with darker border.
  'Purpureus Grandiflorus', deep violet-blue with silvery sheen.
  'Queen of the Blues', light blue.
  'Remembrance', purple-violet.
  'Striped Beauty', white with lilac stripes.
  'Zulu', blackish-blue.

Moderately early
  'King of the Blues', dazzlingly blue.
  'Peter Pan', ivory white.
  'Twinborn', white with deep violet stripes.

Late
'Kathleen Parlow', white, orange stigma.
'Snowstorm', pure white, very large flowers.
'The Bishop', dark violet-blue.

Autumn Crocus
Late-autumn and winter flowering species in exposed positions or cold areas need winter protection with loose conifer twigs. All species and cultivars about 15 cm (6 in).

Flowering time: August/September

Crocus kotschyanus
Rosy-lilac, opening yellow cup with red ring; Asia Minor, Lebanon.
– – 'Albus'
White.
– *speciosus*
Steel-blue, good-tempered; Asia Minor, Caucasus.
– – 'Albus'
Snow white, easy-to-grow.
– – 'Artabir'
Pale blue with dark veining, large-blossomed.
– – 'Oxonian'
Deep-violet, well-formed flowers, less spreading than other cultivars.
– – 'Pollux'
Light violet opening, outer petals silver-grey, large-blossomed.

Flowering time: September/October to November

Crocus asturicus 'Atropurpureus'
Narrow, dark lilac flowers; Spain (Asturia).
– *byzantinus* (syn. C. iridiflorus)
Varying shades of violet; Romania (Transylvania).
– *cancellatus*
Lilac-coloured; Greece, Asia Minor.
– *longiflorus*
Purple-lilac, hardy, scented! Southern Italy.
– *medius*
Purple-lilac; southern coast of France.
– *nudiflorus* · Naked Ladies
Large, violet flowers, hardy; northern Spain, Pyrenees.
– *pulchellus*
Lavender blue with violet veins; southern Bulgaria, Asia Minor.
– – 'Zephyr'

White, outer petals pearl-grey, dependable form.
– *salzmannii*
Large lilac flowers; southern Spain, Morocco
– *sativus* · Saffron
Lilac-blue, flowering varies according to origins. From southern Europe to eastern Turkey.
– *speciosus* var. *aitchisonii*
Light blue.
– – 'Cassiope'
Very large, light blue flowers.

Flowering time: late autumn and winter

Crocus boryi
Cream, outer petals feathered with black; Greece, Crete.
– *hyemalis*
White with purple veining, flowers into January; Syria, Palestine.
– *ochroleucus*
White, flowers into December; Lebanon, northern Palestine.
– *tournefortii*
Bright lilac-blue, weather-resistant; Greek islands.

Cyclamen · Primrose Family (Primulaceae)
All about 8 cm (3 in). ☀ to ◐ ⊕ Υ ✕ ⟳ H2

Flowering time: from about first half of February

Cyclamen coum ssp. *hiemale*
Deep rosy-red; western Turkey.

Flowering time: mid February/end March

Cyclamen coum
Deep rosy-red with darker eye; southern Bulgaria, Asia Minor.
– – 'Album'
White.
– – ssp. *caucasicum*
Similar to the species, but striking silver markings on upper side of leaves; subalpine areas of southern Caucasus.

Flowering time: April/May

Cyclamen pseudibericum
Deep rosy-red, leaves marbled with edges often milled or rounded; Asia Minor.
– *repandum*

Fragrant rosy-pink flowers and silver marbled leaves. S. France to Asia Minor.

Flowering time: from mid July

Cyclamen purpurascens (syn C. europaeum) · Common Cyclamen
Deep carmine flowers; Alps, parts of Tatra, Hungary to southern Moravia and central Yugoslavia.

Flowering time: end August

Cyclamen hederifolium (syn. C. neapolitanum) · Sowbread
Pale pink flowers surmounting wonderfully shaped and coloured foliage; south-east Europe, Mediterranean region, Asia Minor.

Eranthis · Winter Aconite · Buttercup Family (Ranunculaceae)
☀ to ● ⊕ ⅄ ○ ♂ Hı

Flowering time: end February/mid March

Eranthis hyemalis · Winter Aconite
Yellow cups, hardy and self-seeding; Southern Europe, native to some parts of northern Europe.

Flowering time: March

Eranthis cilicica
Narrower, divided ruff of leaves.
Eranthis × tubergenii
Cross between *E. cilicica* and *E. hyemalis*, large yellow flowers, fresh-green leaves, propagate by division only!
– – – 'Guinea Gold' another cross of the two above species, large yellow flowers, bronze leaves, again division only!

Erythronium · Lily Family (Liliaceae)
☀ to ◐ ⊕ ≃ ⅄ ✕ ○ ♂ Hı

Flowering time: around end March/beginning April, all about 15 cm (6 in)

Erythronium dens-canis · Dog's Tooth Violet
Rosy-white, very hardy, grows up to 1700 metres, likes southern faces; southern and central Europe, Siberia and Japan.
– – 'Album', white.
– – 'Lilac Wonder', light-purple.

– – 'Pink Perfection', clear pink.
– – 'Purple King', cyclamen-purple.
– – 'Rose Beauty', dark rose, leaves flecked with dark bronze.
– – 'Rose Queen', clear pink, striking lightly speckled leaves.
– – 'White Splendour', pure white.

Flowering time: around mid April/May

Of the American trout lilies, the hybrids are most rewarding as garden plants.

Erythronium americanum
Only 15 cm (6 in), yellow, single-flowered; south-east Canada to Kansas and Florida.
– *hendersonii*
Light lilac, 30 cm (12 in); SW Oregon and NW California.
– *oregonum* (syn. E. giganteum)
Cream matt, 30 cm (12 in); Oregon to Vancouver.
– *revolutum* · Trout lily
Deep rose, 30 cm (12 in), one of the most beautiful species; Southern California to southern Canada.
– *revolutum* hybrid 'White Beauty'
(Probably crossed with E. oregonum), white, yellow centre.
– *tuolumnense*
Deep yellow, 30 cm (12 in); California.
– *tuolumnense* hybrid 'Pagoda' (*E. tuolumnense* × E. – 'White Beauty')
Sulphur-yellow, spreading, 30 cm (12 in).

Fritillaria · Fritillary · Lily Family (Liliaceae)
Small types and varieties of the snakeshead group.
○ ≃ ⅄ ✕ ▢ Hı

Flowering time: March/April

Fritillaria acmopetala
Hardy, but less popular than other species owing to its unremarkable flower colour. Yellowish-green pendant bell-shaped flowers with purplish tips. Almost 60 cm (2 ft); Cilician Taurus, Cyprus, Syria, Lebanon.
– *aurea*
Large, golden-yellow, bell-shaped flowers, around 15 cm (6 in); Cilician Taurus.
– *pallidiflora*
Flowers in early April, hardy, pale yellow,

opening lightly flecked with red, Snakeshead, 30 to 50 cm (12 to 20 in); Central Asia.

Flowering time: second half April to early May

Fritillaria latifolia
Dark purplish-brown, 30 cm (12 in); Caucasus.
– *meleagris* · Snakeshead
Mostly purple checkered with whitish-mauve, 30 cm (12 in); native to damp meadows of Europe.
– – 'Alba', white.
– – 'Aphrodite', pure white, large flowers.
– – 'Artemis', grey with purplish-red.
– – 'Charon', dark purple.
– – 'Orion', purplish violet to lilac.
– *pontica*
Unusual flower colouring from yellow to green with brownish-purple checkering. Flower stems grow to 60 cm (2 ft), usually only one pendant, bell-shaped flower; Turkey, north-western Greece, Bulgaria.
– *pyrenaica* · Pyrenean Snakeshead
Wine-red to purple-brown, inner petals yellow-green, 30 cm (12 in) or more; Pyrenees, northern Spain. Naturalizes well.
– *tubiformis*
Dark purple, large-blossomed, only 15 cm (6 in); Maritime Alps to southern Tirol.

Flowering time: mid May/June

Fritillaria camtschatcensis · Black Sarana ◐ ⊖
Maroon-purple, almost black, likes slight shade and cool ground, 30 cm (12 in); Kamchatka, Alaska to Oregon.

Large Fritillaries
○ to ○○ ≃ ⊥ Y ✂ ♁

Flowering time: beginning of April

Fritillaria imperialis · Crown Imperial
Orange coloured, 75 to 120 cm (30 to 48 in); south-eastern Turkey to north-west Himalayas.
– – 'Aurora', bright orange-red.
– – 'Lutea Maxima', strong growing, tall, yellow flowers.
– – 'Orange Brillant', large, orange-brown flowers.
– – 'Rubra Maxima', reddish orange with red shading.
– *raddeana*
Straw-yellow, about 60 cm (2 ft); eastern Iran, Turkestan.

Galanthus · Snowdrop · Daffodil Family (Amaryllidaceae)
All species: ☼ to ● ⊕ ≃ Y ✂ ⬡ ♅ H1

Flowering time: December/February

Galanthus elwesii
Large flowers, erect leaves, 15 cm (6 in); Asia Minor.
– *nivalis* · Snowdrop
One of the most familiar spring flowers, usually from mid February.
– – ssp. *cilicicus*
In flower from December, plant in sunny, sheltered spot; Turkey, Lebanon.
– – ssp. *reginae-olgae*
Flowers from October, best in a sunny, sheltered spot; Greece.

Flowering time: from first half March

Galanthus caucasicus
White flowers, larger than *G. nivalis*; Caucasus.
– *ikariae*
Broad, grass green leaves.
– *plicatus* · Crimean Snowdrop
Large-blossomed, rather slow-growing; Crimea.
– – 'Atkinsii' and 'Sam Arnolt' are hybrids with *G. nivalis*, strong and free flowering.

Gladiolus · Iris Family (Iridaceae)
All winter-hardy except in cold areas.
○ to ○○ Y ✂ H2

Gladiolus byzantinus
Rosy-purple, 60 to 75 cm (2 to 2½ ft), May/June; Mediterranean area, south-east Europe.
– × *colvillei*
Almost hardy, to 45 cm (18 in), scarlet flowers marked with yellow;
– – – 'The Bride', a pure white form much used in hybridization.

Hyacinthus · Hyacinth · Lily Family (Liliaceae)
○ to ○○○ ⊕ ✂ ⛀ F H1

– *orientalis* · Hyacinth
Requires dryness in summer.

Flowering time: early to mid April

'Anne Marie', pure rose.
'Delft Blue', dark porcelain blue.
'Jan Bos', carmine red.
'King of the Blues', deep blue.
'L'Innocence', pure white.
'Ostara', light blue.
'Pink Pearl', dark pink.

Flowering time: late April

'Carnegie', pure white.
'City of Haarlem', pale yellow.
'Myosotis', forget-me-not blue.
'Queen of the Blues', light sky-blue.
'Queen of the Pinks', carnation pink.
'Tubergen's Scarlet', blood-red.

Flowering time: end April/May.

All double flowered:
'Hollyhock', carmine-red.
'Madame Sophie', pure white.

Ipheion · Spring Star Flower · Lilac Family (Liliaceae)
Ipheion uniflorum (syn. *Triteleia*)
◗ to ○ ⎕ ≃ H2

Tufted grassy leaves and single, pale blue starry flowers in spring; S. America.
– – 'Wisley Blue', deeper purple-blue flowers.

Iris · Iris Family (Iridaceae)
Bulbous irises, almost all 15 to 30 cm (6 to 12 in).
○ to ○○ ⊕ Y ⤫ ⎕ ○ ♔ F H1

Flowering time: February/March

Iris bakerana H2
Violet-blue, needs warm, sheltered position; Euphrates area.
– *danfordiae*
Lemon-yellow with brown spots, fragrant; Turkey to Syria.
– *histrio* var. *aintabensis*
Light-blue dwarf iris, hardier than the type plant; southern Turkey.

Flowering time: mid March

Iris histrioides 'Major'

Small dwarf iris, deep blue with yellow spots, good-tempered. Origin of the species: central Turkey.
– *reticulata*
Deep violet-blue; Iran, Caucasus to Iraq.
Iris reticulata hybrids (crosses with *I. histrioides* and possibly also *I. bakerana*)
– – – 'Blue Veil', bright sky-blue, a new hybrid with a great future.
– – – 'Cantab', water-blue.
– – – 'Harmony', sky-blue, yellow central strips on lower petals.
– – – 'J. S. Dijt', reddish-purple.
– – – 'Pauline', purple-violet.
– – – 'Violet Beauty', silky violet with slightly darker lower petals.

Flowering time: early to mid April
About 30 cm (12 in) and taller:

Iris bucharica
Winter-hardy, perennial rock-garden iris, five to seven flowers per stem, cream coloured, lower petals with large yellow speck; Pamir.
– *graeberana*
Uniform light blue, also multi-flowered; Turkestan.
– *magnifica*
Pale lavender-blue, up to seven flowers per stem, lower petals flecked with orange, good-tempered; rocky cliff faces of Pamir.
– × *warlsind* (*I. warleyensis* × *I. aucheri*)
Many-flowered hybrid, upper petals blue, lower yellow with blue edges. The name is a combination of the parent types, *Iris warleyensis* and *Iris sindjarensis* (now known as *I. aucheri*).

Flowering time: June/July

Iris xiphioides (syn. *I. anglica*) · English Iris
≃ to ≙
Perennial bulbous iris, does not like too dry a position, leave in ground for several years, do not store bulbs in the dry for too long. The true species is dark blue, 60 to 75 cm (24 to 30 in); damp mountain meadows of central and western Pyrenees. Mostly available only as mixed colours of white, pink, red, violet and blue.

Leucojum · Snowflake · Daffodil Family (Amaryllidaceae)
All species and forms need damp soil: ☀ to ●
Υ ✕ H1

Flowering time: end February/beginning March

Leucojum vernum · Spring Snowflake
Green-tipped; Europe.
– – ssp. *carpaticum*
Yellow-tipped, taller, often with two flowers; Carpathians.

Flowering time: May/June

Leucojum aestivum · Summer Snowflake
Grows to around 50 cm (20 in), four to eight flowers per stem; Europe, Asia Minor.
– – 'Gravetye Giant', more and larger flowers than the type plant.

Lilium · Lily · Lily Family (Liliaceae)
○ to ● ≃ ⊥ Υ H1

Flowering time: June/July

Lilium amabile
Orange-red, up to 90 cm (3 ft); Korea.
– *bulbiferum* · Orange Lily ○
Tangerine-orange, bowl-shaped flowers, up to 90 to 120 cm (3 to 4 ft); mountain pastures of Central Europe.
– – ssp. *croceum*
Dark orange, a little shorter; Alps to central Italy, Corsica.
– *carniolicum* ○ ⊕
Reddish-orange turk's-cap flowers, up to 120 cm (4 ft); eastern Alps to Romania.
– *cernuum*
Extremely graceful, unusual violet colour with darker spots, only up to 75 cm (30 in); North Korea, Ussuri region.
– *chalcedonicum* · Scarlet Turks-Cap Lily ○
Bright red, 100 cm (3 ft); Greece, not always easy to grow.
– *hansonii* · Japanese Turks-Cap Lily ●
Orange-yellow, speckled, very early, up to 90 to 120 cm (3 to 4 ft)
– *hansonii* hybrids ●
Orange to yellow, speckled, 90 to 120 cm (3 to 4 ft)
– *maculatum* hybrids
Many cultivars ranging in colour from apricot, yellow, orange to deep red; some grow up to 90 cm (3 ft), long-lasting and easy to grow.
– *martagon* · Martagon Lily ● not ✕
Pale purple, 1 m (40 in) and taller.
– – 'Album', glorious white form.

Flowering time: March

Narcissus · Daffodil · Daffodil Family (Amaryllidaceae) oto (●) ≃ Υ ✕ FH1
Narcissus cyclamineus · Cyclamen-flowered Daffodil ● ⊖
Small, bright yellow, about 15 cm (6 in), from Spain and Portugal, likes moisture. April-flowering forms are hardy.
– ✕ *johnstonii* 'Queen of Spain'
Wild cross between Spanish wild daffodil *(N. pseudo-narcissus)* and angel's tears (N. triandrus).

Flowering time: March/April

Narcissus bulbocodium (syn. Corbularia bulbocodium) · Hoo-petticoat Daffodil ○ to ○○ ≃ Υ ✕ H2
About 10 cm (4 in), deep yellow, number of subspecies known with varying winter-hardiness, foliage developing in autumn. Naturalise well in short grass; Portugal, Morocco (Atlas).
– – var. *citrina*
Pale lemon-yellow.
– – – *conspicua*
Deep yellow, naturalises readily. H1
– – – *romieuxii* var. *tenuifolia*
Dark yellow, funnel-shaped, early-flowering, dwarf variety, narrow leaves. Most tender. H3
– ✕ *odorus* · Campernelle Jonquil
Orange-yellow, fragrant daffodil, 30 cm (12 in); Mediterranean countries.
– *pseudonarcissus* ssp. *moschatus*
Sulphur-yellow, 15 cm (6 in); Spain and southern France.
– *triandrus* · Angel's Tears
White, 30 cm (12 in); Spain.
– – ssp. *albus*, pure white
– – ssp. *concolor*, golden-yellow

Flowering time: April/May

Narcissus gracilis
Delicate, sulphur-yellow, late wild daffodil from southern France.

– *poeticus*
The well-known poet's narcissus, white, 30 cm (12 in); southern Europe.
– – 'Actaea', snow-white with red eye.

Flowering time: small-flowered autumn species (only for real enthusiasts)

Narcissus elegans H2
Autumn daffodil in white and yellow, 60 cm (2 ft); Italy, Sicily, Algeria.
– *serotinus* H2
White-yellow October daffodil, 30 cm (12 in); Mediterranean.

Puschkinia · Striped Squill · Lily Family (Liliaceae)
○ to ◐ ⊕ ⅄ ○ H1

– *scilloides* var. *libanotica* · Lebanon or Striped Squill
Small pale blue flower of March/April; Asia Minor, Caucasus.
– – 'Alba', snow white striped squill.

Scilla · Squill · Lily Family (Liliaceae)
All species and cultivars:
○ to ● ≃ ⅄ ✕ ▤ ○ ♔ H1

Flowering time: around first half March

Scilla bifolia · Alpine Squill
Low-growing, bright blue squill; Alps, Asia Minor, Caucasus.
– – 'Alba', pure white, early.
– *mischtschenkoana* (syn. S. tubergeniana)
Prettiest of the early types, light blue with darker stripes, increases well but seldom produces seed! 15 cm (6 in); northern Persia.

Flowering time: early April

Scilla sibirica · Siberian Squill or Spring Beauty
Deep-blue, 15 cm (6 in); Crimea, Yugoslavia, Asia Minor.
– – 'Alba', snow-white.
– – 'Spring Beauty', deep-blue, large-flowered.
– – var. *taurica*
15 cm (6 in), paler blue than the type *S. sibirica*. Earlier flowering than the species; Taurus.

Flowering time: end April/beginning May

Scilla amoena
Low-growing, deep blue, 15 cm (6 in).

– *hispanica* (syn. S. campanulata) · Spanish Bluebell
Deep blue squill with bell-shaped flowers, 30 cm (12 in), May, grows well even in semi-shade; Spain, Portugal, southern France. (Most garden bluebells are hybrids with *S. non-scriptus*)
– – 'Blue queen', shining sky-blue.
– – 'Excelsior', deep blue, large bells.
– – 'Myosotis', pure blue.
– – 'Rose Queen', pale pink.
– – 'Sky Blue', dark blue, late variety.
– *pratensis*
Later violet-blue squill of meadows, to 30 cm (1 ft), May/June; Bulgaria, Yugoslavia.

Flowering time: summer to autumn

Scilla autumnalis · Autumn Squill
Reddish-purple flowers, 15 cm (6 in), July/September, flowers richly; north-west Europe, western Mediterranean.
– *peruviana* · Cuban Lily H1
Rosettes of fleshy leaves, flower spikes 25 cm (10 in) tall with wide cluster of starry blue flowers; Portugal, Spain, Italy.
– – 'Alba', white.
Sternbergia · Daffodil Family (Amaryllidaceae)
○ ⅄ ✕ H2
– *lutea* · Common Sternbergia
Bright yellow autumn sternbergia, often begins flowering as early as September, sheltered position only as the leaves appear in autumn; Sicily to Persia.

Trillium · Wake-Robin · Lily Family (Liliaceae)
◐ to ● ≃ ⅄ ✕ ♂ H1

– *catesbaei* (syn. T. stylosum)
30 cm (12 in); south-eastern United States.
– *cernuum* · Nodding Trillium, Bashful Benjamin
White or pale pink, 30 to 45 cm (12 to 18 in), dark red berries; woods of Newfoundland.
– *chloropetalum* (syn. T. sessile var. californicum)
White; mountain forests of California.
– *erectum*
Dark red, red berries, 30 cm (12 in); United States.
– – var. *album*, white subspecies.
– *grandiflorum* · Wake-Robin
The most handsome of the genus, around

40 cm (16 in), pure white, black berries; United States.
- *nivale* · Dwarf White Trillium
  15 cm (6 in), March/May; United States.
- *recurvatum*
  Erect brownish-red flowers, 30 cm (12 in); woods of Mississippi.
- *sessile* · Toad Trillium
  Deep red, 30 cm (12 in); eastern United States.
- – var. *luteum*, greenish or lemon yellow; origin same as type
- *undulatum* · Painted Trillium
  White with purple markings, leaves wavy at edges; United States.

Tulipa · Tulip · Lily Family (Liliaceae)
○ to ○○○ ⊕ ✕ ⬚ ○ ⦙ H1
Wild and garden tulips

Flowering time: around end March

Tulipa kaufmanniana · Water-lily Tulip
  Pale yellow March tulip, 30 cm (12 in), outside petals striped with red, most cultivars 15 to 20 cm (6 to 8 in); Turkestan.
- – 'Ancilla', lemon to ivory, early, red markings.
- – 'Berlioz', yellow buds, gold inside, mottled foliage.
- – 'Fritz Kreisler', large salmon-pink flowers, 20 cm (8 in)
- – 'Gaiety', creamy-white, very large flowers, short stems.
- – 'Gluck', red and cream with cream inside, strongly marked foliage.
- – 'Heart's Delight', rose red and white, broad, well marked foliage.
- – 'Shakespeare', salmon pink-apricot colour, 15 cm (6 in).
- – 'Showwinner', scarlet flowers and striped foliage.
- – 'Stresa', golden petals with strong scarlet markings.
- – 'The First', pure white, outer petals with carmine-red band, very early, 20 cm (8 in).
- *violacea* (syn. T. pulchella var. violacea)
  Violet or purple, black centre, very early, pendant buds; northern Persia.

Flowering time: around first half April

Tulipa australis
  Small yellow wild tulip with red markings; western France, Spain.

- *batalinii*, small, pale yellow, dwarf tulip from Turkestan.
- – 'Bronze Charm', hybrid with *T. linifolia*, bronze-flushed flowers.
- *biflora*, small white tulip opening to flat, starry flower; Siberia, Caucasus.
- *clusiana* · Lady Tulip
  Starry white flowers with purple markings, 30 cm (12 in); Mediterranean to Iran.
- – var. *chrysantha*
  Golden-yellow wild tulip from Iran, 30 cm (12 in), outer petals orange-brown.
- *eichleri*
  Bright red with black and yellow throat; Transcaucasia.
- *fosterana* 'Cantata'
  Large-flowered, scarlet-red dwarf with black throat; Turkestan.
- *greigii*
  Orange-scarlet with black throat; Turkestan.
- – 'Aurea', golden-yellow.
- *hageri*
  Red tulip from Greece, wide starry flower, 15 cm (6 in), from the hills of Parnassus.
- *kolpakowskiana*
  Yellow wild tulip, outer petals marked with red, 30 cm (12 in); Turkestan.
- *praestans*
  Glowing orange, several flowers on each stem, 15 cm (6 in); Pamir.
- *tarda*
  Dwarf tulip with bright gold, white-tipped, starry flowers, three to five flowers per stem; east Turkestan.
- *turkestanica*
  Small white tulip with yellow eye; Turkestan.
- *urumiensis*
  Buttercup yellow flowers opening from bronze-red buds; N. W. Iran.

Flowering time: around second half April

Tulipa armena
  Blood-red with black and yellow throat; Armenia.
- *linifolia*
  Small tulip, carmine-red with black throat, 30 cm (12 in); central Asia.
- *ostrowskiana*
  Large orange-red flowers, 15 cm (6 in); Turkestan.
- *stellata*
  White starry-flowered tulip with blue throat

and red outer petals, opens wide in sun; Himalayas.

Flowering time: around first half May

Tulipa acuminata · horned tulip
Yellow and red-white tulip, 30 cm (12 in); origin unknown but probably a very ancient cultivated form.
– *maximowiczii*
Light red dwarf tulip, similar to *T. linifolia*; Turkestan.
– *montana* (syn. T. wilsoniana)
Crimson-scarlet dwarf tulip with glossy black blotch, open bell-shaped flowers, 15 cm (6 in); mountains of Iran.
– *sylvestris* 'Tabriz'
A wild form named after the place where it was discovered, buds almost as pendant as type, but the flowers with outer petals of green and pale yellow opening are larger. Around 15 cm (6 in).

Flowering time: end May/June

Tulipa sprengeri
Latest of all the tulips, beautiful, scarlet-red throughout; Armenia.

Garden tulips

Flowering time: early to mid April

Early single tulip group in early cultivars.

Flowering time: second half April

Larger garden tulips, low-growing forms.

Flowering time: end May/beginning June

Lily-tulip cultivars for wild garden areas.

Miniature deciduous shrubs

The huge realm of dwarf shrubs, whose longevity and compactness the coming years will show, is one of which gardeners are only just becoming aware. Those who remain ignorant are neglecting a group of plants that are extremely versatile, neat and compact, and which complement and link our smaller and larger garden plants in a way all their own.

In the wild these hardy plants are to be found in all types of habitat. It is now time for the gardener to make full use of them for our gardens will profit greatly from their ability to give an air of space and dimension. By using them with mat formers and one or two larger shrubs we can achieve contrasts of height at every turn.

Too many rock gardeners restrict themselves exclusively to rock plants, instead of viewing shrubs and herbaceous plants as inseparably linked. If you want to provide fully for the beauty and peculiarities of dwarf shrubs, you will have to plan a rather larger rock garden from the outset.

It is possible to achieve a wide variety of decorative effects right through the year. The best effects are provided by dwarf conifers with their unbelievable charm at times when the garden lacks other interest, and the freshness of their new spring shoots, which often go unappreciated. Then there are the berried dwarf shrubs which offer attractive fruits in summer and autumn, and even throughout the winter in the case of some medlars.

They are followed by the flowering shrubs, which offer a host of surprises even for experienced gardeners. They used to be rather too large for rock gardens, but now exist in dwarf forms which can be included anywhere.

Now that the adaptability of these plants has been recognized, the whole area is found to be full of special cultivars with increased hardiness and different flowering times, new species and varieties. It is an area of constant change. No one can become familiar with the whole field; even the experts have been overwhelmed by the avalanche of new plants. And anyone who believes that he knows all there is to know about his collection of dwarf maples, his gorse bushes or dwarf rhododendrons, will be repeatedly surprised by completely new additions, which are as common here as in all other areas of the rock garden.

Common miniature deciduous shrubs

Acer japonicum 'Aureum', golden Japanese maple, 90 cm (3 ft) or more. ○ to ◑ ⊖ ≃ ⊥ ⊔ ⟡ ♠ H1

- *palmatum* var. *dissectum*, Japanese maple, 90 cm (3 ft) or more.
- – – – 'Ornatum', red-leaved form, 90 cm (3 ft) or more.

Berberis candidula, a silver dwarf barberry, yellow flowers and black fruits, 30 cm (12 in); China. ☀ to ◑ ≃ ⊥ ◯ ⧇ ≢ H1
- *empetrifolia*, yellow, 30 to 60 cm (12 to 24 in); Chile. H2
- *hookeri*, a dwarf barberry from the Himalayas, yellow, 120 cm (4 ft). H2
- × *stenophylla* 'Irwinii', smallest of the barberry hybrids, pale yellow. H2
- *thunbergii* 'Atropurpurea Nana', dark purple-red foliage, yellow flowers, to 60 cm (2 ft); type from Japan. H1
- *verruculosa*, a blue-leaved dwarf barberry, 1.5 m (4½ ft) and taller. H1
- *wilsoniae*, coral berries, makes mounds of arching stems to 90 cm (3 ft); China. H2

Betula nana, dwarf birch, 60 to 120 cm (2 to 4 ft). ◯ ≃ ⊥ H1

Buxus microphylla, dwarf box from China, to 1 m (3 ft) or less. ◯ to ◑ ⸽ Y ≢ H1

Clematis alpina, a climbing alpine clematis, violet. ◯ to ☀ ⊕ ≃ ⊥ H1

Corylopsis pauciflora, sulphur-yellow, 1 to 2 m (3 to 6 ft). ◯ ≃ Y ✕ H2

Cotoneaster adpressus, a pink flowered dwarf cotoneaster, 30 cm (12 in). ◯ to ◑ ⸽ ◯ ⧇ H1
- *congestus*, 45 to 75 cm (18 to 30 in). ◯ to ◑ ⋙ Y ◯ ⧇ ≢ H1
- – 'Nanus', dwarf form to 30 cm (12 in) or less.
- *dammeri*, 15 cm (6 in). ◯ to ◑ ▢ ⋙ Y ◯ ⧇ ≢ H1
- – var. *radicans*, quick-growing variety of above.
- *horizontalis*, 60 to 90 cm (2 to 3 ft) when grown flat. ◯ to ◑ ▢ ⊥ ◯ ♠ ⧇ H1
- – *perpusillus*, dwarf cultivar, pink, 30 cm (12 in).
- *microphyllus* var. *cochleatus*, a rock spray from China, white with black centre, 30 cm (12 in). ◯ to ◑ ⸽ ▢ ⊥ ◯ ⧇ ≢ H1

Cytisus × *beanii*, Bean's Dwarf Broom, pale yellow, 30 cm (12 in). ◯ to ◯◯◯ ⊕ ◯ ≢ F. H1
- *decumbens*, a dwarf spring broom, yellow, 15 cm (6 in). H1
- × *kewensis*, ivory-coloured dwarf broom, 30 cm (12 in). H1
- *purpureus*, purple broom, mauve, 30 to 45 cm (12 to 18 in). H1

- – 'Atropurpureus', with dark-red flowers.

Daphne arbuscula, pink, 15 to 30 cm (6 to 12 in). ◯ to ☀ ⊕ ≃ ⸽ ♢ ≢ H1
- *blagayana*, creamy-white flowers, 15 cm (6 in). ◯ to ☀ ⊕ ≃ ⸽ ♢ ≢ ⋙ H1
- × *burkwoodii* 'Albert Burkwood', pale pink, scented, 1 m (3 ft). Sister seedling 'Somerset' is taller and looser in growth. ◯ ⊕ Y F. H1
- *cneorum*, Garland Flower, rich pink, 30 cm (12 in). ◯ to ◑ ⊕ ≃ ⸽ ⊥ ◯ ≢ F. H1
- *collina*, rose pink flowers, 60 to 90 cm (2 to 3 ft). ◯◯ to ◑ ≃ ⊥ ◯ ≢ F. H2
- *mezereum*, Mezereon, carmine-red, 90 to 135 cm (3 to 4½ ft). ◯ to ◑ ≃ ⊥ ◯ ⧇ F. H1
- – 'Album', white.

Deutzia discolor, pink dwarf deutzia, 1.5 to 2 m (4½ to 6½ ft). H1
- *gracilis*, white dwarf deutzia, to 2 m (6½ ft). ◯ to ◑ ⸽ H1

Dryas octopetala, mountain avens, white, just under 15 cm (6 in). ◯ ⊕ ▢ ⋙ ♢ ⧇ ≢ H1
- × *suendermannii*, an even finer evergreen than the above, creamy-yellow.

Euonymus fortunei 'Coloratus', purple foliage in winter, 15 cm (6 in), ◯ to ◑ ≃ ▢ ⋙ ♢ ≢ H1
- – 'Minimus', flat carpeting growth, 15 cm (6 in).
- – 'Variegatus' (syn. 'Gracilis'), leaves white margined, 30 cm (12 in).
- – var. *radicans*, climbing dwarf form, can be grown on ground, 30 cm (12 in).
- – var. *vegetus*, 30 cm (12 in) and more.

Fuchsia magellanica 'Riccartonii', red-blue dwarf fuchsia, 60 cm (2 ft). ◑ ⊖ ≃ ⸽ Y H2

Genista lydia, wide mounds of yellow flowers, to 60 cm (2 ft). ◯ to ◯◯◯ ⊥ Y ≢ H2
- *hispanica*, Spanish gorse, golden yellow flowers, tight hummocks, 30 to 60 cm (1 to 2 ft) high. H2
- *pilosa procumbens*, dwarf greenweed, golden-yellow. H1
- *tinctoria*, Dyer's greenweed, golden-yellow, 60 to 120 cm (2 to 4 ft). H1
- – 'Plena', double variety of Dyer's greenweed, yellow, 30 cm (12 in).

Hedera helix 'Conglomerata', dwarf ivy, 30 cm (12 in). ◑ to ● ▢ ⋙ Y ♢ ≢ H2
- – 'Minima', dwarf ivy, 30 cm (12 in).

Helianthemum, rock rose, all around 15 cm (6 in). This and all following hybrids and cultivars ◯ ⊕ ▢ ⸽ ◯ ♢ ≢ H2
- 'Amy Baring', apricot yellow.

– 'Ben Heckla', copper gold.
– 'Cerise Queen', double rose-red.
– 'Fireball' (syn. 'Mrs Earle'), double red.
– 'Fire Dragon', red-orange, foliage grey.
– 'Firefly', fire-red.
– 'Golden Queen', golden-yellow.
– 'Jubilee', double yellow.
– 'Old Gold', golden yellow, deep green leaves.
– 'Orange Surprise', double orange.
– 'Praecox', single yellow, early.
– 'Supreme', deep carmine-red.
– 'Wisley Pink', soft pink flowers, silvery-grey leaves.
– 'Wisley Primrose', pale yellow, large-flowered, silver-grey leaves.
– 'Wisley White', white with grey foliage.
– *nummularium* (syn. H. chamaecistus), common rock rose, deep yellow, 8 cm (3 in), earliest in May. ○ ▭ ⦙ ⬡ ♡ ⧧ H2
– *oelandicum* ssp. *alpestre* (syn. H. alpestre), Alpine rock rose, yellow, 5 cm (2 in). ○ ▭ ⦙ ⌓ ♡ H2
Hypericum 'Hidcote', glorious golden-yellow flowers and reddish wood, to 1.5 m (4½ ft). ○ to ◐ ≃ ⊥ H2
– *patulum* var. *henryi*, very large flowers, golden-yellow, to 1 m (3 ft). ○ to ◐ ≃ ⊥ ♡ H2
Iberis, see Herbaceous plants, p. 000.
Ilex crenata mariesii, slow growing, to 90 cm (3 ft). ○ to ◐ ≃ ⊥ ♡ ⧧ H2
Lavandula angustifolia, lavender, evergreen, in cultivars of varying height, most up to 60 cm (2 ft). ○ to ○○○ ⊕ ▭ ‖ ⬡ ⚘ F. H2
Leiophyllum buxifolium, sand myrtle, 15 to 45 cm (6 to 18 in). ◐ ⊖ ≃ ▭ Y ♡ ⧧ H1
Mahonia aquifolium 'Moseri', red-leaved Oregon Grape, yellow flowers, 1 to 2 m (3 to 6 ft). ○ to ● ▭ ⦙ Y ⬡ ♡ ♣ ⧧ H1
– *repens,* creeping barberry, creeper, yellow, 30 cm (12 in). ○ to ● ▭ ⋙ Y ⬡ ♡ ♣ H1
Moltkia petraea, a gromwell from Greece, bright blue, 30 cm (12 in), flowers in summer! ○ to ○○○ ▭ ⦙ ⬡ H2
Pachysandra procumbens, bronze-leaved, 30 cm (12 in). ◐ to ● ≃ ▭ ⋙ Y H1
– *terminalis,* evergreen, 30 cm (12 in). ◐ to ● ≃ • ▭ ⋙ Y ⧧ H1
Perovskia atriplicifolia, Russian sage, a blue sage, 90 cm (3 ft) or more. ○ to ○○○ ▭ ⊥ ♡ F. H1
Philadelphus lemoinei hybrids, mock orange, white, 1 to 2 m (3 to 6 ft).
This and the following cultivars ○ to ◐ ⦙ ⊥ ✂ ⬡ F. H1
– – – 'Manteau d'Hermine', double-flowered.
– *microphyllus,* a delicate mock orange, white, 1.5 m (4½ ft) and above. ○ to ◐ ⦙ ⊥ ✂ ⬡ F. H2
Polygala chamaebuxus, box-leaved milkwort, dwarf, clear yellow or brownish flowers, 15 cm (6 in). ○ to ✹ ⊕ ≃ ‖ ⋙ ♡ ⧧ H1
– – 'Grandiflora', yellow and purple flowers.
Potentilla fruticosa 'Daydawn', shrubby cinquefoil, pinkish yellow, 75 cm (2½ ft). ○ ▭ ⦙ ⊥ ⬡ H1
– – 'Manshu' (syn. P. mandshurica), white, 60 cm (2 ft).
– – 'William Purdom' (syn. 'Purdomii'), pale yellow, slow growth, 1.5 m (4½ ft).
Prunus laurocerasus 'Schipkaensis', a dwarf cherry laurel, white flowers, to 1½ m (4½ ft). ◐ to ● ≃ ▭ ⦙ ⊥ Y ♡ ⧧ H2
– – 'Otto Luyken', wide vase shaped, to 90 cm (3 ft).
– *tenella,* dwarf Russian almond, pink, 60 to 90 cm (2 to 3 ft), spreads by means of underground runners, but will not spread quickly. ○ to ○○○ ⋙ ✂ ⬡ ♣ H1
– – 'Alba', white variety.
Ribes alpinum 'Pumilum', mountain currant, yellow, 60 cm (2 ft). H1
Rosmarinus lavandulaceus, blue flowers, prostrate to 15 cm (6 in). ○ to ○○○ ▭ ✂ ⬡ ⚘ F. H2
Ruta graveolens, rue, a decorative herb with blue green foliage, 75 cm (2½ ft). ○ to ○○ ▭ ⬡ ⚘ F. ⧧ H2
– – 'Jackman's Blue', very blue foliage.
Salix caesia 'Nana', dwarf willow, pale yellow catkins, 30 cm (12 in). ○ ≃ ⊥ H1
– *hastata* 'Wehrhahnii', silver dwarf willow, 60 to 90 cm (2 to 3 ft) or more.
– *herbacea,* least willow, 15 cm (6 in), quite prostrate.
– *purpurea* 'Gracilis', purple osier, 60 to 90 cm (2 to 3 ft).
– *repens,* creeping willow, yellow, 30 cm (12 in).
– *reticulata,* net leaved willow, creeper, under 15 cm (6 in).
– *retusa,* yellow, 15 cm (6 in).
– *serpyllifolia,* yellow, 30 cm (12 in).
Santolina chamaecyparissus (syn. S. incana), cotton lavender, silver grey leaves and yellow button heads of flowers. ○ to ○○ ⊕ ▭ Y ⬡ ♡ H2

– – *virens,* bright green, compact bushes.

Spiraea bullata, dwarf spiraea, dark rose, 30 cm (12 in). ○ to ◑ ▯ ⊥ H1

– *decumbens,* dwarf spiraea, white, 30 cm (12 in). ○ ⊕ ▢ H1

Dwarf conifers
in the rock garden

There are many rock gardens where dwarf conifers have been allowed to grow until finally you can see nothing else. Sometimes this can give wonderful colour effects of bluish-green, golden-green, dark green, bright emerald green, or variations of form with wide bushes, upright trees or bushes whose branches cascade towards the ground, but it can also give an overgrown, neglected appearance if shrubs such as *Juniperus chinensis* 'Pfitzeriana' are allowed to become too large. It is easy to forget that many dwarf shrubs will eventually grow quite large and should be restricted to the edges of the rock garden, while other smaller, slower growing types are more suitable for the rock garden proper. I have seen Japanese dwarf False Cypress (*Chamaecyparis obtusa* 'Nana Gracilis') which had grown to only 50 or 60 cm (18 to 24 in) over twenty years, while *Chamaecyparis obtusa* 'Nana' can grow to 200 cm (6 ft) over the same period. One often ignores the importance of the differences between "dwarf", "more dwarf" and "most dwarf" in the rock garden and the different growth rates they indicate in plants which are often closely related. It is also important to distinguish between plants with "slow growth", "moderate growth" and "quick growth". The quick-growing plants should be kept in the background or to form a transition to larger shrubs.

Of course when plants become too thick they can be kept in check by pruning. Planting too many dwarf conifers can not only spoil the appearance of the garden above ground, but can also make for a thick tangle of roots below the surface. It is difficult to conceive of the density of the fine mesh of roots belonging to each plant. In an effort to keep certain sections of soil free from roots I have often adopted the old far eastern method of sinking thin slabs of stone into the soil to keep back the roots and to maintain the balance between weaker and stronger young plants.

Pruning conifers can add greatly to their charm. Good results can be obtained by planting erect conifers with flatter types; the closer they are together the greater the contrast. Try planting a group of contrasting dwarf shrubs, evergreen and deciduous, blue-green with red-brown leaves very close together, almost in the same planting holes.

Be bold, my friend; nature will temper and transform your risks and follies, which may at first seem over-done. If you plant a drooping juniper in a flat plot you create a kind of waterfall effect while at the same time providing some winter protection. It is always advisable to look at a planting of dwarf conifers which has been established for some time, then it is possible to get a better idea of the potential growth form and size that the attractive mini-conifers can attain.

New dwarfs are moreover continually appearing from all corners of the world and one can only wonder that they have never been used before and that their adaptability and beauty has so long been neglected. Many from Central Europe have been in existence far longer than the whole art of the rock garden and have recently begun to add their charm to the garden setting. Many were growing in plantations as curiosities, many come from mountain wildernesses, descendants of old bent trees on inaccessible mountain slopes, such as the Hudson Balsam Fir (*Abies balsamea* var. *hudsoniana*) which takes fifty years to reach 90–120 cm (3–4 ft).

The whole realm of dwarf conifers is a labyrinth of bizarre beauty whose windings no one has yet fully penetrated. It is important to remember that ornamental gardening now consists of millions of small gardens, where small plants and shrubs will play an increasingly important part. Dwarf conifers are the very plants to show off the value of the small space, making a celebration of smallness, turning constricted areas into places of regal proportions. If more was known of the effects that can be achieved with dwarf conifers, many more people would try their hands at rock gardening.

In choosing miniature plants and in our attempts to make them grow and increase, we can all consider ourselves pioneers of a new extension in gardening, which can only develop further in the future. Certainly it is clear that even in the smallest garden they will come to be much appreciated as time goes on.

The species and forms included in my select list are only a few of the plants included and described in recent literature. My aim has not been to include as varied a list as possible, but to include little-known plants of great beauty.

The main dwarf conifers

Abies balsamea var. *hudsoniana*, Hudson Balsam Fir, natural shape, 60 cm (2 ft) eventually more, round and compact, dark green.
- *cephalonica* 'Nana', dwarf Grecian Fir, just over 60 cm (2 ft) in height, compact, dark green.
Cedrus deodara 'Golden Horizon', semi-prostrate with pendulous branches, golden foliage, 75 to 90 cm (2½ to 3 ft).
Chamaecyparis lawsoniana 'Forsteckensis', Dwarf Lawson cypress, up to 120 cm (4 ft), slow-growing, thick, wide cone-shape, grey-blue.
- *lawsoniana* 'Globosa', dwarf Lawson cypress, 60 cm (2 ft), rounded with flat top, light green.
- *obtusa* 'Nana Gracilis', dwarf Hinoki cypress, grows to 1.5 m (5 ft) after several years, irregular conical shape, glistening dark green.
- *pisifera* 'Nana', dwarf Sawara cypress, just over 15 cm (6 in), rounded, blue-green.
- - 'Plumosa Compressa', dwarf thread cypress, 90 cm (3 ft), rounded, compact, yellowish-green.
Juniperus chinensis 'Blaauw's Variety', dwarf Chinese juniper, blue, up to 2 m (6 ft), upward spreading branches, grey-blue.
- *communis* 'Compressa', dwarf common juniper, extremely slow-growing, 60 cm (2 ft) at maturity, narrow torch-shape, light green.
- - var. *depressa*, prostrate juniper, rarely up to 60 cm (2 ft), upward-spreading flat branches, creeping, light green.
- - - - 'Aurea', around 15 cm (6 in), bushy, creeping, light green with golden tipped shoots.

- - 'Hornibrookii' a carpeting juniper, rounded cushions, spreading, light green.
- *conferta*, wide spreading but prostrate, grass green.
- - 'Blue Pacific', slower growing with blue-green foliage.
- *horizontalis*, creeping juniper, 15 to 30 cm (6 to 12 in), prostrate creeper, bluish-green.
- - 'Alpina', over 15 cm (6 in), slow-growing, single erect branches in maturity, bluish-green, purple in winter.
- - 'Glauca', steel-blue cultivar of creeping juniper, 15 cm (6 in), slow-growing, flat, deep blue.
- - 'Humilis', carpeting juniper, good 15 cm (6 in), upright cushions, green.
- *sabina* 'Tamariscifolia', tamarix savin juniper, good 30 cm (12 in), flat and low-growing, dark green.
- *virginiana* 'Globosa', a rounded pencil cedar, to 120 cm (4 ft), compact, rounded, fresh green.
- - 'Grey Owl', up to 2 m (6 ft), grows similarly to *Juniperus chinensis* 'Pfitzeriana', blue-grey.
- - 'Nana Compacta', dwarf pencil cedar, to 90 cm (3 ft), greenish-blue.
Microbiota decussata, new, little-known plant from south-east Siberia, only 15 cm (6 in)! Forms flat mats of thuya-like foliage, will tolerate aridity and heat, fresh-green, copper-coloured in cold weather.
Picea abies 'Compressa', dwarf Norway spruce, eventually 120 cm (4 ft), wide conical shape, similar to *Picea abies* 'Conica', dark green.
- - 'Echiniformis', spiky dwarf spruce, 60 to 90 cm (2 to 3 ft), slow-growing, compact, rounded, dark green.
- - 'Gregoryana', 30 cm (12 in) and a little more, cushion-shaped, later rounded, grey-green.
- - 'Little Gem', up to 30 cm (6 in), rounded, flattened top, light green.
- - 'Nidiformis', 30 to 60 cm (1 to 2 ft), evenly rounded, intented at centre in nest-shape, grey-green.
- - 'Procumbens', 75 cm (2½ ft), flat cushion, yellowish-green.
- - 'Pygmaea', up to 120 cm (4 ft) but very slow-growing, flat pyramid shape, dark green.
- - 'Tabulaeformis', 60 to 90 cm (2 to 3 ft) and more, flat-topped, low-growing, yellow-green.
- *glauca* 'Alberta Globe', dwarf white spruce, only 30 cm (12 in), rounded, green.

– – 'Conica', up to 2 m (6 ft) in maturity, sharply conical, beautiful light green.

– – 'Echiniformis', very dwarf to 40 cm (16 in), compact and neat, blue-green in colour.

– *pungens* 'Glauca Globosa', rounded blue spruce, up to 120 cm (4 ft), rounded with flat top, deep blue.

Pinus mugo ssp. *mugo* (syn. P. mugo var. mughus), Swiss mountain pine, up to 2 m (6 ft), thick at first becoming thinner, dark green.

– – ssp. *pumilio*, dwarf pine, up to 120 cm (4 ft), drooping branches, compact, dark green.

– – 'Mops', dwarf variety of mountain pine, only around 40 to 60 cm (1 to 2 ft), densely rounded, grey, green.

– *pumila*, from East Asia, little over 180 cm (6 ft), slow-growing, branches extend laterally, dark green. 'Glauca' is smaller.

– *strobus* 'Umbraculifera', dwarf Weymouth pine, around 90 cm (3 ft), umbrella-shaped on low trunk, bluish-green.

– *sylvestris* 'Beuvronensis', very dwarf Scots pine, around 60–75 cm (2–2½ ft), dense and soon more broad than high. Grey-green in colour.

– – 'Nana', 60 cm (2 ft), rounded to torch shape, blue-green.

– *wallichiana* 'Compacta', long blue needles make this 200 cm (6½ ft) pine a striking specimen.

Taxus baccata 'Compacta', dwarf English yew, up to 90 cm (3 ft), rounded, shining dark green.

– – 'Repandens', 45 cm (18 in), creeping, shining dark green.

– – 'Standishii', tall and narrow to 120 cm (4 ft), old gold.

– – 'Summergold', semi-prostrate at 40 to 50 cm (16 to 20 in), bright golden foliage in summer.

– *cuspidata* 'Minima', dwarf Japanese yew, 15 cm (6 in), bushy but not too compact, shining dark green.

Tsuga canadensis 'Jeddeloh', dwarf eastern hemlock, about 90 cm (3 ft), interesting shape with nest-like, overhanging growth, shining light green.

– – 'Nana', dwarf hemlock, growing to just under 1 m (3 ft) in maturity, flat-topped, rounded, overhanging, light green.

Taller conifers for rock garden borders

(Recommended for edging and also with herbaceous plants without rocks)

Abies koreana, korean fir, to 5 m (15 ft), slow-growing, compact pyramid, very beautiful and hardy, shining dark green, notable for its prolific coning on young plants.

Chamaecyparis lawsoniana 'Ellwoodii', blue Lawson cypress, up to 2.5 m (8 ft) and more, narrow torch-shape, blue-green.

– *pisifera* 'Squarrosa', silver Sawara cypress, up to 8 m (25 ft), grows to beautiful pyramid, silver-grey.

Juniperus chinensis 'Pfitzeriana', Chinese juniper, up to 4 m (12 ft), wide vase-shape, quick-growing, light green.

– *communis* 'Sentinel', up to 1.5 m (5 ft), slow-growing, narrowly columnar, grey-green.

– – 'Stricta', an Irish juniper, up to 4 m (12 ft), compact, narrow torch-shape, blue-green.

– – 'Suecica', a Scandinavian juniper, up to 10 m (30 ft) at maturity, but usually shorter, rather wider than previous form, overhanging shoot tips! Light green.

– *pachyphlaea*, alligator juniper, a silver juniper to 10 m (30 ft) with narrow form. Not for coldest areas. H2

– *virginiana* 'Burkii', a pencil or red cedar, up to 3 m (10 ft), wedge-shaped, blue-green towards winter turning to purple-red as weather turns colder.

– – 'Canaertii', up to 5 m (15 ft), upright and not too dense, dark green.

– – 'Glauca', 7 m (22 ft) and occasionally up to 10 m (30 ft), pyramid-shaped, steel-blue.

Picea abies 'Acrocona', variety of Norway spruce, up to 4 m (12 ft), wide wedge-shape, cones even on young plants, dark green.

– *breweriana*, Brewer's weeping spruce, up to 20 m (60 ft) but slow-growing, horizontal branches with pendant branchlets, graceful, dark grey-green.

Pinus aristata, bristle-cone pine, slow-growing, takes years to become large, bushy, needles in clumps like brushes, dark green.

– *cembra*, arolla or Swiss stone pine, ideal, slow-growing, beautiful conifer, do not plant close together but free-standing, usually only 10 m

(30 ft), dark green with creamy-blue shimmer.
- *koraiensis,* Korean pine, up to 15 m (45 ft) but slow-growing, similar to arolla pine, bluish-green.
- *parviflora* 'Glauca', Japanese white pine, usually only 5 m (15 ft), more cones on younger plants, finer needles, beautiful bluish-grey.

Taxus baccata, English yew, very slow-growing, bushier when young, tolerates thorough pruning, not for draughty position, top of needles shining dark green, underside light green.
- – 'Aurea', shoots golden, bushy, in later life needles partially striped in gold or yellow.
- – 'Dovastonii', erect to bushy, slow and flat-growing, branchlets hang over at tips, dark green.
- – 'Dovastonii Aurea', slow and flat-growing, needles yellowish-green with yellow edges.
- – 'Dovastonii Aurea Pendula', shoots obliquely upwards at first then downwards as stems lengthen.
- – 'Fastigiata', golden Irish yew, up to 5 m (15 ft), upright column, but less dense with more main branches, not for overexposed positions.
- *cuspidata,* Japanese yew, bushy and compact, equally slow-growing, completely impervious to frost, dark green.

Rhododendrons in the rock garden

The following lengthy list of wild and cultivated rhododendrons is the result of years of experience in several different European gardens and includes some species that will withstand severe frosts. The smaller wild species will form a centrepoint for any rock garden while the larger species and garden cultivars can be used in larger rock gardens together with the coniferous and evergreen leafy shrubs included in my previous lists.

In larger or municipal gardens rhododendrons can be used *en masse* to form shrubberies bordering paths. Here it is advisable to combine larger with smaller species and for ground-cover to plant evergreen grasses, ferns or any ground-covering herbaceous plant that tolerates shade. To add variety rhododendrons can be combined with any mountain shrubs or, for smaller or mediumsized gardens, with any of the coniferous shrubs listed on p. 125 ff, with the exception of the *Juniperus* types. This section also includes other ericaceous plants, both heathers and some lesser known shrubs, almost all of which need lime-free soils to thrive. Unlike most of the rhododendrons, these are small or needleleaved shrubs which are suitable for open sites, though few do really well in hot sun.

Hardy rhododendron species

1. Dwarf species and up to around 80 cm (2½ ft)

Rhododendron atlanticum, white, 60 cm (2 ft), May, F, H1
- *calostrotum,* pink flowers in May, 30 cm (1 ft), ⚹ H1
- – 'Gigha', fine form with deeper flowers, ⚹
- *campylogynum,* pink bells in June, 30 cm (1 ft), ⚹ H2
- – *myrtilloides,* plum purple bells, 15 cm (16 in), ⚹ H2
- *camtschaticum,* purplish-red, 10 cm (4 in), May, usually flowering again in September, H1
- *canadense,* lilac, 60 cm (2 ft), April, H1
- *cephalanthum crebrifolium,* aromatic foliage and pink flowers, 15 cm (6 in), May, ⚹ H2
- *fastigiatum,* purplish-lilac, 50 cm (18 in), early spring, ⚹ H2
- *ferrugineum,* Alpenrose, dark purplish-red, 50 to 80 cm (18 to 30 in), mid May, ⚹ H1
- *forrestii* (syn. *R. repens*), crimson-red, up to 15 cm (6 in), April, ⚹ H2
- *hanceanum* 'Nanum', rounded shrublet, creamy yellow, 35 cm (14 in), May, ⚹ H3
- *hirsutum,* Alpenrose, carmine-red, 50 to 80 cm (18 to 30 in), June, H1
- *impeditum,* purplish-violet, 40 cm (16 in), April/May, ⚹ H2
- *keleticum,* purplish red, 15 cm (6 in), end May, ⚹ H2

- *kiusianum,* pinkish red, 60 cm (2 ft), May/June, ⚑ H2
- – – 'Album', smaller with pure white flowers, ⚑ H2
- *kotschyi,* deep pink, 50 cm (18 in), May, ⚑ H2
- *leucaspis,* white with bristly leaves, 50 cm (20 in), March/April, ⚑ H2

pemakoense, large pale pink flowers, 25 cm (10 in), March/April, ⚑ H2
- *radicans,* purple, 10 cm (4 in), June, ⚑ H2
- *russatum,* dark violet, 60 to 80 cm (2 to 2½ ft), May, ⚑ H2
- *scintillans* (R. polycladum), lilac to blue, 50 cm (18 in), April/May, ⚑ H2
- *williamsianum,* pink, 50 cm (18 in), rounded bush, April, many good hybrids, ⚑ H2
- *yakusimanum,* pale pink, carmine or white depending on origin, slow-growing, rarely reaches 1 m (3 ft), May, many good hybrids, ⚑ H2

2. Medium-height, 80 to 150 cm (2½ to 4½ ft)

Rhododendron ambiguum, yellow with green fleck, perfumed, 100 to 150 cm (3 to 4½ ft), April/ May. ⚑ H2
- *calendulaceum,* yellow or orange to scarlet, 100 to 150 cm (3 to 4½ ft), June. H1
- *dauricum,* lilac-pink, very hardy Siberian species, up to 150 cm (4½ ft), more rarely up to 200 cm (6 ft), flowers as early as January in mild winter, otherwise by March. H1
- *hippophaeoides,* lilac-pink, 100 to 150 cm (3 to 4½ ft), April, ⚑ H2
- *japonicum,* salmon-pink to orange with distinctive orange fleck, usually up to 150 cm (4½ ft) but sometimes up to 200 cm (6 ft), April/May. H2
- *micranthum,* milk-white, 80 to 150 cm (2½ to 4½ ft), May/June. ⚑ H1
- *mucronatum,* pure-white and perfumed, up to 150 cm (4½ ft), May. ⚑ H2–3
- *mucronulatum,* violet-pink, up to 150 cm (4½ ft), very early, flowers as early as January in mild winter, requires protection from damaging weather. H2
- *nudiflorum,* (syn. R. periclymenoides), rose or pale rose, about 100 cm (3 ft), occasionally up to 200 cm (6 ft), April/May. H1.
- *occidentale,* white to pale rose with yellow fleck, good perfume, up to 150 cm (4½ ft), occasionally up to 200 cm (6 ft), June. H2

- *viscosum,* white, strongly perfumed, 150 cm (4½ ft), July. H1

3. Tall, over 150 cm (4½ ft).

Rhododendron albrechtii, pale to purplish-red, up to 200 cm (6 ft, April/May. H1
- *arborescens,* white sometimes toning to pink, up to 300 cm (9 ft), June. H1
- *brachycarpum,* creamy-white, occasionally pink with green fleck, 200 to 300 cm (6 to 9 ft), June/July. ⚑ H2
- *catawbiense,* mountain rose-bay, lilac flowers with greenish speck, up to 400 cm (12 ft), end May, not often grown as its hybrids are better. ⚑ H1.
- *luteum,* common yellow azalea, golden-yellow, strong perfume, up to 200 cm (6 ft), May. H1
- *makinoi,* pale rose, up to 200 cm (6 ft), mid May. ⚑ H2
- *prinophyllum,* (syn. R. roseum), pink, up to 300 cm (9 ft), May. H1
- *reticulatum,* violet, 200 cm (6 ft), May. H2
- *schlippenbachii,* pure pink, 200 cm (6 ft), April/May. H1
- *smirnowii,* varying pink tones, 100 to 300 cm (3 to 9 ft), May/June. ⚑ H2
- *ungernii,* pale pink, up to 200 cm (6 ft), July. ⚑ H2
- *vaseyi,* pink with red fleck, up to 200 cm (6 ft), April/May. H1

Rhododendron hybrids

Evergreen hybrids

This group contains both low-growing and very tall sorts. Hybrids are divided by flowering time.

March/April

Rhododendron × *praecox* (syn. R. ciliatum × R. dauricum)

Early spring Alpenrose, deep carmine-pink, 100 to 150 cm (3 to 4½ ft), shrubby to compact. ⚑

Sun-loving perennials, such as varieties of the *Iris barbata nana* group and *Euphorbia polychroma* (text p. 175), should be planted between stones, as in nature. The stored warmth of the stones stimulates growth.

A springtime path, showing the variation in form of bulbs and dwarf perennials. Although many varieties have been used, the colours are not too scattered.

1. *Primula florindae*, a
tall scented primula
from Tibet (text p. 224).
Planted in fairly large
groups it will maintain
its effect over several
weeks.

2. *Pulmonaria saccharata*
'Mrs Moon', the Bethle-
hem Sage, with its
highly decorative
leaves, is always an in-
spiration.

3. *Primula denticulata*
'Alba', is a white ball
primula which should
find a place in every
garden! One of the
most popular spring
flowers, together with
the deep violet and
even red varieties.

4. *Ranunculus aconitifo-
lius*, the White Butter-
cup (text p. 242), is a
streamside plant of the
mountains of central
Europe, which is an in-
dication of how it
should be used in the
garden.

Campanula persicifolia, the Peach-leaved Bellflower
ext p. 165), thrives in semi-shade. Its seedlings can
metimes get out of hand.
  Anemone vitifolia (text p. 155), in several varieties,
owers from August to October.

3. *Lathyrus vernus*, the Spring Vetchling (text p. 207),
loves semi-shade. Even more attractive is the pink
variety 'Albo-Roseus'.
4. *Melittis melissophyllum*, the Bastard Balm (text p. 211),
is a garden treasure that is still little-known.

1. *Aster alpinus* 'Sabine' – a novelty with doubled pale mauve flowers.

2. *Aster alpinus* 'Suzanne', is a white-flowered double variety related to the pale mauve 'Sabine'. Both varieties can only be increased by division.

3. *Adonis vernalis*, the Yellow Adonis (text p. 152), opens its golden starry flowers towards the end of March.

4. *Inula ensifolia* 'Compacta', carries yellow flowers from July to August. Very effective with the dark blue varieties of *Campanula carpatica* (text p. 163).

Right-hand page:

1. *Iris ruthenica* (text p. 204) – a beautiful little iris with narrow grass-like leaves. Best transplanted shortly after flowering.

2. 'Path of Gold', is one of the most free-flowering and vigorous of the dwarf *Iris barbata nana* group.

3. 'Jerry Rubin', also belongs to the *nana* group. Its dark, velvety, ruby-red solitary flowers are a triumph of the plant breeder's skill!

1. *Haberlea rhodopensis* (text p. 195), will only thrive in a north-east facing situation.

2. *Oxalis adenophylla* (text p. 215), is not a plant for the beginner and will require much attention and a gravelly soil if it is to prosper.

3. *Viola biflora*, the Yellow Wood Violet (text p. 277), likes a damp shady rock cleft.

1. *Ramonda myconi*, the Pyrenean Ramonda (text p. 242) – an easy-to-grow type which also likes a north-east facing situation.

2. *Hutchinsia alpina* ssp. *auerswaldii* (text p. 202), forms beautiful flat green mats with cascades of white flowers.

1. *Paeonia tenuifolia* 'Plena', the double Narrow-leaved Peony, adds a touch of elegance to the garden with its narrow leaves. Very slow to develop to full size.
2. *Paeonia mlokosewitschii* (text p. 215), is a pale yellow Caucasian peony with bluish-green leaves. In flower by May.
3. *Paeonia tenuifolia* (text p. 215), is a plant of the southern European steppes. It needs humus-rich soil and full sun.

1. *Paeonia peregrina*
'Fireking' achieves its
effect chiefly through
the conspicuous sta-
mens within the cup-
shaped, orange-red
flowers.
2. Another variety of
Paeonia peregrina is
'Sunshine', with sal-
mon-orange flowers.
3. *Paeonia peregrina* (text
p. 215) – another dwarf
peony, which should be
left undisturbed, re-
wards us with its rich
flowers in May and
June.

1. *Campanula punctata*
(text p. 165) – grass-like
leaves and non-inva-
sive.
2. *Campanula pulla* (text
p. 164), likes a damp,
well-drained, humus-
rich soil.
3. *Campanula portenschlagiana* (text p. 164), is
the longest-flowering of
all the campanulas – a
real 'long-player'.

1. *Campanula glomerata* 'Superba', a Clustered Bellflower, has deep mauve flowers and is suitable for cutting.
2. *Campanula carpatica* 'Spechtmeise' belongs, with 'Karpatenkrone', 'Blaumeise' and 'Zwerg-möve' to the compact-growing, very free-flowering Bornim varieties.

1. *Campanula carpatica*, the Carpathian Bellflower (text p. 163), is truly one of the longest-flowering of rock garden perennials. Hybridization has improved it greatly. 'Kobalt' (text p. 163), the variety illustrated, has beautiful erect flowers.
2. *Campanula portenschlagiana* 'Birch Hybrid' – a 'long-player' which is crowded with flowers from June to August.

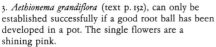

3. *Aethionema grandiflora* (text p. 152), can only be established successfully if a good root ball has been developed in a pot. The single flowers are a shining pink.
4. Dry walls planted with *Alyssum saxatile* 'Plena' and other cushion-forming dwarf perennials, provide a feast of colour in spring.

1. *Dianthus gratianopolitanus*, the Cheddar Pink (text p. 170), comes in several varieties. One of the most reliably-flowering and one which forms a thick, even cushion is 'Compactus Eydangeri'. It goes well with colour-contrasting *Sempervivum* species and hybrids.

2. A real 'long-player' is *Coreopsis verticillata* 'Grandiflora', its flowers continuing from June to September.

1. Successful planting with subjects that go well together will give years of pleasure. Shown here: *Carex montana* (Mountain Sedge) (text p. 106), with *Astilbe* varieties, *Rodgersia podophylla* and, in the background, *Carex pendula*.

2. *Gentiana asclepiadea*, the Willow Gentian (text p. 176), likes damp soil and light shade in the garden, as in the wild. Once well established it should not be transplanted.

1. and 2. *Gentiana sep-temfida* var. *lagodechiana* (text p. 176) from the Caucasus, is a beautiful blue summer plant which no garden should be without.

3. *Gentiana acaulis* (text p. 175–6), is usually found in the wild asso-ciated with *Primula lon-giflora*, as here in the Karawanken Moun-tains.

1. *Cypripedium reginae* (text p. 169), must have slightly acid, continually moist soil and light shade.

2. *Cypripedium calceolus*, the Lady's Slipper Orchid (text p. 169), is a protected species which likes a chalky soil. It needs quite a lot of attention and careful choice of position.

3. *Pleione bulbocodioides* var. *limprichtii*, the Tibetan Orchid (text p. 218), like all terrestrial orchids, needs special care.

End April

Caucasicum hybrid 'Jacksonii'
Pale pink, outer petals with deeper stripe, compact and rounded.
impeditum hybrid 'Blue Wonder'
Dark blue, compact and rounded.
repens hybrid 'Elisabeth Hobbie'
Transparent dark scarlet, one of the top cultivars, wide bush.
williamsianum hybrid 'Treasure'
Rose bells on a dwarf mound of foliage.

Early May

catawbiense hybrid 'Cunningham's White'
White with yellow eye and pale pink veining on outer petals, standard very hardy hybrid, strong rounded growth.
impeditum hybrid 'Moerheim'
Lavender, compact and rounded, quicker-growing than the species.
repens hybrid 'Baden-Baden'
Scarlet-red, strong sideways growth.

Mid May

catawbiense hybrid 'Daisy'
Pale carmine-red, low-growing.
caucasicum hybrid 'Coule de Neige' white with pale yellow markings, thick growth.
impeditum hybrid 'Blue Tit'
Bright azure-blue, rounded.
repens hybrid 'Axel Olsen'
Blood-red, more sideways than upward growth.
williamsianum hybrid 'Bow Bells'
Cerise buds opening paler. Coppery young foliage.

Late May

catawbiense hybrid 'Alfred'
Dark violet, curled, tall growth.
– – 'Allah'
Light purplish-pink with yellow markings, compact, grows moderately quickly.
– – 'Caractacus'
Violet, strong, erect growth.
– – 'Charles Dickens'
Ruby-red, flecked, moderately quick, rather uneven growth.

– – 'Humboldt'
Pale lilac with dark red fleck, wide compact growth.
– – 'Leopold'
Dark violet with brown markings, tall, quick growth.
– – 'Mexico'
Ruby-red with darker fleck, moderate growth.
– – 'Old Port'
Deep violet, more sideways than upward growth
– – 'Parson's Gloriosum'
Pale lilac-pink, strong erect growth.

Evergreen hybrids (Japanese Azalea)

These are particularly richly-flowering, winter-hardy descendants of Japanese wild species. They like a shady to semi-shady position and a moist, acid soil. Protection against winter sun is advisable. Avoid draughty situation. None grows particularly densely. Height varies with hybrid group and cultivar. *kaempferi* hybrids will reach 80 to 140 cm (2 to 4 ft) and *kurume* hybrids up to 100 cm (3 ft).

April–May

kaempferi hybrid 'Orange Beauty'
Orange-red with scarlet toning.
– – 'Betty'
Pink with light-red markings
– – 'Pink Treasure'
Pure pink with reddish-brown markings.
kurume hybrid 'Aladdin'
Orange-red.
– – 'Hatsugiri'
Purplish-carmine.
– – 'Helena'
Pure pink.
– – 'Hinodegiri'
Bright carmine-red.
– – 'Hinomayo'
Pale pink flecked with light red inside.

Mid May

kaempferi hybrid 'Alice'
Carmine with reddish-brown markings.

– – 'Jeanette'
Dark pink with reddish-brown markings.
– – 'Kathleen'
Deep pink with pale reddish-brown markings.

Deciduous, large-flowered hybrids (Summer Azalea)

This group includes the familiar 'Summer azaleas'. Many cultivars have bright orange or red leaves in autumn. They are quick-growing and require less moist soil than the evergreen hybrids. They originate from several rhododendron species in the *Azalea* series.

Ghent, occidentale and *rustica* hybrids usually grow to 200 cm (6 ft), occasionally to 300 cm (9 ft). *Mollis* hybrids on the other hand only grow to 150 cm (4½ ft) or occasionally to 200 cm (6 ft).

Early May

rustica hybrids
– – 'Byron'
Pure white.
– – 'Phidias'
Pale orange-yellow, reddish buds, petal tips pale pink, double.
– – 'Phoebe'
Sulphur-yellow with pink tones.
– – 'Velasquez'
When first open pale pink, turning to pure white.

Mid May

Ghent hybrid 'Gloria Mundi'
Salmon-pink with orange marking, edge of flower slightly fringed.
– – 'Goldlack'
Golden-yellow with salmon-pink bloom.
– – 'Narcissiflora'
Pale yellow with golden yellow fleck, perfumed.
– – 'Pallas'
Orange-red with yellowish-orange fleck.
mollis hybrid 'Directeur Moerlands' ('Golden Sunlight')

Golden-yellow with olive-brown markings.
– – 'Dr. Reichenbach'
Orange with pale salmon toning and dark-red markings.
– – 'Hugo Koster'
Scarlet with brown, red markings.
– – 'J. C. van Tol'
Salmon-pink to scarlet.
– – 'Koster's Brilliant Red'
Scarlet with orange markings.
– – 'Spek's Brilliant'
Orange-red with yellowish-orange markings.
occidentale hybrid 'Irene Koster'
Pale pink with small yellow fleck, perfumed.

Late May

occidentale hybrid 'Magnifica'
Creamy-yellow turning to pale pink with orange markings, some central veins deep carmine.
rustica hybrid 'Aida'
Pale lilac-pink with pale orange fleck.

Mid June

Ghent hybrid 'Coccinea Speciosa'
Bright orange-red.
– – 'Rose-Marie'
Blood-red.

Other ericaceous shrubs

Andromeda polifolia, bog rosemary, 30 cm (12 in). ○ to ◑ ☒ ⅄ ♂ ‡ ⊖ ⦸ H1
– – 'Macrophylla', broader deep green leaves and darker flowers.
– – 'Minima', pale pink, under 15 cm (6 in).
Arctostaphylos nevadensis, pine-mat manzanita, white flowers and carmine-red fruits, 15 cm (6 in). ○ ⊖ ≃ ⋙ ⅄ ‡ ⦸ H1
– *uva-ursi,* bear berry, 15 to 30 cm (6 to 12 in).
Calluna vulgaris, common ling, pink, foliage can turn bronze in late winter, 15 to 30 cm (6 to 12 in). ○ ⊖ ▢ ▏ ⋊ ○ ‡ ❦ H1
– – 'Alba Plena', double white flowers.
– – 'Beoley Gold', golden foliage all year, white flowers.

– – 'Darkness', dark purplish-red flowers and dark green foliage.

– – 'H. E. Beale', most attractive of the double varieties, silver-pink.

– – 'Silver Knight', silvery foliage and pink flowers.

– – 'Sister Anne', greyish woolly foliage, flowers pink.

Cassiope ◐ ⊖ ≃ ‡ H2

– 'Edinburgh', white bells in April, erect growth to 25 cm (10 in).

– *lycopodioides*, prostrate stems to 7½ cm (3 in) with neat small leaves and white bells from red stems.

– – 'Randle Cooke', free flowering hybrid with erect stems, to 15 cm (6 in).

Empetrum nigrum, crowberry, pink to purple flowers, glossy black fruit, 15 to 45 cm (6 to 18 in). ○ to ◐ ⊖ ▭ ⋙ ⧂ ‡ H1

Erica erigena (syn. E. mediterranea) 'Silberschmelze', white flowers. ○ ⊖ ▭ Y ✕ ⬡ ‡ H2

– *herbacea* (syn. E. carnea), spring heath, pink, 15 to 30 cm (6 to 12 in). ○ to ☀ ▭ Y ✕ ⬡ ‡ H1

– – 'Aurea', golden foliage and pink flowers.

– – 'Cecilia M. Beale', white heath.

– – 'James Backhouse', light pink, late.

– – 'King George', rose pink.

– – 'Vivellii', ruby flowers, bronze foliage.

– *tetralix*, cross-leaved heath, pink, 30 cm (12 in). ○ to ☀ ⊖ ≃ ▭ Y ✕ ⬡ ‡ H1

– *vagans*, Cornish heath, pink, 15 cm (6 in). ○ to ☀ ⊖ ≃ ▭ Y ✕ ⬡ ‡ H2

– – 'Alba', white variety.

– – 'F. D. Maxwell', dark salmon colour.

– – 'Lyonesse', pure white.

– – 'St Keverne', light salmon colour.

Gaultheria ◐ to ● ⊖ ≃ ‡ ⋙ ▭ ⧂ H2

– *cuneata*, glossy foliage, white flowers followed by white fruits, 25 cm (10 in).

Kalmia angustifolia 'Pumila', a dwarf sheep laurel with narrow leaves and pink flowers, 30 cm (12 in). ◐ to ● ⊖ ≗ ▭ Y ⟁ ‡ H1

– *polifolia*, swamp laurel, lilac flowers, 30 cm (12 in).

Parahebe catarractae, white flowers veined pink or purple, 15 to 30 cm (6 to 12 in). ○ to ☀ ≃ ▭ Y ‡ H2

– – 'Delight', purple-blue flowers.

Pernettya mucronata, red-berried, white flowers, up to 90 cm (3 ft). ◐ ≗ ▭ Y ⟁ ⧂ ‡ H2

– – 'Alba', white-berried form, 30 cm (12 in).

– – 'Bells Seedling', carmine-red berries.

Vaccinium myrtillus, bilberry, white flowers, 15 to 30 cm (6 to 12 in). ○ to ◐ ⊖ ▭ ⋙ Y ⬡ ⟁ ⧂ H1

– *vitis-idaea*, cowberry, white flowers, 15 to 30 cm (6 to 12 in). ○ to ◐ ⊖ ▭ ⋙ Y ⬡ ⟁ ⧂ ‡ H1

147

An A to Z of Herbaceous Rock-Garden Plants

It is a great pleasure to be able to shed new light on the immense treasure house of small plants, which are increasingly proving their worth to owners of small gardens where, despite their apparent frailty, they can become a permanent feature. All these tiny but enduring plants are capable of living for a whole generation and many years beyond, for as long as it takes a sapling to become a mature tree.

Today we can be brought closer to strange, magical, far-away places in ways that were unimaginable in the past—these small plants can crystallize our feelings and ideas in ways which no words can express.

We are living in the great age of discovery for new plants and varieties, all capable of becoming permanent companions to the gardener, and we must be prepared not only to try individual new plants, but to introduce a whole new range of tones and harmonies into the garden.

Some readers might say—and I am sure many will—'What is the point of trying to remember all this and trying to feel one's way through your maze of small plants. Wouldn't it be better to stick to essentials?' These people forget that the plants they consider to be essential would never have been discovered if their advice had been followed in the past.

There is one thing we should all bear in mind and that is that gardening and gardening problems are now being taken more seriously and are providing more pleasure for both young and old than ever before. Most people would soon become bored if every garden always contained the same plants. Variety alone can ensure that every garden has something different to offer.

The range of these small plants and shrubs is being widened every year by crossing species together to try and produce new hybrids with all the best characteristics of their parents as well as the necessary strength and durability. One could devote a whole book to this topic alone.

The following A to Z of the main herbaceous rock-garden plants is more detailed than was possible—for reasons of space—in the lists of water plants, grasses, ferns, bulbs and shrubs.

Cultivars are given in normal typeface within inverted commas as is standard horticultural and botanical practice. (eg. *Carlina acaulis* ssp. *simplex* 'Bronze').

Distribution maps refer to the type plant immediately preceding and are usually placed at the end of the description, otherwise a caption makes it clear to which species they refer.

Note on Hardiness

All the plants mentioned in the text have been given a rating for their hardiness within average temperate climates. H1 indicates a plant which will grow happily in continental climates where temperatures can be expected to fall to zero fahrenheit ($-18\,°C$) most winters. H2 is used for plants which will grow happily in more maritime climates, such as those experienced in most of Britain and W. Europe, but will need protection in colder regions. H3 indicates plants which will suffer if temperatures fall much below 20°F (−7°C) and so will need protection in all but the most favoured areas of Britain and cannot be considered permanent where cold winters regularly occur.

In the high mountainous regions of most of the world the plants are covered with a blanket of snow throughout the winter season. They are, in effect, in cold storage and completely protected from the exigencies of the weather. At high altitudes, when the snows melt the sun is strong and hot and the plants react by flowering quickly, remaining dwarf and compact.

The same plants grown in a milder, maritime climate will have to withstand (often without their cover of snow) periods of cold and frost alternating with mild, rainy days which will trigger off spring re-growth long before the season is really suitable. Summer sunshine is also far less intense, and dull, damp weather will encourage leafy growth at the expense of flowers. In continental climates the seasons are more definite and many alpines are better adapted to these conditions.

There are also those rock plants which come from coastal areas, and especially from Mediterranean climates. These cannot be expected to withstand severe winters and have been rated accordingly.

Key to symbols and abbreviations

Light requirements

○	sunny position
○○	very sunny position, also tolerates dryness
○○○	extremely sunny position, thrives on drought
☀	partial shade
◐	prefers or will tolerate semi-shade
●	prefers or will tolerate full shade

Soil requirements

⊕	prefers chalky soil
⊖	prefers lime-free soil
≃	requires well drained soil
≊	requires moist soil

Suggested uses

△	rock garden
‖	particularly for crevices
⌒	cushion-forming
▭	suitable for ground-cover
⋙	spreading
⏃	border plant
⊥	for planting in isolation as specimen plants
Y	for planting in front, under and between other plants

⊔	for pools and streams
⋀⋀	marsh plant
⋙	water plant
✄	for cutting
❦	suitable for drying
⊟	suitable for container-planting
◌	attracts bees
⊌	attracts butterflies

Descriptive symbols and abbreviations

♧	with attractive foliage
♠	striking autumn coloration
⚭	fruit-bearing
‡	evergreen
F	fragrant
H1	will withstand temperatures to 0°F (−18°C) and below.
H2	Not suitable for areas with temperatures below 10°F (−12°C)
H3	Not suitable for areas with temperatures below 20°F (−7°C)
×	hybrid (between types or families)
o	country of origin
A	Associates
syn.	former name
ssp.	sub-species
var.	variety
' '	garden variety, cultivar (indicated by inverted commas)

Aceana · New Zealand Burr · Rose Family (Rosaceae)

○ to ○○ ◐ □ ⋙ ♂ ⬟ H₂

Brown or bluish-green flat carpeter, bearing spiny burr-like fruits during the summer months. In many situations, such as large dry slopes or flat beds in a natural garden, their one fault, that they spread rampantly, can be used to advantage. O: New Zealand, southern South America, Falkland Is. and Australia. A: as ground-cover for bulbs, small *Festuca* type grasses.

– *buchananii*
Brownish silver-grey foliage, creeping underground shoots, green or yellow burrs, 5 cm (2 in). O: New Zealand.

– *microphylla*
Brown-green foliage with both under-and overground shoots, glistening red burrs, 5 cm (2 in). O: New Zealand.

– – 'Copper Carpet' ('Kupferteppich')
A much slower spreading cultivar than the type and more suitable for smaller areas, beautiful copper-coloured foliage, 5 cm (2 in).

Acantholimon · Prickly Thrift · Sea Lavender Family (Plumbaginaceae)

○○○ ⊕ △ ‖ 🝙 H₂

– *glumaceum*
Type of single ·prickly thrift which looks attractive anywhere. Requires warm, porous, dry soil. Mature plants form mounds of spiny leaves like grey-green hedgehogs, deep pink flowers, 15 cm (6 in). O: Turkey and Russia. A: silver-leaved milfoil, quick-growing. *Sempervivum* hybrids, *Chrysanthemum haradjanii*.

– *venustum* (syn. A. olivieri)
Much slower growing and difficult to propagate. Thick, spiny, blue-green foliage, beautiful light to dark pink flowers, 15 cm (6 in). O: Cilician Taurus. A: as for previous species.

Acanthus · Bear's Breech · Acanthus Family (Acanthaceae)

○○ ⊕ ⊥ ⋊ ♂ H₁.

Dwarf species suitable for rock gardens, ornamental plants whose leaves and blossoms were a popular motif in Greek decorative architecture. O: southern Europe, Asia Minor.

– *balcanicus* (syn. A. longifolius)
Largest of the species suitable for rock gardens, bronze-green-pink flowers, 100 cm (3 ft), July/August. O: Dalmatia. A: blue-stemmed grasses, also for borders.

– *dioscoridis* var. *perringii* · Dwarf Acanthus H₂
Likes warm, chalky, loamy soil, leaves thick and deeply toothed-edged, pinkish-red flowers, 30 to 50 cm (12 to 18 in). O: eastern Asia Minor, sunny positions from 1500 to 2000 m (4500 to 6000 ft) in Cappadocian foothills of Taurus. A: hardy *Opuntia, Sempervivum, Acantholimon, Yucca*.

– *spinosus* · Spiny Bear's Breech
Leaves deeply ‹lobed and, as in other varieties, spiny; greenish-pink flowers, 60 to 80 cm (2 to 2½ ft), July/August. O: Dalmatia, Greece, Aegean, south-east Italy,

Algeria, eastern Mediterranean. A: as for *A. balcanicus*.

Achillea · Yarrow or Milfoil · Daisy Family (Compositae)
An extremely hardy genus which includes small plants with silvergrey foliage and sturdy border plants. Flowers can be golden-yellow, white or red. Some are evergreen. They include spring and summer flowering plants as well as long-flowering summer and early autumn species.

1. Small silver-leaved, white-flowered species

○ *to* ○○ ⊕ ‖ 🝙 ♂ H₁.

This group grows to only around 15 cm (6 in) and prefers porous, slightly shaded soil and a sunny position. All species produce white flowers in May and June, and flower for longer a second time later in the year. Silver-grey foliage.

Achillea ageratifolia
Leaves deeply toothed, large single flowers. O: south-east Europe and Asia Minor. A: *Sedum spurium* 'Purple Carpet'.

– *clavennae* · Silvery Milfoil
The Styrians used to crown their cattle with these flowers when they drove them down from the alpine pastures. Another plant that likes chalk in the soil. Clusters of beautiful large white flowers, foliage greyish-green. O: chalk cliffs and stony meadows between 1500 and 2500 m (4500 to 7500 ft) of eastern and southern Alps and chalk formations into Illyria, Croatia, Dalmatia and Albania. A: dwarf blue-flowered veronicas 'Firebird'

– × *wilczeckii*
A hybrid of *ageratifolia* and *lingulata*, this is a superior, large-flowered form which flowers from May until July. Has extremely beautiful silver-grey foliage which is very striking in winter. Sub-alpine. O: south-east Europe. A: *Hieracium* × *rubrum*, *Hieracium villosum*.

– umbellata
Highly superior species, white downy foliage and beautiful flowers which can be white or yellow. Indented leaves. July/August, sub-alpine. O: Greece.

2. Large silver-leaved, white-flowered species

O to OOO ⊕ ≃ ✕

Achillea ptarmica
Large flowering plant which grows wild in Europe and Asia, 60 cm (2 ft), June/August. A: Carthusian pinks.
– – 'The Pearl' ⋙
Tall, double variety of white sneezewort, long-flowering, effective close to and from a distance, 60 cm (2 ft), June/July. A: low-growing delphinium. (Better suited to large scale rock garden.)
– – 'Snowball'
Double garden cultivar which, with pruning, will flower for up to five months. The most compact and least spreading form. 35 cm (14 in), June/July. O: Europe, Asia, North America. A: dwarf delphinium, *Chelone*. (Better suited to formal rock garden.)
– – 'Nana Compacta'
A low-growing, compact cultivar of silver milfoil, 35 cm (14 in), June/July. A: tall campanula, *Oenothera tetragona*.

3. Small, yellow-flowered species

O to OOO ⊖ ‖ ⋙ 🛢

Achillea tomentosa · Yellow Milfoil
Clusters of flat yellow flowers above flat grey-green leaves which grow to around 15 cm (6 in). Longer-lasting than *A. chry-*

socoma (syn. *A. aurea*). Plant in full sun as it usually is in the wild. O: sunny, dry cliff faces of south-west Europe, southern Soviet Union to western Siberia in dry meadows together with *Stipa*, *Aster linosyris*. A: blue Carpathian bellflowers.

4. Large, yellow-flowered species.

O ✕ ❦

Achillea filipendulina 'Coronation Gold'
Long-flowering golden milfoil, grows to 60 to 70 cm (2 to 2 ft 3 in) with flowers in flat golden clusters from spring to late summer. A: *Salvia × superba*, *Eryngium alpinum* and blue oat grass.
– – 'Flowers of Sulphur'
Glorious colour, extremely attractive to butterflies. Both these are excellent dried for winter floral arrangements. A: *Nepeta*, *Linum*, dwarf red-leaved barberry and as for previous species.

Acinos · Calamint · Mint Family (Labiatae)
O to OO ⊕ ‖ ▭ ⋙ 🛢 ◯ HI
– *alpinus* (syn. Calamintha alpina, Satureja alpina) · Alpine Calamint
Long-flowering, violet or less frequently pink or white flowers in July, growing from low cushioned foliage. Porous soil and full sun essential. 8 cm (3 in), May/August. O: southern Albania, north-west Yugoslavia, Spain. A: *Sempervivum* species and hybrids, *Petrorhagia (Tunica) saxifraga*.

Aconitum · Monkshood · Buttercup Family (Ranunculaceae)
O to ◑ ⊥ ✕ ◯ HI
All these tall flowers of the mountain meadow, even the slowest growing types, *A. lamarckii* and *A. napellus* 'Sparks Variety', like nourishing, humus-rich or humus-loam soil, which can easily be provided where it does not already exist. They

prefer to be left to grow undisturbed. All are very poisonous.
– × *arendsii* (Syn. *A. carmichaelii* × *A. carmichaelii* var. *wilsonii*)
This hybrid has beautiful deep violet flowers, opening late in September/October. Up to 150 cm (4½ ft)
– *carmichaelii* var. *wilsonii*
A beautiful autumn monkshood with erect amethyst-blue flowers and leathery foliage. Up to 150 cm (4½ ft), August/October. O: central China. A: effective with dwarf pines.
– *lamarckii* (syn. *A. pyrenaicum*)
The tall, pale yellow Pyrenean monkshood is perfectly formed and is at its best in a picturesque rock garden. Likes slightly shady, not too dry position, to 150 cm (4½ ft), July/August. O: sub-alpine southern Europe. A: Martagon lilies, tall campanulas.
– *napellus* · Common Monkshood
The familiar blue monkshood of the Alps and the village garden, which grows from 1–1.5 m (3–4½ ft), likes rich soil and thrives on well manured ground, for even in the Alps it is found in cow pastures. July/August. O: up to alpine level (3 000 m, 9 000 ft) in Alps and Carpathians. A: Beautiful with *Coreopsis verticillata*, *Echinops humilis*, *Monarda*, *Salvia nutans*, dwarf pines. Often found wild with *Veratrum nigrum* and later with yellow columbines and *Deschampsia cespitosa*.

– – 'Bicolor'
Charming cultivar of blue-white monkshood, July/August. A: as above, flowering lamiums, *Cimicifuga racemosa*.
– – 'Sparks Variety'
The modest, dark blue garden

monkshood, July/August. A: *Cimicifuga dahurica.*

Acorus, see Water Plants p. 69

Actaea · Baneberry or Herb Christopher · Buttercup Family (Ranunculaceae)
◐ to ● ≃ ⅄ ⅋ H1
– *pachypoda* (syn. A. alba) · White Baneberry
With its white, red-stalked berries this is one of the finest of the herb Christophers; this woodland plant spreads by seed and prefers fairly moist soil. 60–90 cm (2–3 ft). Berries last several months. O: United States. A: *Cimicifuga,* smaller *Astilbe,* ferns, shade grasses.
– *rubra*
Another plant native to North America. The preceding remarks also apply to this Herb Christopher with its dark red berries.

Adenophora · Bellflower Family (Campanulaceae)
○○ △ ⫾ H1
(Variation on the bellflower!)
– *coronipifolia* (syn. A. himalayana)
Lilac-blue dwarf *Adenophora,* just under 45 cm (18 in), July/August. O: Himalayas.
– *liliifolia*
Pale lilac-blue. Drooping pale blue bells on panicles 1 m (3 ft) tall; hardly spreads at all. July/August. O: east and south-east central Europe to Siberia. Grows in moist woodland soil, thickets and damp meadows together with *Viburnum opulus, Crataegus oxyacantha, Corylus, Brachypodium sylvaticum.*

Adiantum, see Ferns p. 108

Adonis · Pheasant's Eye · Buttercup Family (Ranunculaceae)
Flowers in early and mid spring, pale or golden yellow. *Adonis* are one of the best spring flowers, but are still fairly uncommon in gardens. Young plants in containers are best to ensure good growth. Transplanting is not recommended. Mature plants look

sensational planted with mature ragged robin, a combination which is often found in the wild. Plants ten to fifteen years old will provide at least a square foot of blossom.
– *amurensis* ◐ ≃ ⅄ ⅋ ○ H1
A wonder of the winter garden which, impervious to frost, will sometimes begin flowering in January, sometimes not until March. A conspicuous feature in early spring covered in golden flowers. An indestructible plant but does not like too dry a position. Early spring is nothing without these plants. After flowering large ferny leaves develop, to disappear once more in June. O: Amur area, Sakhalin, Korea, parts of Japan. A: snowdrops, *Hepatica angulosa.*

– – 'Pleniflora'
Petals resemble canary feathers. Flowers last longer than the species, almost until *A. vernalis* comes into flower.
– *vernalis* · Yellow Adonis ○○ to ○○○ ⊕ △ ○ H1
The European spring adonis whose fabulous yellow star-shaped flowers open in late March or later. The wild species is

finer than many cultivated forms. Grows wild in dry and semi-dry meadows in light oak and pine forests and in a variety of situations. Seeds are difficult to germinate which makes it less easily available than it deserves. The flowers open and close with changes in light conditions. A mature plant will close its flowers every time storm clouds gather on the horizon and spread them wide to welcome the returning sun. O: widespread in south-east and central Europe, but found as far as central Asia. A: *Pulsatilla vulgaris,* crown imperial, *Iris reticulata* hybrids.

Aethionema · Grecian Candytuft · Mustard Family (Cruciferae)
○○○ ⊕ △ ‖ ○ ⚏ H1
(This genus includes many small and insignificant species, which are not relevant here.)
– *grandiflorum (pulchellum)*
Pale salmon-pink, May/June, an unforgettable jewel in a porous, light soil in sunny position. Pale grey-blue foliage. Clusters of pink flowers. Can be used to follow the fading *Iberis.* 15 to 20 cm (6 to 8 in) tall. O: Caucasus, Turkey to Iran. A: Carthusian pinks, *Sempervivum* hybrids, dwarf bearded irises.
– 'Warley Rose'
A superior cultivar with deeper pink flowers.

Ajuga · Bugle · Mint Family (Labiatae)
○ to ◐ ≃ ▱ ⋙ ⅋ ♢ H1
– *reptans* · Common Bugle

Adonis vernalis

Ajuga reptans

The bugle is a good-natured plant which will grow long and well. Its rampant spread may have to be checked from time to time, but this is not difficult. Lilac-blue flowers, leaves normally green. May sometimes have a beautiful metallic shine particularly in the 'Atropurpurea' form. April/May. O: throughout Europe, as far north as southern Sweden, across the Baltic as far as the north-west Soviet Union and the Near East. From lowlands up to 1700 m (5000 ft). Grows in thickets and poor grassland, light deciduous and coniferous woods. No particular soil requirements, but not too sunny or dry.

Three of the best cultivars of *Ajuga reptans* are:

– – 'Atropurpurea'
The purple flowered spikes rise up to 20cm (8in) above brownish foliage. Foliage retains its colour throughout the winter providing beautiful splashes of colour, even in rather dry soil. A: *Alsine*, *Arabis* 'Variegata', and yellow flax.

– – 'Multicolor'
Beautiful red-yellow-brown variegated leaves whose colours change over succeeding months. Blue flowers. A: *Sedum ewersii*, blue fescue grass, *Anthemis marschalliana* (syn. biebersteiniana)

– – 'Variegata'
Charming white-yellow variegated leaves, flowers pale blue to lilac. One of the best variegated small herbaceous plants. Goes well with the true species. A:

bright-coloured *Sedum kamschaticum* and forms of blue fescue grass.

Alchemilla · Lady's Mantle · Rose Family (Rosaceae)
– *conjuncta* · Alpine Lady's Mantle
○ to ☀ □ ♂ H1
Tops of leaves shiny, backs silver-white. Modest plants that like damp and shade. Often grown as *A. alpina* but far superior to that species. 10 cm (4 in), June/August. O: Carpathians, Caucasus, north as far as Greenland, Iceland and Scandinavia. Found in meadows, light woods and on cliffs. A: ferns and shade grasses.

Alisma, see Water plants p. 69

Alyssum · Mustard Family (Cruciferae)
○○ to ○○○ ⊕ △ ‖ □ ✂ ⬡ H1
Alyssum thrive on drought; they can grow hanging from steep rock cliffs for several years where they reach enormous size. All have grey foliage and like a dry position. Usually short-lived in rich soil.

– *argenteum* · Italian Alyssum
Large, flat clusters of egg yolk-yellow flowers. One of the fastest growing and most attractive species. 15–45 cm (6–18 in) May/June. O: eastern Europe, Orient. A: spring-flowering speedwell, *Santolina*, *Scutellaria baicalensis*.

– *montanum* · Mountain Alyssum
The earliest of the species flowering in late March/early April and into June. For early spring

beds and effective if allowed to hang on a dry wall. Round yellow clusters of flowers. O: foothills to sub-alpine, central Europe, Asia Minor, eastern Mediterranean. Dry, sunny situations. A: *Draba aizoides*, *Daphne cneorum*, *Adonis vernalis*, *Pulsatilla vulgaris*.
– *prostratum*

Dwarf mat-forming, shining pale yellow, 15 cm (6 in), also has prostrate, grey-leaved stems.
– *saxatile* 'Citrinum' · Gold Dust
The best of the species with delightful ivory-yellow flowers, 15 to 30 cm (6 to 12 in), April/May. O of type: central Europe, French Jura, Danube region, northern Balkans to Crete, eastern Mediterranean. Dry, sunny, rocky terrain. Grows wild with *Aster alpinus*, *Dianthus gratianopolitanus*.

– – 'Compactum'
Low-growing, compact form of Gold Dust in golden yellow, end April/May, 15 cm (6 in)
– – 'Dudley Neville'
Similar but with flowers a creamy-buff yellow.
– – 'Plenum'
Golden-yellow, double cultivar.

Anaphalis · Everlasting · Daisy Family (Compositae)
○ to ○○ ⊕ △ □ ⋙ ⫴ ✂ ♥ ♂
H1

153

– triplinervis
One of the finest species. Forms domes of silver leaves which are in themselves highly decorative in addition to a wealth of ever-lasting flowers shaped like large pearls. In partial shade these flowers will remain white well into October. This makes it one of our "long-players", for white is a very useful colour to com-bine with other shades. 30 cm (12 in), July/October. O: Himal-ayas. A: *Campanula carpatica, Fes-tuca* types, *Alyssum montanum.*
Old *A. margaritacea* is poor in comparison and more fit for the compost-heap.

Anchusa myosotidiflora, see *Brunnera* p. 162

Androsace · Rock Jasmine · Primrose Family (Primulaceae)
Highly decorative rock jasmines, small as miniature phlox, are a must for every rock garden. There can be no excuse for not including them. Some are ex-tremely delicate, others more ro-bust. A: small speedwells, whit-low-grass.
– carnea ssp. *brigantiaca*
○ to ☀ ⊕ ‖ ▯ ‡ Hı
White flowers, only 10 cm (4 in) in height, pretty but sturdy. May. O: Alps. Effective with *A. carnea* ssp. *laggeri.*

– – ssp. laggeri
○ to ☀ ⊕ ‖ ▯ ‡
Another extremely delicate, long-flowering plant. Needs quite careful treatment. April/May, 10 cm (4 in), dark red flowers. O: Pyrenees.
– cylindrica
White or pale pink flowers and grey-green softly-hairy foliage, 3–6 cm (1½–2½ in) May/June. O: Pyrenees.
– primuloides
○ to ☀, also ◐ ‖ ⋙ ‡
Begins flowering in early May. Low-growing, only 8 cm (3 in) in height, so should only be planted with dwarf plants. Rosettes of leaves with pink-white flowers. O: south-west China.

– sarmentosa
○ to ◐ ‖ ⋙ ‡
One of the larger rock jasmines with rosettes of silky-haired leaves. Pink flowers in primula-like clusters. Like *A. primuloides* forms loose cushions of leaves by overground runners, but this plant spreads less quickly. Mid May/June. O: Himalayas, western China.
– sempervivoides
☀ ⊕ ≃ ‖ ▯ ‡
A miniature plant around 5 cm (2½ in). The small, green, smooth rosettes are quite different from the other species listed. Delight-ful bright pink flowers. It prefers shady ledges. Comes from the world's highest mountains. O: Kashmir, Tibet.

Anemone · Wind Flower · Buttercup Family (Ranunculaceae)
The wonderful name anemone exemplifies the poetry of the whole genus. The rock garden is the real realm of the perennial anemone cwhereas the brightly coloured St. Brigid anemones which are not reliably perennial are better in traditional flower beds.
Anemones will flower in the rock garden from the beginning of March and, with only a short summer break, will continue un-til the autumn frosts, usually un-til late October. Real rock-garden anemones can be described as "delicate-looking, but strong and enduring". We have yet fully to appreciate their undoubted charm, especially of well-esta-blished plants and colonies.
Wind flowers are usually thought of as a white-pink mass covering damp woodlands in April, and it will come as a sur-prise to many to learn that they can form brightly coloured car-pets of blue, white, red and yel-low. The anemone kingdom is full of surprises and of a deep, dependable beauty.
I have listed species and cultivars according to flowering time:

1. Spring anemones

◐ ≃ ▢ ⋙ ⅄ ✕

Anemone apennina, see Bulbs p. 111
– blanda, see Bulbs p. 110
– nemorosa, see Bulbs p. 111
– hepatica, see *Hepatica nobilis* p. 200
– pulsatilla, see *Pulsatilla vulgaris* p. 242
– × lesseri
Hybrid of the *sylvestris* with *mul-tifida,* carmine-red flowers, rather smaller than *sylvestris* but other-wise similar in character. May. A: *Viola sororia.*
– narcissiflora · Narcissus-flowered Anemone
The apple-blossom anemone of the Alps, white with sea-green sheen, flowers in broad clusters, likes damp soil, 60 cm (2 ft), May/June. O: Found in many parts of the world, in the mountains of Asia, North America and Eu-rope, from the mountains of south-west and central Europe, through the Balkans and the Near East to Japan and Kams-chatka. Often found among small shrubs at heights of 1600 to 2000 m (4800 to 6000 ft) and above. In the wild grows with *Veratrum, Anthyllis* and *Lotus corn-iculatus.*
– sylvestris · Snowdrop Windflower
Perennial, gradually forms small

Anemone narcissiflora

stretches of greenery, 45 cm (18 in), April/June and may flower a second time. O: distributed throughout Europe from Stockholm to Piedmont, Alps, especially in the mountains of central Germany, the Caucasus, and Siberia to Kamschatka. Likes sunny cliffs and dry, light woods. Thrives best in chalky soils. A: small ferns and evergreen grasses, *Lilium martagon*.

2. Late summer and autumn anemones

◐ to ● □ Υ ✕ Hɪ

Anemone hupehensis 'Splendens'
The true rock-garden anemone of summer and early autumn, pink to dark carmine-red, 60 cm (2 ft), mid August to mid October. Also has other highly recommendable cultivars. O: China.
– – × *hybrida*
Flowers as early as late July, pinkish-red, to 60 cm (2 ft). A: ferns, woodland grasses. The cultivated white, pale pink and clear pink Japanese anemones are an essential feature of any wild garden. The foliage is, however, unsuitable for the smaller rock garden.
– – 'Honorine Jobert'
the most wild looking cultivar with single white flowers, 60 to 90 cm (2 to 3 ft).
– – 'Lady Gilmour'
larger in habit, reaching 90 cm

(3 ft) with pink, semi-double flowers.
– – 'Queen Charlotte'
a good single pink, an old but reliable sort.
– – 'Louise Uhink'
semi-double and pure white.
– – 'White Queen'
strong growing with pure white flowers, 90 to 110 cm (3 to 3½ ft).
– *vitifolia*
Tall pink and white summer and autumn anemone, which years of experience have shown to be completely hardy. 60 to 90 cm (2 to 3 ft), July/September. Decorative fruit. O: Himalayas, alpine. A: *Aster amellus*, *Anaphalis*, autumn crocus. Not to be confused with *A. hupehensis* which is lower-growing. *A. vitifolia*'s mass of white feathery seeds look good with red-berried cotoneasters.

Antennaria · Catsfoot · Daisy Family (Compositae)
○ to ○○ ⊖ △ ⋀⋙ Υ ⭘ Hɪ
– *dioica* 'Rubra'
Silver-leaved carpeting plant with pinkish-red flowers in June/July, never leaves bare patches like *A. dioica* var. *borealis* (syn. A. tomentosa), can replace lawn in dry areas, beautiful intermingled with other 'grey' plants. This small grey plant is native to three continents (Europe, Asia, North America) and is the best and longest-lasting of the many species. O: Europe, central Asia to Siberia and eastern United

States, where it inhabits lowland and mountains up to 2500 m (7500 ft). Found wild with pine trees, *Potentilla cinerea*, dry ground herbaceous plants, in duneland, between bilberries, alpine roses and whortleberries, heather and small grasses. Dislikes over-fertile soil.

Anthemis · Dog Daisy or Chamomile · Daisy Family (Compositae)
○○ to ○○○ △ □ ⎮ ⋀⋙ Hɪ
– *marschalliana* (syn. A. biebersteiniana)
It is difficult to exaggerate the beauty of the silver filigree of foliage which supports the golden daisy-like flowers of this dependable plant. Likes porous soil, 15 cm (6 in), May/June. O: Asia Minor. A: small bellflowers, carpeting speedwell and other small brightly coloured plants.

– *nobilis* 'Plena' (syn. *Chamaemelum nobile*)
Double form of sweet chamomile. Pure white flowers from June/September above fresh green cushions of feathery foliage, 15 cm (6 in), likes porous, well-drained soil. A: Cheddar pinks, dark-leaved *Sempervivum* hybrids, *Campanula portenschlagiana* 'Birch Hybrid'.
– 'Treneague' is the non flowering form excellent for small lawns without using grass.

Anthyllis · Kidney Vetch · Pea Family (Leguminosae)
○○ to ○○○ ⊕ △ ‖ ⋀⋙ ○ ⭘ Hɪ
– *montana* · Mountain Kidney Vetch
Carmine-red flower heads above carpet of hairy, grey leaves, 15 cm (6 in), June/July. O: sub-alpine to alpine mountains of southern

and south-east Europe. A: dwarf bellflowers, dwarf cinquefoil. Found in dry, stony chalkland.

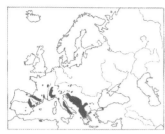

Aquilegia · Columbine · Buttercup Family (Ranunculaceae)
Unlike large garden cultivars, small columbines are ideal for the rock garden where they are often more effective than in traditional beds.
- *alpina* hybrid, 'Hensol Harebell' · Alpine Columbine
  ◐ ≃ ✕ H1
  Not at all like the low-growing 'alpina' which will not thrive in most gardens, forms thick, opulent, 30 cm (1 ft)-high bushes with dark blue flowers which make an excellent plant for corners of the rock garden. Not suitable for wild gardens. May/June.
- *caerulea* · Rocky Mountain Columbine
  ○ to ◐ ≃ ✕
  Bright and muted tones, often two-coloured, with double white centre and short spurs, 30–60 cm (1–2 ft), May/June.
- *discolor*
  Dwarf columbine from Spain, small pale blue and white flowers, delicate but sturdy, to 15 cm (6 in). A real garden treasure: May. O: Cantabria.
- *einseleana* · Einsel's Columbine ⊕
  Dwarf columbine from the southern chalk Alps, likes gravelly, cool soil, violet-blue, to 45 cm (18 in).
- *flabellata* 'Nana Alba' ☀ to ◐ △ ‖
  Large-flowered, white dwarf columbine, to 15 cm (6 in), May/June. O of type: Japan.
- *vulgaris* hybrids
  ○ to ◐ ⅄ ✕

These bright-coloured, short-spurred hybrids will cheer up any part of the rock garden for they will tolerate both sun and shade, 60 cm (2 ft), May/June.

Arabis · Rock Cress · Mustard Family (Cruciferae)
○ to ☀ ≃ △ ‖ ⋙ ✕ ♔ ⚘ H1
- × *arendsii* 'Rosabella'
  Bright pink hybrid of *A. aubrietioides* × *A. caucasica*, beautiful thick cushions of foliage, 15 cm (6 in), April/May. A: *Aubrieta* varieties, low red wild tulips, dwarf iris, white carpeting phlox, horned pansy.
- *caucasica* · Garden Arabis
  White, single-flowered rock cress for borders and to trail down corners. Now superseded by its cultivars which are hardier and more beautiful. The type plant *A. caucasica* and its 'Rosea' form can give an untidy look to the garden in winter and spring! O of type: mountains of Europe, south-east Carpathians, south-west Sierra Nevada to the northern ice-cap, Iceland, Greenland and from Himalayas through Siberia to Novaya Zemlya, Labrador and Alaska; on damp scree, sand and scree slopes, between 400 and 3300 m (1200 and 10,000 ft). Grows wild with hart's tongue fern and *Asplenium viride*.
- – 'Plena'
  Double white form which flowers a little later. More compact growth than the original wild *A. caucasica*.
- – 'Superb'
  Popular cultivar produces plenty of white flowers and thick foliage, April/May.
- – 'Variegata'
  Leaves variegated with yellow-white, not so strong-growing as other cultivars, single flowers.
- *fernandii-coburgii*
  makes small evergreen mats, a very reliable sort with white flowers. To 10 cm (4 in).
- – 'Variegata', a charming cultivar, attractive all the year.

- *procurrens*
  ◐ ▢ ⋙ ⅄ ⚘ ♔
  Thick clusters of white flowers above compact completely evergreen cushions of foliage; you can be quite lavish with this plant in the garden and give it free rein in difficult parts of the rock garden. O: Carpathians, northern Balkans; on scrubby cliffs, mountain to sub-alpine. A: Greek violets, carpeting phlox.

Arenaria · Sandwort · Pink Family (Caryophyllaceae)
○○ △ ‖ ⌒ H1
- *grandiflora* · Large-flowered Sandwort
  Sandwort with large white flowers and cushions of foliage, forms a carpet of large, semi-erect bells. Plant on flat areas with a few dwarf sedges or festucas. 12 cm (5 in), July. O: Spain, northern and central Italy, Alps.
- *montana*
  The largest flowers of all the sandworts, white. 10 cm (4 in), May/June. O: high mountains in Mediterranean countries.
- *procera* ssp. *glabra* (syn. A. graminifolia)
  White-flowered climbing sandwort. A good but rarely used substitute for pearlwort even in dry conditions! Will climb up vertical stone walls!
- *purpurascens* · Pink Sandwort
  Pink sandwort from the Pyrenees, strong-growing, 12 to 15 cm (5 to 6 in). Tolerates partial shade.
- *tetraquetra*
  Likes damp, so do not plant in too dry situation. White flowers, 5 cm (2 in); beautiful with *Campanula cochleariifolia*, *Linaria alpina* and small-leaved *Sempervivum* species. Forms tight flat cushions

and delightful flowers. June. O: mountains of southern France, Pyrenees, Alps.

Armeria · Thrift · Sea Lavender Family (Plumbaginaceae)
○ to ○○ △ ‖ ⌒ ⚕ H1
– *juniperifolia* (syn. A. cespitosa)
A dwarf thrift with small rounded cushions of short, rigid leaves. For gravel, clefts and cracks, requires protection from wet winter weather, silvery-pink. End April/May, flowers three weeks before *A. formosa*, two weeks before *A. maritima*. Plant with *Linaria alpina*. O: alpine levels of mountains of central Spain, Sierra de Guadarrama, 2500 m (7500 ft).
– – 'Alba'
Quite low-growing, white flowers.
– – 'Beechwood'
Low-growing, with pale pink flowers.
– – 'Rubra'
Low-growing, dark pink flowers.
– *Maritima* 'Alba'
White variety of sea pink. 15 cm (6 in), one of the main long-flowering plants. May/June. Sprinkle amongst mat of following sorts. O: type plant boreal mountains, also common on west coast of Europe, often covering large areas and forming nesting places for sandpipers.
– – 'Dusseldorf Pride'
Best colour to date, shining carmine-red, compact and hardy cushions of foliage, only 15 cm (6 in), May/June and flowers a second time.
– – 'Rosea Compacta'
Carmine-pink sea pink which flowers frequently, on compact cushions. A: preceding cultivar, *Paradisea*, *Ornithogalum*, horned pansy, low-growing speedwell and *Minuartia*.

Arnebia · Prophet Flower · Borage Family (Boraginaceae)
○ to ☀ ≃ △ H1
– *pulchra* (syn. A. echioides, Echioides longiflora)
This yellow flower gets its name from the large black spots supposed to represent the prophet's fingerprints. These spots fade as the flower ages. April/May. O: Orient, mountains to sub-alpine, Caucasus, Armenia, Persia. Although a good seeder, not always easy to grow in the garden. A: dwarf iris, *Mertensia virginica*, *Veronica armenia*.

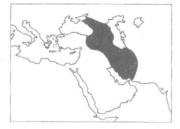

Arrhenatherum, see Grasses p. 106

Artemisia · Wormwood · Daisy Family (Compositae)
○○○ ⊕ △ ‖ ⚲ H1
Both large and small plants providing silver-grey foliage for the garden. Three classic wormwoods with decorative foliage are:
– *nitida* · Narrow-leaved Wormwood
Shining silvery cushions for south-west facing aspects, requires dryness, should be planted out of winter morning sun. Combine with deep blue, brown or clear red plants. Only up to 20 cm (8 in). O: alpine regions of southern Alps, Dolomites, Austrian Alps, Taurus, 1300 to 2000 m (4000 to 6000 ft) on cliffs and stony outcrops.
– *schmidtiana* 'Nana'
A Japanese dwarf wormwood with thick, shining silver cushions, also likes sunny, dry situation, more hardy than *A. nitida*. Plant of incomparable beauty. 15 to 20 cm (6 to 8 in). O: high mountains of Japan. A: as above.
– *vallesiaca*
Insignificant flowers as in all wormwoods, but delightful foliage, 20 to 40 cm (8 to 16 in). O: southern Switzerland. A: *Oenothera missouriensis* and blue oat grass.

Arum, see Bulbs p. 111

Asarum · Birthwort Family (Aristolochiaceae)
◐ to ● ≃ ▢ ⋙ ⅄ ♁ ⚕ H1
– *europaeum* · Asarabacca
Small evergreen with thick, dark green, leathery, kidney-shaped leaves which hide brown, lobed, bell-shaped flowers. The flowers trap flies which drown in the nectar. This plant is an extremely tough, neat and attractive evergreen carpeter which will tolerate any conditions, shade or sun, damp or dryness. Becomes extremely well established despite lack of growth in first year. O: southern and central Europe, Asia Minor, Siberia; deciduous woods, clearings of fir woods, alder woods, streambanks, shady ravines, from sea-level to 1500 m (4500 ft). A: ferns and shade grasses, snowflakes, hepaticas, *Lilium martagon*.

Asarum europaeum

– *hartwegii*
Similar but with leaves white mottled. An attractive evergreen. O: California, Oregon. A: as above.

Asarum europaeum

Asperula · Woodruff · Bedstraw Family (Rubiaceae)
○○○ ⊕ △ ‖ ⬚ H2
– *nitida*
This delicate pink-flowered carpeter comes from Olympus and Greece and grows well in gardens. Needs protection from winter damp and requires dry, porous soil. Flowers May/June with many other dwarf perennials with which it goes well.

Asperula odorata, see *Galium odoratum* p. 175

Asplenium, see Ferns p. 108

Asphodeline ·Asphodel · Lily Family (Liliaceae)
○ ⊕ ⊥ H2
– *lutea* · King's Spear or Yellow Asphodel
This plant forms short runners and has a tuft of triangular, blue-green leaves. The yellow, spike-like clusters of flowers appear around the end April/May. 90 cm (3 ft). Ideal for meadow garden! O: Mediterranean region. A: *Helictotrichon sempervirens, Stipa barbata, Stipa pennata, Cerastium tomentosum* var. *columnae, Sedum spurium* 'Purple Carpet'.

Herbaceous asters for the rock garden

Those suitable for the rock garden can be divided between spring, early summer, summer, autumn and late autumn asters.

Colours: white, pink, blue. Height: 30 to 60 cm (1 to 2 ft). I have also included a few taller asters for larger rock gardens or rock-garden borders, while excluding many types whose flowers are destroyed by frost or which become untidy in extremely dry or wet conditions, which lose their beauty as they mature or are insufficiently hardy. I have also excluded types which, while of moderate size, are not really suitable for the rock garden. I offer my services as guide through the area of rock-garden asters for I have learnt about then and the best new cultivars over many decades of gardening experience.

1. Flowering time: May to June

Aster alpinus · Alpine Aster
○ ⊕ ‖ ✂ ⬚ ○ H1
Delightful, cushion-forming dwarf aster, around 15 cm (6 in) with rosettes of basal, spoon-shaped, hairy leaves. The real rock-garden aster! Protect from accumulating moisture with gravel if necessary. Replanting essential every few years. O: Extremely widespread across the world, also at wide height range from sea-level to 3000 m (9000 ft), in sunny meadows, sometimes even on moorland, cliffs of alpine and medium-height mountains, poor alpine

Aster alpinus

pastures and overgrown hay fields, from the Pyrenees through the Alps, Jura, Harz, Carpathian and Balkan Mountains into the Caucasus and Armenia, through Siberia to northern Asia, in arctic United States and northern Rocky Mountains. A splendid plant that is well worth growing. A: all three colour varieties with *Aubrieta* hybrids, dwarf *Achillea* and *Papaver* types, *Festuca vallesiaca*.
– – 'Albus'
An extremely beautiful white "giant", far superior to the white variety found in the wild. 15 to 30 cm (6 to 12 in)
– – 'Beechwood'
Blue-rayed, yellow centred flowers. 15 cm (6 in)
– – 'Goliath'
Large blue flowers on plants to 20 to 25 cm (8 to 10 in).

2. Flowering time: June

– *andersonii*
○ ≃ □ H1
Mat-forming dwarf species, only 8 cm (3 in) tall. Dainty lilac flowers. Flowers at end of spring in June. O: western United States. A: Dwarf bearded irises.
– *tongolensis* (syn. A. subcaeruleus)
○ ≃ ‖ ✂ ○ H1
Beautiful large flowers of shining violet with orange centre. This and the following sort can grow to 30–45 cm (12–18 in).
– 'Wendy'

Excellent colour contrast of lilac petals with glowing golden-orange centre. O of type: western Himalayas, alpine, A: white *Phlox* hybrid 'Hilda'.

3. Flowering time: June to July

– × *alpellus*
O ≃ ‖ ✕ ◯ H1
Excellent lilac-blue summer asters for the rock garden which will require additional moisture in dry weather. About 20 cm (8 in) high. A cross between *A. alpinus* and *A. amellus* which flowers before the mountain asters.
– × – 'Triumph'
Violet-blue hybrid, up to 20 cm (8 in). Uses as for alpine aster.

4. Flowering in late July.

× *Solidaster luteus*
An interesting cross of species between *Aster ptarmicoides* and *Solidago*, suitable for use between dwarf shrubs in rock-garden borders. 60 to 75 cm (24 to 30 in), but untidy until well-established, so use carefully. Not to be planted with weak-growing plants. Light support with twine advisable. Charming contrast between the golden-yellow full blooms and blossoms fading to cream.

4. Flowering time: July to August.

Aster thomsonii 'Nanus'
Only 45 cm (18 in) at most with lavender blue flowers which last through late summer.

5 and 6. Flowering time: August to October

– *amellus* · Michelmas Daisy
O to OO ⊕ ✕ ◯ ♡ H1
These autumn daisies of the European mountains and moorland are available in high-quality cultivars which are indispensable to the late summer and autumn rock garden and any type of wild garden.

The first list comprises small, compact forms and the second larger, but still compact ones for larger rock or wild gardens. The beauty and richness of mature examples of the best cultivars have surprisingly gone unrecognised up to now. At the beginning of the century there were no cultivated varieties of these excellent autumn plants.

These daisies with their scent of vanilla grow in the wild in many mountain and moorland areas of southern, south-eastern and central Europe and stretch as far as western Siberia. To the south they extend to south-eastern Europe, central Italy and southern France. They are found from sea-level to 1500 m (4500 ft). There are species which grow to 30 to 60 cm (1 to 2 ft) in height. Even in the most adverse conditions these plants can survive for up to ten years. Restriction of growth by lack of water is sometimes welcome. For autumn planting it is essential to use container plants. Spring planting can be as late as June. A: They go well in the garden with autumn colchicums and crocuses, *Anemone hupehensis*, *Anemone japonica* hybrids, and mat-forming asters (*A. dumosus* hybrids).
– × *frikartii* 'Mönch'
Beautiful lavender flowers on tidy plants to 90 cm (3 ft). Best in full sun.

5. Flowering time: end August to mid September

(Small, compact forms.)
– *amellus* 'King George'
Strong, deep blue, 60 cm (2 ft) high cultivar. Will not become 'ragged' through wet, dryness or night frost.
– – 'Cassubicus Grandiflorus'
Lilac-blue, flowers as early as the end of August. A wild variety with all the charm of the best cultivars—also cultivated in Bornim since 1907. Just under 60 cm (2 ft).
– *Linosyris* ·Goldilocks
O to OO ⊕ ✕ ◯ H1
At first glance this beautiful autumn plant with its golden-yellow flowers seems to have little in common with other asters for it does not have ray florets, but flowers in close clusters. Erect growth. The stems have narrow, grass-like leaves. Likes dry, sunny situation. 60 cm (2 ft). O: from south and western France, central Italy through central Europe to the Volga and Armenia. A: violet forms of *Aster amellus*, *Helictotrichon sempervirens*, *Stipa barbata*, *Stipa capillata*.

6. Flowering time: mid and late September to October

(Compact plants growing to 30 to 45 cm (12 to 18 in).
– *amellus* 'Brilliant'
Produces strongly coloured,

Aster amellus

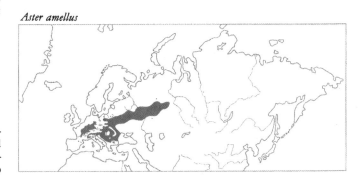

bright pink flowers on sturdy plants. To 60 cm (2 ft).

– – 'Empress'
The palest of the lavender cultivars, extremely long-flowering and clean, compact lines. These qualities are especially apparent in the second year of growth. Reaches 90 cm (3 ft).

– – 'Lady Hindlip'
Large-flowered, pink aster. Flowers less clustered than other cultivars. 75 cm (3½ ft).

– – 'Mrs Ralph Woods'
Erect clusters of silvery-pink flowers on strong stems, almost 60 cm (2 ft). The best of the pinks.

– – 'Nocturne'
Deep rosy lavender flowers, the largest-flowered of all the lavender *amellus* cultivars. Erect, but only 60 cm (2 ft) tall.

– 'Pink Zenith'
Clear pink blooms on an erect plant. Only 60 cm (2 ft).

– 'Violet Queen'
Very free flowering deep violet blooms. 45 cm (18 in).

*7. Flowering time: end September/
early October
and first half October*

Aster dumosus hybrids
○ ≈ □ ⋙ ⋮ ⴼ ✂ ○ ꕥ Hɪ
A cross between *A. novi-belgii* and the wild dwarf *A. dumosus*. These new, small, cushion-forming daisies which flower in late September and October are sensational herbaceous plants. They are unbelievably good-tempered in the garden. When first cultivated, fifty years ago, there were cultivars which ceased to flower in maturity, but this has now been overcome. Cushioning daisies are extremely versatile in the garden, but are especially effective in the autumn rock garden with autumn crocuses and colchicums, autumn anemones and *Cimicifuga* which flower in September and October.
Growth is often much too fast and sometimes needs keeping in check. This is best done by split-

ting away newly formed clumps around the plant.

– hybrid 'Dandy'
A small plant which produces masses of purple red flowers. 30 cm (12 in) tall.

– – 'Jenny'
Double, deep-purple flowers, compact, 40 cm (16 in).

– – 'Judith'
Beautiful, double, clear pink flowers, thick cushions, 40 cm (16 in).

– – 'Lady in Blue'
Double form of an amazingly beautiful blue, only 25 cm (10 in) tall.

– *ericoides*
Very neat, long lasting plants reaching 75 cm (2½ ft) at most. The flowers are carried in charming sprays.

– – 'Cinderella'
Pale blue starry flowers, 75 cm (2½ ft).

– – 'Esther'
Small pink daisies in graceful sprays. Smaller in growth reaching 60 cm (2 ft).

Astilbe · Saxifrage Family (Saxifragaceae)
◑ ⌢ ⴼ ⊔ ✂ ○ Hɪ
It is essential to stress, as far as rock gardens are concerned, how well the Japanese dwarf astilbes (*Astilbe simplicifolia* hybrids) will tolerate a dry sunny situation. The flowers of the early, medium-late and late sorts extend throughout the whole summer. The fern-like leaves are not rigid like conifer foliage, but light and swaying, combining extreme grace with great strength.
Astilbe × *arendsii* hybrids are more particular about soil and air moisture requirements. But here again there are a great number of differences. All astilbes will perform better if mulched with coarse rotted compost or peat. These beautiful astilbes make wonderful waterside plants for formal water gardens and look best in light, semi-shaded poolsides used sparingly with blue-leaved plantain lilies. They can

be planted in sunny situations if planted in a moist depression which will allow thorough watering from time to time. If planted in the sun you will usually find that they seem to bake in the summer sun, produce few flowers and lose their leaves, but in September beautiful new leaves will appear. New cultivars with blue-red and blue-pink backs to the leaves are excellent if alternated with those with red and pink flowers. For wild waterside gardens it is better to choose the more restrained, wilder-looking astilbes.

Astilbe × *Arendsii* 'Cologne'
Bright pink spikes of flowers, June/August, 50 cm (20 in).

– – – 'Deutschland'
Wonderful white cultivar, by far the best of this group, June/July, 50 cm (20 in).

– – – 'Europa'
Thick, pale-pink flowers, earliest of this hybrid group, June/July, 50 cm (20 in).

– – – 'Fanal'
Compact, garnet-red flower panicles, less elegant but incomparable in colour. Less strong growing. Dark foliage. Beginning July, 60 cm (2 ft).

– – – 'Federsee'
Dark wine-red flowers and brownish-red leaves, flowers resemble plume of feathers. Tolerates extreme dryness, June/July, 60 cm (2 ft).

– – – 'Fire'
Fiery salmon-red flower panicles above pale green foliage, end July, up to 75 cm (2½ ft).

– – – 'Irrlicht'
White flowers with very dark green foliage, June/July, 50 cm (20 in).

– – – 'Ostrich Plume'
Light, overhanging, veil-like flower panicles giving an extremely elegant effect. Reliable and ideal. Beginning July, 75 cm (2½ ft).

– *chinensis* 'Pumila'
A hardy dwarf astilbe with lilac-pink flowers. Fading flowers un-

fortunately unattractive! A creeper with flat, carpet-like growth. Tolerates sun and dryness. Later flowering in August, often lasting into Semptember, 25 cm (10 in). Will make wide, weed smothering mats in moist soil.

– *crispa* 'Perkeo'
Very low growing to 25 cm (10 in) only with short, pale pink flowers.

Astilbe simplicifolia hybrids 'Aphrodite'
Delightfully mellow colouring. Dark-leaved version of 'Atrorosea'. Brilliant red flowers whose effect is increased by the dark stems. July/August, 50 cm (20 in).

– – – 'Atrorosea'
Clear dark pink gracefully pendent flowers, August, 40 cm (16 in).

– – – 'Praecox Alba'
Pure white, erect, branching flower panicles. Just as quick-growing and versatile as the other named cultivars. July, 50 cm (20 in).

– – – 'Sprite'
Excellent and low-growing with dark green foliage with striking dark bronze sheen. Elegant, pale-pink, swaying, veil-like flowers, very late in August and extremely long-flowering. 30 cm (12 in). The best sort for the rock garden!

Astragalus · Milk Vetch · Pea Family (Leguminosae)
○○○ ⊕ ⊥ ⟡ Hı
– *alopecuroides* (syn. A. centralpinus)
⊥ ⟡
Too tall for most rock gardens but excellent for borders. This strange plant has an unfamiliar, cheering beauty. Extremely hairy with yellow flowers in July/August, 70 cm (2½ ft). O: southern and south-eastern Europe, western Asia. A: *Helictotrichon sempervirens*, *Carlina acaulis* ssp. *simplex*.
– *angustifolius*
△ ‖ ⌒ ♯ ▯
Heads of white flowers growing

from cushions of grey foliage, about 30 cm (1 ft) across. Likes scree and rocks, chalky soil, 20 cm (8 in), July/August. O: Balkan peninsular, Asia Minor.

Astrantia · Masterwort · Carrot Family (Umbelliferae)
○ to ◑ ⊕ ≃ ⅄ ✕ ○ ⟡ Hı
– *carniolica*
Beautiful pale salmon-pink, from 30 cm (12 in) tall, June/August. O: south-eastern Alps.
– *major* · Masterwort
Varied tones of pale pink, especially when in bud. 40 cm (16 in) tall, June/July. O: Mountain to sub-alpine meadows from sea-level to 2 000 m (6 000 ft). Pyrenees to Balkans and Carpathians and as far as western USSR. A: wild garden, alpine meadow garden with dwarf pines and grasses.

Athamanta · Carrot Family (Umbelliferae)
○○○ ⊕ ✕ ⟡ Hı
– *turbith* ssp. *haynaldii* (syn. A. matthioli)
One of the world's most remarkable plants which grows between rocks in almost no soil at all and seems to require no nourishment. 40 cm (16 in) tall, growing to 80 cm (2½ ft) across in maturity. I have seen this beautiful species survive in unbelievable conditions for up to sixteen years. White flower panicles growing from a filigree of green foliage. June/July. O: dry cliffs of southern Alps, Jura, from Danube Valley and Carinthia to the Adriatic, through Hungary and Balkans. A: bellflowers, speedwell, grasses.

Athyrium, see Ferns p. 108

Aubrieta · Purple Rock Cress · Mustard Family (Cruciferae)
○○ ⊕ △ ‖ ⌒ □ ▯ ○ ♯ Hı
Purple rock cresses flower from the end of April to June, pale lilac to dark velvet-red, and pale pink to fiery carmine red.
It is difficult to keep one's head above water in the ocean of modern aubrieta cultivars. One comes across too many that look no better than existing sorts, which only flower when they are young or which are very slow-growing. Wide, flat plants will only flower for a few years. As with violets, plant individually as small plants, discarding large, woody pieces. I am especially fond of these plants with their huge range of spring colours particularly when contrasted with many other more muted tones. Flowering times for the different forms do not vary much. 'Red Carpet', a beautiful carmine-red, is the earliest and longest-flowering. In exposed situations flowering begins with the glorious and incomparable 'Tauricola'. The differences between the cultivars listed here are so great that none can be omitted. The colour effects are amazing in the sinking sun with shadows producing unbelievable new tones. *Aubrieta deltoidea* was introduced into the gardens of Europe as long ago as 1700. O of type and sub-species: alpine areas to Italy, Orient, Greece, Taurus. A: dwarf iris, carpeting phlox, *Alyssum saxatile* 'Citrinum'.

Aubrieta hybrid 'Astolat'
Small with silvery-edged foliage.
– – 'Blue Emperor' with large, dark violet flowers, long-flowering and forming dense cushions.
– – 'Dr Mules'
Shining velvet-violet with bluish sheen.
– – 'Lobelia'
Best of the blues, early with many flowers. An exceptional plant due to the lasting beauty of

the regular domed shape even of mature examples in unfavourable conditions.
– – 'Red Carpet'
Longest-flowering and deepest ruby-red. Flowers up to a week earlier than the others and 10 days longer.
– – 'Tauricola'
This lilac-blue hardy aubrieta will cling to steep rocks and cracks in walls for up to ten years, continually increasing in size. Light and shade produce amazing colour gradations in the thick foliage. Only 5 cm (2 in).
– – 'Wanda'
A double-flowered, crimson cultivar.

Avena, see *Helictotrichon* (Grasses) p. 106

Azorella · Carrot Family (Umbelliferae) (syn. Bolax glebaria)
○ to ◐ ⊕ △ ⌒ ☐ ♁ ✽ H1
– *trifurcata*
This low grower provides the ideal flat mossy carpet with greenish-white flowers. Hardy and enemy of weeds. Best planted as small plants from containers. Sets off other taller flowers planted in the carpet to perfection. May/June. O: southern tip of South America (Magellan Straits).

Blechnum, see Ferns p. 108

Bletilla · Orchid Family (Orchidaceae)
○ to ◐ ⊕ ≃ H2
– *striata*
Rosy-purple flowers between bamboo-like leaves. Leaves produced very late, not completely hardy in cold areas, protection with thick layer of branches advisable against winter wet. In very cold areas pot-culture recommended. Pots buried in soil in summer can winter in a cool cellar from October, but should not be allowed to dry out. June/July. 30 cm (12 in). O: China, Japan.

Bolax, see *Azorella*

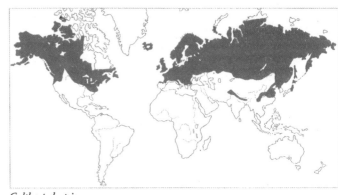

Caltha palustris

Bouteloua, see Grasses p. 106

Briza, see Grasses p. 106

Brunnera · Borage Family (Boraginaceae)
○ to ◐ ☐ Y ♁ H1
– *macrophylla* (syn. Anchusa myosotidiflora)
A unique and welcome addition to the early spring garden, with large sprays of clear blue flowers which will grace any situation. Beautiful foliage up to end October. Flowers from end March to end May. Difficult to have too many of these in the garden. Variegated forms are not so strong growing. To 45 cm (18 in). O: Caucasus. A: woodruff, *Trollius, Iris,* columbines and all early spring flowers.
– – 'Langtrees'
This form has similar flowers but the leaves are cream speckled.
– – 'Variegata'
Cream striped leaves show up the bright blue flowers.

Buglossoides purpurocaerulea (syn. Lithospermum purpurocaeruleum) · Blue Gromwell · Borage Family (Boraginaceae)
○ to ◐ ⊕ ☐ ⋙ Y H1
A delightful and reliable plant with red and later blue flowers for dry, sunny as well as difficult, very dry, shady situations in the rock or wild garden. The blue is a deep gentian colour. The sight of this plant in mountain wood-

land is one that will never be forgotten. Prefers chalk. O: From western Europe to Caucasus and northern Iran. Do not plant with less strong growing plants as it spreads rapidly. A: *Brunnera macrophylla,* strong-growing shade grasses, *Actaea* species.

Buphthalmum speciosissimum, see *Telekia speciosissima,* p. 255/256

Butomus, see Water plants p. 69

Calla, see Waterplants p. 70

Caltha · Marsh Marigold · Buttercup Family (Ranunculaceae)
○ also ◐ ≌ ☐ Y ⊔ ⋙ ✕ H1
– *palustris* · King Cup or Marsh Marigold
Wild marsh marigold, 30 cm (12 in), March/May. O: throughout Europe, meadows and watersides up to 2500 m (7500 ft). Wide areas of Asia and Americas. An excellent garden plant for its early spring colour. A: grasses, *Brunnera macrophylla, Omphalodes verna.*

162

– – var. *alba*
Only around 20 cm (8 in) tall with dark green leaves; compact and white-flowered, flowering earlier than *C. palustris*. Does not like too much moisture in winter. Usually flowers richly a second time in autumn. O: Kashmir. A: *Primula rosea*, blue *Primula denticulata*.

– – 'Flore Pleno' (syn. 'Multiplex')
The best, longest-flowering, double form of marsh marigold for gardens, superior to every' other. 30 cm (12 in).

Campanula · Bellflower or Harebell
Bellflower Family (Campanulaceae)
From some 300 known species I include sixty of the greatest beauty and durability, together with their cultivated varieties. Everyone, both young and old, looks forward to their appearance. Bellflowers occupy an important position in the realm of plant distribution and there are many areas in which they dominate everything else. In high alpine meadows they spread in wide carpets as if undisturbed by any human footfall. There are early, mid and late summer bellflowers.
There are extremely small dwarf species as well as the wood bellflowers which tower above head-height. I know of garden sites where bellflowers have flourished for decades.
Their countries of origin are mainly the alpine meadows and rocks of the European mountains, from Italy and south-eastern Europe to the Caucasus. Dwarfs from the mountains of East Asia have recently been introduced, but their lasting worth for gardens has yet to be proven. I list here the 'elite' of the garden bellflowers arranged in two lists according to size.
The smaller group begins flowering in May and with a later second flowering goes right into autumn.

The flowers of the larger species last from the end of June until late August.
I would also refer the reader to the *Codonopsis*, see p. 168 and Chinese Bellflower *(Platycodon)* p. 218 which are similar to the bellflowers. See also *Adenophora*, p. 152.

1. Smaller Bellflowers

Campanula aucheri
○ to ☀ ⊕ △ ‖ H1
The earliest of the dwarf bellflowers, shining dark violet, single, often erect flower. Hardy with a little attention, 10 cm (4 in), April/beginning May. O: Caucasus.

– *carpatica*
○ to ○○ ⊕ △ ‖ H1
Up to 30 cm (12 in), July/September, if faded flowers pruned will flower for up to fourteen weeks. The species has been improved and replaced by excellent cultivars, yet with its varying dark blue tones it embodies all the beauty of the bellflowers. A: dwarf delphiniums, *Heuchera* hybrids (second flowering!), *Dianthus gratianopolitanus*, *Linum flavum* 'Compactum'.

– – 'Blue Clips'
Seed-cultivar, 20 cm (8 in) tall, sky-blue flowers. Even growth but lacks the charm of the more popular forms.

– – 'Blue Moonlight'
Small and blue-flowered, only 15 cm (6 in) in height.

– – 'Bressingham White'
Strong growing with pure white bells, grows taller and straighter than other cultivars, 25 cm (10 in).

– – 'Chewton Joy'
Low-growing, China blue bells, charming and popular, 10 to 20 cm (4 to 8 in).

– – 'Kobalt'
Deep-violet, erect cups, long flowering and good second flowering, grey foliage, grows quickly, 10 cm (4 in).

– – 'Lavender'
Produces many silver-blue flowers. Will flower again after pruning. 20 cm (8 in).

– – 'Snowsprite'
Snow-white, combines astonishing growth-rate with rich flowers, a plant two to three years old can have up to 200 or 300 flowers at any one time, 15 cm (6 in).

– – 'White Clips'
White seed-cultivar, similar to 'Blue Clips' apart from colour, 20 cm (8 in).

– *turbinata*
Later, smaller and more compact than *C. carpatica*. The species has fine white hairs, violet, erect cups with flared tips. Seldom cultivated individually, but usually crossed with one of several *C. carpatica* varieties. Early and long-flowering, 10 to 15 cm (4 to 6 in), from June. O: Transylvania.

– – 'Alba'
White form of the above with same qualities as the species, 10 cm (4 in).

– – 'Wheatley Violet'
Wide-open, deep blue cups. Dark green leaves, less hairy than usual. 20 cm (8 in).

– *cochleariifolia* (syn. C. pusilla) ·
Fairy's Thimble
○○ ⊕ △ ‖ ⋙ H1
This enchanting, energetic dwarf will survive for decades, being extremely reliable. Can be grown successfully between the foliage of almost any other herbaceous plants. Excellent flowering amongst red thyme or white sandworts. Cannot be praised too highly. Even in the wild colour varies from white to lilac-blue. 10 cm (4 in). O: from Pyrenees, across mountains of central France, Jura, Vosges, Black Forest, Alps, Carpathians, chalk formations. On rocks, in gravel and scree, creeper, up to 3000 m (9000 ft), also in chalk moorland and rocky river banks. Grows wild with *Linaria alpina*, *Gypsophila repens*.

– – 'Alba'
White dwarf bells, most attractive with deep blue forms, 10 cm (4 in), June/July.

– – 'Miranda Bellardii'
This cultivated variety is smaller-

flowered and longer-blossoming than the species. It is one of the earliest of the garden dwarfs. Pale blue flowers. May/beginning August, 5 cm (2 in).

– – 'Miss Willmott'
Pale silvery-blue and large-flowered. Plant with *Moeringia muscosa*, 10 cm (4 in), June/July.

– – 'Oakington Blue'
Deep blue dangling bells with dark green leaves, 10 cm (4 in), June/July.

– – 'R. B. Loder'
Dark-blue double bells, 10 cm (4 in), June/July.

– *collina*
○ to ◑ ≃ △ ▢ ⋙ ✕ H1
Likes rich soil and shady to semi-shady situation, carpeter. 15 cm (6 in), June. O: Caucasus.

– *garganica*
Forms rosettes of leaves without runners, good for walls, particularly effective with reddish stone. One of the many southern plants successfully established in the north. Blue, starry flowers, 15 cm (6 in), May/June. O: Dalmatia, Italy (Monte Gargano). A: *Heliosperma alpestre*, *Geranium dalmaticum* 'Album'.

– – 'Hirsuta'
Grey-leaved with pale lilac stars, otherwise like the true species.

– – 'Hirsuta Alba'
Attractive white flowered form.

– *glomerata* 'Acaulis' · clustered bellflower
○ to ○○ △ ▢ ⋙ ‖ H1
Dwarf form of clustered bellflower with deep violet flowers, in flower from May/August, carpeter, 15 cm (6 in).

– – 'Nana Alba'
Pure white contrast to the deep

violet cultivar with single blossoms on smaller plants than the type. Hemispherical shape in full bloom, 15 cm (6 in). A: *C. glomerata* 'Acaulis'.

– *portenschlagiana*
○ to ◑ ⊕ △ ‖ ◿ ⫶ ⋙ H1
One of the best long-flowerers of the rock garden with three flowering periods from end May to early November. Soft, reddish-lilac, erect bells. Leaves smooth, broadly kidney-shaped. Not to be confused with *C. poscharskyana* and *C. garganica*. 10 cm (4 in). O: Dalmatia, Serbia. A: *Hypericum olympicum*, *Linum flavum* 'Compactum', red-leaved *Sempervivum* hybrids, *Helianthemum* hybrids, *Campanula carpatica* var. *turbinata* 'Alba'.

– – 'Birch Hybrid'
Hybrid between *C. portenschlagiana* and *C. poscharskyana*, light purple and quick-growing with dark leaves, extremely versatile, June/August and certain to flower again later, 15 cm (6 in). A: as for species.

– *poscharskyana*
○ to ◑ ⊕ △ ‖ ▢ ⋙ H1
With its great strength, wealth of flowers and ability to spread by underground runners, this plant has many uses for wilder areas where it can be contained. It combines moderation of growth with striking colour. 15 cm (6 in). O: Dalmatia (around Dubrovnik). A: as with *C. portenschlagiana* but keep an eye out for spreading.

– – 'Alba'
Pure white flowers, on long stalks, long-flowering, from June to October, 20 cm (8 in).

– – 'E. H. Frost'
White flower with blue star, quick-growing, pale-leaved form, May/August, 15 cm (6 in).

– – 'Lisduggan Var.'
The only lavender-pink cultivar to date, less quick-growing, extremely popular, June/August, 20 cm (8 in).

– – 'Stella'
Flowers and shoots more compact and, with violet-blue flowers to the end of October, more attractive than the species. Much more slow-growing than other blue cultivars, 15 cm (6 in).

– *pulla* · Solitary Harebell
☀ ≃ △ ‖ ⋙ 🗊 H1
Popular dwarf with deep violet swinging bells on separate stems. Likes moist, porous, humus soil, sheltered from full sun. Forms masses of rosettes of leaves. May/June, up to 10 cm (4 in). O: eastern Alps. A: *Saxifraga oppositifolia* var. *latina*, *Haberlea rhodopensis*.

– ✕ *pulloides* (*C. pulla* × *C. c.* var. *turbinata*) 'G. F. Wilson'
○ to ☀ ≃ △ ‖ ⋙ 🗊
This beautiful hybrid has all the hallmarks of the parent plants. The cross has produced an early-flowering, wide-belled, deep lilac dwarf, an excellent garden plant. Same growing requirements as *C. pulla*. May, 10 cm (4 in).

– *raddeana*
○ to ◑ ≃ △ ‖ ⋙ H1
From glossy, dark-green rosettes of leaves grow reddish-brown stems each supporting several small violet bells. Remains small even into maturity. End May/July, 10 to 20 cm (4 to 8 in). O: Caucasus.

– ✕ *wockei* (*C. waldsteiniana* × *C. tommasiniana*)
○ to ☀ ≃ △ ‖ 🗊
A hybrid which stands exactly half way between the parent plants. Pale violet bells, several hanging from each stalk. Good for cracks. Responds well to care—rich in flowers. 10 cm (4 in), July/August.

2. Tall and medium-height Bellflowers

○ to ◐ ⊕ ≃ ✕ ⋙

Campanula glomerata 'Purple Pixie' · clustered bellflower.
A new cultivated variety with short, compact, deep violet flower heads. 30 cm (12 in), July.

– – 'Alba'
Pure white flowers, therefore useful to combine with deep purple forms. 50 cm (18 in), July.

– – 'Superba'
Deep violet cultivated variety. Charming example of the type with whorl-like flowers. 40 cm (16 in), June/July. O of type: spread from Europe to Kamtshatka. A: *Oenothera tetragona, Potentilla nepalensis* 'Miss Willmott'.

– *lactiflora*
H1–2
This pale blue bellflower looks like a loose lilac phlox. Flowers for longer if supported. Comes in white, blue and very pale lilac-pink. Plant the three colours in close proximity. If *C. lactiflora* is to grow well, it requires rich soil and a lot of moisture. Up to 2 m (6 ft), June/August. O: Caucasus, usually by streams.

– – 'Alba'
White flowers, July/August.

– – 'Loddon Anne'
Pale lilac pink, only 90 cm (2 ft 9 in), July/August.

– – 'Pouffe'
Pale blue, almost dwarf, about 30 cm (12 in), July/August.

– – 'Prichard's Variety'
Amethyst, 60 cm (2 ft), July/August.

– – 'White Pouffe'
○—similar to its blue counterpart but with white bells.

– *latifolia* var. *macrantha* · Giant Bellflower
This deep-violet woodland bellflower is a noble variety which will tolerate arid conditions. The species itself is not so good as it tends to wilt with shade or dryness. *C. latifolia* var. *macrantha* has stronger stems which give a better shape. 80 to 120 cm (2½ to 3½ ft), June/August. O: Caucasus,

northern Iran, Siberia, thickets and woodland up to 1250 m (4500 ft). A: *Digitalis grandiflora*, goatsbeard, ferns.

– – – – 'Alba'
Attractive white flowered form.

– – – – 'Gloaming'
Unusual smoky blue bells.

– *persicifolia* · peach-leaved Bellflower
The typical bellflower, attractive glistening flowers, but untidy when flowers fading, likes to grow amongst grasses or other plants of similar height. Prune after flowering. 70 to 100 cm (2 ft 3 in to 3 ft), June/August. O: almost whole of Europe, Armenia, Siberia, light woods and wooded cliffs, on sandy-loamy, fresh soil. Grows wild particularly in mixed woodland with: *Lychnis viscaria, Anthericum ramosum, Dianthus carthusianorum*. A: wood grasses, ferns, mullein, sage, *Lysimachia, brown-flowered small heleniums*. Do not plant as whole areas but use individually or in informal groups. Additional loam required in light soil.

– – 'Grandiflora Alba'
Long-established with white flowers, 80 to 100 cm (2½ to 3 ft), June/July.

– – 'Grandiflora Caerulea'
Bright blue, large-flowered, 80 to 100 cm (2½ to 3 ft), June/July.

– – 'Moerheimii'
Old double cultivar of great charm.

– – 'Telham Beauty'
Large bright blue flowers, June/August.

– – ssp. *sessiliflora* (syn. C. grandis)
H2
Open blue or white (in Alba variety) cups rise from decorative foliage. Pruning recommended immediately after flowering. Evergreen shoots appear later. Originates in Greece therefore requires airy winter protection against long periods of exceptional frost. 80 to 120 cm (2½ to 3¼ ft), June/July. A: ferns, woodland grasses, also for borders.

– *punctata*
△ ⋙ H1

Unique among the bellflowers with creamy bells, flecked inside with purple, and lax rosette of leaves. 30 cm (12 in), June/July. O: Siberia, Japan.

Cardamine · Bittercress · Mustard Family (Cruciferae)
☀ to ◐ ⊕ ≌ H1

– *pratensis* · Cuckoo Flower or Lady's Smock
Looks best in the rock garden amongst grasses, also for wild grassy areas where it is one of the most effective plants. 30 to 60 cm (1 to 2 ft), April/May, white to lilac. O: Europe, northern Asia, Kamchatka, North America up to the Arctic Circle, in woodland meadows, from lowland up to 200 m (600 ft). A: *Caltha palustris, Geum rivale, Myosotis palustris*.

– – 'Plena'
Double, lilac-pink and white flowers. This popular rock-garden plant is often found in abundance in the wild and grows in alpine meadows like a small garden flower. Must be kept unrestricted by larger plants in the garden.

– *trifolia*
△ ▢ ⋙ H1
Charming coloration with white flowers against dark evergreen leaves. These flat-growing plants which love shade will set off nearby plants to perfection. Likes chalky soil. 20 cm (8 in), May/June. O: Alps, northern Carpathians, Apennines, northern Yugoslavia.

Carex, see Grasses p. 105/106

Carlina · Carline Thistle · Daisy Family (Compositae)

○○ to ○○○ ⊕ △ ⊥ ✕ ♥ ○ ♔ ♤ H1

– *acanthifolia* · Acanthus-leaved Carline Thistle
These sturdy, low-growing, flattish carline thistles like heat. Flowers up to 15 cm (6 in) in diameter, golden-brown. July/August. O: chalk formations of south-east Europe, rising to 1800 m (5500 ft), occasionally also in western Alps.

– *acaulis* ssp. *simplex* (syn. C. var. *caulescens*) Alpine Carline Thistle. Silvery-leaved, 15 cm (6 in), July/September, will survive for decades in a rock or wild garden. (It is worth mentioning here other cultivated thistles for the garden, *Eryngium* and *Cirsium*. Both are valued in the rock garden and for herbaceous beds where many sorts find a home). O: from south-western Europe to Italy and Balkans, mountains to sub-alpine (2500 m, 7500 ft), Alps and foothills, central Europe to central USSR. In hedgerows with *Sesleria*, *Pulsatilla vulgaris*, *Gentiana cruciata*, *Achillea*. They produce a single, thick tap root so cannot be transplanted or divided. I once counted forty peacock-butterflies around one such thistle, and they also attract bees. Over fifteen years a plant can grow to two feet in width. Attractive with dwarf conifers; excellent for cutting for dried-flower arrangements with their silver and pale blonde coloration.

– – – – 'Bronze'
The bronze-leaved and stemmed alpine carline thistle is most attractive both in the garden and for cutting. It makes a fine con-

trast to paler plants. A: *Nepeta* × *mussinii*, *Artemisia vallesiaca*, *Festuca cinerea*, *Sempervivum* hybrids, *Dianthus gratianopolitanus*.

Centaurea · Cornflower or Knapweed · Daisy Family (Compositae)
○○ ⊕ □ ⊥ ✕ ᄿ ♔ H1

– *montana* · Mountain Cornflower Blue, 45 to 60 cm (18 to 24 in), mid May/June. O: mountains to alpine (2000 m, 6000 ft), from Spain and France, through southern Germany, Alps to Carpathians and Caucasus; mountain pastures, woods and damp rocks with *Ranunculus aconitifolius*, *Astrantia*, *Cypripedium calceolus*. A: plant all the following cultivars together with columbines, cinquefoils, masterworts.

– – 'Alba'
Tall, white cornflower, which takes two years to develop fully.
– – 'Grandiflora'
Shining blue, 40 cm (16 in).
– – 'Rosea'
Pink flowers.
– – 'Sulphurea'
Yellow mountain cornflower.
– – 'Violetta'
Deep violet.

– *pulcherrima*
Extremely attractive, silver-grey leaves, pink flowers, 30 cm (12 in), June/July. (C. *dealbata* can wilt, C. *sternbergii* becomes over-rampant, C. *ruthenica* is not very interesting.)

Centaurea rhapontica, see *Leuzea rhapontica*, p. 208

Cerastium · Chickweed · Pink Family (Caryophyllaceae)
○○ to ○○○ △ ‖ ᄿ ⁞ H1

– *biebersteinii*
White flowers. Suitable only for areas where it can be allowed to spread, or walls where it can hang freely. Will survive for decades in the right conditions. Flowering time: May/early June.

– *tomentosum* var. *columnae* · Snow in Summer

The noblest of this dwarf species, compact, low-growing, snow-white flowers on silvery foliage, extremely attractive but likely to overgrow neighbouring plants. O: southern Italy. A: *Sedum spurium* 'Purple Carpet', *Geranium sanguineum*, *Campanula portenschlagiana*.

Ceratostigma · Sea Lavender Family (Plumbaginaceae)
○ to ◐ △ □ ᄿ ✕ H2

– *plumbaginoides*
Masses of deep blue flowers from beginning of September to end October. Leaves with reddish autumn tints. Not for very cold sites! O: China. A: excellent with white autumn colchicums and crocuses (*Crocus speciosus* 'Albus') and dwarf asters.

Ceterach, see Ferns p. 108

Chelone obliqua · Turtle Head · Figwort Family (Scrophulariaceae)
○ ≈ ⅄ ✕ H1
Suitable for moist rock-garden borders. The whole plant gives a rather stiff effect. Dark pink flowers similar to those of familiar snapdragon. 60 to 90 cm (2 to 3 ft), long-flowering from July/September. O: central and southern United States.

Chiastophyllum · Stonecrop Family (Crassulaceae)
☀ to ◐ ≈ △ ‖ ♤ H2

– *oppositifolium* (syn. Cotyledon oppositifolia) · Lamb's Tail
Charmingly attractive golden catkins on 5 cm (2 in), arching stems above succulent leaves. Do not plant in full sun. June. O: Caucasus. A: *Saxifraga cuneifolia*, *Saxifraga umbrosa*, *Ramonda pyrenaica*.

Chrysanthemum · Garden Chrysanthemum · Daisy Family (Compositae)

○ to ◑ △ ☐ ⋙ ✕ ○ ♨ H₁

(All *Chrysanthemum indicum*, *koreanum* and *rubellum* are too 'cultivated' for the rock garden or wild garden.)

– *arcticum* (syn. C. yezoense)
Will survive for decades in its original position. In poorer soils it will soon cease to flower unless well mulched. The white flowers are unaffected by October frosts. Arctic Chrysanthemums flower earlier in their native habitat because of the northern sun, from the end of August. O: Arctic countries of Europe, Asia, America. A: *Aster amellus* and *A. dumosus* in late varieties. Late autumn colchicums make excellent neighbours too.

– – 'Roseum'
Pale pink flowers turning to white, flowers one to two weeks earlier than the species. A real treasure of the October garden. Both tolerate semi-shade. A: blue fescue or other coloured grasses.

– *haradjanii* (syn. Tanacetum haradjanii)
○ to ○○○ ‖ ⛢ ♁ H₂
Also found under the names *C. hosmariense* and *Tanacetum haradjanii*, this chrysanthemum is semi-shrubble with silver-grey feathery leaves and white petalled daisy-like flowers. Shoots thick and rather erect. July/August. O: Asia Minor. A: *Sempervivum* species and forms, *Acantholimon* types, *Festuca punctoria*, *Asphodeline lutea*.

– *leucanthemum* · Marguerite or Dog Daisy
The most attractive of all the perennial, white marguerites which flower in May/June. Extremely hardy, suitable for any rock garden situation. Reaching 60 cm (2 ft), it flowers for up to two months. Do not plant in too dry a position.

– *nipponicum*
H₂
Remarkable for its late flowering, this plant is semi-shrubby with dark green leaves, then in October and November covered with large, single pure-white daisies. It is best in a warm site where its flowers can open before the worst of the winter weather arrives. 60 cm (2 ft). O: Japan.

Cimicifuga · Bugbane · Buttercup Family (Ranunculaceae)
The six classic types of the glorious *Cimicifuga* flower over a period of four months, and I have arranged them according to flowering times, a useful way of distinguishing between them, and important for anyone who plans to use them. They range in size from the dwarf September cimicifuga, *C. acerina* to the huge *C. cordifolia* which, with its attractive foliage, towers above head-height.
They are all so "wild-looking" that it would be impossible to omit them from any book which claims to deal with the wild garden. Their hardiness and durability makes them extremely easy to grow.
The beauty of the foliage is best exemplified in *C. cordifolia* and *C. ramosa*.

Cimicifuga arranged by flowering times

– *racemosa* · Black Snakeroot
This July cimicifuga grows to 1 m (3 ft) across and 2 m (6 ft) tall in maturity. Arched flower panicles. O: United States, Canada.

– *cordifolia*
Wide, flat bushes of heart-shaped leaves with erect candles. 1.5 m (4½ ft) tall. Beginning August. O: north-eastern United States.

– *dahurica*
A large August cimicifuga from the Amur region and northern Korea. Has up to fifty-five erect, branching flower spikes on every stem, from overhanging branches. Mid August.

– *ramosa*
Flowering in September it has incomparable foliage topped by erect candles up to 2 m (6 ft) tall. O: Japan.

– *acerina*
A dwarf September-flowering species. Grows to only 80 cm (2½ ft) and likes less sun than the others. O: Japan.

– *simplex* 'Elstead'
Noble October-flowering species, growing to 1 m (3 ft) tall. Best flowers of all, white, opening from purple buds. O: Kamchatka.
A: for all species, ferns, cultivated grasses, autumn anemones and autumn-flowering monkshood, hostas with autumn colouring, *Aster amellus*.

Cirsium · Thistle · Daisy Family (Compositae)
○ to ○○○ ⊕ △ ‖ ✕ ♥ ○ ♨ ♁ H₁

– *acaule* · Stemless Thistle
Stemless, completely hardy thistle, with purple flower growing direct from attractive basal leaves in July. O: Europe to Siberia, England, Scandinavia to Spain, Italy, western Balkans and western Asia; from sea level to 2000 m (6500 ft), in sunny rocky places or undisturbed dry grassland. Dry, calcareous soil.

Clematis · Buttercup Family (Ranunculaceae)

○ to ◑ ⊕ △ ⊥ Ⴗ ⚹ ○ ஃ H1

– *recta* 'Grandiflora'
The white bush clematis sometimes has an excellent perfume, sometimes none. It is only in maturity that the true qualities of this indestructible plant are revealed. To 1.5 m (4½ ft). Needs support if used between other herbaceous plants or support of other shrubs. June. O: central to southern Europe, northern Asia. A: *Salvia nemorosa*.
– – 'Purpurea'
Attractive reddish-brown foliage.

Codonopsis · Bellflower Family (Campanulaceae)

○ to ◑ △ Ⴗ H1

– *clematidea*
Pale porcelain blue bells with freckled inside to the throat hanging from branching stems, up to 75 to 100 cm (2½ to 3 ft). This species is perennial and is often confused with the more delicate *C. ovata*. June/July. O: Kashmir, Turkestan.

Convallaria · Lily of the Valley · Lily Family (Liliaceae)

◑ to ● △ Ⴗ ♉ F H1

– *majalis* · Lily of the Valley
Perennial with creeping rhizome with beautiful perfume, white flowers, 24 cm (9 in) high. O: temperate climates in Europe, Asia, Japan and North America. Likes light woodland. Begins to flower early to mid May. Can become invasive in heavy soils over the years, extremely hardy. Should be included in every garden.
– – 'Grandiflora'
Extremely rich, large flowers.
– – 'Rosea'
Flowers have delicate pink toning. A: *Hepatica triloba*, *Asperula*, *Lathyrus vernus*, ferns.

Coreopsis · Daisy Family (Compositae)

○ □ ⚹ H1

Leaving out semi-perennial or highly hybridized sorts, I am in-cluding only one completely hardy perennial species and one cultivar.

– *verticillata*
Above a fine network of leaves, everlasting flowers of yellow stars, completely different in tone from all other coreopsis. To 60 cm (2 ft), June/September. O: North American prairies. A: *Veronica longifolia*, *Eryngium planum*, *Carlina caulescens* 'Bronze', delphiniums, sage, bellflowers.
– – 'Grandiflora'
Improvement on the species with more flower heads and larger flowers, justifiably popular and common. A: as for type.

Cornus · Dogwood · Dogwood Family (Cornaceae)

☀ to ◑ ⊖ ⚌ ᙭ Ⴗ ♢ ஃ H1

– *canadensis*
Extremely decorative, indestructible carpeter for shade or partial shade, but rather slow spreading. White blossoms, set low upon the leaves. Cool, acid soil essential, 10–25 cm (4 to 90 in), May/June. O: Canada from Alaska to Labrador, Manchuria, Sakhalin to mountains of Japan. A: dwarf ferns, sedges, dwarf rhododendrons.

Corydalis · Fumitory · Poppy Family (Papaveraceae)

☀ to ● ≃ ‖ · Ⴗ H1

Many fumitories grow very well in crevices in dry walls. The genus includes charming plants of great beauty which need to be seen at close quarters and other coarser types for the wild garden. They are extremely reliable and long-living. The small tuber types are included in the section on bulbs.

– *bracteata*, see Bulbs p. 112

– *cava* 'Alba', see Bulbs p. 112

– *densiflora*, see Bulbs p. 112

– *solida* 'Transsylvanica', see Bulbs p. 112
– *cheilanthifolia*

Pale yellow flowers. Ferny foliage ranges from bluish-green, golden brown to pinkish-green, yet delicate rather than over-obtrusive. Free-seeding in some soils. Protect from standing moisture in winter. April/May and beyond. O: western China.
– *lutea* · Yellow Fumitory
Good climber for walls. Along with Canadian violets, one of the longest-flowering perennials. Seeds itself freely. Can easily be kept in check, but should have sturdy neighbours. End April to mid November. O: from Pyrenees, southern France, through northern and central Italy, Switzerland, Austria and the Carpathians. On shady, damp rocks and walls up to 1500 m (4500 ft). A: *Polemonium* × *richardsonii* cultivars.
I have seen twenty-year-old plants growing happily in cracks between bricks with no sign of any soil.
– *nobilis*
April to May, golden-yellow with black markings, flowers in large, thick clusters. Early spring garden. 15 to 60 cm (6 to 24 in). A: *Doronicum caucasicum*, *Mertensia virginica*, *Brunnera macrophylla*. O: Siberia.
– *ochroleuca*
Beautiful plant with cream flowers with golden tips. 15 to 30 cm (6 to 13 in), otherwise like *C. lutea*, but produces few seeds. O: southern Europe.

Cotula · Daisy Family (Compositae)

○ to ◑ ≃ △ □ ᙭ Ⴗ ≢ H2

– *squalida*
Forms flat, ferny, brownish-green, compact mats with insign-

ificant flowers. Plant not too dry in semi-shade where it has room to spread. O: New Zealand. A: *Ornithogalum montanum* or other sturdy bulbs.

Cotyledon oppositifolia, see *Chiastophyllum oppositifolium*, p. 166

Crucianella stylosa, see *Phuopsis stylosa*, p. 217

Cypripedium · Slipper Orchid · Orchid Family (Orchidaceae)
– *calceolus* · Lady's Slipper Orchid
☀ to ◑ ⊕ ≃ Hɪ
Likes chalky, humus-rich soil in partial shade. One of the most exotic of our native plants, now threatened with extinction. Each flower has a large, yellow lip and smaller brownish petals behind. Where possible leave undisturbed after planting. 15 to 25 cm (6 to 10 in) in height. O: central, south-eastern and northern Europe, western Siberia, widespread in southern Europe in coniferous and deciduous forest; on scrubby cliff-faces, from sea-level to 1 600 m (4 800 ft), particularly in mountain beech forest. Wild with: *Lilium martagon*, *Thalictrum aquilegifolium*, *Aquilegia vulgaris*.
– *reginae* (syn. C. spectabile)
☀ to ◑ ⊖ ⬤
Suitable only for quite moist, acid soils and partial shade. Do not plant too close to other plants, and leave undisturbed! The flowers are pink and white. Needs care to grow successfully. 15 to 25 cm (6 to 10 in) and beyond, June/July. O: United States. A: slow-growing grasses and delicate ferns. Will add magic to the garden year after year.

Cystopteris, see Ferns p. 108

Delphinium · Buttercup Family (Ranunculaceae)
○ ⊕ ✕ ◯ Hɪ
The father of the garden delphiniums, *D. elatum*, is native to areas stretching from the Pyrenees, through the Alps to the Carpathians and into central Asia—mountain meadows, high pastures, streambanks at heights from 1 300 to 2 000 m (2 000 to 6 000 ft). A: woodland hairgrasses, large milfoils, orange lilies, recommended wild roses, white astilbes, yellow loosestrife. With the blue delphinium, the king of the mountain meadow, it is best restricted to the edge of the rock garden, while low-growing, compact, less-cultivated types are used for the rock garden proper. There are always possible uses and suitable sites, sometimes bordering trees, as with the taller sorts one finds wild in the Alps. I have, however, included only small rock-garden delphiniums which are extremely effective with dwarf astilbes and low-growing, early *Anemone japonica* hybrids, both for the rock garden or wild garden. No perennial plant grows higher than the 'Glacier Delphinium' discovered in 1905 in Kanchenjunga at a height of 6 300 m (19,000 ft). Delphiniums which flower twice in the right situation, in summer and late summer, can be combined with completely new partners in autumn.

Delphinium grandiflorum (syn. D. grandiflorum var. chinense) · Larkspurs △
A dwarf delphinium in gentian-blue, pale blue and white. Needs a good, sunny situation which should not be allowed to dry out. Pruning advisable immediately after flowering. This is often neglected with these dwarf plants in a mistaken effort to prolong their lifespan. With time some extra feeding will be worthwhile, giving excellent results for little effort. 30 to 60 cm (1 to 2 ft), June/July and September/October. O: China. A: yellow rockrose types, low green grasses.

Delphinium hybrids (Belladonna group)
All the following cultivars are low-growing and have slightly loose, richly branching flower panicles. Their ability to flower again after pruning is worth noting. Begin flowering in June/July.
– – 'Lamartine'
Loose, violet-blue flowers. To 120 cm (4 ft).
– – 'Piccolo'
Compact growth, bright blue flowers. This plant has remarkable rigidity. 100 cm (3 ft).
– – 'Pink Sensation'
Unusual rose-pink flowers. Up to 90 cm (3 ft).

Delphinium hybrids (Elatum group)
Small and medium cultivars of this group are suitable both for rock-garden borders and wild gardens. Must be pruned at the right time if they are to flower twice. Need no support in sunny weather, but should be supported with twine to protect against storm damage. If in shade require support of pole in rainy climate.
– – 'Blue fountains'
Bright blue with white eye, flowers around end June, only 90 cm (3 ft).
– – 'Blue Heaven'
Old, sturdy form, clear blue with white eye, flowers from end June, goes well with red tones. 75 to 90 cm (2½ to 3 ft).

Dentaria · Toothwort · Mustard Family (Cruciferae)
☀ to ◑ ⊕ ⬤ Hɪ
– *enneaphylla* (syn. Cardamine enneaphylla)
From late April through May this toothwort produces pale yellow flowers. The plant is 20 to 30 cm tall (8 to 12 in) and has dark green, basically trifoliate leaves.
– *heptaphylla* (syn. D. pinnata, Cardamine heptaphylla)
The lilac umbels of flowers open in April. 30 to 60 cm (1 to 2 ft)
– *pentaphyllos* (syn. D. digitata, Cardamine pentaphyllos)
This spring (April) toothwort grows to 40 cm (16 in) and has

deep lilac umbels of flowers. This hardy plant is surprisingly little grown but is becoming more readily available. Disappears in summer. O: Pyrenees, south-western Alps and foothills to Croatia; in fresh, shady places and woodrows from 400 to 1700 m (1200 to 5000 ft). A: small grasses and ferns.

Dianthus · Pink · Pink Family (Caryophyllaceae)
○ to ○○ also ☀ △ ‖ □ ⁞ ✕ ⚘ F H1–2
This list includes only wild pinks, the larger carnation types being omitted as less suitable for the rock garden. Wild pinks are gradually beginning to make their way into gardens as their beauty and perfume are recognised by more and more gardeners.
I have chosen the best of the types that flower from May to the end of July, together with the most beautiful and sturdy cultivars. Tiny dwarf pinks begin to appear as early as spring, making small splashes of beauty. A: small grasses, small bellflowers, milfoil, speedwell.

1. Flowering time:
early May into June

Dianthus microlepis
Dwarf of only 6 cm (2½ in), forms compact dark-green foliage. Like all true rock pinks forms long, little-branched roots, so plant only young specimens. Do not overfeed or it will not survive long. All shades of pink, also white. O: mountains of Bulgaria and Yugoslavian region of Macedonia.

2. Flowering time:
end May and throughout June

Dianthus gratianopolitanus (syn. D. caesius) · Cheddar Pink
Pink and rarely white, 15 cm (6 in). O: western and central Europe. Likes warmth. Rock clefts and rocky meadows. Scented.

– – 'Flore Pleno'
A very dwarf form which bears double, pink flowers, which are very long lasting. Scented.
– *plumarius* · Common Pink
Single flowered as the bigger doubles are too artificial for our purpose. 20 cm (8 in), perfumed. O: western and south-eastern European Alps.
– – 'Apollo', salmon-pink.
– – 'Cyclop' pinkish-red.
– – 'Jupiter', red with darker eye.
– – 'Scoticus', large, pink flowers.

3. Flowering time:
mid or late June

Dianthus cruentus
Up to 50 cm (1 ft 6 in) tall in flower. Hardy plant with gleaming velvet-red flowers and compact, dark green leaves. O: Balkans.

– *deltoides* · Maiden Pink
Their bright red colour comes as quite a shock when we come across them in the wild. Deep pink, 10 cm (4 in). O: dry grass-land and woodedges of Europe and temperate Asia. From sea-level to 1500 m (4500 ft). Grows wild with heather and small grasses. Plant in garden with speedwell and bellflowers.
– – 'Albus', white flowered.
– – 'Brillant'
Glowing red, much better and hardier than 'Splendens', bronze-green leaves. A: small, silver-grey foliage plants.
– – 'Flashing Light'
Shining salmon scarlet, bright green foliage, 10 cm (4 in).

4. Flowering time:
June to July

Dianthus pavonius (syn. D. neglectus) · Three-veined Pink
☀ ⛉
8 to 10 cm tall (3 to 4 in). Best planted in pots, then knock the bottom out and stand in gravel. Keep moist while becomes established but will tolerate dryness later. With careful attention mature plants, with their gleaming, salmon-pink flowers, can grow to the size of a soup-plate. Dislikes chalk. O: throughout the alps from east to west, subalpine to alpine.
– *pinifolius*
○○ ⊕ ‖
White pink from Macedonia, popular species, 12 cm (5 in).
– *spiculifolius*
⊕ ‖
Small, ragged, pink and white flowers and thick, spiky foliage. Likes chalk. O: eastern Carpathians (especially Transylvania).
– *strictus* var. *integer*
Small white flower with unbroken edge, leaves green and grass-like. Good 15 cm (6 in). When in flower, 8 cm (4 in). O: Balkan mountains.
– *superbus* · Superb Pink
Finely-frayed, deep pink flowers. Grows in moist, acid meadows, but will tolerate fairly dry garden position. Good for marshy stream and pool sides. To 60 cm (2 ft). O: Europe to Japan. Many small cultivated pinks are

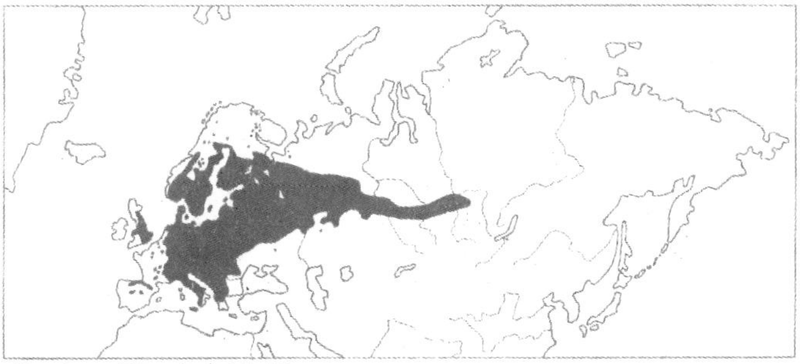

Caption: *Dianthus deltoides*

suitable for rock garden culture, flowering freely on grey foliage.

'Fanal'

Single flowers of a deep, intense red. 15 cm (6 in).

'La Bourbille'

An old favourite with silvery-blue leaves and bright pink flowers. 'Alba' is white. Only 8 cm (3 in).

'Spark'

A green-leaved dianthus with rich red flowers. 15 cm (6 in).

5. *Flowering time: July to August*

Dianthus alpinus · Alpine Pink

✹ ⊍

Carmine-pink with darker shading, leaves flat and dark green. Likes barely moist soil with a little gravel and a few rocks. Requires shady spot and additional loam. O: eastern Alps, alpine to 2200 m (6600 ft).

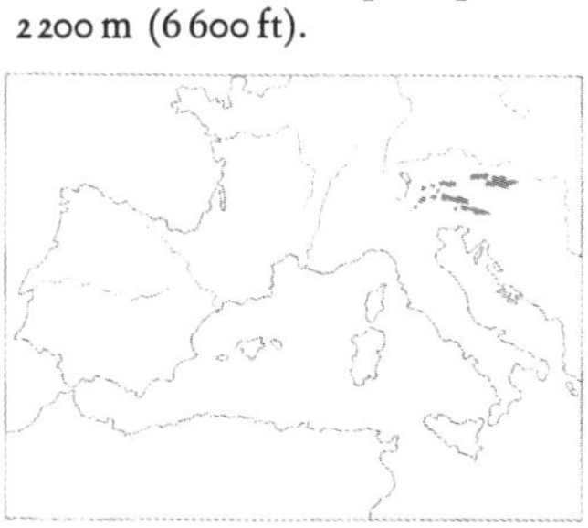

– *carthusianorum* · Carthusian Pink

○○ ⊕

Astonishingly long-flowering throughout June/August. In maturity the flat foliage becomes almost bony. These plants like to roast in full sun on poor sandy soil, and are found on the edges of coniferous woods or on dry scree, but like chalk. Deep carmine-red, 25 cm (10 in) tall. O: distributed from western to south-eastern Europe.

– *knappii*

○ ≃

40 cm (16 in) tall, pale ivory yellow. Likes light soil. Similar to *D. cruentus*. O: Bosnia, Herzegovina.

– *petraeus* ssp. *noëanus* (syn. D. noëanus)

○○ ⊕ ‖

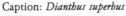

Latest of all, small white flowers, 20 cm (8 in) tall, prickly foliage. O: Balkan peninsula.

Caption: *Dianthus superbus*

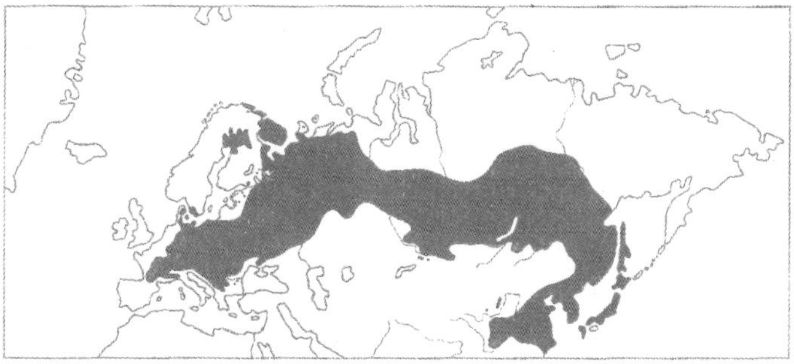

Dicentra · Bleeding Heart · Poppy Family (Papaveraceae)

○ to ◐ △ ⋘ Y ✂ ⬡ ♁ H1

– *eximia*

Small cousin of bleeding heart with 30 cm (1 ft), pendent, pink flowers and green, fernlike foliage, spreads in moist soil. Likes semi-shade and will not be affected by roots of flowering shrubs. Beginning May/September. O: north-eastern America. A: small ferns and shade grasses.

– – 'Alba'

Much slower growing, pale green foliage, a "long-player" like the type. White flowering.

– – 'Luxuriant'

Rich ferny foliage in profusion with bright red flowers from May to October. 30 cm (1 ft)

Dictamnus · Rue Family (Rutaceae)

○ to ○○○ ⊕ △ ⊥ ✂ ♁ F H1

– *albus* (syn. D. fraxinella) · Burning Bush
The red dictamnus and its beautiful white form deserve a place in the rock or wild garden and will grace them for decades. The aromatic scent can be lit on a hot, still evening to give a brief, green flame. 70 cm (2 ft), June, likes warmth and chalky soil. Leaves remain fresh into autumn. Once planted do not move. O: widespread from central and southern Europe to China. A: *Veronica longifolia*, strong grasses, wormwood.

Digitalis · Foxglove · Figwort Family (Scrophulariaceae)
○ to ◑ ≃ □ ⊥ H1
– *grandiflora* (syn. D. ambigua) · Large Yellow Foxglove
Hardy, yellow, perennial foxglove. Height 80 cm (2½ ft). Pale, yet warm shade of yellow. O: from central and southern Germany in mountain scrub, as far east as Siberia. A: tall, white and blue bellflowers, medium-height grasses, ferns and other June flowers of the heather and hedgerow landscape.
– *purpurea* · Common Foxglove
Noble red foxglove, up to 2 m (6 ft) tall, flowers flecked with red all to one side of the stem. Usually, flowers for only two years, but immediate pruning of fading flowers can prolong flowering for up to four years. Likes moorland hillsides, clearings and grows amongst grasses, ferns, goatsbeard and tall bellflowers. Flowers June/July. O: originally confined to western Europe, but now much spread by hand of man. A plant which is much loved.

– – 'Excelsior'
A marvellous improvement on all aspects of the foxglove. Grows to 160–200 cm (5–6 ft) in height and instead of pendent flowers has a mass of inclined flowers in a wide variety of shades all around the stem. Correct pruning is even more rewarding here and will produce more shoots, which will all remain low-growing. You can leave a few of the best plants to go to seed, they are usually self-seeding and will produce dense banks of plants. Irreplaceable for the border of a shady rock garden amongst ferns, though in the truly wild garden, the unimproved form is more in keeping.

Dodecatheon · Shooting Stars · Primrose Family (Primulaceae)
○ to ◑ ≃ △ ⅄ ✕ ♉ H1
– *meadia*
A shooting star with clusters of flowers in May, 50 cm (20 in). Comes from woods and prairies of eastern U.S.A. Leaves die away in summer and can be replaced with annuals. Plant with *Epimedium*, small grasses, fumitory.
– – 'Alba'
Wonderfully effective, long-flowering, white form, up to 30 cm (1 ft).

Doronicum · Leopard's Bane · Daisy Family (Compositae)
○ to ◑ ≃ △ ⅋ ⅄ ✕ ○ H1
– *orientale* (syn. D. caucasicum)
Looks best in the rock garden. The longest-flowering of all the species 30 cm (1 ft), April. O: Caucasus, alpine to subalpine, also in Apennines, Carpathians, Balkans, Asia Minor to Syria. Other closely related species are much more difficult to grow in the garden.
– – 'Miss Mason'
A hybrid of *D. orientale* which has longer flowering stems and is more free flowering.
– – 'Spring Beauty'
Great improvement on the yellow leopard's bane, with double

flowers. Probably a hybrid. 30 cm (1 ft), April/May.

Douglasia vitaliana, see *Vitaliana primuliflora*, p. 000

Draba · Whitlow-Grass · Mustard Family (Cruciferae)
○ to ○○ ⊕ △ ‖ ♉ ○ H1
After long, intensive screening I have been able to select a few of the best, small species from this very large genus. The main source of the whitlow-grasses are the mountains of Asia Minor, but they are distributed from the Caucasus to the Urals and west as far as Spain. Those listed are impervious to frost and aridity. It is marvellous that these small rock-climbing and desert plants have survived the centuries and passed into the age of the European rock garden! A: all types of saxifrage, early, dwarf bellflowers, *Veronica armena*, *Sempervivum arachnoideum*, *Iris reticulata* hybrids, Cheddar pinks, *Globularia*, *Hutchinsia*.

Whitlow-grasses arranged by flowering time.

Draba aizoides · Yellow Whitlow-Grass
(Begins flowering end March.)
Earliest yellow whitlow-grass, 10 cm (4 in), alpine regions of central and southern Europe, on rock faces and ledges, 1000 to 3500 m (3000 to 10,000 ft), sometimes covering entire rock faces.

– *haynaldii*
Beginning April, more attractive version of the above.
– *bruniifolia*
Attractive, moss-like cushions in

second half April. (Often listed in catalogues as *D. olympica*.) O: subalpine regions of Asia Minor.
– *sibirica* (syn. D. repens)
Latest and longest flowering, prelude to alyssum. Prune when flowering is over. O: subalpine and alpine regions of Caucasus, Urals, Siberia.
– *dedeana*
8 cm (3 in), most robust of the white species. O: mountains of Spain.

Dryas, see Miniature Deciduous Shrubs p. 122

Dryopteris, see Ferns p. 108

Echinops · Globe Thistle · Daisy Family (Compositae)
○○ ⚹ ♥ ○ ♔ Hɪ
– *humilis* 'Blue Globe'
Deep blue, dwarf globe thistle, 60 to 90 cm (2 to 3 ft), mid to end July. O: Altai. A: dwarf conifers, blue grasses, dwarf golden-rod, yellow loosestrife, *Lavatera thuringiaca*.

Edraianthus · Wahlenbergia · Bellflwoer Family (Campanulaceae)
○ ⊕ ‖ ⌷ Hɪ
– *dinaricus*
Most attractive species with blue toning to violet, bell-shaped, single, short-lobed flowers. Grey-green cushions without silvery sheen of only 5 cm (2 in) height. All *Edraianthus* species require good drainage in clefts or cracks. They require a sunny position and chalky soil. O: Dalmatia. A: *Jovibarba* species, *Dianthus gracilis* var. *simulans*.
– *pumilio*
Correctly held to be the most

beautiful. Only 5 cm (2 in). Silvery cushions and single, violet-blue flowers. Same requirements as *E. dinaricus*. O: Dalmatia. A: as above.

Epilobium · Willow Herb · Willow-Herb Family (Onagraceae)
○ to ◑ ≃ △ ⋙ Hɪ
Tall willow herbs are untidy and should have no place in the rock garden.
– *nummariifolium*
A cheerful, flat-growing, rock-garden plant, a dwarf willow herb with tiny, pink, long-lasting flowers. Can spread widely on light soil. July/October. O: alpine meadows of New Zealand. A: dwarf golden-rod, bellflowers.

Epimedium · Barren-wort · Barberry Family (Berberidaceae)
◑ ≃ △ ⬚ ⋙ ⟳ ♠ (⚘) Hɪ
All types listed 20 to 40 cm (8 to 16 in), April/May. Barren-worts may look delicate and frail, but are in fact extremely robust plants which can live as long as man. One lifetime is insufficient fully to appreciate what excellent garden plants they make.
The beautiful autumn colouring lasts into November, and is improved when the leaves are wet and reflect the blue of the sky. One April day there is nothing to be seen, then the next warm day the flower stalks shoot up to 15 cm (6 in) through the old leaves, which must be cut away. The colourful new leaves develop quickly amidst the mass of flowers. The leaves of all types have their own individual charm, and one can admire the magic of the changing leaf tones well into autumn. Even in November these plants are unwilling to give up their leaves.
– *alpinum*
Heart shaped leaves, often flecked with brown, topped by reddish flowers.
– *grandiflorum* (syn. E. macranthum)
Largest-flowered species, white, slow-growing. O: Japan. A: San-

guinaria canadensis, Carex and Luzula species, Pulmonaria azurea, Hepatica nobilis, Primula juliae hybrids.
– *pinnatum* ssp. *colchicum*
Yellow barren-wort from Caucasus and Iran. Flowering time and neighbours as for above. Best subspecies of *E. pinnatum*. Light winter protection necessary in very cold areas. In a milder climate the leathery foliage keeps its beauty into the new year.

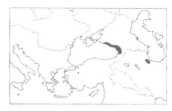

– × *rubrum* (hybrid between *E. alpinum* × *E. grandiflorum*)
More attractive than *E. alpinum* and without runners, carmine-red with yellow star.
– × *versicolor* 'Sulphureum'
Long-flowering barren-wort with evergreen foliage. In April/May produces delicate, sulphur-yellow clusters of short-spurred flowers. Glorious pale green leaves flecked with brown and red. Evergreen foliage lasts particularly well if the plant is out of the winter sun.
– × *youngianum* 'Niveum'
Extremely charming, small, white barren-wort, 25 cm (10 in), much later flowering; golden-brown leaf tones.
– × *youngianum* 'Roseum'
Pink form of this hybrid which is so unlike other barren-worts. 25 cm (10 in). A: *Asplenium scolopendrium* (plus cultivars), *Carex morrowii* 'Variegata', *Trillium grandiflorum*.

Eriophorum, see Grasses p. 106

Eriophyllum · Daisy Family (Compositae)
○○ to ○○○ ⊕ ⬚ ○ Hɪ
– *lanatum* (syn. E. caespitosum) · Oregon Sunshine
This golden daisy, just under

25 cm (10 in), should find a place in every rock garden. The silvery foliage sets off the golden flowers admirably. One aim of this book is to collect together a list of the many lesser-known plants to provide more variety for our gardens. June/July and flowers a second time. O: north-western America. A: *Linum perenne, Nepeta*.

Erodium · Storksbill · Geranium Family (Geraniaceae)
○○ to ○○○ ⊕ △ ‖ 🖰 ↻ H1
The flowers of these delightful, undemanding plants last unbelievably from May through to October. Their full beauty comes out when planted amongst small, white neighbours: white dwarf bellflowers, *Minuartia, Moehringia*, white self-heal, *Globularia, Limonium binervosum, Veronica spicata*. Their only requirement is to be away from standing moisture! Heavy soils need lightening with chalky gravel. 15 cm (6 in) in height.
– *chrysanthum*
Pale yellow, up to 15 cm (6 in), whole plant grey-green, May/June. O: Greece.
– *corsicum*
H2
Dwarf, up to only 5 cm (2 in), dark green leaves and finely hairy in small rosettes, carmine-pink with dark veins. Needs dry spot and protection from wet winter weather. O: Corsica, Sardinia.
– *petraeum* ssp. *glandulosum* (syn. E. macradenum) · Rock Storksbill
Lilac pink with distinctive dark veining. Some forms, known as *supracanum*, have dark markings on the petals. May/June. Similar to a dwarf geranium. The most attractive of all the storksbills. O: Pyrenees.
– *reichardii* (syn. E. chamaedryoides)
White storksbill. Forms 5 cm (2 in) cushions of small, long-stemmed, hairy leaves. May/September. O: Balearic islands.

Eryngium · Eryngo or Sea Holly · Carrot Family (Umbelliferae)
○ to ○○ ≃ ⊥ ✿ ✂ ○ ♨ ↻ H1
This genus includes several excellent rock-garden plants. Flower from mid June/August. A: *Stipa barbata, Helictotrichon sempervirens, Stachys byzantina, Sedum spurium* 'Purple Carpet'.
– *alpinum* · Alpine Eryngo or Queen of the Alps
Silvery-blue filigree of leaves and cone-shaped flower heads with a ruff of feathery bracts. To 70 cm (30 in).

O: from Maritime Alps across the Alps to central Balkans, from 1500 to 2000 m (4900 to 6500 ft), rocky mountain pastures. After planting protect from prolonged drought.
– – 'Superbum'
Improvement on the species with larger flowers and more intensely coloured foliage.
– *amethystinum*
H2
40 to 60 cm (16 to 24 in). Spine-tipped bracts beneath the blue heads. O: Sicily, Italy and Balkan peninsula.
– *bourgatii* · Pyrenean Eryngo
30 cm (1 ft) and taller, small, white flowers with steel-blue leaves.
– *maritimum* · Sea Holly
H2
The native sea holly is more suitable for a wild garden than the rock garden, especially for a dune garden, and will only do well in sandy, moist soil. Looks best planted with sea lavender, *Heuchera*, grasses, gypsophila and white bellflowers.
– × *oliveranum*
A hybrid of alpine eryngo but with smaller heads and bigger, metallic blue bracts.

– *planum*
At maturity this rigid species forms a compact plant and is excellent for rock gardens. Steel-blue, 60 to 90 cm (2 to 3 ft). A: gypsophila and sage hybrids. O: From Austria and the Oder to the Urals and into the Altai. Grows on sandy riverbanks, dry meadows and steppes.
– × *zabelii*
Large, starry, reddish-violet flowers, about 60 cm (2 ft). The best coloration of all garden thistles and tolerates more dryness than others. Hybrid of E. *alpinum* and E. *bourgatii*, combining the best qualities of both.

Euphorbia · Spurge · Spurge Family (Euphorbiaceae)
○ to ○○ ⊕ △ ‖ ⅄ H1
– *capitulata*
Charming alpine to subalpine rock-garden plant. A dwarf at only 5 cm (2 in). Flowers are familiar mixture of green with dull gold. Slowly spreads by underground runners. June/July. O: south-eastern Europe, Dalmatia to Greece. A: *Linaria, Minuartia*, rosette-leaved saxifrage.
– *myrsinites* · Glaucous or Blue Spurge
H2
Rhythmic arrangement of rolled, pale bluish-green leaves, insignificant yellow-green flower. Leaves will disappear in extremely harsh winters, but reappear unharmed. O: Mediterranean countries, mountain to subalpine. A: Plant in mat of blue-green grasses and sedum with early dwarf irises and *Allium* which also flower in early May. May/June.
– *palustris* · Marsh Spurge
H1
100 cm (3 ft) or more tall, intense autumn colouring. Can be planted in tubs under up to 5 cm (2 in) water. In highly fertile soil old plants are so beautiful that in many countries, Denmark for instance, they are planted individually in the lawns of public parks. O: extensive, throughout

Europe except for extreme south, through Siberia, Urals and Altai. Often grows in shrubs beside water. May/June. A: beautiful with *Iris pseudacorus* and blue-green rushes, *Lysimachia, Lythrum.*

– *polychroma* (syn. E.epithymoides)
This species forms rounded bushes, 1 m (3 ft) across, regular in form and with green-gold leaves. During the long flowering time from early April to end May will make even the most difficult positions attractive. O: south-eastern Europe with isolated instances in central Europe.

A: *Brunnera macrophylla*, tulips, red maple.

Festuca, see Grasses p. 106

Filipendula · Meadow Sweet or Dropwort · Rose Family (Rosaceae)
○ ⊕ △ ▭ ✂ ↻ H1
– *vulgaris* (syn. F. hexapetala) · Dropwort
Cream with pale pink sheen, flowers twice. Extremely attractive in its double form 30 to 45 cm (12 to 18 in). From sturdy, flat rosettes of leaves grow long-stemmed, flat, cream flowers and pink buds. O: widespread from Caucasus to Siberia, Asia Minor to North Africa from southern Europe to Scotland and Finland. A: grows wild in dry meadows with *Aster amellus.*
– – 'Plena'
Double, garden variety, second flowering even better than first, most attractive with bellflowers and pinks. Droops frequently in rain.

– – 'Rosea'
Beautiful, single, pink cultivar, which unfortunately is rarely found today.

Gaillardia · Daisy Family (Compositae)
○ to ○○○ ✂ ○ ♔ H1
Only dwarf forms are suitable for the rock garden. Usually short-lived, pruning essential around mid September. O all species: southern United States.

Gaillardia hybrid 'Goblin'
Red with yellow, 30 cm (12 in), suitable for rock gardens. Long-flowering July/September.

Galium · Bedstraw · Bedstraw Family (Rubiaceae)
◑ to ● ⋙ ⅄ ↻ H1
– *odoratum* (syn. Asperula odorata) · Sweet Woodruff
White flowers around mid May; mats of woodruff are highly effective in any shady or semi-shady situation where they form a thick carpet of snow. Dried sprays will scent a room over a long period. The permeating perfume of the garden plants is excellent with other perfumed flowers that blossom at the same time, violets for instance. O: from northern to central Europe to Balkans, Italy, North Africa and as far as Siberia; woodlands rich in humus from sea-level to 1800 m (6000 ft). A: *Brunnera macrophylla*, many woodland flowers, ferns.
– × *pomeranicum* (syn. G.ochroleucum)
Yellow hedge bedstraw, hybrid of *G. mollugo* × *G. vernum*, 30 cm (12 in), tolerates dry conditions, cushioning plant which forms runners. This bedstraw will tolerate extreme aridity. Flowers for about four weeks from end May. Do not plant with weak-growing neighbours. O: southern Europe. A: bellflowers.

Gentiana · Gentian · Gentian Family (Gentianaceae)
The following list includes the most common gentians whose blue flowers extend from end April/beginning May right through to October. I have omitted a large number of insignificant or difficult species. It is certain that in the near future more beautiful gentians will be imported from a wide variety of distant mountain settings. I hope that my list will help to make the gentian more popular as a garden plant.
I have abandoned the usual alphabetical listing and list the gentians according to flowering time. The true age of the gentian is just beginning. These plants are now starting to bring the delights of the wild and mountain landscape to our gardens. The sight of a carpet of gentians in a highland meadow or woodland clearing is one of the best nature has to offer. One can wander through these carpets of deep blue for a whole day as April changes into May. The crocuses have long since given way to primroses and daisies, and just as these are fading the carpets of beautiful spring gentians suddenly appear. There are of course some gentian species which are unsuitable for the garden, but this only increases our love of the gentian, for there are plenty that are highly suitable.

*1. Flowering time:
May to beginning July*

Gentiana acaulis · Trumpet Gentian
○ to ☀ ▭ ✂ ♯ H1
This gentian of an unforgettable velvety-blue and dark green foliage is delightful with yellow auriculas and small primroses. In light soil it requires additional loam and a quite moist, semi-shady position. In many gardens it will grow more luxuriantly than in the alpine meadow. It will live for a long time in a poor soil but will not blossom well. In moist soil it will spread well. O: from western to eastern Alps, from Jura to Vienna woods and

even into the Carpathians; infertile pasture, mountain meadows and flat moorland at heights of 800 to 2700 m (2600 to 8700 ft). Grows wild with Cheddar pinks, primroses and soapwort.

– *dinarica*
○ to ☀ ≃ □ ✕ ≢

The most common and best wild gentian species for the garden. Begins flowering end May. Deep gentian blue, only 10 cm (4 in). Has similar flower to *Gentiana acaulis*. Flowers richly over many years! O: south-western Yugoslavia, Albania, Abruzzi.

– *freyniana*
○ to ☀ ≃ □

Shimmering light-blue flowers for weeks on end; 15 cm (6 in). In mature plants flowers form a circle around the plant.

– *septemfida* var. *lagodechiana*
○ to ◑ ≃ ‖ ✕

Later-flowering plant which looks best if allowed to grow quite large. 10 cm (4 in), long-flowering. More dwarf than *G. freyniana*. July/September. O: eastern Caucasus.

– – – – 'Doeringiana'

If you want to introduce gentians into the garden it is probably best to start with the summer-flowering 'Doeringiana' cultivar which produces rich blossoms. It

is marked by its compact, erect growth.

2. Flowering time: July to beginning August

Gentiana septemfida var. *latifolia*
○ ◑ ≃ ✕

Good examples of this plant show it to be the real king of the summer gentians, growing to 20 to 30 cm (8 to 12 in) and with pure deep blue flowers. The seeds germinate well and, as with delphinium seedlings, each plant is different from its neighbours. Many only flower up to mid-day, others to evening. O: high mountain meadows in Balkans where it grows luxuriantly.

– *cruciata* ssp. *phlogifolia*
○ to ◑ ≃ ✕

Flowers beginning July, 15 cm (6 in), like *G. cruciata*, one of the gentians that produces seedlings of a particularly attractive blue. It is time that these improved plants were given cultivar names. O: Carpathians.

– *cruciata* · Cross Gentian
○ to ◑ ≃ ✕

Flowers July/August. Mature plants which grow to above 15 cm (6 in), will fight off weeds for tens of years and will continue to produce their unusual blue flowers. O: subalpine and alpine, dry meadows, hills and mountains, from sea-level to 2000 m (6500 ft); Europe through Asia Minor to Caucasus, Turkestan and Siberia.

– × *macaulayi*
☀ ⊖ ≌ △ □ ✕

Attractive long-flowerer of summer and late summer, only 10 cm (4 in) tall with quite large, light blue trumpets. Cross between *G. sino-ornata* and *G. farreri*. Requires same treatment as *G. sino-ornata*.

3. Flowering time: August to October

– *dahurica*
○ to ◑ ≃ ✕

60 cm (2 ft), medium-blue, August. O: China.
– *decumbens*
○ to ◑ ≃ ✕

Like the previous species, tolerates both slight shade and a dry, sunny position. Bright blue well into August, 40 cm (16 in). O: central and northern East Asia, Siberia.

– *asclepiadea* · Willow Gentian
◑ to ● ≌ ⊥ Ⴗ ✕ ↺

Colours range from clear gentian blue to lilac-blue. Likes light, moisture-retentive soil in a rock garden situation with partial shade for its long flowering period in July/September. To 60 cm (2 ft) or more if in rich soil. O: original home extends from Pyrenees and Alps—in ten separate areas—to Caucasus. A: small ferns and grasses, wood strawberries (without runners), Turk's cap lilies and rhododendrons.

4. Flowering time: beginning September to October

Gentiana farreri
☀ ≃ △ ‖ ✕

An unusual light sky-blue. Flowers to 5 cm (6 in) from zebra-striped buds end August/September. Extremely beautiful plant, which grows wild at great heights, tolerates full sun and extreme dryness if in moderately good soil. O: western China. A: *Sedum cauticolum*, *Sempervivum* species and hybrids, *Carex firma*, small ferns.

1. Only the rock garden offers the chance of gathering so many plants into so small a space. Properly constructed, it is an unbeatable source of gardening pleasure.

2. *Allium oreophilum* (text p. 110), is one of the most beautiful of the dwarf flowering alliums.

1. *Cerastium tomentosum* var. *columnae*, the Snow-in-Summer (text p. 166), is more attractive and much slower-growing than *C. biebersteinii* (text p. 166).

2. Part of a rock garden, including, from front to back: *Sedum album* (text p. 249, 250), *Arabis caucasica* 'Variegata', *Armeria maritima* (text p. 157) (in flower), *Campanula carpatica* (text p. 163), *Pulsatilla vulgaris* (text p. 242) (in fruit).

3. *Alyssum montanum*, the Mountain Alyssum (text p. 153), is most at home between rocks.

1. *Edraianthus pumilio*
(text p. 173), is a dwarf
species with mauve
flowers.
2. *Androsace primuloides*
(text p. 154), forms
loose cushions of ro-
settes.
3. *Edraianthus dinaricus*
(text p. 173), like all
Rock Jasmines, is sus-
ceptible to wet and is
best planted in a rock
cleft.
4. *Phlox subulata*
'Vivid' – a warm sal-
mon-pink variety
whose growth improves
with careful soil prepa-
ration. This colourful
variety is unfortunately
not always available.

1. *Phlox subulata* (text p. 217), looks very well when planted on top of walls. Its peak flowering time is mid-April.
2. This section of a show garden gives some idea of the variety that can be achieved in a very small space.

. Sedum spathulifolium
'Purpureum', is slow-
growing. The blue-
white centres of the ro-
settes contrast beauti-
fully with the reddish
outer leaves.

2. and 4. *Chrysanthemum
haradjanii* (text
p. 167) – a delightful
new garden plant that
requires well-drained
soil and a dry sunny
position. The rather in-
significant yellow flow-
ers give little indication
of their kinship with
our autumn chrysanthe-
mums.

3. *Lavandula angustifolia*
– a popular, summer-
flowering dwarf shrub
which likes a warm
sunny position. This is
one of the best varie-
ties – 'Hidcote Blue'.

Hypericum olympicum (text p. 202), with blue-green foliage and bright yellow flowers, forms a small cushion. It is also distinguished by its long flowering season, from June to August.

1. *Saponaria caespitosa*, the Tufted Soapwort (text p. 243), does best in a sunny rock cleft.
2. *Androsace carnea* ssp. *laggeri* (text p. 154), has needle-like foliage of only 3 cm (1¹/₂ in) and attractive deep pink flowers.

3. One of the most indestructible plants is *Dianthus deltoides*, the Maiden Pink (text p. 170), which likes a poor, acid soil and a sunny position.
4. *Dianthus gratianopolitanus*, the Cheddar Pink (text p. 170), is available in a number of forms.

1. *Saxifraga* X Irvingii
(text p. 244–5), grows
well in shady crevices.
2. *Saxifraga* X *rubella*
(text p. 245), is one of
the most beautiful and
prolifically-flowering
hybrids.
3. *Saxifraga ferdinandi-
coburgi* (text p. 245), was
first discovered in the
Pirin Mountains. It is
one of the most vigo-
rous of the *Kabschia*
species.
4. *Saxifraga burserana*
(text p. 245), reaches a
height of only 8 cm
(3 in).
5. *Saxifraga oppositifolia*
(text p. 245), flowers
freely in the rock gar-
den, given careful culti-
vation.

1. No rock garden should be without saxifrages. Especially vigorous are the yellow-flowering. *S. X haagii* (text p. 245), (left) and *S. pseudo-sancta* (right). Both form large, stiff, rather pungent cushions.

2. These saxifrages all go very well with each other. Even in early spring their cushions are covered with flowers. Illustrated here are: *S. X ochroleuca* (text p. 245) (above); *S. X Irvingii* (text p. 244–5) (centre) and *S. X apiculata* (text p. 245) (below).

1. *Euphorbia polychroma* (text p. 175), can justifiably be
described as the most beautiful yellow species. Old
plants can be up to 1 m (3 ft) across, even in an
unpromising site.

2. *Polygonum affine* 'Superbum', is one of the longest-
flowering rock garden plants. Its white flowers later
turn to deep red, toning in well with other autumn
colours.

1. and 2. *Carlina acanthifolia*, the Acanthus-leaved Carline Thistle (text p. 166), never ceases to amaze with its gigantic flower heads, but in many cases it will prove rather short-lived.

3. *Carlina acaulis* ssp. *simplex*, the Alpine Carline Thistle (text p. 166), is by contrast a hardy garden plant, less susceptible to wet than the Acanthus-leaved species.

4. *Eryngium alpinum*, the Alpine Eryngo (text p. 174), with its beautifully-shaped, steel-blue flowers, belongs to the Umbellifer family.

Sempervivum species and hybrids are extremely undemanding rock garden plants. With a little nutritious soil their colourful, and sometimes cobwebbed rosettes are excellent for dry walls, rock clefts and tubs.

1. *Sempervivum* hybrid 'Silberkarneol' – a well-known Bornim hybrid.

2. *Sempervivum arachnoideum* ssp. *tomentosum* – a Cobweb Houseleek (text p. 253).
3. *Sempervivum arachnoideum* – the Cobweb Houseleek (text p. 253).
4. *Sempervivum* hybrid 'Rubin' – its rosettes are flushed with ruby from April onwards.

Hardy opuntias are becoming increasingly popular. To be grown successfully, they require sun and protection from winter wet.

1. *Opuntia phaeacantha* var. *albispina* (text p. 214).
2. *Opuntia phaeacantha* var. *camanchica* 'Rubra'.

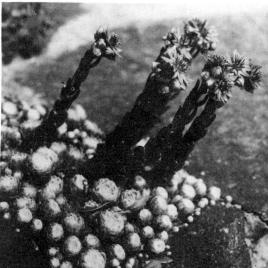

1. and 2. *Orostachys spinosus*, the Stonecrop (text p. 214), comes from Mongolia. The beautifully-formed, succulent rosettes are blue-green in colour. Thrives in light shade.

3. *Sempervivum arachnoideum*, the Cobweb Houseleek (text p. 253), has the most beautiful pink flowers of all sempervivums.

4. This close-up of *Sempervivum arachnoideum* (text p. 253), reveals all its magic and charm.

1. *Hieracium villosum*, the Shaggy Hawkweed (text
p. 200–1), has a thick covering of hair. It is the most
attractive of the yellow hawkweeds and causes no
problems with seedlings.
2. *Alchemilla alpina*, the Alpine Lady's Mantle, is
worthy of greater popularity. Its beautiful silver
shoots contrast excellently with the dark green
leaves.
3. *Onosma alborosea* – a fine Golden Drop, but less
suitable for the garden than *O. stellulata*.

1. Evergreen *Rhododen-dron kaempferi* hybrids, should be in every garden. They like a sheltered spot out of the wind, and a moist atmosphere.

2. *Magnolia stellata* will resist all frost, but flowering as it does in March/April, it requires careful choice of situation in a warm position.

3. *Viburnum carlesii* is a delicately fragrant viburnum which reaches only 1 m (3 ft) in height after years of growth.

4. Even younger specimens of *Pinus mugo* ssp. *mugo*, the Mountain Pine (text p. 126), will flower and produce cones in the garden.

– *sino-ornata*

☀ ⊖ ⊆ △ ▢ ⋙ ✂

15 cm (6 in), colour like that of Trumpet Gentian, likes acid soil, moist situation and additional loam or leaf mould. Best in partial shade out of direct rain. Many gardeners have no luck with this plant—or the plant has no luck with them. Introduced sixty years ago. 'Brins Form' is the easiest form of this species.

O: mountains of south-east China. A: white autumn crocuses, *Saxifraga fortunei*.

– – – 'Praecox'
Flowers two weeks earlier than the species, less striking colour, slower-growing and narrower-leaved.

– – – – hybrid 'Kingfisher' (*G. farreri* × *G. sino-ornata*)
Selected from many seedlings of beautiful cobalt-blue. Begins flowering after *G. farreri* and before *G. sino-ornata*, in mid-August, extending through to early October. Has inherited the strong growth of *G. sino-ornata* while being less demanding.

Geranium · Cranesbill · Geranium Family (Geraniaceae)
For most people the word geranium means the familiar geraniums or pelargoniums of our balconies and window-boxes, introduced into Europe from South

Gentiana cruciata

Africa. It was only at the turn of the century that people became aware of hardy, perennial geraniums and there are still some people who have never heard of them. All are extremely long-flowering.
I have listed the smaller rock-garden geraniums by their flowering times.

1. Flowering time: early May

Geranium himalayense (syn. G. grandiflorum, G. meeboldii)
○ to ● ≃ ⅄ H1
A most attractive blue, 30 to 45 cm (12 to 18 in), should not be confused with the native European meadow geranium which can cause havoc with its seedlings. A pleasing shape and a real treasure in a shady corner. Flowers from May. O: Sikkim, Turkestan. A: white bloody cranesbill which flowers a little later.

2. Flowering time: early June

– 'Ballerina'
Beautiful small, silvery pink flowers with lilac veins, flowering throughout summer. 15 cm (6 in), garden hybrid between *G. cinereum* and *G. subcaulescens*.
– *subcaulescens* 'Splendens'
○ to ○○ △ ‖ ⌀ H1
Thick bushes of bright, carmine-red flowers with black eye. Extremely bold colouring. This cultivar is a great improvement on

the pink-flowered, less easily grown type plant and its long flowering time should make it a feature of any rock garden. Likes warm, sunny, well-drained situation. 15 cm (6 in), June/July. O: Pyrenees, Balkans, central and southern Italy, Asia Minor. A: a host of small plants which flower at this time.

– *sanguineum* 'Album' · Bloody Cranesbill
○ to ○○○ ▢ ⋙ ⅄ H1
15 to 30 cm (6 to 12 in). The red species is found from the Caucasus to Sicily, from England to Finland, that is throughout Europe and as far as the southern Urals. Often grows with *Stipa pennata*, *Anthericum*. Flowers until late July. A welcome companion throughout the long months.

– – *lancastrense*
○ to ○○○ □ ⋙ Υ
Pale pink flowers with red veins in June/July. Despite its small size, an energetic and strong plant. 10 cm (4 in) tall. Can be used for ground-cover. By far the best form of *G. sanguineum*. O: Walney Is, Lancashire, now Cumbria.

– – *prostratum*
Similar to *lancastrense* but with the red flowers of the type.

– *dalmaticum*
○ to ○○ △ ‖ □ ⏁ H1
Long-lasting, warm pink flowers and evergreen foliage. Dwarf.

– – 'Album'
Finally a good white dwarf geranium to go with the long-flowering *G. sanguineum* var. *prostratum* and the deep-red dwarf *G. subcaulescens* 'Splendens'. With the three colours planted together, white, pink and red, they cry out for a touch of blue. Try *Scutellaria alpina*.

– *psilostemon* (syn. G. armenum)
⏀ H1
At its best in June and early July it makes clumps to 120 cm (4 ft) with elegant, deeply toothed leaves which have the bonus of colouring in autumn. The flowers are a rich magenta with a black eye. O: Armenia, USSR. A: Silvery artemisias and other geraniums.

– *traversii*
H2
A tufted, low growing geranium making 15 cm (6 in) silvery-green mounds. The light pink flowers are surprisingly large. O: New Zealand (Chatham Is.)

3. Flowering time: early July

Geranium farreri
○ to ☀ ≃ △ ‖ ⏁ H1
Apple-blossom-pink geranium with black anthers. Flowers July/August, 15 cm (6 in) tall. Wonderful autumn colouring. This slow-growing dwarf likes partial shade. O: northern China, Korea.

– *endressii* · Western Cranesbill
○ to ◑ □ Υ ⏀ H1
(20 cm to 8 in), flowers July to September, an attractive plant with warm pink flowers. Goes well with any small herbaceous plants.

– *macrorrhizum* · Rock Cranesbill
◑ to ● □ ⋙ Υ ⚏ H1
Excellent plant for covering shady, poor soil with permanent carpet of evergreen leaves, 30 cm (1 ft). Light pink flowers and good perfume. Prevents growth of weeds. O: Balkan peninsular, Carpathians, southern Alps, Appennines.

– – 'Album'
White flowers opening from a pink calyx.

– – 'Walter Ingwersen'
Evergreen, deep pink.

– – 'Spessart'
Pale pink, slightly taller than other varieties, evergreen, quick-growing.

– *renardii*
H2
As attractive for its sage-green, wrinkled leaves as its white, purple-veined flowers. O: Caucasus.

Geum · Avens · Rose Family (Rosaceae)
○ to ◑ ≃ △ □ ✕ H1
The completely hardy avens of the rock garden provide a range of orange-red, dark-red tones to fill a gap in the rock-garden colour scheme. They are used much too rarely; but there is no doubt that the near future will produce beautiful cultivars suitable for rough terrain as well as the formal rock garden.

Smaller, hardy Geums for the rock garden

(early, medium and late cultivars and species arranged by flowering time)

Geum rivale · Water Avens
20 cm (8 in), April/May, orange-pink with reddish-brown throat. O: throughout northern temperate zones. The following cultivars are most suitable for garden use.

– – 'Leonard'
Improved coppery-pink form with nodding flowers. A: other waterside plants such as *Caltha palustris* and *Myosotis palustris*.

– – 'Lionel Cox'
Distinct form with yellow petals.

– *coccineum* 'Borisii' (*G. × borisii*) · Scarlet-flowered Avens.
Bright orange-red, 30 cm (12 in), flowers for up to one month, which will continue to flower in maturity in untended situations, where other orange Geums of similar age have ceased to flower. Flowers twice, more frequently as it grows older. May/June and later. A: *Doronicum, Brunnera, Veronica, Potentilla aurea*.

– *montanum* · Alpine Avens
A charming pale-yellow, dwarf Geum. To 15 cm (6 in), June/July. O of type: Europe and high mountains of Europe.

– hybrid 'Georgenberg'
Hardy, bright orange-yellow hybrid with deep green leaves, 25 cm (10 in), end April/June.

Gillenia · Rose Family (Rosaceae)
◑ ≃ ⊥ Υ ✕ H1

– *trifoliata* · Indian Physic
60 to 120 cm (2 to 4 ft), June, white flowers with reddish throats, sparsely-branching, indestructible plant, seen to best advantage with similar shrubs. O: North America.

Globularia · Globularia Family (Globulariaceae)
○○ to ☀ ⊕ △ ‖ □ ⋗⋗ 🯄 ♯ H1
– *cordifolia* · Matted Globularia
Forms mats of deep green, small leaves; semi-woody, likes chalk, effective on moist, porous rock faces. Excellent summer flowerer. Lilac-blue, 5 to 10 cm (2 to 4 in), May/July. Plant together with its white and pink forms. O: Alps to southern Europe.
– *trichosantha* · Globe Daisy

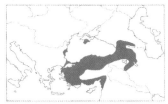

Almost twice as tall and a much brighter blue than the above, produces more flowers even in old age. Forms runners and quickly covers soil or rocks. Hardy and evergreen. May/June (later than *G. cordifolia*!). O: south-eastern Europe, Crimea to Asia Minor.

Gypsophila · Pink Family (Caryophyllaceae)
○○○ ⊕ △ ‖ □ ⊥ ✂ 🯄 H1
– *repens* · Creeping or Alpine Gypsophila
10 cm (4 in), end May/June. This species and the following cultivars are excellent for dry walls where they trail down like a waterfall of blossom. O: alpine level, Pyrenees to Alps, Carpathians and into Poland.
– – 'Letchworth Var.'
This 15 cm (6 in), tall deep-pink cultivar is an excellent rock-garden gypsophila.
– – 'Rosea'
Beautiful, double, pale pink

flowers. 10 cm (4 in), June. A: *Veronica prostrata* 'Caerulea'.

Gypsophila repens hybrid 'Rosy Veil'
The only pale pink, double gypsophila that looks right for the rock garden. 40 cm (16 in), a compact, rounded plant that can reach 1 m (3 ft) across in maturity. June/September. With correct pruning can flower three times a year. Attractive beside steps.

Haberlea · Gloxinia Family (Gesneriaceae)
☀ to ● ⊕ ≃ △ ‖ 🯄 ♡ ♯ H1
– *rhodopensis*
Flat rosettes of dark green, evergreen leaves, mottled lilac flowers similar to a dwarf gloxinia. 10 cm (4 in), June/July. O: Rhodopi mountains, Balkan mountains, alpine, likes chalk. A: small ferns, small grasses such as *Carex firma*, *Festuca glacialis*. Plant in shade on north-east side of rocks.
– – 'Virginalis'
A pure white cultivar, the flowers making a striking contrast to the deep green leaves. Needs a similarly shaded site with a cool root run.

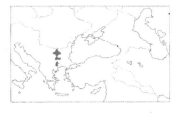

Hacquetia · Carrot Family (Umbelliferae)
☀ to ● ⊕ ≃ □ Y ♡ H1
– *epipactis* · Hacquetia
Charming little spring flower

producing gold and green flowers in April/May, 15 cm (6 in). From a distance resembles a small spurge. O: south-eastern chalk Alps to the Carpathians. A: *Hepatica* and *Pulmonaria*.

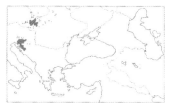

Helianthemum · Rockrose · Rockrose Family (Cistaceae)
○ ⊕ △ □ 🯄 ○ ♯ H2
The rockroses grown in gardens are mostly derived from the mountains of central and southern Europe and dry grassy places elsewhere on the continent. The cultivated garden varieties are being continually improved. Dark green, blue-green or silver-grey foliage forming a remarkable contrast to the bright flower colourings in early and late summer. The early, low-growing, golden-flowered, evergreen Alpine Rockrose is without parallel! The double forms in pale yellow or ruby-red flower continuously from May to October. Plant in a sunny spot. To keep them neat and compact they can be pruned right back in spring, though this is not essential if you have plenty of room for them to spread. Do not be worried about over-pruning. The rate of growth varies a lot from type to type, but in most species it is rapid and, despite spring pruning, you will inevitably find you have planted rockroses too close to neighbouring plants. As they have very deep tap roots, typical of plants from dry habitats, they cannot be moved. Most nurseries have supplies of potted plants even in summer, which will allow you to plant by colour, but when planting in groups remember to allow $\frac{1}{3}$ m² for growth. It is a good idea to intersperse them with a flat *Sedum* or

Thymus villosus which is also evergreen. A: small and medium-sized bellflowers, small grasses, speedwell, dwarf conifers to provide good colour contrast, for example yellow, brown, blue-green or pale yellow, ruby-red, clear blue. Flowering time generally end May to early July, double forms end May to beginning October; most species flower a second time even later in summer.

1. Small wild types of the Alps and Carpathians

Helianthemum nummularium (syn. H. chamaecistus) · Common Rockrose
Single, deep-yellow flowers, about 8 cm (3 in). Earliest in May/August. O: Europe, Asia Minor, northern Iran; dry, warm situations such as poor grassland.

– *oelandicum* ssp. *alpestre* (syn. H. alpestre) · Alpine Rockrose
Single, yellow flower, thick, dark-green cushions of foliage. 5 cm (2 in), June/August. O: Alps, Carpathians; damp, chalky soil.
– – 'Serpyllifolium'
Golden-yellow, single flower, 10 cm (4 in), June/August, forms thick carpet.

2. Garden varieties suitable for rock gardens

(Double varieties flower twice as long as single ones!)
The following colour forms are either single or double, around 15 cm (6 in) tall, June/July, evergreen.

Helianthemum hybrid 'Amy Baring'
Apricot-yellow. Only 10 cm (6 in).

– – 'Bronze'
Golden-brown.
– – 'Citronella'
Lemon-yellow.
– – 'Fire Dragon'
Flame-coloured, particularly reliable, strong and long-flowering.
– – 'Golden Queen'
Golden-yellow.
– – 'Jubilee'
Lots of double, lemon-yellow flowers, 15 cm (6 in), June/October.
– – 'Lawrensons Pink'
Pale pink with lighter centre.
– – 'Red Orient'
Single and dark red.
– – 'Rose Queen'
Pink.
– – 'Rubin'
Lots of dark-red, double flowers, 15 cm (6 in), June/October.
– – 'Supreme'
Deep carmine-red; words cannot express the beauty of the colour! Requires good winter cover, shorter flowering time than others.
– – 'Wisley Primrose'
Astonishingly large, pale yellow flowers and silver-grey foliage.
– – 'Wisley White'
Attractive silvery-grey foliage.

Helleborus · Hellebore or Bear's Foot · Buttercup Family (Ranunculaceae)
◐ ● ⊕ ≃ △ ▱ Ⴢ ✂ ◯ ♢ (⚘) H1
The real garden life of the hellebore still lies ahead of us, when nurseries and gardeners will inevitably recognise the full worth of the queen of them all, *Helleborus niger*, the Christmas Rose. To date this hellebore from the eastern Alps has not been treated seriously enough. The form known as 'Praecox' begins to flower in October and, in mature plants, can last through to Christmas. It produces more flowers on longer stems than any other hellebore, and produces better seeds than the later-flowering types. Young plants develop quicker and are correspondingly earlier flowering.
It is extremely easy to grow suffi-

cient young plants from seed to supply both yourself and your neighbours. In April/May when the seeds are ripe, choose a semi-shady spot and dig a hole 15 cm (6 in) deep with sloping sides, large enough to take a seed-box. Fill the seed box with sandy compost and sow the seeds in rows 1 cm (½ in) deep. Water and press down the soil quite firmly and cover the entire hole with a piece of wood to prevent the soil drying out. Some of the seeds will germinate during the summer and the rest a little later. Even new seedlings which appear late in autumn should survive the winter. Do not remove the wooden covering until germination is well advanced, and keep the wood nearby to use for hot, dry periods. The strongest seedlings can be transplanted in late summer or even earlier to a special semi-shady bed where they will continue to develop until well into December. By the second spring they should be quite sturdy and can be transferred to their final position—although in this second year they will produce no, or very few, flowers. Flowering begins in the third year and is well worth waiting for. Plants should flower well for years and it will be a long time before they need dividing and transplanting. Transplant once a plant has stopped producing flowers, preferably in April. The seed pods are used to the protection of snow in their native habitat and may not develop well during a winter with little snow. It is worth taking the precaution of putting a few plants in a small sheltered situation in an early-spring bed, to prevent the seeds being damaged in such winter conditions.

In the garden, plant hellebores with their usual wild neighbours, ferns and spruce, choosing slow-growing species. If soil is kept moist hellebores will tolerate a sunny situation and can be combined with forms of the winter-flowering heather *Erica herbacea* which will not tolerate continuous shade. Hellebores make excellent cut flowers and will keep for weeks. Their attractive leaves are ideal in a vase together with winter heather, ferns and woodland grasses.

In the wild garden hellebores can be combined with other winter-flowerers, October-flowering saxifrage, winter jasmine, *Adonis amurensis*, violets, snowdrops, early rhododendrons together with the striped variety of the wonderful, evergreen, Japanese sedge, *Carex morrowii*. The flowering time of the early hellebores usually precedes the winter snows, while later species and forms often flower in deep snow. The whole atmosphere of the declining days of late autumn changes as hellebores and *Saxifraga fortunei* begin to put out their white flowers in the garden. The hellebores are listed here by flowering time from October to April.

Modern gardens are becoming more and more attractive during this period of the year; the rock garden with its fresh, varied greens and its winter flowers and buds has played an important part in this development. The refreshing appearance of the hellebores lasts into the spring. Each of the numerous long-flowering species has its own role to play in the garden through the long winter months. Throughout the hellebore family there have been important new additions, the glorious, tall Christmas rose, *Helleborus niger* var. *altifolius*, follows the pink 'Madame Fourcade' of late autumn and flowers right up to the flowering time of the true Christmas rose. All these plants are extremely well-behaved and reliable, if you have the patience to wait for two years and take care to provide the necessary loam and compost and to plant in a shady spot. In the sun they need to be kept moist. Only the hybrids will tolerate dryness in shade or sun and even these will become rather limp at first after transplanting.

Try to include at least a few of the beautiful species listed here in your wild or rock garden, in an early-spring or shady garden, at the corners of herbaceous borders and especially in a bed of cutting flowers.

It is always a pleasure to be able to cut long-stemmed flowers outside the main garden flowering time—providing you do not have to wade through deep snow—which can be combined with other innumerable beauties of the winter garden.

White-flowered Hellebores

Helleborus niger · Christmas Rose
The wild Christmas rose of the Alps, whose varieties include not only stronger, better-flowering plants like those listed here, but also early and late-flowering forms which extend the flowering time over a long period. In the Alps flowering begins from mid November to the beginning of December, much earlier than in low-lying gardens. Despite its name, Christmas rose, in mild winters it will come into flower much later, but there are great discrepancies between plants of the same family group. Thus, for example, the true *niger* flowers in January, but some smaller plants may begin to produce flowers in autumn. The same variation of flowering times in our gardens is evident as in summer flowers. An extremely hot, dry year can weaken and delay the flowers. On rare occasions some hellebore species, especially when not yet fully established, will fail to flower at all, which would seem to justify the doubts of some gardeners who remain sceptical about hellebores. They are just as loud in proclaiming the realisation of their misgivings as they are silent in a normal year when plants flower in the usual way.

In the Alps the Christmas rose is found up to 1800 m (5800 ft), often growing in huge expanses in the moist, humus-rich soil at the edges of the forest. These wonderful flowers grow wild amidst *Hepatica*, *Oxalis*, *Cardamine*, *Actaea*, columbines, cyclamen, daphne, *Asplenium scolopendrium*. Colonies in the northern and central Apennines, through Istria to the northern Danube, in a wide range of climates and at varying heights, make for such varied flowering times, that one could pick wild Christmas Roses somewhere in Europe any time from October to April.

– *niger* ssp. *macranthus*
Large flowers of pure white and luxuriant blue-green foliage, 30 to 40 cm (12 to 16 in) tall, end January to March. O: southern Alps.
– – var. *altifolius*
Long-stemmed Christmas rose, 30 cm (12 in). A: evergreens, ferns, daphne, evergreen grasses, red-leaved *Bergenia*, winter jasmine.
– – 'Praecox'
A cultivar which grows to almost 30 cm (1 ft). October/December. A: small late asters, October saxifrage, autumn-flowering violets, autumn colchicums.

Yellow-green-flowered Hellebores

Helleborus foetidus · Stinking Hellebore
A green, European species which seems to enjoy turning nature upside down by producing pale green flowers and dark green leaves throughout the winter months. No wild garden and many rock gardens would be in-

complete without it. There are many garden situations where it will not thrive, although at other times you may find seedlings all over the garden, even in cracks in walls. Up to 50 cm (18 in) tall! Native to western and southern Europe, England, Belgium, Tirol to Calabria; edges of woods and thickets, dry cliff-faces. Also grows in mountains up to 1800 m (5800 ft); grows with hazel, black-thorn, clematis, cinquefoil, grom-well, wood vetch and lily of the valley. Unlike *H. niger*, needs less moist or humus rich soil.

– *lividus* ssp. *corsicus*
H2
Beautiful, semi-woody hellebore, up to 80 cm (2½ ft), leathery, deeply toothed, evergreen leaves with bluish tinge. Greenish-yellow flowers in March/April. Sometimes self-seeding. O: Corsica, Sardinia.
– *odorus*
H2
Yellow-green nodding flowers with slight scent of elder. Above 30 cm (1 ft), end February to beginning March, seems to survive any conditions. O: from Bulgaria and Romania to Hungary in the east and to northern Italy and southern Tirol in the west. Likes chalky grassland and woods, scrubby faces and woodland clearings, up to 1700 m (5000 ft), grows with *Lamium*, grass-leaved irises, sweet williams, purple broom and *Hacquetia*.

Red and coloured Hellebores

Helleborus abchasicus
Red Caucasian wild species, earliest of the deep violet to red forms which flower February/April, 30 to 40 cm (12 to 16 in) and even taller. O: Caucasus (Georgia), eastern slopes of Black Sea.
– *guttatus*
Later-flowering, wild species with large white, pink-edged flowers, 30 cm (12 in). Unlike *H. abchasicus*, evergreen leaves. March/April. O: Caucasus.

Helleborus hybrids

White, pink, mottled and dark red early spring hellebores. These cannot be too highly praised. Large, old plants on parkland slopes can dominate the landscape for weeks on end and form a wonderful contrast in early spring with coniferous shrubs. In good soil, especially in Switzerland, old individual plants have summer foliage which looks like rhododendrons from a distance and are equalled only by the *Helleborus lividus* ssp. *corsicus* in the wild.

In the first year these plants respond to planting in full sun, which they can tolerate even when the ground is dry, with ominous wilting, but they soon recover. The flowering time is extremely long, with many seedlings flowering well in advance of the rest, often as early as February. Others seem totally confused and come into flower in autumn, continuing to do so every year. Since they tolerate sun better than *Helleborus niger*, the hybrids are more frequently planted with winter heather and a wide selection of other early-spring flowers.

In severe winters coloured helleborus hybrids can suddenly stop flowering, and even the usual fine green winter foliage may be affected, although I have never yet seen one of these plants die.

Helleborus hybrid garden varieties

These seem unfortunately to have disappeared from cultivation and this is particularly regrettable for they provided many unique colours for the spring garden. One always knew what one was getting as far as colour was concerned. Is there anyone who is still growing them? Perhaps the modern trend of growing seed-raised plants and discarding all but those with the best flowers has made their preservation unnecessary.

Helleborus hybrid 'Bridesmaid', speckled greenish-yellow.
– – 'Diadem'
Pale pink.
– – 'Ibericus'
Yellowish-pink.
– – 'Rosa Perfection'
Pale lilac-pink.
– – 'Tea Rose'
Pale violet on yellowish background.
– – 'The Sultan'
Deep violet.
– – 'White Queen'
Pure white.

Hemerocallis · Day-Lily · Lily Family (Liliaceae)
○ to ◑ ≃ to ⌒ ⊥ Ⅴ ✕ ⊔ H1
New, dark brown, velvet-brown, orange or even red, late and long-flowering garden varieties of *Hemerocallis* have helped make these willing and undemanding plants much more popular. Since *Hemerocallis* plants are sometimes naturalized in meadows it is excellent for wild gardens either with or without rocks, especially combined with the noble forms of the meadow iris *(Iris sibirica)*. Both have a role to play in the wild garden and the formal waterside garden and for months on end will complement the form and colour of many other plants.

Hemerocallis species and cultivars are still rather daring for rock and wild gardens and you will have to think carefully about neighbouring plants!

There are some amazing new Hemerocallis cultivars, which I have found excellent, and which

I could not resist including. My list begins with small wild species, suitable for the rock garden, for natural-style watersides and any part of the rock garden that includes grasses. These are followed by hybrids and their forms arranged by flowering time.

1. Wild species

Hemerocallis citrina
Funnel-shaped, lemon-yellow, perfumed flowers, 90 cm (2 ft 9 in), flowers from first half July. O: central China.
– *dumortieri*
Orange-yellow flowers with brown shading outside, flowers often low over leaves. 40 cm (16 in), long-flowering from May/August. O: eastern Siberia, north-eastern China, Korea, Japan.
– *middendorffii*
Many open funnel-shaped, deep orange-yellow flowers, 50 cm (18 in), end May/June. O: northern China, Amur area, Sakhalin, Korea, Japan.
– *minor* · Grass-Leaved Day Lily
Lemon-yellow, funnel-shaped flowers; the whole plant has the delicate look of grass, 50 cm (18 in). The species mainly used to produce dwarf *hemerocallis* hybrids. May/June after *H. middendorffii*. O: East Asia.

2. Garden hybrids

Miniature Hemerocallis hybrids
Popular for the charm of their elegant little flowers, 3 to 4 cm (1 to 1½ in) in diameter. Low, grass-like foliage, usually 40 to 50 cm (16 to 18 in) with a few growing to 80 cm (2½ ft). Very similar to wild *H. minor*. A few years of cultivation of this group has produced fantastic results for colours now include every possible tone of yellow and some pinks. All are excellent for the rock garden.
Hemerocallis hybrid 'Corky'
Pure medium-yellow flowers on dark branching stems, July, 75 cm (2½ ft).

– – 'Golden Chimes'
Clear golden-yellow, branched stems, long-flowering, June/July, 70 cm (2 ft 4 in).
– – 'Half Pint'
New colour in the group, pink flowers with lighter rim, May/June, 50 cm (18 in).
– – 'Thumbelina'
Delightful dwarf plant, only 40 cm (16 in) tall, small orange flowers. July.
– – 'Tinkerbell'
Again small, but orange-yellow flowers on branching stems, May/June, 50 cm (18 in).

Large-flowered cultivars

The main hallmark of this group is a flower diameter in excess of 6 cm (2¼ in), and it includes dwarfs of only 50 cm (18 in) and larger plants that grow to over 1 m (3 ft). Here again a few years of cultivation has brought a range of impressive colours, which it is too soon at present to evaluate fully. I scarcely dare contemplate the shades of yellow and red that will be achieved. There are even forms with rims and centres in different shades and the very latest include bluish and almost white colours. It will be many years, however, before these find their way into our gardens.
All the large-flowered cultivars have inherited the grace and longevity of the parent wild species without the sometimes stocky growth of the older forms they replace. Where can these beautiful plants be used? All are excellent for formal pools, while in rock gardens they should be kept to the borders.
Hemerocallis hybrid 'Atlas'
Huge, pale-yellow flowers with wavy edges, July, 110 cm (3 ft 4 in).
– – 'Burning Daylight'
Deep orange flowers with pale brown bloom, extremely beautiful, colour does not fade in full sun, August, 60 cm (2 ft).
– – 'Buzz Bomb'
Rich velvety red, one of the best

cultivars in this colour, slow-growing, June/July, 60 cm (2 ft).
– – 'Chartreuse Magic'
Canary-yellow flowers with a very distinctive green throat. Another that will not fade! June/August, 90 cm (3 ft).
– – 'Doubloon'
Richly-flowering cultivar with very large, golden-yellow flowers in July and August, 90 cm (3 ft).
– – 'Frans Hals'
Popular two-coloured flower with orange-red petals and cream sepals. Richly-flowering and strong-growing, July/August, 90 cm (3 ft).
– – 'Hesperus'
Deep lemon-yellow, large, starry flowers, long-flowering, July/August, 100 cm (3 ft).
– – 'Hornby Castle'
Deep, brick-red flowers with a yellow throat on small plants, June/August, to 45 cm (18 in).
– – 'Hyperion'
Fine, pure canary-yellow flowers which are long lasting and carried freely, June/July, 100 cm (3 ft).
– – 'Knighthood'
Dependable, rich-flowering and quick-growing sort in deep mahogany-red with golden-yellow central vein to petals and orange throat, June/July, 90 cm (3 ft).
– – 'Morocco Red'
A very exotic dusky red, yellow in the throat, June/August, 60 cm (2 ft).
– – 'Pink Damask'
Enchanting, unique pink form, grows well and flowers profusely. Justly popular. July, 80 cm (2½ ft).
– – 'Rajah'
Profuse flowers, quick-growing, orange. Paler central vein to petals and red-flecked throat, July/August, 100 cm (3 ft).
– – 'Stafford'
An old favourite with deep red flowers shown up by an orange-yellow throat, June/August, 90 cm (3 ft).
– – 'Whichford'
Beautiful, large flowers in a delicate shade of primrose, the

throat a light green. June/August, only 45 cm (18 in).

– – 'Wideyed'
Pale yellow flowers with bright mahogany-red border, highly effective. Guaranteed to flower profusely twice. June/September, 80 cm (2½ ft).

– – 'Zora'
Another low growing sort to 45 cm (18 in) with a clear orange flower.

Hepatica nobilis · Hepatica · Buttercup Family (Ranunculaceae)
◖ to ● ⊕ △ ⅄ ○ ♔ ♂ ≢ Hı
The blue jewel of our spring woods. I would sacrifice all the anemones of the world for this flower. Its bright blue, star-shaped flowers in the brown of the early-spring wood are an essential part of the spring landscape. The flowers of every plant are different; the most attractive are those of the deepest blue with contrasting white stamens, but the white and pink forms are also unbelievably beautiful. All have a very long history. In a well-established plant cushions of flowers can be the size of a frying pan. Beautiful with yellow primulas, pheasant's eye, daphne. Double varieties have been in existence for centuries. March/April. Often evergreen or at least winter-green. Early spring beds. O: extremely widespread in woodland throughout Europe with the exception of far northern and a few western and southern countries. Deciduous forest and thickets from sea-level to foothills, seldom alpine. A: wild with *Anemone nemorosa, Pulmonaria, Maianthemum bifolium, Oxalis acetosella*; in mountain woods with *Cyclamen purpurascens, Pyrola* types, *Luzula sylvatica, Luzula pilosa, Helleborus niger, Soldanella montana.*

– – 'Alba'
Snow-white.

– – 'Rosea'
Rose-pink cultivar in unusual gradations of pink. There are double forms of all three colours,

but these require care. All hepaticas like occasional addition of well-rotted leaf mould.

– *transsylvanica* (syn. H. angulosa)
The best adapted to the garden, surpassing other hepaticas in its tolerance of dry ground. Flowers up to two weeks earlier, producing large, blue flowers. Leaves hairy and sinuate. Healthy plants will quickly form small carpets. White and pink forms also known. O: only in Transylvania. A: *Erythronium dens-canis, Galanthus nivalis, Cyclamen coum, Pulmonaria rubra.*

Heuchera · Alum Root · Saxifrage Family (Saxifragaceae)
○ to ◖ ≃ □ ⅄ ✕ ⬡ ♔ ♂ Hı
The original species, most of which reached Europe during the last ten years of the last century, had dull pink or white-green flowers. After crossing and various improvements in cultivation these have produced glorious garden plants, whose red is so often needed in the weeks from June to August. Now they grace our rock gardens, flower beds, colour gardens and cutting beds with their glowing reds and delicate pinks for up to eight weeks. They will tolerate both semi-shade and moist soil with full sun. O: Species come from North America from Ontario to Minnesota, Nova Scotia. Most of the best cultivars raised in England, France and Germany. *H. sanguinea* is from sub-alpine and alpine regions of Mexico and flowers from the end of May to the end of July. *Heucherella tiarelloides* flowers from end May to mid June. Earliest flowering

form is 'Freedom' from last third of May.

A: *Mertensia paniculata*, small *Hosta* species, summer-flowering *Primula alpicola*, white-flowered *Primula japonica* and *Polystichum setiferum* 'Plumosum Densum', *Saxifraga trifurcata, Tradescantia andersoniana* hybrids. All are 45 to 75 cm (18 to 30 in).
These plants like rich soil and dislike prolonged drought, though the soil must be well drained and not remain wet in winter.

Heuchera hybrid 'Firebird'
Deep-red, bell-shaped flowers, 75 cm (30 in).

– – 'Greenfinch'
Unusual greenish-sulphur. 75 cm (30 in).

– – 'Hyperion'
Most beautiful deep-pink colour with stiffly erect spikes.

– – 'Palace Purple'
Named for its purplish leaves. The flowers are white. 60 cm (2 ft)

– – 'Scintillation'
A very bright heuchera, the pink flowers edged with red. 60 cm (2 ft)

– *sanguinea* 'Alba' · Coral Bells
White variety with brown stems.

– – 'Splendens'
Dark crimson. O: North America, New Mexico.

✕ *Heucherella tiarelloides* (species hybrid between *Heuchera* and *Tiarella*) 'Bridget Bloom'
◖ to ● □ ⋙ ⅄ ♂ Hı
Glistening pink flower candles above pale green and beautifully marked winter-green leaves. 45 cm (18 in). Forms runners. Not for dry garden plots. End May/August.

Hieracium · Hawkweed · Daisy Family (Compositae)
○ to ○○○ △ □ Hı
15 to 30 cm (6 in to 1 ft), June/July, and sometimes into autumn.

– *villosum* · Shaggy Hawkweed
By far the most beautiful species with its hairy leaves and more manageable in the garden as it

spreads much less freely. Golden-yellow flowers on stems up to 25 cm (10 in) tall. Likes dry, chalky soil. O: Alps, Apennines, Abruzzi, Balkans.

Hippuris, see Water plants p. 70

Horminum · Dragonmouth · Mint Family (Labiatae)
○ to ◑ △ ‖ H1
– *pyrenaicum* · Pyrenean Dragonmouth

Violet-blue dragonmouth, evergreen with dull green rosettes of wrinkled leaves. No special soil requirements. 20 to 30 cm (8 to 12 in), June/July. O: Central Europe, Pyrenees.

Hosta · Plantain Lily · Lily Family (Liliaceae)
◑ to ● ≃ □ ᵞ Υ ⊔ ✕ ♧ ♠ F H1
I have attempted here to sort out the confusion that surrounds these beautiful, ornamental plants and to give each with its correct name. Plantain lilies are well represented here for three reasons: firstly there are six forms small enough for the rock garden proper; secondly all plantain lilies will live well and long in the shadiest situation; thirdly they are unbeatable for any type of waterside garden. Some, like

H. plantaginea or *H. crispula* will even tolerate full sun and a light, dry soil.

If plantain lilies have not so far enjoyed the popularity they deserve it is because many people are unfamiliar with the best species and forms or have been wrongly put off by the supposed ugliness of their flowers, for it is true that only two types, *H. plantaginea* and *H. sieboldii*, produce really striking flowers.
O: Japan, Korea, China.
Plantain lilies are delightful plants. One cannot overstress the great length of time, from early April to the end of September and beyond, that these indestructible and undemanding plants and their hybrids provide glorious decorative effects in the garden.
Smaller plantain lilies are here denoted by the suffix 'rock garden'.

1. Blue Plantain Lilies

Hosta sieboldiana 'Aureomarginata'
Blue foliage edged in yellow. 90 cm (3 ft).
– – 'Elegans'
Large blue-green leaves. 90 cm (3 ft).
– *tokudama*
Blue, spoon-shaped leaves which are ribbed and puckered. Best in moist ground.

2. Gold and gold-green Plantain Lilies

Hosta fortunei 'Aurea'
Gold, spring plantain lily. (rock garden)
– – 'Aureomaculata'
Yellow leaves with green border.
– – 'Aureomarginata'
Green leaves with gold border.
– – 'Frances Williams'
Golden margins to glaucous blue leaves.
– – 'Semperaurea'
Ever-gold leaves. (rock garden)
– *sieboldiana* 'Golden'
Equally vigorous but with golden-yellow leaves which re-

tain their colour through the summer. 90 cm (3 ft).
– 'Wogon Gold'
A small, golden leaved hosta. 35 mm (1.4 in) in flower. (rock garden)

3. White- and green-edged Plantain Lilies

Hosta crispula
Large green leaves edged in white.
– *decorata*
Green leaves, ribbed and margined cream. 45 cm (18 in). (rock garden)
– *undulata*
Green-white, wavy-edged leaves. (rock garden)
– – 'Univittata'
White, feather-like markings on leaves. (rock garden)
– 'Thomas Hogg'
Broad green leaves with white margins. 60 cm (2 ft). Flowers mauve.

4. Green Plantain Lilies

Hosta elata
Large green leaves.
– *longissima*
Narrow-leaved, the earliest species. 15 cm (6 in), a natural border plant.
– *minor*
Very small, neat dark-green leaves. 'Alba' is white flowered. (rock garden)
– *plantaginea* · Large White Plantain Lily
Late flowering white and scented.
– – 'Honey Bells'
A hybrid of *H. plantaginea* with scented, purplish flowers.
– *sieboldii* (syn. *H. albomarginata* 'Alba')
White-flowered dwarf plantain lily. (rock garden)
– *venusta*
A very dwarf species only 15 cm (6 in) tall in flower. The leaves are green and make close mounds of foliage. (rock garden)

Hottonia, see Water plants p. 70

Hutchinsia · Chamois Cream · Mustard Family (Cruciferae)

○ to ☀ ≃ △ ‖ ▢ 🗍 ○ ⚞ H1

– *alpina* · Chamois Cream

Dense clusters of tiny white flowers above rosettes of flat, evergreen, fern-like leaves, 8 cm (3 in), April/June, very long-flowering if not in too sunny position. The sub-species listed below is better adapted to garden use. O: high mountains of Europe, growing wild in damp, stony-sandy soil in full or partial shade. Found from 400 m to 3 000 m (1200 to 9 000 ft), from the Pyrenees in the west to the Carpathians in the east. A: *Primula rosea*.

– – ssp. *auerswaldii*

An excellent, reliable spring plant, later flowering, even more evergreen. Ideal for the rock garden. Like the type plant prefers slightly humus soil and not too much sun. May/June. O: high mountains of Spain.

Hypericum · St John's Wort · St John's Wort Family (Hypericaceae)

○ ⊕ △ 🗍 H2–3

– *coris*

Slender stemmed shrublet covered in gold flowers June/July onwards. 10 to 40 cm (4 to 16 in). O: southern slopes of Alps.

– *olympicum*

H2

From Olympus in Asia Minor, 10 cm (4 in) tall, flowers in June. Individual plants or larger groups are equally effective.

– *polyphyllum*

H2–3

Incomparable golden-yellow flowers, June/July. A beautiful

St John's Wort with a potential spread of 1 m (3 ft) or more, best planted at the base of a terrace of natural rock. Can be cut back or even killed in very severe winters. 15 cm high (6 in). O: Sicily, Asia Minor, southern Balkans.

– – 'Sulphureum'

Similar in growth but the large flowers are paler.

– *reptans*

H2

This charming mat former to only 8 cm (3 in) has very large, solitary golden flowers. From June onwards. O: Himalayas.

Iberis · Candytuft · Mustard Family (Cruciferae)

○ to ○○ ⊕ △ ▢ ⦙ ⚞

These dwarf woody plants which produce masses of flowers over many years cannot be praised highly enough.

– *saxatilis*

H1

An early-spring candytuft producing cushions of snow-white flowers in April/May, flowers quite well a second time over several weeks in autumn. 15 cm (6 in). Older plants are extremely attractive. O: southern Europe, northern coast of Black Sea.

– *sempervirens* · Evergreen Candytuft

H2

The type plant is less often grown now as it has been surpassed by the cultivars listed below. O of species: from Spain, across south-eastern France, Swiss Jura, Italy and into Sicily, Crete, Asia Minor and Crimea, mountain to subalpine. A: early tulips and dwarf irises. For borders it is worth remembering that thickly

planted areas will only flower well for six to eight years and even renewal of the soil will not bring back the richness of blossom. I have found it best to remove several plants from the row to leave a gap of 40 cm (16 in) between the ends of the twigs; this will allow the shrubs to flower well once more, and can more than double the flowering life of the plant. This also applies to poorer, dry soils. You can fill the gaps you create with dark blue, dwarf iris.

– – 'Little Gem'

Smaller-growing, neater cultivar to 15 cm (6 in).

– – 'Snowflake'

Form with dazzling white flowers. Flowers three weeks later than *I. saxatilis* until well into June. 25 to 30 cm (10 to 12 in) tall, profuse flowers.

Incarvillea · Bignonia Family (Bignoniaceae)

○ ⊕ △ ⊥ H2

These showy plants, suggestive of small gloxinias, add a touch of far eastern magic to the garden. It is difficult to imagine that the turnip-like rhizomes will in summer produce such glorious trumpet-shaped flowers. Careful planting of the brittle rhizomes, preferably in early spring, will ensure years of blossoms. It is best to plant quite deep, covering with about 10 cm (4 in) of soil. All the species listed are hardy in normal weather conditions. Prefer porous, chalky, rich soil. A: plant in small groups or individually with not too thick ground covering plants.

– *compacta* 'Bees Pink'

The dwarf of the family at only 30 cm (12 in) tall, with up to ten large, pale-pink flowers per stem. May/June. O: north-west China.

– *delavayi*

A large, hardy species, excellent in the garden, 60 cm (2 ft). Smaller flowers than others listed here, but up to twelve per stem, beautiful rose-red with yellowish throat. Although this is the hardiest species, some winter protection is advisable in very cold areas. June/July. O: west China (Yunnan).

– *mairei* var. *grandiflora*
Grows to only 20 cm (8 in) with usually only one or two flowers per stem. Paler rose-red colour. The species grows wild in mountain meadows up to 3500 m (10,500 ft). O: west China

Inula · Daisy Family (Compositae)
○ to ○○○ ⊕ △ ☐ ◯ 🗱

– *ensifolia* 'Compacta'
A dwarf narrow-leaved *Inula*. Flowers profusely in July/August, forming rounded bushes of 25 cm (10 in) height and breadth, covered with small yellow daisies. Most attractive with *Campanula carpatica* and other summer-flowering herbaceous plants. O of type: southern Europe, Austria, south-east Europe, northern Turkey, on dry, sunny slopes. Sub-alpine to alpine. A: garden thistles, skullcap.

Iris · Iris Family (Iridaceae)
I want here to mention the important, yet widely unrecognised, pioneering work carried out in iris cultivation and to suggest new forms which have recently become available for you to try in the garden. The iris can offer a host of unfamiliar, highly varied and beautiful plants, both large and small. The various species flower from March right through to late summer (see also Hardy flowering bulbs and corms. p. 108 ff). The species,

varieties and cultivars include both small and large plants, both cultivated and wild, suitable either for a formal waterside or water garden or for a natural rock, waterside or wild garden. No other plant can offer such variety as is found in the small, modest wild irises and the large, imposing garden cultivars. The iris is well on the way to becoming the most popular garden plant throughout the world, even surpassing its popularity with gardeners of the past and its place in mythology.
The smaller irises will add beauty to the smallest garden from March to the end of July. For months on end the gardener can gaze at them in amazement, overwhelmed by the brilliant, jewel-like beauty that they give us.
This book also includes the new dwarf irises, 'Chamaeiris' and 'Lilliputs', produced by crossing large bearded iris with *I. pumila* or *I. chamaeiris* and giving a much more delicate feel to the iris. These small (usually less than 15 cm, 6 in) plants in a variety of colours which flower in early May can be used in rock-garden positions where the bearded hybrids would be unsuitable. Great progress has been made in the cultivation of 'Lilliputs' and other dwarf forms both in Europe and North America, and the cultivars listed are only a small part of those available. One advantage of the iris is that it will flower well in both sun and semi-shade, providing it is not too closely over-shaded. Any list of larger irises for the rock garden must include not only the modest, wild species such as *Iris sibirica*, *I. orientalis* and *I. monnieri* (which look equally right in a formal water garden) but also the two most highly bred, long-flowering irises, *Iris germanica* and *I. kaempferi*, which complete my list, for these are excellent for the more formal water and waterside garden of dressed stone.

Using iris all round the garden

The great host of small, perennial irises, which I have divided into four flowering groups, so ideal for the rock or waterside garden or any herbaceous bed, are as unfamiliar to many gardeners as the larger wild species of river banks, meadows and steppes such as *Iris sibirica*, *I. orientalis* in yellow and white, and *I. monnieri*.
These large, wild irises, both early and late species (up to *I. pseudacorus*) are suitable for formal water gardens and can be combined with the bearded *I. germanica* groups as well as *I. xiphioides* and *I. kaempferi* which also have long-lasting flowers, interspersed with early and late varieties of *Hemerocallis* (day lily). The individual requirements of iris species and hybrids vary considerably and you should pay close attention to these when choosing irises for the garden.

Small Herbaceous Iris

in four flowering groups from March to beginning June

1. Flowering time: March to April

See list of bulb iris, p. 117 ff.
All the early species and cultivars in the bulb list like moist soil with quite a good compost content. During their resting time in summer and early autumn they need a dry position with good drainage.

2. Flowering time: mid and late April to May

Dwarf rhizome iris for a variety of garden positions
○ to ○○○ ⊕ △ ‖ ⋮ ✕ 🗒 H1

Iris aphylla
An early, wine-red, dwarf iris, 10 to 20 cm (4 to 8 in), one of the few rock or wild-garden plants of

this colour to flower so early. Leaves fall soon after flowering. O: Found central and south-east Europe, Caucasus, Asia Minor.

Iris aphylla

– *lacustris*
An American dwarf iris with pale blue, perfumed flowers. Flowers from May and sometimes until October. Likes moist, slightly acid soil. Forms attractive green carpet rather like grass. Native to rocky shores of North American lakes.

– *mellita*
Dwarf iris, 10 to 20 cm (4 to 8 in). Pale smoky-brown petals, shaded and veined with reddish purple. O: Balkans to Asia Minor.

– *pumila* · Dwarf Iris
A small iris found in all colours in the wild, but less often cultivated as dwarf bearded group hybrids grow better and are less demanding. O: Central Europe, Balkans to southern Urals.

3. Flowering time: end April to mid May and beyond

Dwarf bearded irises
Later flowering than *I. pumila* and larger, 20 to 30 cm (8 to 12 in).
○ to ○○○ ⊕ △ ‖ ⋮ ✕ 🗑 H1

– – – 'Ablaze'
Yellow standards, orange-brown falls, 15 cm (6 in).
– – – 'Blazon'
Uniform gleaming wine-red, 15 cm (6 in).
– – – 'Blue Denim'
Uniform shimmering medium-blue, 15 cm (6 in).
– – – 'Blue Pet'
Pale blue with darker markings. Only 10 cm (4 in).
– – – 'Coerulea'
Pure sky-blue, 15 cm (6 in).
– – – 'Cyanea'
Pure ultramarine-blue, 15 cm (6 in). Available since 1899 and still unsurpassed.
– – – 'Fairy Flax'
Shimmering pale blue, falls with darker fleck, 20 cm (8 in).
– – – 'Green Spot'
White, striking green veining to standards and falls, 25 cm (10 in).
– – – 'Jerry Rubin'
Bright ruby-red, flowers profusely, 30 cm (12 in).
– – – 'Lemon Flare', sulphur yellow. 30 cm (12 in).
– – – 'Lilli White'
Profuse, pure white flowers, 20 cm (8 in).
– – – 'Lutea'
Golden-yellow, extremely rich flowering, 25 cm (10 in).
– – – 'Path of Gold'
Profuse, bright golden-yellow flowers, stocky variety, 20 cm (8 in).
– – – 'Pogo'
The chrome yellow falls have a reddish brown central blotch. Very distinctive. 40 cm (16 in)
– – – 'Ragusa'
Medium-blue standard, violet-blue falls, dependable and rich-flowering, 15 cm (6 in).
– – – 'Snow Cap'
Snow-white, 30 cm (12 in), one of the older cultivars with profuse flowers.
– – – 'Yellow Pet'
Very dwarf canary yellow. Only 8 to 10 cm (3½ to 4 in).

4. Flowering time: end May to early June
○ to ◑ ≃ ♂ H1

Iris chrysographes
Velvety purple to deep violet wild iris with yellow markings on falls, 30 to 50 cm (12 to 18 in) with reed-like foliage.

– *gracilipes*
Rhizomatous iris with pale lilac petals and orange crest from dense fans of flat spear-like foliage. Likes rich soil, 25 cm (10 in). O: Japan. 'A continual reminder in the garden of the thousand isles of Matsushima' (Farrer).

– *graminea* · Grass-Leaved Iris
○○ ⊕ ‖ H1
20 cm (8 in), unusually shaped blue and violet flowers. O: southern Europe, Spain to Balkans, southern Soviet Union, north into Austria.

– *ruthenica*
○○ ⊕ ‖ 🗑 H1
20 to 30 cm (8 to 12 in), pale lilac with white and violet toning. When not in flower looks like a small grass. Likes porous, rather chalky soil. O: from Transylvania to East Asia.

Larger Iris for Wild Gardens or Formal Waterside Gardens

Flowering time: June to July

○ to ○○○ ⊕ ⊥ ✕ ♂ H1
Like the larger irises listed in the fourth group, the taller summer-flowering irises listed here are suitable for both the wild rock or waterside garden and are extremely beautiful in a formal rock or waterside setting. They are noble forms of the wild iris of the steppes of Asia Minor.

Iris monnieri

Golden-yellow iris from the Greek Islands, 45 cm (18 in) and above, but will grow to 100 cm (3 ft) and more in shallow water!

– × *monspur* (hybrid of *I. monnieri* and *I. spuria*)

Blue-white, almost 1 metre (3 ft) tall, needs warm, sunny but not too dry position if it is to flower well.

– *orientalis* (syn. I. ochroleuca) 'Gigantea' · Yellow Iris

Beautiful iris, excellent for cutting, white flowers with attractive yellow fleck on falls, 70 to 90 cm (2 ft 4 in to 2 ft 9 in).

– – 'Sulphurea', pale yellow with blue.

The thick foliage of both the species and its forms is equally attractive in either dry or marshy conditions. O of species: Syria, Asia Minor.

– *pseudacorus* · Yellow Flag

⊔ ⩓ ⩘ ✕ H1

Golden-yellow, native iris with flowers almost 1 m (3 ft) tall from imposing foliage. Will tolerate constant shallow water and is almost indestructible. Plant between *I. sibirica*. Varieties with paler flowers or variegated leaves are available and can be used mixed with the true species.

– *sanguinea*

⩗ ⊔ ✕ H1

Beautiful wild iris whose erect leaves are similar to *I. sibirica*. Reliable garden plant that will flower profusely for years, deep blue, 60 cm (2 ft). O: Japan, Korea, north-east China, Baikal area, east Siberia to Ussuri area.

– – 'Snow Queen'
Uniform ivory-white, 100 cm (3 ft), May/June.

Iris sibirica

– *sibirica* · Siberian Iris

⩗ ⊔ ✕ ♂ H1

Native to Central Europe but now disappearing with intensive grazing of much meadowland, 40 to 100 cm (1 ft 4 in to 3 ft), deep and pale blue. O: Central Europe to Siberia.·

– – 'Blue Moon'
Large, flattish, two-tone flowers of violet and pale blue, very similar to *I. kaempferi*.

– – 'Caesar'
Beautiful flowers of dark velvet-blue.

– – 'Lime Heart'
The large white flowers have central lime-green markings.

– – 'Mrs Rowe'
Silver-white with lavender-pink.

– – 'My Love'
Branched stems bearing soft, medium-blue flowers, even plants of several years flower profusely. Beautiful veining on falls.

– – 'Ottawa'
Slender foliage with clear blue flowers.

– – 'Perry's Blue'
Pale blue, most beautiful of the older cultivars.

– – 'Phosphorflamme'
Blue with phosphor-coloured markings.

List of the two garden iris groups

These plants of the formal rock or water garden include the bulbous iris of the Pyrenees, the hardy *Iris xiphioides* and its hybrids, together with the tall and intermediate bearded iris groups and *Iris kaempferi*, the last of which is indispensible in the formal water garden.

These tall irises should be well spaced when planting to prevent overcrowding, to which they are prone. The soil should be enriched with compost and this will need topping up at intervals. For a more informal look combine with a few attractive grasses and semi-shade plants with attractive leaves.

1st Garden Iris Group

1. Flowering time: from mid May

Iris germanica

○ to ○○ ⊕ ‖ ⊔ ✕ H1

Intermediate or Median group, 25 to 75 cm (10 to 30 in) in height. Intermediate bearded hybrid 'Andalusian Blue'

Pale blue, very early-flowering, 70 cm (2 ft 4 in).

– – – 'Black Hawk'
Deep velvety violet, reliable cultivar with profuse flowers, 60 cm (2 ft).

– – – 'Langport Chimes'
Wonderfully rich-flowering and stocky, deep golden-yellow, early flowering, 50 cm (18 in).

– – – 'Langport Sultan'
Large, plum-purple flowers, 45 cm (18 in).

– – – 'Libellula'
Delicate pale blue, rich-flowering, grows well, 30 cm (12 in).

– – – 'Ruby Glow'
Shimmering wine-red, early, 40 cm (16 in).

– – – 'White Swan'
Pure white, 30 cm (12 in).

2. Flowering time: around end May

Tall group of bearded irises, 85 cm (35 in) and over in height
○ to ○○ ⊕ ‖ ⊔ ✕ H1
(The long flowering period of the tall group brings it into several flowering periods, including the third flowering time which follows below.)
Tall bearded hybrids 'Black Taffeta'
Deep, satiny blue-black, wavy petals, fascinating! 70 cm (2 ft 4 in).
– – – 'Blue Glow'
Smooth-petalled, medium blue, very attractive, 80 cm (2 ft 8 in).
– – – 'Blue Sapphire'
Elegant, wavy, pale lavender-blue flowers, very rigid, 100 cm (3 ft).
– – – 'Cloud Cap'
Profusely flowering, pure pink, 80 cm (2 ft 8 in).
– – – 'Desert Song'
Large, pale-yellow flowers, falls have small white splash, 80 cm (2 ft 8 in).
– – – 'Dotted Swiss'
White flowers delicately pencilled in blue, 90 cm (3 ft).
– – – 'Elizabeth Arden'
Apricot-pink with cream falls and orange splash, 88 cm (34 in).
– – – 'Glory of June'
Very large flower, creamy yellow with white falls, 100 cm (39 in).
– – – 'Lugano'
Large, cream flowers with gold throat, in right position will flower into autumn, 100 cm (3 ft).
– – – 'Magic Hills'
Pale violet with orange mark on falls. Very strong growing, 90 cm (3 ft)
– – – 'Melrose'
Apricot with pinker falls and orange centre, 100 cm (39 in)
– – – 'Powder Pink'
A clear flesh pink with orange beard, 100 cm (40 in)
– – – 'Sable Knight'
Purple-black, 80 cm (2 ft 8 in).
– – – 'Seagull'

Profuse, pure white flowers, weather-resistant, 80 cm (2 ft 8 in).
– – – 'Xantha'
Very large golden yellow flowers. 90 cm (35 in)

3. Flowering time: early June

Tall bearded iris 'Arctic Snow'
White with bluish sheen, profuse flowers, 90 cm (2 ft 10 in).
– – – 'Black Hills'
Uniform blue-black, 100 cm (3 ft).
– – – 'Blue Rhythm'
Bright medium-blue, 100 cm (3 ft).
– – – 'Blue Shimmer'
White with blue edging and veining, 80 cm (2 ft 8 in).
– – – 'Danube Wave'
Shimmering medium-blue, slightly wavy flowers, 100 cm (3 ft).
– – – 'Extravaganza'
Cream standards, plum-coloured falls, unique colour combination, very late flowering, 80 cm (2 ft 8 in).
– – – 'Firecracker'
Beautiful reddish-brown markings on gold petals, another profuse flowerer, 80 cm (2 ft 8 in).
– – – 'Golden Sunshine'
Pure yellow, very weather-resistant, 90 cm (2 ft 10 in).
– – – 'Harriet Thoreau'
Lilac pink with light brown throat, 90 cm (2 ft 10 in).
– – – 'Honey Gold'
Golden with deep crimson-red falls and a golden-brown throat. Profuse in its flowering, 100 cm (39 in).
– – – 'Jane Phillips'
Best of the pale blue cultivars, dependable, 80 cm (2 ft 8 in).
– – – 'Lela Dixon'
White petals with conspicuous blue markings, flowers profusely, 90 cm (2 ft 10 in).
– – – 'Mystic Melody'
Cream, almost white standards, deep gold falls, beautiful colour combination, 80 cm (2 ft 8 in).
– – – 'Ola Kala'
Excellent deep-gold, late blooming, smallish flowers but irreplaceable, 90 cm (2 ft 10 in).

– – – 'Pacemaker'
Velvety brownish-red, 80 cm (2 ft 8 in).
– – – 'Party Dress'
Apricot pink with yellow throat, petals wavy at edges, 80 cm (2 ft 8 in).
– – – 'Rosenquarz'
Extremely striking, pure pink variety, grows quickly, flowers profusely, resilient. One of the best pinks! 100 cm (3 ft).
– – – 'Wabash'
White standards, violet-blue, white-edged falls. Older cultivar with smallish but profuse flowers, unsurpassed, 100 cm (3 ft).
– – – 'White City'
Tall, almost blue-white flowers, 120 cm (4 ft).
– – – 'Wild Echo'
Very dark blue-black with golden throat, 100 cm (39 in).

2nd Garden Iris Group

Iris kaempferi
○ to ◗ ≌ ⊔ ✕ H2
Can be described as a 'marsh iris' since it grows well in moist, chalk-free soil and while in flower can be transferred in tubs to the pool where it can tolerate up to 5 cm (2 in) water. Later, particularly in winter, it does not like continual wet. Winter protection advisable in exposed situations. Plants become exhausted after a while and stop flowering; they should then be divided and replanted in spring. Experience has shown that this plant falls into two types, one of which will not flower in the year of replanting and the other which will.
The situation with *Iris kaempferi* around the middle of this century was as follows: the confusion in nomenclature meant that one could not be sure of getting the best cultivars and it was a matter of luck if the nursery actually supplied the best possible sort. But more recently the situation has improved and great steps forward have been made throughout the world. Cultivation of *I. kaempferi* was much adv-

anced by Max Steiger. Six years of work on this species produced varieties better suited to garden use and better able to tolerate chalky soil. (He labelled his varieties 'CARE' = Calcium Resistant). This work involved some 5 000 to 6 000 new seedlings per year.

This iris has now become the great flower of the summer waterside garden. It is too elegant for the wild garden but excellent for formal waterside gardens. It thrives in extremely wet soil.

Iris kaempferi · 'Snowdrift'.
A delightful pure white form. 90 cm (3 ft)

Jeffersonia dubia, see *Plagiorhegma dubium*, p. 218

Jovibarba · Stonecrop Family (Crassulaceae)
○ to ○○○ ⊕ △ ‖ ⬚ ♂ ⚹ H1
A group of plants formerly included in the *Sempervivum* family, which have now been renamed to form a separate family. Despite the new name, I have hopes that these interesting succulents will grow in popularity. All *Jovibarba* types form small lateral rosettes on stolons. They are treated as used in the same way as *Sempervivum*.
– *heuffelii* (syn. Sempervivum heuffelii)
With its flattish rosettes and small, erect flower heads this plant has something of the look of a small tortoise. The beautiful sea-green leaves can best be compared to the colour of jade. Increase is slow by splitting of the rosettes. Likes porous soil and dislikes too much winter moisture. Several variations in rosette colour. Originally discovered in 1874 in Serbia.
– *heuffelii* var. *reginae-amaliae*
Unusual whorls of thick foliage, bronze with some green shading, pale yellow flowers. This plant should not be confused with *Sempervivum reginae-amaliae* and its wild forms, which are very

seldom cultivated. Discovered in 1877 in the mountains of Greece.

– *sobolifera* (syn. Sempervivum soboliferum) · Hen-and-Chickens Houseleek
Forms areas of globular rosettes, both large and small, green in colour and often tinged on the underside with red. A highly individual plant. The English name 'hen and chickens' is extremely apt. Easy to cultivate, with no special requirements. Discovered in 1885. O: northern central and east Europe, found as far north as Archangel.

Juncus, see Grasses p. 105/106

Koeleria, see Grasses p. 105/106

Lathyrus · Vetchling, Pea · Pea Family (Leguminosae)
◐ to ● ▭ ⅄ ○ H1
– *vernus* · Spring Vetchling
Reddish flowers which eventually turn blue. 30 cm (1 ft), April/May. O: damp and also dry woods of Europe, Caucasus, Siberia. A: early spring plants. (Looks best at a distance for unattractive as flowers fade.)
– – 'Alboroseus'
Enchanting little bushes of warm

pink, about 1 ft in height and diameter, which become thicker as the plant matures, extremely undemanding plants. Flowers for only two weeks, but the memory lives on! Difficult to imagine these plants without their natural neighbours, ferns, narrow-leaved lungwort and woodland forget-me-nots. One of the flawless treasures of the garden!

Lavandula, see Dwarf Deciduous Shrubs, p. 123

Leontopodium · Edelweiss · Daisy Family (Compositae)
○ ⊕ △ ‖ ✂ ♥ ⬚ ♂ H1
– *alpinum* · Edelweiss
The name first appeared in writing in 1785 in the Tirol. O: rock clefts from subalpine to alpine levels. The home of the edelweiss family is central Asia. One single species made its home in the European Alps during the ice age where it lives between 1700 (5000 ft) and 3400 m (10,000 ft) in patches of grass and steep, sunny, rocky slopes, sometimes found at lower levels too.

In the garden edelweiss like a sunny but not over-dry position with porous, chalky soil. Feeding will adversely affect flowering. Quality plants can be propagated from cuttings.

Good quality edelweiss will grow just as luxuriantly and produce as many flowers in lowland gardens as in their alpine home. A: *Veronica incana, Thymus serpyllum,*

Lathyrus vernus

Campanula cochleariifolia and *Campanula portenschlagiana*, *Primula auricula*.

– – 'Mignon'
A very dwarf, compact form of *L. alpinum* making close, dense mats with flowers on stems no longer than 10 cm (4 in).
– *palibinianum* (syn. *L. sibiricum*)
Widespread in Siberia, Mongolia, Manchuria and Korea, where it spreads like a weed over mountain and country paths. The longest flowering species.
– *souliei*
Dwarf, mat-forming edelweiss with profuse, small, silver-white flowers, just under 30 cm (12 in), June/August. O: Tibet, Yunnan.

Leuzea · Knapweed · Daisy Family (Compositae)
○ to ○○ ⊕ ⊥ ⟳ H1
– *rhapontica* (syn. Centaurea rhapontica) · Giant Knapweed
A large, vigorous plant with decorative leaves, about 1.5 m (4½ ft), with attractive, rose-purple flowers. The silver-grey flower buds, which can be as large as a hen's egg, are especially attractive. The best place for this plant is a dry wild garden. O: western Alps. A: *Limonium*.

Lewisia · Purslane Family (Portulacaceae)
○ to ☀ ⊖ △ ‖ ⬚ ⚹ H2
– *cotyledon*
White or pink flowers with darker veining, 15 cm (6 in), flowers May/June. O: mountains of California.

L. cotyledon hybrids
L. cotyledon is usually cultivated in hybrid form, crossed with

closely related types such as *L. heckneri*. Colours range from white, pink, red and apricot to orange. If success is to be ensured these plants require porous, acid soil in a sunny or partially shaded position. Protect neck of root with stone chippings against winter wet. A: *Sempervivum, Asperula, Orostachys spinosus*.

Liatris · Daisy Family (Compositae)
○ to ○○ ⊥ ⚹ ○ H1
– *elegans* · Snake-Root
Reddish-purple, candle-like flowers, 45 cm (18 in), prefers dry conditions. August. O: Florida, Texas. A: grasses, *Scabiosa caucasica* (blue and white forms).
– *spicata* · Blue Snake-Root
A plant from the Gulf of Mexico area. Like the above apart from the colour which is usually bluish red. July/August.
– – 'Kobold'
Bright violet flowers, 40 cm (16 in).

Limonium · Sea Lavender · Sea Lavender Family (Plumbaginaceae)
○ to ○○○ △ ⊥ ⚹ ❦ ○
The sea lavenders include both large and small plants, and with their attractive colouring and lines, they are ideal for any rock, dune or meadow garden. They make excellent dried flowers.
– *binervosum* (syn. Statice auriculifolia) · H2
Dwarf, white-flowered sea lavender with heads which form small, silver triangles. The flowers give long-lasting, pleasure and even when faded continue the silver

effect, setting off plants of several seasons. 15 cm (6 in), August. O: southern Europe, sunny mountain sides and clefts in rocks.
– *latifolium*
H1
To 30 cm (12 in), the mature plants become quite wide and resemble a blue gypsophila, although more rigid and lower-growing. July/August. O: grassy meadows of southern Russia to the Volga and Bulgaria. A: blue dwarf globe thistles, dwarf golden rods and other dune garden plants.

– – 'Violetta'
Attractive, dark lilac, late-flowering form. Slower growing than the species. Propagated by root cuttings.

Linum · Flax · Flax Family (Linaceae)
○ to ○○○ △ ⬚
– *flavum* 'Compactum' · Yellow Flax
H1
Compact form of the impressive golden, full-summer flower of the rock garden. 30 cm (12 in), July/August. O of species- alpine regions of south-east Europe to central and southern Soviet Union. A: *Festuca cinerea, Festuca vallesiaca, Campanula carpatica*, skullcap.

– *monogynum*
H2–3
Charming white flowered flax from New Zealand (not to be confused with New Zealand flax—*Phormium*). Growing to 40 cm (16 in) it is a short-lived perennial but easily kept going from seed. June to frosts.
– *narbonense*
H1–2
Azure-blue. In contrast to *L. perenne* which lives for only three to four years, this plant is long-lived. The most beautiful blues are available in cultivars such as the 'Six Hills'. At maturity the plant forms luxuriant bushes of an unforgettable azure-blue, a must for the rock garden. A mature plant of ten to fifteen years of age and 80 cm (2½ ft) diameter is a sight to behold in the blue light of early morning. This plant is semi-evergreen, but the green bushes should be pruned back in spring like *Helianthemum*. By midday the pure blue of the morning fades to pale lilac, as with many types of speedwell. 15 cm (6 in) to 45 cm (18 in), end May to end July.
– *perenne* · Perennial Flax
H1
A plant that has spread far across the world, throughout Europe, through north and central Asia and into North America. Its blue flowers appear over a very long season, as its name implies—from June until well into autumn. Lives for only three to four years but seeds profusely. For a time the blue flowers grace the familiar spot, only to disappear and then to reappear just as suddenly in late summer. 45 cm (18 in), May to October.
– *suffruticosum*
H2
Shrubby white flax, 40 cm (16 in), June/July.
– – 'Nanum' (syn. L. suffruticosum salsoloides)
Very much smaller, scarcely exceeding 15 cm (6 in) but with equally large flowers. O: southern Europe.

Linum perenne

Lithospermum purpurocaeruleum, see *Buglossoides purpurocaerulea*, p. 162

Lotus · Birdsfoot-Trefoil · Pea Family (Leguminosae)
○○ to ○○○ ⊕ △ □ H1
– *corniculatus* 'Pleniforus' · Birdsfoot-Trefoil or Bacon and Eggs
Low-growing (10 cm/4 in), long-flowering, golden plant which always looks fresh. Requires dry, sunny position. End May to October. More attractive than the single-flowered species, which is native to Europe as well as Asia and North Africa and can be invasive.

Luzula, see Grasses p. 106/107

Lychnis · Pink Family (Caryophyllaceae)
○ ⊖ H1

– *alpina* (syn. Viscaria alpina) · Alpine Lychnis or Catchfly
≃ ‖
Under 30 cm (1 ft), dark pink flowers in June/July, also a white form; a small, dainty plant which seems to thrive in a chalk-free, lightish soil. Not as long-living as the species which follows. Easily grown from seed!
O: Pyrenees, Alps, mountains of northern Europe and Arctic regions, usually between 2000 and 3000 m (6000 and 9000 ft), but also lower.
– *viscaria* ssp. *viscaria* 'Splendens Plena' · German Catchfly
✄
Intense magenta-red that seems to flame in the evening sun! 45 cm (18 in), end May/June. A difficult colour to use naturally and perhaps better suited to the

Lychnis alpina

formal rock garden. Home of species: throughout Europe and beyond Arctic Circle, western Siberia, Transcaucasia. A: *Veronica latifolia*, blue grasses. Grows wild with maiden pinks and *Corynephorus*. Type grows on dry, sunny turf, rocky cliff faces and edges of coniferous forest.

Lysimachia · Loosestrife · Primrose Family (Primulaceae)

◐ ≃ □ Y ⊔ Hɪ

– *clethroides*
Extremely fine, white-flowered, completely indestructible plant to 90 cm (3 ft) in height. Unusual, over-hanging flowers. Flowers July/August. O: Japan, China. A: woodland campanula, *Veronica incana*.

– *nummularia* · Creeping Jenny
ᴍᴧ
Forms flat carpets of beautiful golden flowers, but also attractive when not in flower. Beautiful in large areas. June to September. Protect small plants from being overshaded by stronger neighbours. A popular plant both in the wild and in the garden. For a long life requires humus-rich and preferably moist, soil. O: Europe. A: *Myosotis*, grasses, dune sedge, speedwell.

– – 'Aurea'
Requirements as for species. In moist, nutritious soil will tolerate full sun. A popular pot plant in England, in Sweden grown hanging from tubs in almost every garden. Considered a 'lucky' plant by country folk.
– *punctata* · Large Yellow Loosestrife
Most attractive of all the erect, yellow loosestrifes. Beautiful yel-

low whorls. An excellent plant for either sun or shade, excellent with delphiniums. Really a 'plant of all work'. Almost 90 cm (3 ft), flowers May to August. Can be invasive. O: Europe, northern Asia.

Lythrum · Loosestrife · Loosestrife Family (Lythraceae)

○ to ◐ ♎ ⊥ ⊔ ᴍᴧ ○ ☖ Hɪ

Grows to 90–120 cm (3–4 ft), lilac-pink flowers from June to September, garden varieties include taller plants and deep salmon-pink flowers. O: throughout northern temperate zones, and has even made its way to Australia. Has spread extremely far for several reasons, one being that it is truly amphibious and can live in dry conditions or shallow water (with *L. virgatum* tolerating water extremely well). It flowers for months on end surrounded by white butterflies and tossed by the wind. In ditches found growing side by side with meadow sweet.
There are several cultivars in beautiful colours and of impressive size.
– *salicaria* 'The Beacon' · Purple Loosestrife
Rose-red flowers up to 100 cm (3 ft 3 in). Most beautiful of all the loosestrifes.
– – 'Robert'
A salmon-pink cultivar which grows to only 75 cm (30 in), excel-

lent for the smaller rock garden. A: *Lysimachia clethroides*, white dwarf astilbes, *Tradescantia andersoniana* hybrids.
– *virgatum* 'Rose Queen' · Slender Loosestrife
A loosestrife whose salmon-pink flowers will grace the garden for up to two months. Grows to only 60 cm (2 ft) so suitable for a variety of rock and waterside-garden uses. O: from south-east United States to Europe. A: beautiful with white and pink *Tradescantia andersoniana* hybrids and blue-green sedges.

Maianthemum · May Lily · Lily Family (Liliaceae)

● ⊖ ᴍᴧ ♢ Hɪ

– *bifolium* · May Lily
Forms white, 10 to 20 cm (4 to 8 in) high carpets in shady positions. A quality plant, delightful growing amongst small fern fronds. The Canadian species, *M. canadense* is stronger and quicker-growing. O: northern temperate zones. Sea-level to sub-alpine. Grows in shady woods and thickets rich in leaf mould, also in dunes, moorland and rocky places, up to 2 000 m (6 000 ft).

Malva · Mallow · Mallow Family (Malvaceae)

○ to ○○ Hɪ

– *moschata* · Musk Mallow
A delightful plant for the wild

Lythrum salicaria

garden, keeping itself going by seeding, but never so invasive that it becomes a nuisance. It can reach 75 cm (2½ ft) and in summer is covered in rosy pink flowers for weeks on end, flowering from June till late August and beyond. O: Europe.

– – 'Alba'
A pure white form which comes true from seed. One of the last plants to be still visible on a summer evening.

Mazus · Figwort Family (Scrophulariaceae)
○ to ◑ △ ⋙ H2
– *pumilio*
This dwarf from New Zealand is a low-growing carpeter with small mauve flowers. Winter protection advisable in cold areas if severe frost is forecast.

Meconopsis · Poppy Family (Papaveraceae)
☀ to ● ⊖ ≃ ⊥ Υ ⋔ H1–2
– *betonicifolia* (syn. M. baileyi)
The unsurpassable blue poppy of the Himalayas. No one can ever forget their first sight of these amazing blue flowers. It is advisable to cut off the flower stems immediately after flowering—as with *Digitalis* and *Verbascum olympicum*—for this will extend the flowering life to three to four years. Requires sheltered, shady, moist position with rich but well drained soil. One scarcely dares to mention neighbouring plants, but this poppy looks good with wavy hartstongue fern or the tall, late-flowering *Primula florindae*. Cannot be transplanted easily as it has a strong tap root. 1 m or more (3 ft 3 in).
– *integrifolia* · Lampshade poppy
○○
Beautiful nodding yellow flowers with rounded petals. O: China.

Melittis · Mint Family (Labiatae)
◑ ⊕ Υ ⋔ F ○ H1
– *melissophyllum* · Bastard Balm
A beautiful wild plant for the shade, grows to 45 cm (18 in) with white and rose-purple flowers in

July/August. Is not as popular as it deserves to be. Likes chalk and warm soil. O: western, southern and central Europe to the Ukraine. A: woodruff, small ferns and grasses.

Menyanthes, see Water Plants p. 70

Mertensia · Borage Family (Boraginaceae)
○ to ◑ ≃ △ □ Υ ⋔ H1
(Listed in order of flowering)
– *virginica* · Virginian Cowslip
Refined and unusual pale blue. Blooms in hundreds of thousands in the fields and woods of its native North America. A spring flower. Dies down completely after flowering and spends three-quarters of its life underground. Should be planted before leafing. 45 to 60 cm (18 to 24 in), early April. A: beautiful with similar spring plants—pale-yellow, black flecked prophet flowers, grasses, yellow primroses, white *Fritillaria meleagris*.

– *primuloides*
A small plant which produces roughish, creeping leaves and clear blue flowers. Suitable for the early spring bed, beds with partial shade and rock gardens.

Must have light, humus-rich soil. 30 to 45 cm (12 to 18 in), April to May.
Stronger than *M. echioides*, although less attractive. A: beautiful with small barrenworts, *Waldsteinia*, ferns.

Meum · Carrot Family (Umbelliferae)
○ to ◑ ≃ Υ ⟐ ⋔ F H1
– *athamanticum* · Baldmoney or Spignel
White umbels of flowers from green, feathery leaves in May/June. One plant will be sufficient for the rock garden. O: mountain to sub-alpine, woodrows throughout Europe up to 2000 m (6000 ft)—often with *Ranunculus aconitifolius*, *Arnica*, *Achillea millefolium*, *Geranium*. A: *Campanula persicifolia*. Also suitable for scattering over large areas of lawn.

Micromeria · Mint Family (Labiatae)
○○ to ○○○ ⊕ △ ∥ ⟐ H2
croatica
An unpretentious, pink-flowered, shrubby plant. Likes sunny position between limestone rocks. Self-seeding but not invasive. Just under 15 cm (6in), semi-woody. O: Balkans. A: *Campanula carpatica* ssp. *turbinata*, *Sempervivum* hybrids.

Minuartia · Sandwort · Pink Family (Caryophyllaceae)
○ to ☀ △ ∥ □ ⋙ ⟐ ⋔ ✴ H1
– *graminifolia* · Apennine Sandwort
This sandwort is a true climber! Planted at the base of an upright wall it will climb right up it forming a flat, mossy covering that is quite unlike any other plant. Of course it takes time to develop.

Seldom flowers but is nevertheless extremely attractive. O: northern Italy, southern Tirol to Balkans, alpine and sub-alpine. A: dwarf bell-flowers, rock roses.

– *laricifolia*
Forms loose mats of leaves and umbels of white flowers in late summer. With only a brief intermission flowers for months on end over a very long lifespan. One of the most serviceable plants in the rock garden and deservedly popular. Goes well with dwarf bell-flowers but the flowers will outlast any others planted with it. In the wild, almost always on granite. Alpine to sub-alpine. June to September. Native to Pyrenees, Apennines, Alps and into Romania. A: speedwell, *Sedum, Campanula, Dianthus cruentus, Silene schafta, Sempervivum.*

Mitella · Mitrewort · Saxifrage Family (Saxifragaceae)
◗ to ● ≃ ⋙ Y Hi
– *diphylla*
Produces excellent ground-cover for semi-shady, not too dry positions, produces runners to cover large areas quickly. 15 cm (6 in). Insignificant white flowers in April. O: North America.

Moehringia · Sandwort · Pink Family (Caryophyllaceae)
☀ to ◗ ⊕ ≃ △ ‖ ⟳ Hi
– *muscosa* · Mossy Sandwort
Loose, mossy foliage and very small, white, starry flowers. An attractive, long-flowering plant from end May to September. No other plant has leaves of a more vivid green. Plant over wide areas out of full sun, or better still in shade in a position free from roots of shrubs. Will set off to the full whatever you plant with it, such as dwarf bell-flowers, *Primula marginata, Ramonda myconi*, quick-growing saxifrages. O: Alps and foothills, mountain to alpine up to 2300 m (7000 ft). Damp spruce forests and en masse in southern Alps in semi-shady clearings in beech and chestnut woods, also found in similar woods throughout mountains of western Europe and into Transylvania.

Molinia, see Grasses p. 000

Morina · Teasel Family (Dipsaceae)
○○ to ○○○ ⊕ △ ⊥ ⋊ ○ ⟳ Hi
– *longifolia*
A long-living plant which is really not difficult to grow. Foliage reminiscent of thistle, attractive whorled flowers initially white turning to pink. Almost 100 cm (3 ft 3 in), July/August. Grows almost anywhere except exposed position, so light winter protection necessary. O: Himalayas. A: blue-stemmed grasses, plant in carpets of Sedum.

Myosotis · Forget-Me-Not · Borage Family (Boraginaceae)
○ Y ⋊ Hi
– *alpestris* · Alpine Forget-Me-Not
Useful plant for shady rock or wild gardens with beautiful azure-blue flowers. Usually a fairly short-lived perennial. O: Europe, Asia, North America; sub-alpine to alpine.
– – *rupicola*
Forms with congested foliage and brighter blue flowers are often available under this name.
– *australis*
Short-lived perennial 20 to 30 cm (8 to 12 in), leaves often a coppery colour contrasting with the white flowers. O: New Zealand, Tasmania. Forms from Australia have blue flowers.
– *scorpioides* 'Semperflorens'
≅
The perennial forget-me-not of azure-blue. Will be kept under control and grow quite tall if planted amongst tall grasses, particularly sedges, where it can reach 70 cm (2 ft 4 in). In poor soil flowers will be short-lived, especially in mature plants, 20 to 30 cm (8 to 12 in), from May intermittently throughout the summer. O: Many variations on this forget-me-not can be found in both northern and southern tem- perate zones, with our native variety not being exclusive to Europe. Found everywhere in marshland and ditches, damp fields and mountains up to 2000 m (6000 ft). A: water and marsh grasses, also marsh ferns. Requires frequent cutting back.

Nepeta · Catmint · Mint Family (Labiatae)
○○ to ○○○ ▭ ○ ᙡ ⟳ F Hi.
– × *faassenii* (*N. mussinii* × *N. nepetella*)
Flowers from end of May to end of September, would be an irreplaceable rock-garden plant if it only flowered a quarter as long. A: this greyish-leaved, long-flowerer can be planted with a whole series of other plants; best with pale yellow cinquefoil. In maturity individual plants cover up to half a square metre. Extremely attractive to butterflies!
– × *faassenii* 'Six Hills Giant'
Tall, free flowering form to 90 cm 3 ft. Clear blue flowers into September.

Nuphar, see Water plants p. 70

Nymphaea, see Water Plants p. 70

Oenothera · Evening Primrose · Willow-Herb Family (Onagraceae)
○○ to ○○○ ▭ 🝫 Hi
The evening primroses include four wonderful, long-flowering perennials which seem to have been specially created for the garden but have yet to gain general recognition.
All *Oenothera* originate in the dry grassland and hills of North America and are extremely undemanding. Only *O. caespitosa* prefers fairly rich soil with perhaps a sprinkling of partially buried stones. Beautiful in shrubberies with blue-green grasses.
– *caespitosa*
The most fragrant of the evening primroses. Beautiful planted between small grasses, dwarf junipers, dwarf gorse or *Yucca*. Flowers open during the day to be at their best in the evening and

night. Unfortunately not very long-lived and best in warm positions. White, 30 cm (12 in), June/July.

– *fruticosa* 'Yellow River'
The queen of the evening primroses with gleaming pale yellow flowers. Unbelievably long-flowering from June/August—an incomparable garden flower. New flowers in September. 15 to 30 cm (6 to 12 in). I tend to think this cultivar a cross between *O. missouriensis* and *O. tetragona*.

– *missouriensis*
The longest-flowering of all the evening primroses with the largest blooms. Ten-year-old plants hanging down a wall can sometimes have up to thirty or forty large flowers open at the same time. Lemon-yellow. 15 to 30 cm (6 to 12 in), June to October. O: south-west United States. A: This long-flowerer of the rock garden needs several partners to set it off to the full throughout its long flowering time. Try *Genista tinctoria* 'Plena', double-flowered broom, Chinese balloon-flowers, *Gentiana cruciata* and *G. septemfida*, *Campanula carpatica*, garden varieties of *Veronica spicata*.

– *tetragona*
From brown rosettes of leaves rise brown and reddish stems supporting panicles of yellow flowers interspersed with reddish-brown buds. 15 to 45 cm (6 to 18 in), depending on soil. Mid-June to mid-July. A very striking plant. O: southeast United States north of Florida. A: *Campanula*

persicifolia, Delphinium grandiflorum, Geum coccineum 'Borisii', *Helianthemum*.
– – 'Fireworks'
The golden yellow flowers open from June/August from bright red buds, 45 cm (18 in).

Omphalodes · Navel-Wort · Borage Family (Boraginaceae)
◐ to ● ≃ □ ᴍᴧᴧ Υ H1
– *verna* · Blue-Eyed Mary
An early spring flower of shimmering sky-blue, native to the southern and eastern Alps. Blue-eyed Mary looks magical flowering beneath bleeding hearts *(Dicentra spectabilis)*. When well spaced the plant will put out long shoots which take root, but if closely planted their ability to spread is somewhat restricted. Happiest in slight shade; in full sun it will lie dormant for many weeks before suddenly beginning to grow, providing the soil is not over-dry. A beautiful ground cover plant with light green foliage. O: southern Alps, also Romania and into Portugal. In the wild this plant prefers mountain forests providing slight shade. Known as 'Reine Marie' in the Paris region after Queen Marie Antoinette who missed the plant in France and

had it brought from her native Austria. A: *Epimedium, Pulmonaria angustifolia*, ferns, *Luzula* and *Carex* types, *Dicentra spectabilis*, both white and pink.
– – 'Alba'
White form of blue-eyed Mary —an extremely charming variety but a slow-growing one.
A: as above.
– – 'Grandiflora'

Larger flowers combine with the good qualities of the species.

Onosma · Golden Drop · Borage Family (Boraginaceae)
○ to ○○ ⊕ △ ‖ 🝙 ♂ H1
– *stellulata*
The most garden-worthy of the golden drops, which like poor, dry soil and full sun. Spreads by self-seeding, a welcome feature of this plant. 15 to 30 cm (6 to 12 in), May/July, lemon-yellow. O: south-east Europe, Caucasus, Armenia, Asia Minor and even Himalayas, mountain to sub-alpine. A: *Veronica austriaca* ssp. *teucrium* 'Shirley Blue'.

Opuntia · Prickly Pear · Cactus Family (Cactaceae)
○○ to ○○○ △ ‖ 🝙 ✳ H1 (dry winters)
In America, the great cactus-centre of the world, they grow high up into the mountains, venture quite far north and even overgrow railway embankments.
What better place could there be in the garden for these plants other than near or framed by rocks? Since these small, comparatively recent garden plants respond well to a winter covering of spruce twigs, there is no reason why these succulents should be restricted to the rock garden and banned from the remainder of the garden. All they require are the right neighbours and the necessary sun and dryness together with the good drainage of a low hill.
A: *Bouteloua gracilis, Helictotrichon sempervirens, Festuca cinerea, Acantholimon glumaceum, Chrysanthemum haradjanii, Sedum* types, *Sempervivum* types and hybrids, *Yucca filamentosa*.
– *engelmannii* · Prickly-Pear Cactus
In Europe grows flat or rising slightly from the ground; large, pale-green, rounded joints; spines whitish with brownish bases, up to 5 cm (2 in) long. Large, yellow flowers. O: southern United States (as far as New Mexico).

– – var. *discata*
Similar size but with bluish-green joints and black spines and large yellow flowers.

– *fragilis*
Stocky plant with dark-green, cylindrical, heavily-spined, yellowish-brown joints, 3 to 5 cm (1½ to 2 in) long. Flowers yellow to pale reddish-yellow inside, greenish-yellow outside. Often produces few flowers but very hardy. O: British Columbia. Oregon to Arizona and western Texas.

– – var. *brachyarthra*
A variety with thick turf-like growth. Stronger spines than the species. Pale yellow flowers. Resistant to wet. O: Colorado.

– *humifusa*
Creeping growth with rounded or oval joints. Usually without spines. Sulphur-yellow flowers with reddish centre. Very hardy! O: south-east United States.

– *phaeacantha*
Low growing, but can form small bushes in right position. Oval joints up to 15 cm (6 in) long. Thick spines up to 6 cm (2½ in) long. A hardy species that comes in a variety of shapes. In winter edges of joints turn reddish or purple (the main distinguishing feature of this species). Large, pale-yellow flowers. O: Texas to Arizona, New Mexico.

– – var. *albispina*
Garden variety with white-tipped spines. Pale yellow flowers which turn to brown.

– – var. *camanchica*
Strong-growing, low to horizontal form with large, rounded, pale green joints, up to 17 cm (7 in). Reddish-brown spines up to 6 cm (2½ in) long, with lighter tips. Pale green flowers with brownish centre. O: South Colorado.

– – var. *longispina*
Beautiful variety with long spines up to 7 cm (3 in) and large, striking joints. Cup-shaped, pale-yellow flowers which fade to brown.

– – var. *salmonea*

Another garden variety with quite large, oval joints. Less densely spined than the type. Interesting chamois-brown flowers turning to salmon.

– *rafinesquei*
The type name is a subject of some argument, but it seems advisable to stick to the name *O. rafinesquei* for the time being. Very hardy plant which will tolerate temperatures as low as −30°C. One of the best flowerers in the garden and recommended for beginners.
Joints up to 10 cm (4 in) long and 6 cm (2½ in) wide with topmost joints spined. White spines with darker tips. Sulphur-yellow flowers which darken as they wilt. O: sandy soil of Lake Erie, Kentucky, Missouri to Texas and west to Colorado.

– *rhodantha*
Forms groups of joints of around 15 cm (6 in), rather horizontal in growth. The tuberous joints are oval, dark-green and with the tops covered with brown spines. Usually red or pink flowers. O: west Colorado to California.

– – var. *pallida*
Variety with pale yellow flowers.

– – var. *schumanniana*
Erect growth with medium-sized joints. Beautiful deep carmine-red flowers.

– *utahensis*
Introduced by C. A. Purpus. Again species name under debate. Low, wide-spread growth, sometimes bush-like. The small joints are inverted ovals or elipses, quite thick, almost free of tubercles with spines on upper portions. Large, impressive, carmine-red flowers. Hardy to frost but susceptible to wet.

Origanum · Marjoram · Mint Family (Labiatae)
○○ to ○○○ △ ⊕ □ ○ 〖〗 F H2.

– *amanum.*
Low growing to 15 cm (6 in) with the small pinky flowers within large red purple bracts. Very striking. O: Turkey.

– *rotundifolium*

Quite a newcomer to the garden making wide clumps to 20 cm (8 in) tall. The flowers are tiny and pink but are carried within large, striking apple green bracts. A real charmer. O: N. Turkey.

– *vulgare* 'Compactum' · Wild Marjoram
The most useful of all the marjorams, as the whole insect kingdom would agree. The plant grows to 30 cm (12 in) in height and width with pale to pinky lilac flowers in a thick carpet of dark leaves. A plant that likes a dry, light position amongst heather or in the shrubbery with blue-green Sedum and grasses. It has been difficult to photograph this plant for on a sunny day they are surrounded continuously by so much insect life. The scent of these dwarf bushes which survive for tens of years is similar to thyme and mint. Start with only one of these plants, but you will soon be tempted to use more, to make entire borders or cover wide areas. O: Britain to the Himalayas, North Africa to Scandinavia where it lives with a wide variety of different plants.

Orontium, see Water Plants p. 70

Orostachys · Stonecrop Family (Crassulaceae)
○ to ☀ △ ‖ ⊟ ♡ ⚕ H1

– *spinosus* (syn. Umbilicus spinosus)
Forms beautiful grey-green, stemless rosettes of leaves, 10 cm (4 in) across. Flowers only after several years with pale yellow flowers in a narrow spike. Dies off after flowering but the many side shoots already produced live on. Likes shady, well-drained position. O: Siberia, Mongolia.

Oxalis · Wood Sorrel · Wood-Sorrel Family (Oxalidaceae)
◐ to ● ⊖ □ ᠕ ⅄ ♡

– *acetosella* · Wood Sorrel
H1
A charming, 15 cm (6 in) shade plant with pink-white flowers on

10 cm (4 in) stems in April. Gives excellent service in a shady rock garden, early spring garden, wild garden or parkland. Likes acid soil with leaf compost. O: woods of Europe, Asia and central United States. A: plant beneath ferns, strong, shade-loving bulbs and rhododendrons.
– *adenophylla*
H2
Beautiful, tuberous plant with silver-grey foliage. The whole plant grows to only 3 cm (1/4 in)! Attractive veined, pale-mauve flowers, averaging about 2.5 cm (1 in) in diameter. Likes sunny position and must have porous soil. Covering with gravel advisable. May/July, dying down in August. O: Cordillera of Chile and western Argentina (sub-alpine to alpine).

Pachysandra procumbens and *P. terminalis*, see Dwarf Deciduous Shrubs p. 123

Paeonia · Peony · Peony Family (Paeoniaceae)
○○ to ◑ ≃ △ ⊥ ✕ ♁ H1
The peonies listed here, almost all of which are native to alpine or sub-alpine regions, are all plants of unpretentious charm which can find no more appropriate home than the rock garden. But they must be used with care in a selected position, possibly in a corner position amongst shrubs or used individually in a more prominent position flanked by large rocks.
– *mascula* (syn. *P. corallina*)
A good species for the garden grown in monasteries as far back as the Middle Ages. Downy undersides to leaves. Purple, 20 to 60 cm (8 to 24 in), April/May. O: light situations in Mediterranean deciduous forests.
– – *arietina* 'Northern Glory'
Pinky-red flowers and attractive, deeply cut foliage.
– *mlokosewitschii* 'Molly the Witch'
Beautiful but slow-growing wild peony from central Caucasus. Distinctive bluish-green leaves.

Pale yellow flower cups in May, 30 cm (12 in).
– *obovata* 'Alba'
Striking in spring with its coppery young leaves and even more so when its large white globular flowers open. One of the best peonies. O: China, Japan, Sakhalin.
– *officinalis* ssp. *humilis*
A true dwarf peony at only 50 cm (18 in)! The leaves are smooth on the surface and hairy underneath. Attractive, red, cup-shaped flowers, up to 13 cm (5 in) across. O: south-west France, Spain.
– *peregrina* (syn. *P. lobata*)
A beautifully proportioned dwarf peony, 30 to 45 cm (12 to 18 in), with deep red flowers which will flower profusely in the same rock garden position with no attention for thirty years. O: Balkan peninsula, southern Alps up to 1700 m (5000 ft). Grows wild with *Campanula pyramidalis* and *Asphodelus*. A: dwarf *Deutzia*.
– *tenuifolia* · Narrow-leaved Peony
The smallest of all the peonies and just right for the rock garden. Attractive and elegant leaves divided into numerous narrow segments. 20 to 30 cm (8 to 12 in), glowing red, beginning May. O: south-east Europe, Asia Minor. A: *Polemonium* × *richardsonii* cultivars.
– – 'Plena'
Long-established cultivar with

dark red, rather plump, double flowers. Usually easier to get hold of than the more attractive species. Not suitable for wild gardens!
– *veitchii*
Delicate light green leaves make a mound to 45 cm (18 in). The single, rose-purple to pink flowers are carried freely in May. O: China.

Papaver · Poppy · Poppy Family (Papaveraceae)
○ to ○○ ⊕ ≃ △ ‖ 🛢 ○ H1
– *burseri* · Alpine Poppy
White with yellow centre. O: Austrian Alps.
– *kerneri*
Usually gold, but occasionally orange. O: eastern Alps, Transylvania. The flowering time of these dwarf poppies with their fine, feathery foliage is June/August. They usually grow to 20 to 25 cm (8 to 10 in). A short garden life indicates wrong handling. They like porous, gravelly, not over-dry soil and it is advisable to cover the planting hole with gravel. Reproduction is usually by self-seeding. Grow wild with *Minuartia verna*, *Linaria alpina*, *Luzula*, dwarf willow, *Ranunculus glacialis* on screes and moraines. A: *Minuartia laricifolia*, dwarf bell-flowers, dwarf pinks. Especially beautiful in troughs.
– *nudicaule* · Iceland Poppy
A plant whose history goes back two thousand years. Found in

Oxalis acetosella

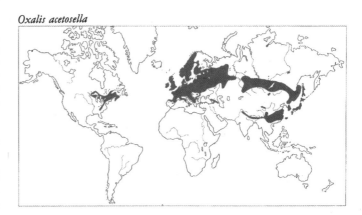

three colours—white, yellow and deep orange. Larger leaves than the preceding species. Long-flowering but may become invasive through self-seeding, so don't be afraid to pull out weaker seedlings or to cut off the seed pods before the seeds ripen. 30 to 45 cm (12 to 18 in), end May/October. O: northern temperate zones.

– *rhaeticum* (syn. P.pyrenaicum ssp. rhaeticum) · Rhaetian Poppy
This species has golden flowers which turn orange as they fade. Similar in appearance to *P. kerneri* but with greener, downy leaves. Under 30 cm (12 in), May/July.

Paradisea · St Bruno's Lily · Lily Family (Liliaceae)
○ to ○○ ≃ ✂ ♧ H1
– *liliastrum* · St Bruno's Lily
This noble-looking, hardy, long-lived plant likes deep, nutrient-rich but light soil and some moisture. 60 to 75 cm (24 to 30 in) stems support large, white, funnel-shaped flowers similar to small Madonna Lilies. May/June. O: found in woodrows and clearings and hedgerows, sub-alpine to alpine, western and eastern Alps, Veneto, northern Pyrenees, northern Apennines. Isolated groups in Spanish and Portuguese mountains. Flowers pollinated by gamma moth. A: dwarf delphiniums, *Lilium martagon, Lilium croceum*, wild geraniums, masterworts, all of which grow together in the wild, with the exception of the delphiniums.

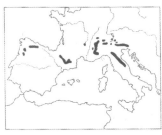

– – 'Gigantea'
Even larger-flowered than the preceding form, but not widely grown since it produces no seed.
– – 'Major'
Up to 90 cm (2 ft 8 in), larger flowers. Propagated easily by seed.

Paronychia · Pink Family (Carophyllaceae)
○○ to ○○○ △ □ ⋙ ♯ H1–2
– *kapela* ssp. *serpyllifolia*
A flat, grey-green carpeter that flowers June to August. Undemanding and hardy groundcover for both large and small areas of the rock or wild garden. Not even thymes compare with it for value, reliability and trustworthiness, for, despite their better colour, they have the disadvantage of spreading too energetically. It is nothing for a *Paronychia* to survive twenty or thirty years in the most difficult and driest spot, even amidst a honeycomb of roots. It will not, however, stand overhead shade from nearby plants and shrubs. Insignificant silver-white flowers.
This carpeter is excellent under dwarf bulbs, which should be planted slightly deeper than usual to keep the roots separate. Also effective with dwarf conifers and clumps of Sempervivum. O: Spain, Maritime Alps.

Patrinia · Valerian Family (Valerianaceae)
○ to ◑ ≃ △ ⅄ ♧ H1
– *triloba*
At first glance its foliage gives it the appearance of a cultivated *Anemone ranunculoides*, flowering for a second time in summer: golden-yellow fragrant flowers in heads. 15 cm (6 in) or more, May/June. O: Japan.

Pennisetum, see Grasses p. 107

Penstemon · Figwort Family (Scrophulariaceae)
○ to ○○ ⊖ ≃ △ ‖ □ 🛢 ○ ♯
– *caespitosus*
H1
A cushion-forming Penstemon, only 10 cm (4 in) tall, with narrow, lanceolate, smooth leaves. Propagated by overground runners. Beautiful turquoise-blue flowers. Dislikes chalky soil. June/July. O: western United States.
– – 'Alba'
White flowers.
– *fruticosus*
H1
Sub-shrubby penstemon to 40 cm (28 in) with lavender-purple flowers. O: Oregon to British Columbia.
– *pinifolius*
H2
With its evergreen needles it looks like a miniature conifer. All shoots are erect, woody and about 15 cm (6 in) tall. Highly attractive bright, light scarlet, labiate flowers, and especially useful as it blooms July/August. O: south Arizona, New Mexico.
– *rupicola*
H2
Low, mat-forming, 10 cm (4 in) high, rather twiggy with age but splendid with its carmine-red flowers. O: Washington State to California.
– *scouleri*
H2
Another woody plant but taller at 30 cm (12 in). The linear, lanceolate leaves are usually deeply serrated. In May/June the whole plant is covered with luminous lilac flowers. Dislikes chalky soil. O: United States.

Petasites · Butterbur · Daisy Family (Compositae)
○ to ◑ ☽ ⋙ ♧ F H2
– *fragrans* · Winter Heliotrope or Sweet Coltsfoot
The winter heliotrope, which is more attractive in scent than in appearance, should be planted only amidst the shrubbery where it is bounded by paths or walls. It is best in damp, shady situations or on the damp banks of a stream. If planted in the protection of rocks it will bloom earliest on a southern aspect with summer shade. Grows to 20 to 30 cm (8 to 12 in), December/

March. Insignificant appearance but beautiful scent. In too dry a situation it will survive but will be flowerless. O: North Africa. A word of warning: this plant spreads continuously by means of underground runners so it is highly advisable to restrain it by planting from the outset in an underground concrete pipe and keeping a careful eye on it.

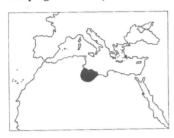

Petrorhagia · Pink Family (Caryophyllaceae)
○ to ○○○ ⊕ ‖ ✕ 🗍 HI
- *saxifraga* (syn. Tunica saxifraga, Kohlrauschia saxifraga) · Tunic Flower
Long-flowering rock-garden plant with delicate rose flowers from July to September. Chalky soil. O: rocky cliffs and meadows, mountain to sub-alpine where it grows with rock roses, thyme, burnet saxifrage, globularia. Throughout southern Europe, into West Germany and French Jura, also in south-east Europe, Asia Minor, Armenia, northern Iran, Caucasus. Can live up to fifty years. A: *Campanula portenschlagiana*, late speedwell, blue grasses.

- – 'Rosette'
A perfumed, double form of this small universal plant, a good pink colour, recommended for its charm and long flowering time.

Phlox · Phlox Family (Polemoniaceae)

Rock-garden Phlox by Seasons

1. Carpeting Phlox

○ ⊖ ≃ △ ▢ ⋙ 🗍 ⚏ HI
O. of all dwarf species: North America. Mid-April to end May, 10 to 15 cm (4 to 6 in) tall. Cut back occasionally when getting straggly.

Phlox subulata 'Atropurpurea'
Deep rose Moss Phlox.
- – 'G. F. Wilson'
Pale lavender flowers.
- – 'Oakington Blue'
Sky-blue flowers.
- – 'Red Wings'
Dark crimson with deeper centre.
- – 'Rosea'
Pale rose, compact foliage.
- – 'Temiskaming'
Brilliant magenta-red.
- – 'Vivid'
Warm salmon-pink. Less robust than some and seldom available.
- – 'White Delight'
Best of the white cultivars with lighter green foliage.

Phlox-douglasii hybrids
As *Phlox subulata* begins to fade, these charming, compact evergreen plants are just coming into their own. Only 5 cm (2 in) tall, evergreen and much slower-growing than *P. subulata*. April/May. O. of type: north-west America.
- – 'Daniel's Cushion'
Large, freely born rose-pink flowers.
- – 'Red Admiral'
Rounded, crimson flowers.
- – 'Rosea'
Wide spreading plant with pink flowers.

2. Early semi-dwarf Phlox

○ to ◐ ⊖ ≃ △

Phlox amoena
This phlox with its narrow, lanceolate leaves grows to only 30 cm (12 in). Heads of carmine-red flowers. Prefers slightly acid soil and also tolerates semi-shade. April/May. O: south-east United States.
- – 'Variegata'
Brightly variegated foliage.
- *divaricata* (syn. P. canadensis) · Wild Sweet William
The glorious, 15 cm (6 in), species has pale mauve flowers from end April to mid-May. Also tolerates slight shade. O: eastern North America. The wild type *P. divaricata* var. *laphamii* is less successful in a hot, dry site, but in shade its pale blue flowers are most attractive.

3. Early-Summer Phlox

for any type of rock garden. June/August.
○ to ◐ ≃ △

× *arendsii*
Name for a group of hybrids between *P. paniculata* and *P. divaricata*.
- – 'Hilda'
White with mauve sheen, pink eye, 40 to 60 cm (16 to 24 in).
- – 'Susanne'
White with large red centre, 40 to 50 cm (16 to 20 in).
These plants will flower repeatedly after cutting back, and look good with wild sage, also early and late speedwell.

Phuopsis stylosa (syn. Crucianella stylosa) · Crosswort · Madder Family (Rubiaceae)
○○ to ◐ △ ⋙ F HI
10 to 20 cm (4 to 8 in) high plant with long-lasting pink flowers. Its only disadvantage is that it spreads and should be planted with sturdy neighbours that will not be over-run by it.
Long-lasting flowers in shade or in dry position is a valuable asset. May/July. O: northern Iran.

Its scent is musky and far pervading. Some people find it pleasant, others describe it as foxy!

Phyllitis, see Ferns p. 60

Phyteuma · Rampion · Bellflower Family (Campanulaceae)
○ to ◑ ≃ △ ✕ 🖱 ○ H1
– *scheuchzeri* · Horned Rampion
A highly unusual little plant which is extremely hardy. 10–20 cm (4–8 in), May/July, deep blue. O: western to eastern Alps and Transylvania, 200 to 3500 m (600 to 10,000 ft). A: plant quite large areas with other small, neat plants such as *Gypsophila repens*, small pinks and bellflowers. Often found in the wild with *Festuca varia* but you can combine with other small *Festuca* species.

Pimpinella · Burnet Saxifrage · Carrot Family (Umbelliferae)
– *saxifraga* · Burnet Saxifrage
○ to ○○ ⊕ ≃ ○ 🖱 H1
Flowers in umbels are so rare among rock-garden plants that athamanta and burnet saxifrage, particularly the pink type, are very welcome additions. Pale pink, 30 to 60 cm (1 to 2 ft) and above, June/July. O: almost throughout Europe, Asia Minor, Caucasus, Armenia, west Siberia. Rocky, barren meadows, moorland, thickets and streamsides. Subalpine to alpine.

Plagiorhegma · Barberry Family (Berberidaceae)
◑ to ● ⊖ ≌ ♂ H1
– *dubium* (syn. Jeffersonia dubia)
A plant with hepatica-like flowers, usually known as *Jeffersonia dubia*. Reddish-brown leaves are folded flat until they develop in late spring. This sturdy, but delicate-looking, woodland plant was introduced earlier this century from Manchuria. Like most woodland plants it prefers semi-shade. Leaves at first dark brown flushed with metallic purple. Plant in semi-shade. Make sure that they do not dry out when

they are newly planted. When young these plants can be damaged by dryness, but once well-rooted the plant is unbelievably long-lived. I have a group of such plants which are still thriving twelve years after planting under a group of dwarf almonds, where they are completely unaffected by dry weather.

Platycodon · Balloon Flower · Bellflower Family (Campanulaceae)
○ to ◑ ≃ △ H1
– *grandiflorus* 'Snowflake'
White bells.
– – 'Apoyama'
An interesting local form from the Apoy Mountains in Hokkaido, Japan. Grows to only 15 cm (6 in). Violet-blue cups. A real rock-garden balloon flower.
– – 'Mariesii'
This bright blue balloon flower is smaller than the species at around 40 cm (16 in). Flowers end July/August. Pentagonal buds open into bells, rather like clematis. Very old plants form thick, woody nodules. I have had a plant for thirty years which is completely hardy and requires no protection. O: China, Japan, Manchuria. A: tall speedwell, *Oenothera tetragona* varieties, *Scabiosa caucasica* 'Miss Wilmott'.

Pleione bulbocodioides var. *limprichtii* · Orchid Family (Orchidaceae)
☀ ⊖ ≌ △ Y 🖱 H3
Exquisite and lovable dwarf orchids that are unbelievably easy to grow. With the right treatment and a little attention these orchids are surprisingly trouble-free. They like a shady spot where the air is moist and overhead protection from wet to-

gether with fairly coarse, acid soil with plenty of humus. They are best kept dry from the end of October to the beginning of March so some form of winter protection is advisable. They grow from pseudo-bulbs which should be planted deeper than one would in pots. Give them an extra covering of peat in winter. The flowers are rose-coloured and a good size, at least 5 cm (2 in) wide. The lighter lip is fringed and marked on the inside with reddish-brown. One to two flowers on each 8 cm (3 in) stem, which appear before the leaves. April/May. O: from 2000 to 3000 m (6000 to 9000 ft), rock crevices in west China (Szechwan, Sikiang).
– – 'Alba'
A charming white flowered form.

Podophyllum · May Apple · Barberry Family (Berberidaceae)
◑ to ● ⊖ ≌ Y ♂ H1
– *hexandrum* (syn. P. emodi) 'Majus' · Himalayan May Apple
In the centre of a red-marbled umbel of leaves, at first only 15 cm (6 in) high, balances a white-pink anemone flower. Initially the plant gives little indication of its future robustness, with large apples growing on 30 cm (12 in) high clumps of leaves. Every part of the plant, except the fruit, is poisonous, but this is no reason to ban it from the garden. This plant will thrive in the most unpropitious situations. 15 to 30 cm (6 to 12 in), April/May. O: Himalayas.

Polemonium · Jacob's Ladder · Phlox Family (Polemoniaceae)
○ to ◑ ≃ △ ✕ ○ ♂ H1
The *P.* × *jacobaea*, 'Richardsonii' (thought to be a cross between *P. caeruleum* and *P. reptans*) which flower as early as the beginning of May, are among my favourite garden plants. This woodland plant, which will also tolerate full sun, is in full bloom in late April when the small bushes of

blue, pale blue, mauve and white are extremely attractive. They need good moist soil. O: *P. coeruleum* is native to mountain river valleys, slightly shady banks of streams and woodlands throughout the temperate zones of Europe, Asia and North America, east as far as Japan, north as far as Lappland.

– *reptans*
Compact plant with a profusion of pale blue flowers. Around 30 cm (12 in), April/May. O: *P. reptans* is found only in North America in woods of Minnesota, Alaska and Arkansas. A: delightful with *Heuchera* hybrids and mossy saxifrage.

– × *jacobaea* ('Richardsonii')
Fresh, delicate mauve.
– – 'Album'
Pure white.
– – 'Pallidum'
Pale blue.
– – 'Superbum'
Dark mauve.

Polygonatum · Solomon's Seal · Lily Family (Liliaceae)
◐ to ● ≃ ⅄ ♂ ⚯ Hɪ
– × *hybridum*
The common Solomon's seal of gardens to 90 cm (3 ft).
– *commutatum* (syn. P. giganteum)
The largest of the Solomon's seals and the most attractive, but best confined to the wild garden or edges of the rock garden because of its size. Survives longer in a vase with *Trollius* than in the garden. 100 to 120 cm (3 to 4 ft), May/June. O: North America. A: *Trollius*, *Uvularia*, ferns, *Podophyllum*.
– *hookeri* A tiny Solomon's seal, only 10 cm (4 in) high with lilac flowers from May–June. O: Tibet, Sikkim, W. China.

Polygonum ·Bistort, Knotweed · Dock Family (Polygonaceae)
○ to ◐ ≃ △ ⋘ ⊔ ✂ ♂ Hɪ
Only the less rampant bistort species are suitable for the rock garden. Apart from *P. bistorta* the rest are little known, but many have recently been introduced to

cultivation and show promise.
– *affine*
An essential rock-garden plant forming thick foliage which turns red in autumn. Spiky flowers turn from white to deep red as the summer progresses. 20 cm (8 in) tall, June/late autumn. O: Himalayas. A: carpeting speedwell, sprinkled amongst grasses.
– – 'Darjeeling Red'
Has deep pink spikes.
– – 'Dimity'
A dainty form with slender white spikes aging pink. Only 15 cm (6 in).

– *amplexicaule* 'Inverleith'
A cultivar with red flowers for months on end from June/October. Only 50 cm (20 in) high. The species is less suitable reaching 120 cm (4 ft) or more. O: Himalayas. A: ideal in front of and between shrubs since it tolerates roots.
– *bistorta* 'Superbum' · Bistort, Snake-Root
Mature plants look excellent with grasses bordering the rock garden or in a wild garden. Likes moisture-retentive soil and sunny position. Although the plant does not spread it should not be planted alongside over-delicate plants. 30 to 45 cm (12 to

18 in), June/July. O: mountain meadows of moderate northern zones. A: *Iris sibirica*, *Trollius* hybrids.

Polystichum, see Ferns p. 108

Polypodium, see Ferns p. 108

Potentilla · Cinquefoil · Rose Family (Rosaceae)
○ ≃ △ ‖ ✂ ♂ Hɪ
This family provides highly varied garden plants: early-flowering, yellow cushion and mat-forming species; 30 cm (1 ft) high with bright, velvety flowers; multi-coloured long-flowering plants and delicate alpines. Flowering of the various species extends from mid-April to well into August. All, with the sole exception of *P. atrosanguinea* 'Gibsons Scarlet', tolerate drought, and even the large-flowered garden hybrids seem unaffected by dryness. All are long-flowering and most, with the exception of the small, yellow, spring and early summer cinquefoils, will flower a second time. They fill the garden from spring to autumn with both delicate and deep, glowing colour. Only by considering the variety of the whole family can one begin to understand these charming little plants and provide them with the right neighbours. Once again I am not listing the types alphabetically but by flowering time.

Potentilla tabernaemontani neumanniana (syn. P. verna) · Spring Cinquefoil
Flat carpeter with golden-yellow flowers from April. The whole plant gives a grey-green effect and grows in the wild in dry meadows and dry coniferous woods. O: Europe.
– – 'Nana'
An unbeatable, long-flowering carpeter for dry, sunny positions. Only 5 cm (2 in), golden-yellow, April/August. Leaves have spicy perfume. A: ideal with blue *Fes-*

tuca, *Sempervivum, Sedum* and dwarf bellflowers.

- *cinerea* (syn. P. arenaria) · Grey Cinquefoil
Forms flat cushions of thick, bright yellow flowers as early as April. 8 cm (3 in). An unrecognised treasure! O: Western Alps to northern fringes of southern Alps. A: *Viola odorata, Iberis saxatilis, Sedum album* 'Murale', *Veronica armena*.
- *aurea* ssp. *chrysocraspeda ternata* (syn. P. chrysocraspeda)
Golden-yellow flowers slightly earlier than *P. aurea*. The deep green leaves are only trifoliate. 8 cm (3 in). O: mountains of south-east Europe.
- *aurea* · Golden Cinquefoil
A charming golden-flowered cinquefoil which grows to 8 cm (3 in). Top of leaves smooth and green with underside hairy and silvery. Likes slightly acid soil with plenty of humus and not too dry. May/June. O: subalpine to alpine between 3 000 and 5 000 m (9 000 to 15,000 ft). A: *Geum coccineum* 'Borisii', small blue grasses, brown-leaved herbaceous plants.

- - 'Plena'
Heightens the effect of the type plant considerably with its unbelievable masses of double golden flowers. A favourite with both gardeners and photographers. May/June.
- *pyrenaica* · Pyrenean Cinquefoil
Irreplaceable plant for June/July when it takes over from *P. aurea* and *P. ternata*. 25 cm (10 in). End June/July. Golden-yellow. O: Pyrenees. A: *Campanula portenschlagiana* and *C. carpatica, Polemonium* × *richardsonii*.
- *fragiformis*
The yellow flowers form an arabesque. Splendid little plant whose charm lies in the silvery, downy shoots, the foliage and the large flower cups. Mid-June/July, 15 cm (6 in). O: Asia, Altai, Alaska.
- *argentea* var. *calabra* · Hoary Cinquefoil
15 cm (6 in) plant with pale yellow flowers, has silver, strawberry-like leaves. The Calabrian variety grows to only half the height of the type species.
- *recta* 'Warrenii' · Sulphur Cinquefoil
Compact plant which grows to 30 to 45 cm (12 to 18 in) and 30 cm (12 in) diameter. Much longer-flowering than all other yellow cinquefoils. Takes over from the Pyrenean Cinquefoil from June to September. Advisable to cut off dead flowers to prolong flowering. O of type: Europe, Caucasus, Siberia.
- *atrosanguinea*
15 to 30 cm (6 to 12 in) and taller with dark red flowers. Flowers in July, earlier than the hybrids listed below. O: Himalayas. A: *Veronica gentianoides* and balloon flowers.
- - 'Gibsons Scarlet'
A beautiful scarlet plant which forms small bushes. A star amongst the summer rock-garden plants. July/August.
- *nepalensis*
Most people would not imagine this plant with its strawberry-like leaves to be a true cinquefoil. Grows up to 45 cm (18 in), salmon-pink with darker base and veining on reddish stems. The following varieties increase the colour range. O: W.-Himalayas.
- - 'Roxana'
30 to 45 cm (12 to 18 in), golden-brown, spreading stems, irrepressibly long-flowering. Very distinctive colouring. A: small blue and yellow herbaceous plants.
- - 'Fireflame'
A hybrid with deep red flowers which are borne above silvery foliage. Three plants at 15 cm (6 in) intervals, surrounded by variegated grasses (*Molinia caerulea* 'Variegata') are delightful when the flowers appear above the grass. Prune after flowering!
- - 'Miss Willmott'
This beautiful pink potentilla has been long cultivated. The single flowers are borne on 30 cm (1 ft) high plants. July/August.
At this point I should warn against *Potentilla reptans*, an extremely rampant plant which can take over whole sections of the rock garden. Many rock-garden books make the mistake of recommending the double variety for sandy inclines. But even this garden variety threatens the whole area around it.

Primula · Primrose · Primrose Family (Primulaceae)
Primroses are delightful in the early spring garden or the semi-shady spring or summer rock garden. There are species suitable for both natural or formal settings. In moist soil they tolerate full, though not strong, sun. Primroses embody the special feeling of spring for everyone and I am glad that an increasing number of ever more beautiful primroses are adding to their effect. Anyone familiar with the enormous variety of primroses throughout the world reels at the thought of their great riches. Next to the crocus we have here the most delicate, and charming of all spring flowers. Without them spring is no longer spring. The family includes popular, rather old-fashioned, garden flowers as well as contrasting strange new forms.

The king of the alpine plant specialists, the writer and gardener Farrer, juggled with thousands of primrose species, subspecies and hybrids in his book, even without including the garden cultivars. There are tiny dwarf primroses as well as giants more than a metre (3 ft) tall; plants that tower like pagodas or give beautiful perfumes. Many have huge crowns of leaves, which when young are eaten by the people of the Himalayas.

At one time garden primroses flowered for four weeks of the year only—now they flower from February to the end of July in an endless stream. The feeling of restlessness of spring which, like youth itself, remains a time of laughter and impulse, now links up with the spring flowers of autumn as spring is reborn in September/October with autumn crocus, bright primroses, scented violets, anemones and blue gentians.

Primulas grow wild in moderately high mountain areas, on cliffs, screes, damp places around springs, moorlands, meadows, lowland meadows and light mountain woods. Endless varieties of primroses are found from Europe to China, and more are wild in N. America. The primrose brings us wonderfully close to its distant homelands.

Just as the mountain landscape is bejewelled by alpine plants for the well-travelled naturalist, so our knowledge of native mountain flowers forms links with the mountain homelands of those plants we come to handle. The scent of many mountain primroses brings a whiff of an eternal freshness and primordiality, fulfilling the words of Goethe, "One should begin a new epoch of one's life with every new day".

Old-fashioned perfumes mingle with the scent of Parisian perfumes like that of the pendent bells of *Primula sikkimensis* which grows at 4 000 m (13,000 ft). The scents of fruit and yellow roses are also echoed in these spring flowers. Indescribably delicate perfumes of the Far East are brought to our western gardens by Siebold's Japanese primrose and its cultivars; our first meeting with them remains fixed in the memory.

It is a long way from such considerations to thoughts of practical garden uses. To make the huge primrose family more accessible and to guide the gardener through this sea of plants I have separated both wild and garden forms into seven flowering periods. With this guide to hand you can be confident of entering uncharted areas of the primrose kingdom with the passing years. At present we are only at the beginning of the age of discovery of the garden primrose.

I have first divided the genus into six groups depending on their basic form.

Cushion primroses
Ball primroses
Umbelliferous primroses
Bell primroses
Candelabra primroses
Spike primroses

These form subdivisions of the flowering-time groups.

1. Flowering time: early March to April
2. Flowering time: second half March to end April
3. Flowering time: second half April into May
4. Flowering time: mid-May to June
5. Flowering time: June to July
6. Flowering time: July
7. Flowering time: July to August

1. Flowering time: early March to April

Cushion primroses
☀ to ◑ ⊕ ≃ ⅄ ✕ ○ F H1
Primula vulgaris (syn. P. acaulis) ·
Primrose
◑ to ● ≃ ⅄
One of the most widespread of the primrose family. In woodrows, shrubby mountainsides and slopes, roadsides and meadows, often so highly scented in the hot midday sun that one can smell them from the road. Sadly depleted now near towns and where hedgerows have been destroyed. O: from north, west and central Europe to North Africa and into the mountains of Asia. A: violets, *Scilla sibirica*, dark blue hyacinths, *Primula rosea*, *Hepatica* species; early spring garden. Best primrose to give a wild look to rock and wild gardens, also in grass near shrubberies.

– – ssp. *sibthorpii*
An extremely strong and hardy plant which will even survive in short grass in a sunny position as long as the ground is not dry. Varying from pink to lilac adding a new colour to the garden cushion primroses. There is also a very charming white form. O: eastern Mediterranean (Bulgaria to Afghanistan). A: small evergreen grasses, evergreen ferns, *Adonis amurensis*, *Eranthis*, *Galanthus* and *Crocus* species.

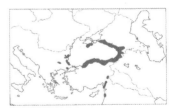

Cultivated cushion primroses
Primula vulgaris (syn. P. acaulis)
'Alba', white.
– – 'Atrorubens'
Velvet red.
– – 'Blue Riband'
Unforgettable shades of blue.

– – 'Snow Cushion'
White.
– – 'Wisley Crimson'
Deep red.
Flowering two weeks later:
Primula vulgaris 'Rosea Plena',
double pink.
– – 'Alba Plena'
Double white.
– – 'Marie Crousse'
Double red.
– – 'Sulphurea Plena'
Double pale yellow.
Once found in all old-fashioned country gardens, and in apothecaries' gardens, they are now very scarce and in demand. Coloured, double primroses need a light, but well-anchored protection of foliage against hard frost if they are to survive the winter undamaged. Increase only by division. Serious gardeners are well advised to help the spread of these small treasures by exchanging them with other gardeners.

2. Flowering time:
second half March to end April

Cushion primroses
☀ to ◑ ⊕ ≃ ‖ Υ ✕ ○ F

Primula juliae ◑ to ● ⧤ △ Υ H₁
Forms mats scarcely 5 cm (2 in) high with a profusion of lilac-pink flowers. To thrive requires moist, nutritious soil and shady position. If the plants fails to flower they must be divided and planted deeper. They also do best with annual light mulch of humus-enriched soil. O: Caucasus. Parent plant of the following hybrids (which are an improvement on the species for length of flowering and toleration of dry conditions!):

P. × pruhoniciana (*P. juliae* hybrids)
◑ to ● ≃ △ Υ ⊔
These hybrids, some of which flower earlier than the species and some later, are among the hardiest of the cushion primroses, many are hybrids with primroses (*P. vulgaris*), others with cowslip (*P. veris*) or oxlip

(*P. elatior*). They almost go underground in winter. I have never yet lost any. Many grow at three times the rate of the others and also flower quite a bit earlier. There are many named cultivars and new ones are continually appearing, adding variety with new colours and larger flowers; others, however, fail to fulfil the hopes we have of them and disappear as quickly as a shooting star in the spring sky.
– – – 'Corinna'
Cream with orange-yellow eye, medium-sized, stemmed flowers.
– – – 'Garryade Guinevere'
Distinctive for its bronze leaves. Pink flowers on 10 to 15 cm (4 to 6 in) stems.
– – – 'Kinlough Beauty'
Very delightful pale pink flowers, long flowering, 10 cm (4 in).
– – – 'Lady Greer'
A well tried cultivar with profuse cream flowers.
– – – 'Mrs McGillevry'
A profusion of lilac-pink flowers.
– – – 'Old Port'
Deep port coloured flowers and purplish-tinged leaves.
– – – 'Purple Cushion' ('Purpurkissen')
Wine-red flowers which, in a mild winter, can open as early as January.
– – – 'Snow White'
A white cultivar. Although the flowers are a little small, it grows quickly and flowers profusely.
– – – 'Sylvia'
Carmine-red sister of 'Corinna', also with orange-yellow eye. The two look excellent together.
– – – 'Wanda'
Beautiful violet sort that flowers long and profusely. There is also a hose-in-hose Wanda with two flowers growing inside each other from each calyx.

Ball primroses

Primula denticulata
◑ to ● ≃ △ Υ ⊔ ✕ ○ ♔ H₁
Balls of pale lilac flowers. Forms thick crowns of leaves after flowering. Although they will grow

and flower in most gardens, for a real show they need moist ground, 15 to 30 cm (6 to 12 in) O: Found from Afghanistan to Yunnan between 2000 and 4000 m (6000 and 12,000 ft). A: *Omphalodes verna* 'Alba' and *Scilla sibirica* 'Alba'.
– – 'Alba'
White ball primrose. A: *Omphalodes verna*, *Brunnera*, *Pulmonaria angustifolia* 'Azurea', pink winter heather and the following primroses.
– – 'Grandiflora'
Large-flowered, seeding primrose in colours varying from pale pink, through mauve to violet.
– – 'Rubin'
Beautiful cultivar in varying shades of ruby-red, not as resilient as the other named forms.

Umbelliferous primroses

Primula rosea
○ to ◑ ⧤ △ ⊔ ○ H₁
Large-flowered pinky red species, only 10 cm (4 in high).
– – 'Delight'
Large-flowered, seeding primrose, brightest pink of all the primroses. If it is to thrive in the garden, requires moist, humus-rich soil and shady position. 10 to 20 cm (4 to 8 in). O: Himalayan mountain meadows, 3000 to 4000 m (9000 to 12,000 ft). A: suitable partners at this time of year are too numerous to list.
– *marginata*
○ to ☀ ≃ △ ‖ ✕ ⊓ ↻ H₁
Pale to dark mauve flowers with silver ring around throat. A sturdy garden plant of 150 years standing and an essential feature of any spring garden. Like *Primula auricula*, forms a stem over the years and should then be planted deeper. March/April. O: Maritime and Cottian Alps in rock clefts. This small, highly serviceable and indestructible primrose has produced a host of named cultivars in a number of delicate shades, including deep blue, pink and white.

The following *Primula marginata*

hybrids were achieved by crossing with *Primula auricula* and *Primula × pubescens*.

– – 'Alba', pure white.
– – 'Hyacinthina', large, lavender flowers with shading.
– – 'Rosea', medium-pink, particularly sturdy growth.
– × *wockei*
○ to ☀ ≈ △ ‖ ✕ ⊟ H₁
Extremely strong-growing, dark mauve flowers, good for division, but has green, less serrated leaves without powdering of farina.

3. Flowering time:
second half April into May

Umbelliferous primroses
Primula elatior hybrids · Oxlip hybrids
◑ to ● ≈ △ Ⴤ ⊔ ✕ F H₁
Cultivated, large-flowered types producing a mixture of deep colours including dark red. The most impressive of all the primulas in colour, form and scent. If plants fade after three or four years or become weak, transplant into fresh soil immediately after flowering.
O: the type plant, *P. elatior*, the oxlip, a European meadow and woodland plant extends to the southern Soviet Union from sea-level to subalpine areas. "Its cymbal-like tones fill whole fields, interspersed with the bassoon-tones of the marsh marigold."
An important step forward in the cultivation of *Primula elatior* hybrids has been the increase in blues, often in unusual shades; the beauty of these blues is unique in the flower kingdom. We must particularly mention the

work of Teicher in this field. Another, by far the largest-flowered group, is the Pacific family, with flowers up to 6 cm (2½ in) across. They are perhaps less suitable for the wild garden than the smaller-flowered sorts.

Like the primula growers, we should not merely accept that these glorious, brightly coloured primulas will cease to flower after three or four years, but keep a careful eye on them and reseed every five years or so from the best plants. In places where these primulas are grown in large quantities beneath fruit bushes for the cut-flower market, one can always find a few plants still flowering where others around them have faded.

Primula auricula · Auricula
○ to ☀ ⊕ ≈ △ ‖ ✕ ⊟ ♂ ⚹ F H₁
Its glorious yellow flowers amidst silver-powdered leaves shine like gold from the alpine rock clefts. Likes damp, light position out of intense sunlight. Tall, mature plants require banking up. Cultivated varieties last twice as long as *Primula elatior* hybrids. O of species and sub-types: subalpine to alpine in Alps, Carpathians and Apennines. Many named cultivars have been grown, reaching their peak of popularity about 100 years ago. Most of these old forms with white meal on their petals are now lost, but hybrid mixtures and a number of more recent, named cultivars are available, extending the colour range to reds,

bronzes and even green. The first brightly coloured auricula

hybrids were discovered in the Alps as long ago as the late Middle Ages. As in the last century, the future will be a great time for the auricula, but for the present it has been overtaken by the longer-stemmed and cushion-forming primulas, which grow at twice the rate. When one tires of the bright colours of the primrose it is a relief to turn to the more subdued shades of the auriculas, which will also tolerate sun and dry conditions better. The brightly coloured hybrids were once available by colour. Auricula societies tended to encourage those varieties, including double ones, which were popular at the time. If one grows mixed hybrids, it is worth sowing the seed and then picking out and propagating the best colour combinations. In doing so one must take good care to remove the many "head-hangers" and to bank up mature plants growing too high above the ground.

– *frondosa*
○ to ◑ ⚌ △ ⊔ ⊟ ♂ F H₁
Rather more permanent than the short-lived birdseye primrose, *P. farinosa*, and an excellent replacement for it in the rock garden. Up to 20 cm (8 in), pink. Its charm lies in its apparent frailty. O: Balkan mountains. Mountain meadows. A: *Gentiana acaulis, Hutchinsia*.

– *saxatilis*
◑ to ● ≈ △ Ⴤ H₁
15 cm (6 in), lilac-pink, better than *P. cortusoides*. A real treasure for the wild garden, excellent for larger, though subdivided areas, excellent with early ferns. O: Manchuria, Amur region. Flowers in rock clefts, first introduced into gardens over a century ago. A: *Cardamine trifoliata*.

4. Flowering time:
mid-May to June

Bell primroses
– *sikkimensis*
☀ to ◑ ⚌ △ Ⴤ ⊔ ✕ H₁

Umbels with pendent bells, deep yellow and beautifully perfumed. Varies as to size of umbels and speed of growth. Calls for the best garden plants to surround it and must have moist, semi-shady position. 45 to 60 cm (1½ to 2 ft). O: Himalayas, 4000 to 5000 m (13,000 to 16,250 ft). A: *Heuchera, Saxifraga, Polystichum setiferum* 'Proliferum'. Also ideal for streamsides with early *Astilbe* cultivars or *Iris kaempferi*.

Primula alpicola
☼ to ◐ ⚌ △ Ⴟ ✕ F H1
A delightful plant with white powdered flowers which grows to 45 cm (18 in). Still uncommon in gardens. Likes moist, semi-shady position. June/July. O: south-east China.
– – var. *alba*, milk-white.
– – – *luna*, pale lemon-yellow.
– – – *violacea*, violet.

Umbelliferous primroses
Primula sieboldii
☼ to ● ≃ △ Ⴟ ✕ H1
Lightly fringed, unusually veined flowers ranging in colour from pale blue, through white to dark red. Dies down completely by summer. 15 to 30 cm (6 to 12 in). O: Japan and Baikal area. A: *Heuchera, Mertensia paniculata*, ferns, dwarf rhododendron.

– – 'Robert Herold'
Strong-growing, large, red flowers with lighter centre.
– – 'Snowflakes', pure white.

5. Flowering time:
June to July

Candelabra primroses
The taller primulas are real sum-

mer treasures and provide a variety of colours. Toughest of all is *Primula japonica*. O: from the mountain woods of Japan and west China. A: *Heuchera, Brunnera macrophylla*, medium-height columbines in various colours, shade grasses, particularly fronded ferns.

Primula japonica
☼ to ● ⚌ △ Ⴟ ⊔ ✕ H1
This beautiful primula is hardy and easy to grow. Like other candelabra primulas it likes a damp, slightly shady position, though preferably not with its roots in water in the winter. Self-seeding in the right conditions. 60 cm (2 ft). There are several hybrids in varying shades of red, as well as white. O: Japan.
– – 'Miller's Crimson', a bright red form to 60 cm (2 ft)
– *beesiana*
Flowering slightly later and growing to 1 metre (3 ft). O: Yunnan.
– *pulverulenta*
Deep red candelabra primula that grows to 80 cm (2 ft 6 in). The flower stems and throats are white-powdered. O: China.

6. Flowering time: July

Candelabra primroses
Primula bulleyana
☼ to ● ⚌ △ Ⴟ ✕ H1
Extremely beautiful, scented species. The flowers orange on strong stems. Up to 80 cm (2 ft 6 in).
– – hybrids
☼ to ● ⚌ △ Ⴟ ⊔ ✕ H1
An ever-fresh range of colours. New hybrids in which a number of candelabra primulas provide a range of sizes and colours in orange, deep red, yellow and pale pink and an increasing number of tones of these.
– *burmanica*
☼ to ● ⚌ △ Ⴟ ⊔ ✕ H1
One of the best primulas with an unusual bright purple-red colour, but must have shade. Astonishingly strong and long-last-

ing. Around 75 cm (30 in). O: Burma. A: grasses and other candelabra primroses.
All these tall candelabra primroses and their hybrids together give a fine display of colour in June and July.

7. Flowering time:
July to August

Bell primroses
Primula florindae · Tibetan Cowslip
☼ to ● ⚌ △ Ⴟ ⊔ ᠕ ✕ H1
Extremely effective with pale yellow flowers rising above thick foliage. By streams will flower half in the water, but also do well in more usual garden positions. 60 to 90 cm (2 to 3 ft). O: south-west Tibet. A: *Heuchera*, rushes, ferns, shade grasses, *Meconopsis betonicifolia*.

Spike primroses
P. vialii · Red-hot Poker Primrose
Remarkable spikes of red and mauve flowers like colourful, dainty red-hot pokers. O: China. A: dwarf rhododendrons, *Meconopsis*.

Prunella · Self-Heal · Mint Family (Labiatae)
○ to ○○ also ◐ ≃ □ Ⴟ ○ H1
Cushions of foliage of 15 cm (6 in), flowers June/September. Try mixing several types. A useful stopgap for difficult areas and an attractive one since it is long-flowering. A: Mullein, bellflowers, perennial flax, milfoil.
– *grandiflora* · Large Self-Heal
Mauve with bronze tones as flowers fade. Native plant.
– – 'Alba', white.
– – 'Loveliness', pure mauve.
– – 'Rosea', extremely beautiful, densely covered with pink flowers.
– × *pinnatifida* (*P. laciniata* × *P. vulgaris*)
Usually found in gardens in the 'Rubra' form. Another "long-player" from July/September, 15 cm (6 in). A: any plant that likes dry conditions, eg. *Anthemis nobilis* 'Plena'.

Juniperus chinensis 'Pfitzeriana', the Chinese Juniper, can grow to 2 m (6 ft) tall and 4 m (12 ft) across and should be planted individually.

1. *Trapa natans*, the Water Chestnut (text p. 70–1), is a floating water plant which sadly has fallen out of favour, possibly because it has to be started afresh each year.

2. and 4. *Hippuris vulgaris*, the Mare's Tail (text p. 70), is one of the most beautiful and interesting of the water plants. Its spread can only be restricted by planting it in tubs.

Left-hand page:
3. Looking at the seeds of *Trapa natans*, the Water Chestnut (text p. 70–1), it would be hard to think of a more appropriate common name.
5. *Sagittaria sagittifolia*, the Common Arrowhead (text p. 70). It is best to plant the bulbs in a wide, shallow basket if your pond does not have a soil base.

A small pool will provide space for a variety of water plants. Prevent spread where necessary by planting in tubs. Small and large waterside plants have been combined to give an attractive effect, avoiding the creation of too much shade, where waterlilies would not flower.

1. Even a small pool can lend atmosphere to the rock garden. Shade-loving perennials are particularly suitable for planting at the margins – for example the *Astilbe simplicifolia* hybrid 'Aphrodite', with its bright red flowers and dark foliage.

2. *Nymphaea pygmaea* 'Alba' is a dwarf white-flowered waterlily suitable for water depths between 5 and 15 cm (2 in and 6 in).

1. *Iris kaempferi* (text
p. 70, 206–7) should
only be planted by the
edge of water for it is
not a truly aquatic spe-
cies. Less well-known
still is its ability to
thrive in fertile, damp
and chalk-free soil.
2. *Menyanthes trifoliata*
(text p. 70), is adorned
in May and June with
entrancing flowers.
3. *N. X marliacea chromatella*, is one of the best
of the yellow *Nymphaea*
hybrids. To display its
splendour fully it needs
large pool and a water
depth of at least 40 to
80 cm (16 to 32 in).

1. Anyone with a stream in their garden is to be envied. The first task is to clear away the grass. Here, *Brunnera macrophylla* (text p. 162), is on the left and various *Bergenia* hybrids on the right of the stream.

2. The best feature of *Sparganium erectum*, the Branched Bur-reed (text p. 70), is its fruits.

3. *Acer palmatum* 'Atropurpureum' hangs over the water. A few strings have been draped across the tree to support a blue Morning Glory, where it flowers regularly for months on end, from half-past-eight to half-past-three.

After a few years small pools can become overgrown
if plants are not contained by pots or tubs. Then only
complete replanting will help. There should always
be an area of clear water, free of plants.

1. Although *Juncus effusus*, the Soft Rush (text p. 106), has insignificant brownish flowers, its erect form makes it attractive beside pools.

2. *Trollius* hybrids, have unfortunately become somewhat forgotten. As long as they have a humus-rich, tolerably light soil they will delight the eye from the end of April until the beginning of June.

3. Before planting waterlilies it is necessary to bear in mind that they need completely still water and full sun to reward us with plenty of flowers. Many varieties suitable for different depths of water remain to be discovered.

1. *Polystichum setiferum* 'Plumosum Densum' – one of the best evergreen forms. Its fronds can grow to 50 cm (20 in).

2. *Polystichum setiferum* 'Proliferum', bears numerous plantlets on the midribs of its fronds, which is surely why this fern is so common.

3. *Polystichum setiferum* 'Wollastonii', the Wollaston Fronded Fern, is by far the largest of the family.

4. *Ceterach officinarum* (text p. 108) – essential requirements are a warm sunny crevice and some protection in winter. This dwarf fern refuses absolutely to grow in the shade!

5. *Phyllitis scolopendrium* 'Crispa', the Hart's Tongue Fern, will delight anew every fern enthusiast. This form is one of the strongest-growing.

Wild ferns contrast well in the rock garden with a
variety of shade-loving plants and shrubs.
1. *Polypodium vulgare*, the Common Polypody (text
p. 108) – one of the best-known, most indestructible
little ferns, forming compact mats.
2. *Asplenium ruta-muraria*, the Wall Rue (text p. 108), is
good for narrow shady clefts.
3. *Asplenium trichomanes*, the Maidenhair Spleenwort
(text p. 108), is a hardy dwarf fern that is easy to
grow and likes a confined space between rocks.
4. *Adiantum pedatum* 'Imbricatum', deserves wider use
in the garden.

Calla palustris, the Bog Arum (text p. 70) and *Thelypteris thelypteroides*, the Marsh Fern (text p. 71, 108), can be planted together in tubs, since neither spreads or interferes with the other.

Picea glauca 'Conica', a dwarf White Spruce, can grow
to 1.5 m (4½ ft) in old age. This should be borne in
mind when planting and neighbouring plants should
not be too near. Too close planting or too heavy
shade will both cause ugly bald patches to appear on
the tree.

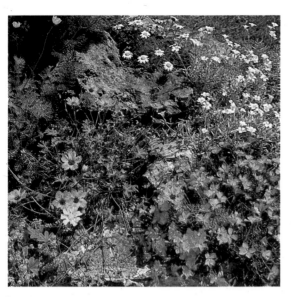

1. *Dianthus gratianopolitanus* (text p. 170), planted in association with *Geranium cinereum* 'Ballerina' and the white-flowered, moderately vigorous *Cerastium tomentosum* var. *columnae* (text p. 166).

2. Rock garden plants look most natural when they do not smother the rocks among which they grow. Illustrated here are *Edraianthus* and *Dianthus* varieties.

3. A mixture of flowering perennials in the rock garden in June. The dominant cushion of *Saponaria ocymoides* (text p. 243–4), is associated with *Veronica austriaca* ssp. *teucrium* 'Knallblau' and encrusted *Saxifraga* species.

Right-hand page:
Numbers of beautiful grasses are beginning to make their way into our gardens but many gardeners are still reluctant to use them.
1. A beautiful specimen of *Festuca cinerea*, the Blue Fescue, with *Iberis saxatilis* (text p. 202) in April.
2. *Festuca scoparia* (text p. 106), forms wide flat carpets in shady places out of the winter sun.
3. *Stipa barbata* (text p. 107), is here planted beside steps. Its silvery fronds provide a decorative effect throughout the summer weeks.

1. to 3. *Dictamnus albus*, the Dittany or Burning Bush (text p. 172), can survive a lifetime in its original site, providing it has sun and a chalky, humus-rich, slightly loamy, fairly dry soil.

Primula japonica (text p. 224), comes in white and
shades of red. In favourable situations it seeds itself
well.

Prunella grandiflora

A: carpeting ivy. Mature plants beautiful amongst white *Arabis* types.

– – 'Highdown'
Very rich-blue flowers and lightly spotted leaves.

– – 'Sissinghurst White'
A pure white form with green leaves.

–. × *webbiana* (thought to be *P. grandiflora* × *P. hastifolia*)
Larger mauve flowers than *P. grandiflora*. Found in gardens since 1600!

Pulmonaria · Lungwort · Borage Family (Boraginaceae)
◑ to ● ≃ □ Y ✗ ○ ♔ ♂ HI
The lungworts are all sturdy, indestructible, early-spring plants which tolerate shade and grow to about 30 cm (1 ft) tall. The following species and cultivars should be an essential feature of any rock garden. They are listed in order of flowering time.

– *rubra*
The earliest and sturdiest of the entire family. In early spring a mass of coral-pink flowers appear from the thick crown of leaves. The flowers tend to be unsightly as they fade. Gives a beautiful overall effect in the sun with white winter heather or in shade with ferns and evergreen grasses, white daphne, lots of

early crocus and the earliest species of *Muscari*. End February/April. O: Carpathians, Transylvania, south-east Europe, in similar locations to our native lungwort.

– *angustifolia* 'Azurea' · Narrow-Leaved Lungwort
From 15 cm (6 in) to almost 30 cm (1 ft), gentian blue, end March/early May. The deep blue of this long-lasting plant which thrives in shade is one of which no gardener should fail to take advantage. One can't have enough of them in the garden. For large areas of wild garden a hundred plants would not be excessive. O: Europe to Caucasus. Isolated colonies found throughout Switzerland, Bohemia, Moravia, mountains of central Germany, Styria, Istria; in semi-shady woodedges, from sea-level to 2700 m (8800 ft). A: beautiful between *Primula elatior* hybrids, *Lathyrus* in various colours, daffodils, *Waldsteinia* and shade grasses.

– *saccharata* (syn. P. picta) · Bethlehem Sage
The earliest-flowering species whose flowers turn from blue to red with age. Very striking marbled leaves. Flowers early April. O: central Italy. Spread northwards as early as the 16th century, now found from Portugal, through Switzerland to Belgium.

Pulsatilla · Pasque Flower · Buttercup Family (Ranunculaceae)
○ ⊕ △ ‖ ⊥ ✗ ○ ⊗ HI
All pasque flowers feature amongst the most popular rock-garden plants and what gardener would be willing to dispense with their purple (or even white or red), silky-haired, bell-shaped flowers? The species and varieties listed here are all excellent for gardens and suitable for a variety of warm, sunny spots with fairly good, porous soil. They always grow wild in sites open to the warmth of the sun and few thrive with overhead shade.

Because of the rather pronounced development of the taproot you should always plant young plants and once in place they do not transplant well. All pasque flowers are long-lived, so that one often forgets how long ago they were planted. After the flowers they produce silver feathery seed heads in early summer.

I have omitted the alpine *Pulsatilla* species that require a lot of attention.

– *halleri* ssp. *slavica* (syn. Anemone slavica, Pulsatilla slavica)
Erect, pure mauve flowers in March/April. In flower two weeks earlier than *P. vulgaris* with attractive, larkspur-like leaves.

241

Taller than *P. vulgaris*. O: Slovakia. A: *Adonis vernalis*, *Stipa* species, *Dianthus gratianopolitanus*.

– *vulgaris* (syn. Anemone pulsatilla) · Common Pasque Flower
In many places comes into flower with the first cuckoo calls. 10 to 20 cm (4 to 8 in), mid-April/May, deep mauve, early-spring in the garden. O: from England and southern Sweden through central Europe to southern Ukraine. Likes chalk but also does well without it.

– – 'Alba'
Charming interspersed amongst the purple species. Unfortunately off-white varieties sometimes supplied.
– – 'Barton's Pink'
A charming pink flowered form which, however, sets little good seed.
– – 'Rubra'
Red variety, extremely effective, colour tends to vary slightly.
– – ssp. *grandis*
Beautiful subspecies with extremely large, mauve flowers. Same requirements as the type and similar uses. Seldom grown. I must warn against plants that are no more than selected, large-blossomed *P. vulgaris*. O: isolated examples found, in Moravia and Austria for instance.

Ramonda · Gloxinia Family (Gesneriaceae)
☀ ⊕ △ ‖ 🛡 ♢ ✿ Hɪ
It is astonishing that this delicate plant from the far subalpine cliffs of Serbia and the Pyrenees, a relative of the hothouse gloxinia, can happily make its home on north-facing rock-garden

slopes. An evergreen plant that will survive over decades continuing to bring forth its blue, pale pink or white blossoms from a rosette of corrugated leaves. Prefers a north-facing position, a preference that one is only too happy to satisfy.
I have omitted *R. serbica* from my list for it is rarely found in gardens and is less attractive than the other two species listed here.
– *myconi* (syn. R. pyrenaica) · Pyrenean Ramonda
Grows to 8 cm (3 in), pale lavender-blue flowers end May/June. A: with *Moehringia* or *Saxifraga* in north-facing clefts.

– – 'Alba'
White flowers. A: small ferns.
– – 'Rosea'
Pink flowers.
– *nathaliae*
Slightly earlier more striking flowers of darker colour with orange ring. Leaves glossy dark green and less corrugated. O: Macedonia.

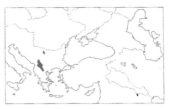

Ranunculus · Buttercup · Buttercup Family (Ranunculaceae)
◐ to ● ≃ △ ⅄ ⊔ ✕ ♢ Hɪ
While the brightly coloured, double-flowered corm buttercups of Asia are rather unreliable, the herbaceous buttercups listed here are excellent.
– *aconitifolius* · White Buttercup, Fair Maids of Kent

White flowers from aconite-like leaves in mid-May, 45 cm (18 in). Likes moist places in the wild and has similar garden requirements. In light woods, damp meadows and banks of streams grows alongside *Trollius*, *Geum*, *Thalictrum aquilegifolium*.
From the mountains of Central Germany, climbs to 2500 m (7500 ft) in the Alps and is even found in some places at sea-level. O: almost all of mainland Europe, principally mountain to subalpine. A: *Brunnera macrophylla*, *Omphalodes verna*, *Myosotis alpestris*.

– – 'Pleniflorus'
A really charming plant with the same uses as the above, but also to border herbaceous beds. Double, ball-shaped flowers.
– *acris* 'Multiplex' · Meadow Buttercup
It is difficult to understand why this old-fashioned little garden treasure, which will grow anywhere and flower for two months on end, should be so neglected by gardeners instead of being given its true worth. 30 to 60 cm (1 to 2 ft), golden-yellow, mid-May to June and beyond. O of type: *R. acris* is found from sea level to 2500 m (7500 ft), is widespread throughout Europe as well as in north and south Asia, North Africa, Ethiopia, the Cape, North America and Greenland. A: columbines and *Tradescantia andersoniana* hybrids (not pink).
– *bulbosus* 'Pleniflorus' · Bulbous Buttercup
Its glossy green and gold flowers are like small, Victorian sofa-cushions. Around 20 to 40 cm (8

to 16 in). This little plant is amazingly undemanding and long-living. Beware however of acquiring the spreading *R. repens* 'Flore Pleno' in error! Mid-May. O: type plant lives in dry meadows, grassland and along the edges of hill paths from sea-level to the alpine foothills, with odd groups found as high as 2000 m (6000 ft). Central and west Europe, western Asia to northern Persia. A: *Polemonium × richardsonii*, blue dwarf irises, *Alyssum saxatile* 'Citrinum'.

– *gramineus* · Grass-leaved Buttercup
H2
A charming perennial with leaves very unlike those of a normal buttercup, making 30 to 45 cm (12 to 18 in) light-green clumps. The golden flowers open in late May to June. O: southern Europe.

– *montanus* · Mountain Buttercup
H1
Low clumps of rounded green leaves to 15 cm (6 in). The wide golden flowers are at their best in late spring. 'Molten Gold' a fine, free flowering form. O of species: Alps, south and west to the mountains of Jugoslavia.

Ranunculus aquatilis, see Water plants, p. 70

Sagina · Pearlwort · Pink Family (Caryophyllaceae)
○ to ◑ ≃ △ ⋙ ⚹ H1
– *subulata* · Awl-Leaved Pearlwort
Use in small groups in dry, semi-shade, otherwise they will lose their leaves. Will also grow in light, damp soil. Beautiful on steps. White, starry flowers in June/July. Unfortunately the flat cushions of foliage tend to become weed-infested. O: southern and central Europe.
– – 'Aurea'
The foliage has a golden tinge.

Sagittaria, see Water plants, p. 70

Salvia · Sage · Mint Family (Labiatae)

○ to ○○○ ⊕ ⊥ ⋊ ◯ ▧ H1
A fine group of plants for a sunny part of the garden.
– *argentea* · Silver Sage
H2–3
Grown both for its broad, silvery woolly leaf rosettes and its pinky-white flowers. Needs a well drained spot and protection in cold areas. O: USA.
– × *superba* 'May Night'
In flower in mid-May, some weeks in advance of the tall, blue unimproved hybrid. This sage which grows to just over one foot tall is worthy of any rock garden for its blue-black flowers can provide an unusual colour for both small and large gardens. Put a few plants close together to get the full effect of this dark blue shade which is quite different from the mauve of the more usual *S. × superba*. The flowers seem to continue endlessly, surrounded by bees. After cutting back will flower again into September. A: *Gypsophila repens* and hybrids, heather, *Oenothera tetragona*, grasses for dry soil.

Sanguinaria · Bloodwort · Poppy Family (Papaveraceae)
– *canadensis*
◑ ≃ ⋙ ⅄ ♂ H1
A plant with beautiful, heart-to-kidney-shaped, blue-green leaves. From them unfold the solitary anemone-like flowers of purest white. Unfortunately the flowers are rather short-lived. Dies away in late summer like our *Anemone nemorosa*. Requires moist, slightly shaded position. 15 to 30 cm (6 to 12 in), April/May. O: eastern United States. A: ferns, shade grasses, shade-loving *Primula* types.
– – 'Multiplex', fully double flowers which are much more lasting. A delightful plant for a moist position.

Santolina · Cotton Lavender · Daisy Family (Compositae)
○ to ○○○ ⊕ △ ⫴ ⚹ H2
– *chamaecyparissus* · Lavender Cotton

A rather shrubby, evergreen, aromatic plant from the Mediterranean which grows to 60 cm (2 ft). Silver-grey feathery foliage with yellow flowers in July and August. There is a certain morbid charm as the flowers fade and shrivel. To the attuned eye in the right light this can be one of the finest sights the flower garden has to offer. O: western Mediterranean coastline as far as Dalmatia. A: blue *Festuca* types.
– – 'Sulphurea'
With more striking flowers than the former, one of the best rock-garden plants at this time of year. Pale yellow flowers which make it particularly useful. July/August. A: *Scutellaria baicalensis*, *Campanula carpatica*.
– – 'Nana'
A dwarf, neater plant growing to only 30 cm (12 in).

Saponaria · Soapwort · Pink Family (Caryophyllaceae)
○ to ○○ △ ∥ ⋙ ⊟ ‡ H1
– *caespitosa* · Tufted Soapwort
Sprays of pink flowers, 5–10 cm (2½–4 in), May/June. O: Spanish mountains.
– *ocymoides* · Rock Soapwort

Large, feathery cushions of leaves. 15 cm (6 in) high but making mats to 100 cm (3 ft) wide. June. O: sunny shingle banks from mountain to subalpine levels in south-west Mediterranean, across Apennines, into central France, southern Spain and Alps. Also in Corsica and Sardinia. A: yellow *Helianthemum*, *Globularia*, *Veronica austriaca* ssp. *teucrium* 'Kapitan' and 'Crater Lake Blue'.

– – 'Splendens'
Beautiful variety in brighter, warmer pink than the species.

– × *olivana* (*S. pumila* × *S. caespitosa*)
This, the queen of the soapworts, forms mats of warm pink flowers, completely covered in blossom in maturity. Will flower magnificently year in and year out. Under 15 cm (6 in), June/July. A: in rock clefts with dwarf *Campanula*, *Saxifraga callosa* var. *australis* 'Superba'.

Satureja · Savory · Mint Family (Labiatae)
○ to ○○○ △ ⇝ ⬡ ✿ F H1

– *montana* 'Alba Compacta' · Winter Savory
Grows to between 15 (6 in) and 30 cm (12 in) high. Undemanding and indestructible. Will survive in the garden for tens of years even in a difficult position.

– – ssp. *illyrica* 'Lilacina'
15 to 30 cm (6 to 12 m), an amazingly compact plant in maturity. Another long-flowering plant in August/September. Winter Savory, particularly the white form, is extremely useful in the late-summer rock garden. O: Along the whole northern Mediterranean and over into Algeria, through southern Soviet Union to Caucasus. A: autumn crocus and colchicums, *Sedum pluricaule, Campanula carpatica* – in fact seems to go well with anything.

Saxifraga · Saxifrage · Saxifrage Family (Saxifragaceae)
The saxifrage genus is practically never-ending and every rock garden is sure to include at least one plant. The species themselves are extremely numerous, quite apart from the beauty and individuality of the hybrids of a plant that hybridizes so readily. It would take decades for the uninitiated to come to terms with all the variety covered by the term "saxifrage". The first task is to overcome the inhibitions of the uninitiated who fear anything new, to remove prejudice and to bring the beginner to an appreciation of new experiences.

Maeterlinck's description of garden flowers as "the means of increasing our level of happiness" is increasingly applicable.

Did you know that there are tiny, silver-grey dwarfs with lilac-pink flowers in March-April from both Arctic regions and the far Himalayas?

Even the smallest saxifrages are great travellers, spreading from the far north to deep into the Mediterranean countries. It would take more than one lifetime to see all the places where they grow.

Few lovers of the tall pyramidal saxifrage *(S. cotyledon)* can be aware how widespread it is; from Iceland, through Lappland and Norway (where it is used in wedding bouquets), then making a leap to the Central Alps where it stands out white against the dark granite of the Simplon before following mountain roads down to the south where the hot dust powders its silver flowers. Even in the least auspicious garden situations it will spread its immortal rosettes of broad leaves.

The tiny *S. burserana*, the finest early-spring flower among the wild European alpine saxifrages, grows in all its beauty in the Dolomites as well as the mountains of southern Spain.

The largest of the saxifrages with rosettes a foot across grow up to 90 cm (3 ft) while one has almost to kneel to see the smallest of the genus. For the sake of the saxifrage alone, the rock garden has become indispensable. The earliest often flower as early as January, the latest in October. From quite a different point of view the dwarf saxifrages will increase in importance. I am convinced that the popularity of miniature gardens in the Far East will spread to the west and remain a permanent feature of our garden culture. Here, though, the trend will be towards the greatest possible variety of tiny plants and in this field the wonderful world of the alpines is invaluable, for in the smallest space they leave us breathless as they develop throughout the year. In March-April *Saxifraga* × *irvingii* opens its tiny flowers and invites us irresistibly into the world of dwarf plants. The following list of garden saxifrages does not claim to be complete. Its aim is something quite different, to pave the way of the saxifrage into numerous gardens; to break down the inhibitions which still keep so many gardeners from these unfamiliar beauties.

I have grouped the saxifrages in quite a new way to distinguish between the various flowering times and the various garden uses, and within the groups themselves I have chosen to arrange them by flowering time rather than alphabetically.

1. Small early-spring saxifrages

✺ △ ‖ ⛁ ⬡ ♁ ≢ H1
(Easy-to-grow early saxifrages from end February to April)
If the following instructions are complied with these are easy to grow anywhere in the garden, providing the soil is kept relatively moist. They should grow well in a damp climate, but also in a continental climate if given a light position out of the sun. In too much shade they will not flower well. In damp climates they can be allowed a more sunny position and the greyer the leaves, the more sun they will tolerate. Buds often appear as early as January.

– × *kellereri* (*S. burserana* × *S. stribrnyi*)
Flowers in January/March, earliest of all the dwarf saxifrages. Pale pink flowers from grey-green rosettes. Flowers weeks before the two parent species.

– × *irvingii* (*S. burserana* × *S. lilacina*)

In flower by mid-March. One of the best miniature plants the world can offer. Masses of silvery-pink flowers breaking out from fine-stemmed red buds. Use around rocks out of sun.

– × *elizabethae* (*S. juniperifolia* ssp. *sancta* × *S. burserana*)
Grey-green cushions and heads of soft yellow around the beginning of April. Unlike most hybrids this one does not flower profusely.

– × *apiculata* (*S. marginata* var. *rocheliana* × *S. juniperifolia* ssp. *sancta*)
Deep green cushions with masses of ivory flowers in early April. Likes more humus than *S.* × *elizabethae*. A: mauve dwarf primroses.

– × *haagii* (*S. ferdinandi-coburgi* × *S. juniperifolia* ssp. *sancta*)
Rather lax mats of dark green and small clusters of bright yellow flowers in early April.

– × *ochroleuca* 'Minor' (*S. juniperifolia* ssp. *sancta* × *S. burserana*)
Mid-April. Flowering time follows on well from the above. Greyer foliage than *S.* × *haagii*.

– *marginata* var. *rocheliana*
Mid-April. Silvery, grey-green cushions with white flowers to 15 cm (6 in) O: Carpathians, Balkans, alpine to subalpine. A: *Primula marginata*.

– *juniperifolia* ssp. *sancta* (syn. S. *sancta*)
Beautiful, sulphur-yellow flowers in early April, 8 cm (3½ in) over flat, green cushions. O: Athos mountains. A: *Chionodoxa sardensis*.

2. Second group of small, early-spring saxifrages

☼ ≃ △ ‖ ⛢ ◯ ⟱ ⟲ ⚓ Hı
(Slightly more difficult to grow than preceding group, particularly in hot, dry sites).
A group of early-spring saxifrages to grow in the shelter of rocks in areas which experience long hot summers. They should have a moist position out of the sun, preferably a north-east or west-facing slope. Use them in rock clefts or gravel where they can be watered easily to give them the moisture they are used to in their mountain habitat.

– *burserana* · One-flowered Cushion Saxifrage
A large-blossomed dwarf, only 6 cm (2½ in) tall, white flowers above silvery cushions. O: alpine and subalpine areas of Dolomites, E. Alps and south to Italian Alps.

– – var. *burserana* (syn. S. burserana 'Minor')
Early April. Flowers less prone to frost damage so often preferred to other forms of *S. burserana*.

– – 'Crenola'
Early white and pink form of *S. burserana* 'Major'. No defects. Same requirements as *S. burserana*.

– – 'Major'
Another early-flowerer, end February/March. Largest blossoms of all the small, early saxifrages and parent of several large-blossomed, early hybrids. Many of these early saxifrages have buds ready to burst open in the depths of winter; one cannot easily manage without them.

– *grisebachii*
In late March, purple-red bracts and flowers rise 10 to 15 cm (4 to 6 in) above the silver rosettes of leaves. O: Alps, Macedonia. A: *Sempervivum tomentosum*.—One of the best forms is 'Wisley Variety'.

– *oppositifolia* · Purple Saxifrage
End March. Forms thick carpets in shady positions in moist, gravelly, humus-rich soil. Requires careful handling since it will not tolerate prolonged drought. The species with its mossy cushions and bright red flowers is extremely widespread. O: Pyrenees, Switzerland, Alps, Apennines, Carpathians, northern Europe, Britain, Scandinavia, Greenland, Lapland, arctic and subarctic North America, polar islands, Rocky Mountains. An arctic-alpine plant that will settle in any place that is at all suitable—ridges, cliffs, shrubland, streamsides, scree, from polar mountains to 3500 m (10,500 ft) in Alps.

– – 'Ruth Draper'
A vigorous form with rosy red flowers.

– – 'Splendens'
Beautiful red-purple flowers.

– × *rubella* (*S. burserana* × *S. lilacina*)
Fairly large, beautifully-formed, pink flowers above delicate carpet of foliage in early April. 7 cm (3 in) tall.

– × *arco-valleyi* (*S. lilacina* × *S. marginata* var. *coriophylla*)
Enchanting hybrid with pale mauve flowers. Only 7 cm (3 in) tall.

– × *suendermannii* 'Major'
The deepest red of all the dwarf hybrids, likes sandy humus soil near rocks. Mid-April, 8 cm (3 in) tall.

– *ferdinandi-coburgi*
The latest of the yellow saxifrages, flowering late April and into May. Graceful, deep yellow flowers on grey foliage. O: Pirin Mountains, first discovered in 1903.

3. Evergreen moss saxifrages

☼ to ◐ ≃ △ ▢ ⟿ ◯ ⟲ ⚓ Hı
(see also Group 4)
A group that thrives in sun even in a hot climate, arranged by flowering time. Unlike the following group, these species and cultivars will tolerate full sun and drought, but will also do well in a damp, semi-shady position. These saxifrages stand out from the rest for the density of

their foliage. After a few years give them a sprinkling of loose soil. The only precaution you need take is to guard against roots and dripping wet from shrubs.

Saxifraga bronchialis
April. Flat-growing, mossy saxifrage with highly unusual white flowers. O: Siberia, East Asia, North America, alpine to subalpine. A: *Scilla sibirica*.
– *arendsii* hybrids
Unless in a rainy climate, they like semi or full shade. They are gradually becoming less demanding by selection and the use of sturdy, undemanding species and cultivars as parents.
– – – 'Ballawley Guardsman'
Sturdy cultivar with large carmine-red flowers.
– – – 'Gaiety'
Deep pink flowers.
– – – 'Pixie's
Small, neat growing form with rose-red flowers which cover the plant from April to May. 15 cm (6 in).
– *hypnoides* · Mossy Saxifrage
Extremely low-growing saxifrage with delicate white flowers. Leaves turn beautiful red in autumn! Late May. O: Atlantic variety from the mossy rocks of the rainy west European mountains from northern Spain through France to Holland, Britain and Iceland. A: often with *Asplenium trichomanes*, *Sempervivum*, *Dianthus*.
– *muscoides* · Musky Saxifrage
Low, mossy foliage with short-stemmed white flowers. Indestructible plant whose leaves turn to striking red in winter which contrasts beautifully with snow or frost on a sunny winter day. Early May, 5 cm (2½ in) tall. O: Pyrenees, Maritime Alps, Arctic, Caucasus at alpine level. A: white daphne.
– – 'Findling'
Extremely quick-growing and tolerates more dryness than other white forms.
– *trifurcata*

Hardiest of the mossy saxifrages with masses of small white flowers over attractive, slightly rounded cushions of leaves. Also good for borders. End May. O: Pyrenees, alpine to subalpine. A: Horned pansy.

4. Evergreen mossy saxifrages susceptible to drought

☀ to ◑ ≃ △ □ ⋘ ◯ ♔ ≢ Hɪ
In dry continental climate require continuously damp soil and shady situation out of full sun and away from roots of shrubs.
In a damp climate, on the other hand, these garden cultivars can be used in normal flower beds or in the rock garden out of intense sunlight. If they are allowed to become too dry or have too much sun the leaves will turn brown. Towards mid-April, throughout May, with the last one listed flowering in June.
Hybrids of S. moschata · Mossy Saxifrages · 'Cloth of Gold'
The white flowers stand out against the cushions of golden leaves. 10 cm (4 in).
– – – 'Triumph'
With right treatment produces masses of glowing red flowers. Must be out of sun! A: scatter with the occasional white cultivar.
– – – 'Pearly King'
Flowers of pure white, the most impressive of all the white saxifrages. Plant areas of this with the cultivars listed above.
– *irrigua*
Latest of the white mossy saxifrages, flowering in June, 15 cm (6 in). Unfortunately seldom seen in gardens.

5. Bulbous saxifrages

◑ to ● △ Hɪ
– *granulata* · Meadow Saxifrage
Its white flowers follow those of the cuckoo flower in May, when they bloom in their thousands on roadsides, thickets and dry meadows. Plant bulbs around 5 to

8 cm deep (2 to 3 in). Equally happy in wet or dry conditions! O: throughout Europe, south into Morocco, north to Finland, east as far as western border of Soviet Union. A mountain plant in the south, but in the north also found at sea-level. A: low grasses.
– – 'Plena'
A double garden form which, like *Lychnis viscaria* 'Splendens', differs markedly from the true species. A: Alpine aster.

6. Dark green rosette saxifrages

◑ to ● ≃ △ □ ⋘ Υ ♔ ≢ Hɪ
End May. For sun or shade in damp climate, in continental climate will tolerate sun in damp soil while in sun will tolerate dryness. Has been used to cover city courtyards with a beautiful, evergreen carpet (hence the name 'London Pride').

Saxifraga umbrosa · London Pride
Stems up to 30 to 45 cm (12 to 18 in) have white flowers with delicate pink markings. Children are told that this is where flies learn their tables! O: northern Portugal, northern Spain, isolated colonies in Ireland, usually in shady, mossy woods like the pinewoods of the Pyrenees. A: *Iris pumila*, *Brunnera macrophylla*. Uncommon in gardens.

The common garden London Pride is a hybrid with *S. spathularis* and known as *Saxifraga × urbium*.
– – 'Aureopunctata'
A plant with golden splashes on its leaves and pink flowers.

– – 'Elliot's Variety'
Pink and white flowers from completely flat, dark green rosettes which become reddish in winter. A: *Primula sikkimensis*, *Phyllitis scolopendrium*, *Epimedium* types.

7. Silvery rosette saxifrages

○ to ☀ ≃ △ ‖ □ ✕ ⊟ ♂ ♯ H1
For normal garden use in any temperate climate. Can also tolerate dryness and can be used for rock clefts and dry walls in either sun or semi-shade. Here a whole casket of silver jewels waits to dazzle the gardener. Amidst the silver are flashes of pink. These plants seem to encapsulate all the beauty of hoar frost. May/June.

Saxifraga paniculata 'Major' (syn. S. aizoon 'Major') · Live Long Saxifrage
From small grey rosettes, which are pure silver in the best forms, white flower heads rise a foot high. Flowers end May. O: polar regions, arctic, and then in three main areas of distribution where forms may differ slightly. 1. Mediterranean area from Spain to Balkans, 1800 m (4500 ft), and central Europe, Alps, mountains of central Germany to Carpathians. 2. Scandinavia. 3. Greenland, arctic regions of North America, eastern Canada. Often found on inaccessible rocks with *Carex firma*, *Draba*, *Primula auricula*, gentians, *Globularia cordifolia*. A: *Linaria*, dwarf bellflowers.
– – 'Rosularis'
Cultivar with white and pink flowers and good rosettes. A: *Veronica*, *Campanula portenschlagiana*, *Campanula cochleariifolia*.
– – 'Atropurpurea'
Good rosettes and deep pink flowers. A: *Veronica prostrata*.
– – 'Lutea'
Pale yellow flowers and light green leaves. A: *Codonopsis clematidea*.
– – 'Rex'
Mahogany-brown stems and

flowers to a foot high. Discovered on the Dossenhorn by Farrer in 1903 and was brought back in the same metal container as *Campanula cochleariifolia* the fairy's thimble. A: dwarf bellflowers.
– *cochlearis*
Delicate silver foliage and white flowers. A charming plant which leads up to *S. callosa* var. *australis* 'Superba'. An essential rock-garden plant and just as rewarding as the unusual *S. callosa*. May/June. O: western Alps.
– *hostii* ssp. *hostii* (syn. S. altissima var. altissima) · Host's Saxifrage
This plant is by far the strongest and the most profuse leafer of all the silvery rosette saxifrages, with white flowers from 15–30 cm (6–12 in). May/June. O of type: southern and eastern chalk Alps from Lake Como to Karawanken range, 600 m to 2000 m (1800 to 6000 ft); upper Styria and northern Alps. A: *Heuchera* hybrids.
– × *andrewsii* (*S. paniculata* × *S. hirsuta*)
This hybrid has unusual dark-green rosettes with slightly lighter edges with white flowers up to 45 cm (18 in). May. A: golden flax.
– *callosa* var. *australis* (syn. S. lingulata var. lantoscana)
Flowers two weeks before the cultivar listed below, with white flowers on slightly shorter, less rigid stems. 20 cm (8 in). O: Maritime Alps. A: bellflowers.

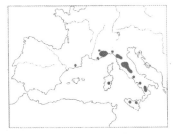

– – – 'Superba'
The noblest of the group capable of surviving for tens of years in the most difficult positions. 30 cm (12 in) flower stems are excellent for cutting. O: southern

Alps, Maritime Alps. A: *Heuchera* hybrids, *Mertensia paniculata*.

8. Silvery rosette saxifrages for damp positions

○ to ☀ ≃ △ ‖ □ ✕ ⊟ ♂ ♯ H1
Will only tolerate dryness for a short time, requires light semi-shade. In the right conditions they are extremely strong and completely hardy.

Saxifraga cotyledon · Pyramidal Saxifrage
The most striking of the silver saxifrages with flower stems 40 to 60 cm (16 to 24 in) tall, and to over 75 cm (2 ft 6 in) in the best forms. Excellent for cutting. June/July. O: central Alps, Pyrenees, Lapland, Iceland, North America, subarctic. Grows wild with *Sempervivum arachnoideum*, *Sedum album*. Forms humus through its own rosette system. *Asplenium septentrionale*. A: *Veronica latifolia*.

– – 'Pyramidalis'
Pyrenean type with particularly tall flowers.
– – 'Caterhamensis'
Flowers with red markings.
– *longifolia* · Pyrenean Saxifrage
For many years its beautiful rosettes will produce no flowers at all, then suddenly flower profusely before the plant dies away. Propagation mainly from seed but a few offsets are produced. No related types are in flower at precisely the same time, but there are many hybrids in addition to the true *S. longifolia*. O: Pyrenees, southern Spain, Atlas Mountains (Morocco).

9. Autumn saxifrages

◐ to ● ♨ △ Ⴁ ✕ ♧ H2

- *fortunei* (syn. cortusifolia var. fortunei)
Attractive, highly polished leaves, which themselves justify the inclusion of this plant in the rock garden; from them rise graceful panicles of white gossamer flowers throughout October. They are best grown in shade where their leaves show to best advantage. O: Japan. A: Mossy green carpeting saxifrages, autumn crocus, small ferns, *Tricyrtis hirta* and early Christmas roses.
- – 'Rubrifolia'
Coppery-red leaves, very red beneath.
- – 'Wada's Form'
Rich purple leaves make this form distinct, 20 to 25 cm (8 to 10 in).

Scabiosa · Scabious · Scabious Family (Dipsacaceae)
○ to ○○ ⊕ ⊥ ✕ ◯ H1

- *caucasica*
A wonderful, unbelievably long-flowering plant which will survive for years in the same spot. June/September. Looks wild enough for either the rock or wild garden, while its cultivars are fine enough for the formal rock garden.
- – 'Miss Willmott'
A good white form. Traditional feature of bridal bouquets in many areas, especially in parts of Germany. A: 'Moorheim Blue', *Potentilla* 'Gibsons Scarlet'.
- – 'Moorheim Blue'
A quick-growing, large-blos-

somed form, excellent with the white 'Miss Willmott'. The deep lavender-blue flowers last throughout the long summer and late-summer weeks. Suitable for wild gardens.
- *graminifolia*
○ to ○○○ ⊕ △ ◯
Long-lived, lilac-pink flowers, 15 to 30 cm (6 to 12 in), July to September. O: southern Alps, subalpine. A: *Micromeria piperella, Satureja montana* 'Alba'

Scutellaria · Skullcap · Mint Family (Labiatae)
○ to ○○○ ⊕ △ ‖ ▭ ⋙ ⎚ ◯ H1

- *alpina* · Alpine Skullcap
An excellent, energetic, long-living little rock-garden plant with mauve and white or pink flowers. 25 cm (10 in). A neglected plant, but one most worthy of inclusion in the garden. May/August. O: one subspecies grows in mountains of Asia, whence through central and southern So-

viet Union and Balkans, Alps, Pyrenees. Mountain scree slopes to subalpine level. Grows wild with small *Carex* and *Festuca* types, *Arabis*. A: red sedum.
- *baicalensis*
Grows to 30 cm (12 in). Bluish-mauve flower heads which gradually grow to form small bushes, almost a metre (3 ft) across. July/August with second flowering in early autumn. This charming skullcap is the best of those listed here and one of the best summer rock-garden plants. Its size makes it most suitable for the edges of the rock garden or with dwarf shrubs. O: from Lake

Baikal to eastern Siberia. A: white *Delphinium grandiflorum*, yellow flax, yellow potentilla and helianthemum.
- *orientalis* var. *pinnatifida* · Yellow Skullcap
H2
The longest-flowering of all the skullcaps; 15 to 30 cm (6 to 12 in), June to August. The grey-green leaves are thickly covered with long, pale-yellow, snapdragon-like flowers. This variety is hardier than the type and seems to be native to more northerly climes. The true species is found from Syria to the Urals, from the Altai to the Adriatic. Provide it with its native habitat—a dry, sunny, rather rocky slope in a warm position, and you will find the effort worthwhile! A: Combine it with other small long-flowerers like *Campanula portenschlagiana, Helianthemum*, blue flax.
- *scordifolia*
H2
A plant which continually amazes one with its good temper and long flowering. Will usually produce dark mauve flowers throughout the summer months, but may fail to flower some years, though it will usually reappear in flower in the same spot. Propagate by small tuber-like growths that the plant leaves behind it in the soil. Pruning sometimes advisable. 15 cm (6 in). July/August. O: Korea. In light soils it can be very invasive.

Sedum · Stonecrop · Stonecrop Family (Crassulaceae)
○ to ○○○ △ ◯ ⋓ ♧ H1
Sedums are plants of astonishing indestructibility, most of which will tolerate extreme drought, while others will form thick carpets in the deepest shade, with both leaves and flowers contributing to their effectiveness. Flowering time is in summer and autumn, when the saxifrages are almost completely over. Sedum is also the cheapest plant to re-

place lawn in areas where turf refuses to grow or where turf would be too expensive. Of course we are not talking here of a lawn with the accepted uses of grass, and it would require narrow paths or stepping stones. In many of the more succulent species any small shoot broken off will form roots and develop a new plant. Both the foliage, evergreen in some cases, and the flowers give a decorative effect throughout the entire year. They thrive on drought, with only a few species failing to prosper in extreme drought on a south-facing slope, but these too will do well with the minimum of watering.

At this point I must warn against a number of sedum species or forms which are untypical of the beauty of the family in general.

Beware of:

Sedum acre, a very devil in the garden.
- *album* (wild type), invasive.
- *anglicum*, short-lived.
- *lydium*, unreliable in the long term, though good where it thrives.
- *sedifome*, unattractive.
- *spurium* 'Splendidissimum', flowers poorly in maturity.

It has taken long years of working with sedums in the garden for me to be able to compile the following ideal list and to be able to list flowering times and colours, leaf colourings and evergreen properties for each plant.

It would be difficult to imagine a more reliable and serviceable assortment of plants, yet many of them are not traditional garden plants. I hope that the colour photos and the distribution maps will help persuade many gardeners of their merits.

The realisation of the immense lifespans of numberless small plants, grasses and ferns can only increase their worldwide popularity.

List of sedums arranged by flowering time

1. Flowering time: May

Sedum krajinae (syn. S. ukrainae)
‖ ᴧᴧᴧ▸ 🗂 ‡
A stonecrop with profuse warm-gold flowers above dark-green, mossy leaves, from southern Slovakia. One of the earliest, low-growing sedums which flowers for weeks on end. Its only drawback is its unattractive brownish colouring after flowering. A: intersperse with a few dwarf blue grasses and red-leaved *Sempervivum* hybrids.
- *roseum* (S. rhodiola) · Roseroot
‖ 🗂 ‡
A tough herbaceous sedum with its 15 to 30 cm (6 to 12 in) stems densely set with blue-grey leaves and terminating in clusters of yellow flowers in spring. O: mountains around the northern temperate zone. Worth growing for its foliage alone.

2. Flowering time: June to July

Sedum album 'Coral Carpet' · White Stonecrop
‖ ▢ ᴧᴧᴧ▸ ‡
A thick, low-growing carpeting form with white flowers in June/July. Beautiful reddish-bronze colouring from early summer through to autumn. In winter the bronze turns to green. At its best in full sun and not over-rich soil! A: blue *Festuca* species, also between bulbs.
- - 'Murale'
A wild variety discovered in the Donau region in 1887. Superior to the species in more orderly growth, durability and richness of flowers. Loses its bronze colouring when in flower in summer but to regain it in autumn. One of the best brown-leaved sedums. The white and pink flowers are better and thicker than in the species. 10 to 15 cm (4 to 6 in). O: Europe, North Africa, Asia Minor.

- *floriferum*
▢ ᴧᴧᴧ▸ ‡
A real treasure with its profuse bright yellow flowers and thick, dark-green shoots. Around 20 cm (8 in). Also attractive with its brown, ornamental fruits. Good ground-coverer. O: north-east China. A: in small groups with blue grasses or as individual, solitary plants.
- - 'Weihenstephaner Gold'
Golden-yellow cultivar, excellent ground-cover.

- *hybridum*
◗ ▢ ᴧᴧᴧ▸ ‡
Has a great future in the garden ahead of it. Tolerates any treatment and responds by forming evergreen carpets which amaze us in autumn when all other *Sedum spurium* varieties lose their leaves. The yellow flowers that rather spoil the effect of the plant do not live long and can be easily removed. This is the best sedum for graves. The name *"hybridum"* is something of a mystery which even escaped the great Linnaeus.

- *kamtschaticum* 'Variegatum'
▢ ᴧᴧᴧ▸
Charming yellow flowers and long-lasting flowers. 15 cm (6 in). It is astonishing that plants like this, or the October cimicifuga *(Cimicifuga simplex)*, come from such exposed areas. A: beautiful with small blue *Festuca* species or blue-green carpeting sedums and brown *Sedum kamtschaticum* var. *middendorfianum*.
- - var. *middendorfianum* 'Diffusum'
▢ ᴧᴧᴧ▸
Flowers weeks before the brown-leaved sedum species, forming luxuriant carpets of yellow flowers which turn reddish-brown as they fade. 15 cm (6 in).

- *reflexum* · Rock Stonecrop
▢ ᴧᴧᴧ▸ ‡
Like *S. rupestre*, is unique in colouring, with its golden flowers. Widespread throughout Europe. Flowers 25 cm (10 in) tall over low carpet of leaves.

– – 'Viride'
A variety of the above, but will not tolerate so much dryness'

– *selskianum*

Comes from the shores of Lake Khanka in east Manchuria. Shining green carpet with yellow flowers. Tolerates more shade than the others and good carpeter in shade. Leaves turn salmon-pink in autumn. Slight scent of mignonette. Only disadvantage is that flowers fade slowly detracting from the beauty of the plant. 15 to 20 cm (6 to 8 in).

– *spathulifolium* 'Cape Blanco'

Its grey, almost white foliage has such a delicate appearance that it is a pleasant surprise to find that it behaves so well in the garden. A few plants will soon cover quite an area. 10 cm (4 in), June/July. O: Cape Blanco, Oregon.
A: any number of neighbours can give a variety of effects. Try carpeting speedwell or red *Sempervivum* hybrids. Effective in tubs.

– – 'Purpureum'

Older leaves are wine-coloured. Much more sturdy growth than *S. spathulifolium* 'Cape Blanco'.

3. Flowering time: July to August

Sedum album · White Stonecrop

Only 8 cm .(3 in) tall. Tolerates less dryness than many other *Sedum* species. O: North Africa, Europe, Asia Minor; isolated examples up to 2 500 m (8 250 ft).

– *dasyphyllum* var. *suendermannii* · Thick-leaved Stonecrop

Spanish form of thick-leaved stonecrop. Bluish-green leaves. Only 5 cm (2½ in) tall. Takes over when true plant stops flowering and has same requirements.

– *divergens* 'Atropurpureum'
From the north-west United States (Oregon). 10 cm (4 in) tall. Copper-coloured cushions of short, thick shoots. Pale yellow flowers.

– *ewersii*

A 15 cm (6 in) dwarf with pink to ruby flowers, which should be snipped off after flowering. For months its charm remains unrivalled (even by *S. cyaneum*). Must be in full sun! O: west Himalayas, Altai, Mongolia.

– – var. *homophyllum*
Heaven knows where this plant originated! A delightful little carpeter, but slightly bushier than most. Extremely even tempered and not used anywhere nearly often enough. Can be shy flowering. Dark pink. Beautiful up to August when it loses leaves.

– *kamtschaticum* var. *middendorfianum*

Attractive yellow and brown starry flowers from bronze cushions of leaves. A precious jewel which makes *S. middendorfianum* 'Diffusum' look coarse. The older the plant, the more its quiet charm increases. The joy of growing such small, indestructible jewels can be quite extraordinarily intense.

– *lidakense*
Trailing mats of green leaves with shining pink flowers. 10 cm (4 in). Flowering from June to August. O: Japan.

– *sarmentosum*

A Chinese creeping *Sedum* which is unique in the genus.

– *sexangulare* · Six-Angled Stonecrop

A delightful plant whose green leaves dissolve into masses of gold flowers. This thick, flat carpeter can never be too highly valued. 8 to 10 cm (3 to 4 in). O: Europe.

– *spurium*

A garden plant for over two hundred years, but cultivars date back only 30 to 50 years. 10 to 12 cm (4 to 5 in).

– – 'Album Superbum'
The most attractive and thickest of the S. spuriums but with short main flowering time and longer second flowering.

– – 'Purple Carpet'
This flat, copper-leaved stonecrop must be the best of all. In its familiar spot becomes more beautiful every year. Deep carmine-red flowers toning beautifully with leaves. 10 cm (4 in).

– – 'Roseum Superbum'
Striking for the beauty and long life of its pink flowers which make this plant particularly attractive.

– – 'Salmoneum'
Salmon pink cultivar, one of the least demanding, and best-coloured forms. Flowers a second time!

– – 'Schorbusser Blut' ('Dragon's Blood')
Beautiful brownish carpets with ruby flowers. One of the most richly flowering cultivars.

– *telephium* 'Munstead Dark Red' · Orpine
○○ ⦙ ⬡
Highly unusual colouring with its dark red leaves, and also one of the longest-lived *telephium* forms in this colour. Quite unique in appearance. 30 cm (12 in) tall, 40 cm (16 in) wide. Carmine flowers. O: Europe.

4. Flowering time: August to September

Sedum anacampseros · Reddish Stonecrop
○○ ‖
Grows to 10 to 15 cm (4 to 6 in). Delightful shape with beautiful bluish tone to leaves but insignificant flowers. O: northern Spain and southern Alps, rising to 2500 m (8250 ft).

– *cauticolum* 'Robustum'
○ to ○○○ ‖ ▭ Y ⬡ ♕ ♁
A much larger variety than the type plant with especially attractive leaves. Bright red flower heads. From thick cushions of leaves (20 cm, 8 in tall) produces its warm red flowers as early as August, so that this colour is now available for three full months.

– *cyaneum* (syn. S. pluricaule)
○ to ○○ ‖ Y ⛁ ⬡ ♁
6 cm (2½ in) high, pinkish-red flowers from flat, blue-green leaves, which begin to develop slowly in the spring. A: principally with *Sempervivum*. O: Japan, Amur region, Sakhalin.

– *pulchellum*
○ ≌
Evergreen species with pink, starfish-like flowers. Best in moist position. 15 cm (6 in). O: eastern United States (Indiana, Missouri, Texas).

– *spectabile*
○ to ○○○ ‖ ⊥ ⬡ ♕ ♁
Forms bluish-green rounded bushes up to 80 cm (2½ ft) diameter and 60 cm (2 ft) tall in maturity; flat carmine flowers.

– – 'Autumn Joy'
In this cultivar *S. spectabile* has finally achieved a really good, salmon-pink colour. Mature plants of 45 cm (18 in) tall and 70 cm (2 ft 4 in) wide are plants of the utmost beauty.

– – 'Brilliant'
Carmine red form, 40 cm (2 ft 4 in) tall, renowned for its luxuriant growth.

– – 'Iceberg'
A fine plant to 30 cm (1 ft) with pure white flowers contrasting well with the foliage.

– – 'Variegatum'
Foliage has buff-yellow variegation

– *tartarinowii*
○○ ‖
A plant which is as delicate-looking as it is indestructible. 8 cm (3 in) tall with pinkish-white flowers. Decorative blue-green leaves for months on end. O: northern China, Mongolia.

– *telephium* · Orpine
○ to ○○○ ≃ ⦙ ⊥ ⬡ ♕ ♁
Adds a new colour to the September garden which continues into October. Mature plants grow to 60 cm (2 ft) tall and 80 cm (2 ft 8 in) wide. A: this sedum is beautiful beneath *Cimicifuga racemosa* and *C. simplex* or alongside white heath asters *(A. ericoides)*. Ideal for heather gardens and edges of rock garden. The sight of the dried-up flowers against the first snow is extremely picturesque, so do not cut back until spring.

5. Flowering time: September to October

Sedum cauticolum
○ to ○○○ ‖ Y ⛁ ♁
Only 12 to 15 cm (5 to 6 in) tall, a flat-growing, grey-leaved plant with leaves edged in mauve. O: Japan.

– *sieboldii* · Siebold's Stonecrop
○ to ○○○ ‖ Y ⛁ ⬡ ♕ ♁
Extremely beautiful, almost turquoise-blue leaves make this one of the most attractive of all sedums. Late-flowering, 15 cm (6 in). O: Japan. A: *Sedum spurium* 'Purple Carpet', blue fescue and red-leaved *Sempervivum* hybrids.

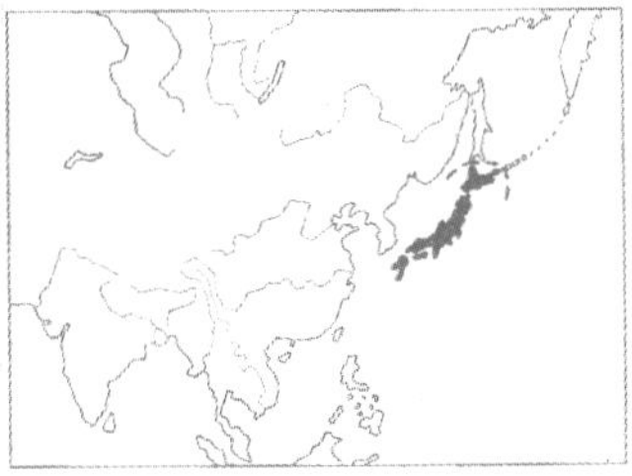

Sedum
(arranged by leaf-colour)

Brown-leaved
Sedum album 'Murale'
– *kamtschaticum* var. *middendorfianum*
– *spathulifolium* 'Purpureum'
– *spurium* 'Purple Carpet'
– *telephium* 'Munstead Dark Red'

Blue-leaved
Sedum anacampseros
– *ewersii* 'Nanum'
– – var. *homophyllum*
– *reflexum*
– *sieboldii*

Variegated leaves
Sedum cauticolum
– *kamtschaticum* 'Variegatum'

Green-leaved
Sedum cauticolum 'Robustum'
– *hybridum*
– *krajinae*
– *pulchellum*
– *reflexum* 'Cristatum'
– *sarmentosum*
– *selskianum*
– *sexangulare*
– *spectabile*
– *spurium* (except for 'Purple Carpet')
– *telephium*

Best evergreen sedums
Sedum album
– – *'Murale'*
– *divergens* 'Atropurpureum'
– *hybridum*
– *reflexum*
– *sexangulare*
– *spathulifolium* 'Cape Blanco'

Sempervivum · Houseleek · Stonecrop Family (Crassulaceae)
○ to ○○○' △ ‖ ▭ ⋀⋀ ⎕ ⭗ ⌁
H1

For the past thirty or forty years I have been grappling with the problem of sempervivums in the garden, during which time many varieties with which I was at first delighted proved over the years to have various defects and had to be withdrawn from circulation, especially with large-rosetted forms. From 70 new wild hybridizations only two proved relevant to the rock garden! Defects included an inclination to flower too early, preventing sufficiently large rosettes being formed. Other plants faded either too quickly or too slowly. Two varieties showed definite diseases which no one had ever mentioned previously. This was one face of the coin. Another was the remarkably uninformed indifference of the gardening public towards sempervivums. I began—and would advise other cultivators to do the same—to rely on colour photography and to construct long boxes beside the most frequented paths in my nursery, where the plants were prominently displayed with their botanical and common names in an attempt to catch the eye of the passer by.

My list of sempervivum species and varieties suitable for the garden cannot pretend to represent the complete range of wild species, varieties and garden hybrids. There are many other wild species in addition to those I have included and cultivars producing improvements in form and colour are also still in their infancy! Large-scale seeding from the best species and hybrids always produces unusual colour tones which no one could anticipate. But it is a long process to produce high quality in the quantities required for worldwide distribution. From the time when *Sempervivum tectorum*, the least demanding of the large-rosetted sempervivums, was planted on roofs to protect against thunderstorms in the early Middle Ages, where they survived for decades without soil, the family has evolved producing immense variety. We continually come across surprising new sempervivums as we go through life. Some have rosettes which are covered in silvery white webs and form tiny indestructible, silver-white cushions from which rise red flowers, reminiscent of underwater plants. The jewel-like quality of their silver leaves or their green and reddish-brown colouring close by buff-coloured rosettes or deep violets tinged with steel-blue are truly a magical sight.

Even the larger plants are beginning to spin silver webs whose beauty no words of mine can portray. How often words fail to convey the fullness of beauty. The day is not far off when these little jewels will come into their own, these northern brothers of the distant cactus kingdom. For hundreds of years the statue of Roland in Brandenburg has worn a crown of sempervivum to protect against lightning. There is no soil for its roots, only the sparrows provide a little manure. The ability of *S. tectorum* to live without soil, found elsewhere only in *Arhemanta* or *Corydalis lutea*, is echoed in other sempervivum types, both large and small, which have been known to live up to fifty years in a crack in a wall. The owners of one such plant recall the stormy contrast between their own lives over the last fifty years and the tranquillity in which this plant has passed its life.

America has no native sempervivum species—most come from Europe and Africa and from there they spread to the mountains of W. Asia.

Botanical names are still a matter of dispute. I have come across three names for one plant, resulting from its tendency to hybridize freely. So I have taken the obvious course and where possible added a common name to the botanical name. One producer of extremely beautiful hybrids has solved the difficulty of thinking up new names by calling his three treasures 'Alpha', 'Beta' and 'Gamma'. But unfortunately the name 'Gamma' gives no indication that it refers to a magical jewel of a plant which plays a special part in the spring garden.

My former list of sempervivums, all of which are completely indestructible and cover a wide variety of properties, has been extended to include eleven new plants, all of which have been successfully tried over several years. These additions to my original list are all completely free of defects. These living jewels are a possession we should value, created to remain with us for ever more.

To achieve the fullest effect do not use too few of each individual sort and place a few runners at the edge of each group leading into neighbouring plants to provide a good colour contrast. Sempervivums are always grateful to be able to sink their relatively strong, long roots into good soil and will profit from a little fresh soil occasionally. Flat carpets of small-rosetted sempervivums will profit from an occasional thorough watering.

None of this is essential, but will prove worthwhile in the long term. You can intersperse the separate clumps with dwarf blue festucas, silver saxifrages and low-growing sedums, together with individual rocks of interesting colour. Some species in the genus *Sempervivum* are now included in the *Jovibarba* and can be found under that heading.

List of sempervivums with species and forms arranged by size

1. Small sempervivums

Sempervivum arachnoideum · Cobweb Houseleek
This little silvery plant has an individual charm which ensures it a lasting place in our garden. First discovered in 1884. O: granite Alps from the Pyrenees to the Apennines from 600 to 2000 m (1800 to 6000 ft).

– – 'Minor'
One of the very smallest Cobweb Houseleeks which grows unbelievably in any available situation. O: unknown.
– – ssp. *tomentosum*
One of the most attractive of the Cobweb Houseleeks. Discovered in 1865 in the high French Alps and later in Switzerland and the Tirol. Not to be confused with 'webbianum' which is prone to disease. Rosettes twice as large as in the species plant *S. arachnoideum*, producing bright carmine-red flowers.
– *arachnoideum* var. 'Iaggeri'
Its white, cobwebbed rosettes form a small dome while the flowers are deep pink.
Sempervivum soboliferum, see *Jovibarba sobolifera*

2. Medium-sized Sempervivums

Sempervivum reginae-amaliae
Medium sized dense rosettes of usually purplish-green leaves,

sometimes almost grey, making an effective contrast to the brighter forms. The smaller forms are generally the most attractive.
– hybrids 'Alpha'
This cultivar forms light brown cushions of leaves spun with silvery threads, which appear everywhere.
– – 'Beta'
Purplish-red with silver sheen.
– – 'Correvon's Hybrid'
Medium sized, velvety, grey-green rosettes, violet tinted in spring.
– – 'Gamma'
To do justice to this treasure of the older sorts any description must take in its unusual green, silver and deep-brown tones and decorative effects.
– – 'Gloriosum'
Medium sized, reddish rosettes at their brightest in summer.
– – 'Granat'
A hybrid which forms striking, medium-sized deep red rosettes. Unfortunately slower-growing than other red hybrids.
– – 'Rubin'
Medium-sized rosettes of strongest and purest red of all *Sempervivum* hybrids. To perform at its best it requires a little more care in feeding and positioning than the others.
– – 'Shirley's Joy'
Green-leaved but so densely covered in white hairs as to appear frosted.
– – 'Snowberger'
Soft jade green with silvery overlay and curled leaves.
– *marmoreum*
The true species is rather like a neater, slower-growing *S. tectorum*, the green rosettes usually with dark tips and an overall reddish flush.
– – 'Chocolate'
Dark, chocolate coloured rosettes which turn red in winter.
– – 'Giganteum'
A significant improvement in size and colour which improves even more in winter and also forms much larger rosettes.

– *montanum*
A very variable species found right through southern Europe. A number of forms have been given separate names.
– – 'Rubrum'
Rosettes a good mahogany red, darkest in summer sun.
– *pittonii*
An attractive species with medium sized dense rosettes, grey-green in colour with purple tips. Yellowish flowers are frequent but so are the short-stalked offset rosettes making tight clumps.
– *ruthenicum*
This species is individualized by its characteristic thick, dark-green leaves with their silver down and is completely different from all other Sempervivums. From its luxuriant flat rosettes rise pale yellow flowers. Found in Transylvania, Ukraine and much of south-east Europe. Discovered 1855.

3. Large Sempervivums

Sempervivum hybrid 'Commander Hay'
This hybrid forms huge rosettes up to 20 cm (8 in) in diameter. Light reddish-brown in colour with green tips.
– – 'Othello'
This hybrid forms extremely flat, well-shaped large, very deep-red rosettes which look really gigantic and is also fast-growing. Pink flowers.
– – 'Silverine'
Very large, silvery-grey rosettes. An excellent contrast to the red-leaved cultivars.
– *marmoreum* (syn. S. schlehanii) 'Maximum'
The strongest and longest-living of the large green sempervivums. While there are larger, more attractive large green species which will delight over many years until they are partly or completely destroyed by severe frost, this one continues in all its glory. I have not been able to make up my mind whether to recommend winter protection. It

may be necessary in very cold areas. O: eastern Alps.

– – 'Metallicum Giganteum'
A cultivar whose colour is that of red sandstone.

– *tectorum* · Common Houseleek
The "protector against lightning" which can cover roofs where there is no soil with large rosettes and grow there happily for decades. O: from Pyrenees through Europe to north of Balkan peninsula.

– – 'Atroviolaceum'
Pinkish-mauve houseleek whose colour tones are unique. Origin and place of discovery remain unknown.

– – 'Giganteum'
In a suitable spot will produce gigantic rosettes. In less propitious situations will grow to moderate size. Colour is same olive-green found in *S.* × *mettenianum* and nowhere else in the plant kingdom.

– – 'Robustum'
Large, bluish-green rosettes with slightly brownish tone.

– – 'Royanum'
Yellowish-green rosettes, the leaf tips flushed red.

– – 'Triste'
The best golden-brown colour of all the wild houseleeks. Experts believe this to be the real species plant rather than the deep-red, small-rosetted plant. Unknown origin, known since 1880.

– – var. *calcareum* · Limestone Houseleek (syn. S. calcareum)
Typified by greenish-blue rosettes with reddish-brown tips. From French Alps.

– – ssp. *mettenianum*
A fine, irreplaceable houseleek with all the good qualities tirelessly producing its large rosettes to form thick carpets over large areas. Retains its beauty in winter. O: central Alps and Pyrenees.

– – ssp. *tectorum* var. *lamottei*
An extremely sturdy plant whose green, red-tipped rosettes will overcome all weeds. Excellent ground cover for shade. Discovered in 1885 on the Puy de Dôme. Found from central and eastern France to Alsace.

Silene · Campion, Catchfly · Pink Family (Caryophyllaceae)
○ to ☀ ⊕ ≃ △ ‖ 🍶 H1
The large Silene family is, with the exception of *Silene maritima*, made up of excellent rock-garden plants from Transylvania, the Carpathians and Caucasus and other high alpine regions.

– *acaulis* · Moss Campion
✤
Pink flowers on a thick, dark green mat in June/July. An extremely striking plant in the mountains where it forms thick, pink mats often up to half a metre (18 in) across. The type plant has, however, proved disappointing in the garden.

– – 'Floribunda'
A cultivar which flowers successfully in the garden and needs some chalk supplement. Plant in fertile but not over-nutritious soil—and be patient. It is best to position the plant where it can grow down over a rock beneath.
The mat itself does not form roots, the whole plant drawing on one deep tap-root. O of type: from the Pyrenees, through the Alps, Carpathians, north-west Balkans to the Urals. Its pink mats also greet the surprised traveller in the west and east Arctic and in some parts of the Rocky Mountains.

– *alpestris* (syn. Heliosperma alpestre) · Alpine Catchfly
White-flowering in mid-May/June. O: southern Alps to Carpathians, mountains of south-

east Europe. This alpine catchfly grows to just under 20 cm (8 in) with dainty white flowers. It is certain that no one could ever tire of it. There is also an excellent double form. O: eastern Alps to Transylvania, northern Balkans, at alpine levels. A: a host of suitable partners at this time of year: gentians, *Helianthemum chamaecistus*, *Viola gracilis*, *Potentilla aurea*, small buttercups.

– – 'Pleniflorum', snow-white double form flowers June/July.

– *maritima* · Sea Campion
A silver-leaved plant with long-lasting white flowers above a completely flat mat of leaves. White is excellent to offset bright colours, and is highly effective even in small quantities. O: western and southern Europe. There is a double form.

– *schafta*
An autumn campion from the Caucasus. Fresh, bright pink flowers which form an excellent prelude to the heathers. August/September. Beautiful with *Satureja montana* 'Alba'.

– – 'Splendens'
A marked improvement on the type plant!

Sisyrinchium · Iris Family (Iridaceae)
○ to ○○

– *angustifolium* · Blue-eyed Grass
H1–2
Dense tufts of iris-like leaves up to 30 cm (1 ft) tall, with mauve flowers in late May and June. Dies back in winter in unpropitious sites but as the plant reseeds itself it is rarely lost. O: North America. A: charming with maiden pinks, *Festuca* species, *Campanula portenschlagiana*, *Hypericum olympicum*.

– *bellum*
H2–3
A dwarf species, only 10 to 15 cm (4 to 6 in) high with relatively large mauve-blue flowers. O: western North America.

– – 'Album'
White flowers. Often confused with or called *S. macouainii*.

Soldanella · Snowbell · Primrose Family (Primulaceae)

– *montana* · Mountain Snowbell
☀ to ◐ ⊖ ≌ ⅄ ⬡ ⏀ ⧧ H1
Fringed, funnel-shaped flowers of bluish-amethyst appear in April. An alpine plant from 800 to 1600 m (2400 to 4800 ft) in moist, humus soil, usually in shade. Excellent in semi-shady garden sites together with its wild neighbours, wood sorrel, *Luzula*, *Maianthemum*. This is a good soldanella for the garden, but better is its subspecies *S. montana* ssp. *hungarica* (which has recently come to be considered a species in its own right). O: Alps, eastern Europe, Carpathians, Balkans. Likes well rotted pine mull and a moist, shady position. With a little care soldanellas will do well in the garden, especially in peaty soil. A: dwarf rhododendrons.

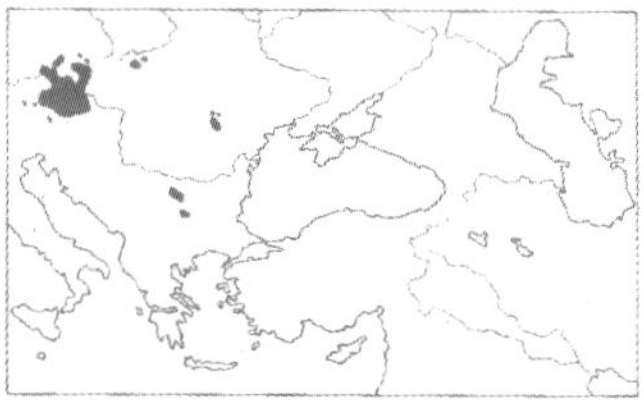

– *alpina*
Not as easy as *S. montana* but successful in peaty soil which does not dry out. Far more dainty, from 5 to 15 cm (2 to 6 in) high. O: mountains of Europe.

– *villosa*
Similar to *S. montana* but the leaves wider and more red-purple beneath. Flower stems to 30 cm (1 ft). An excellent garden plant.

Solidago · Golden-Rod · Daisy Family (Compositae)
○ to ○○○ ≃ ⤫ ⬡ ♈ H1
Only dwarf golden-rods are suitable for the rock garden. Of the taller forms, both well-established species and newer improved cultivars, there are a few smaller ones which can be used for extremely dry sites, but for general rock-garden use even these are too coarse. Use them rather for rock-garden borders between shrubs, blue-green grasses and other robust plants which like dry conditions, and use them individually. The following four non-spreading dwarf species and forms will usually be enough for any garden. Snip off the flowers when they have faded.

Solidago 'Cloth of Gold'
Around 45 cm (18 in) in height, very vigorous in growth with bright yellow flowers.

– 'Crown of Rays'
Grows to around 45 cm (18 in). Bright golden flowers in August. The most attractive shape of all the small golden-rods.

– 'Golden Thumb' ('Queenie', 'Tom Thumb')
Very dwarf and bushy, to 20 to 30 cm (8 to 12 in). The foliage is golden tinted and the flowers bright yellow.

– *virgaurea* 'Brachystachys' · Golden-Rod
Forms small erect bushes of 40 cm (16 in); for the rock or wild garden. Yellow flowers in July/September. O: Europe, northern and western Asia, North Africa.

– – 'Cambrica'
Even smaller with flowering stems only 10 to 15 cm.

× *Solidaster luteus*, see index

Stachys · Woundwort · Mint Family (Labiatae)
○ to ○○○ ▭ ⋙ ⦙ ⅄ ⏀ H1

– *byzantina* (syn. S. olympica, S. lanata) · Lamb's Ears
Insignificant mauve flowers sitting atop masses of silver, woolly leaves and stems. 30 cm (12 in), June/July. O: sunny slopes between *Artemisia pontica* and *Verbascum*: Crimea, Caucasus to northern Iran. A: Beautiful in large areas with blue-green grasses and sedums and interspersed with 'Silver Carpet' and other silver-grey plants.

– – 'Silver Carpet'
At last we have a cultivar which does not flower, thus producing

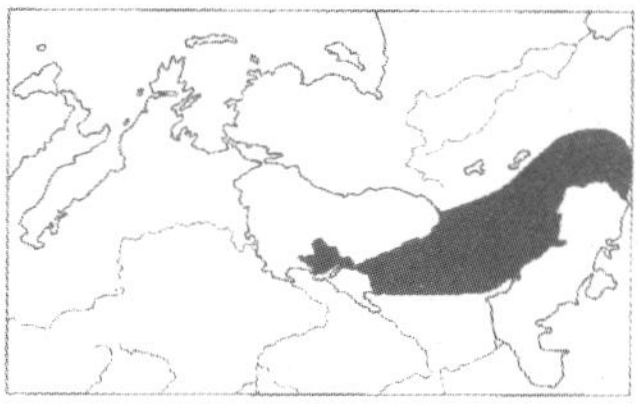

much better quality plant. Excellent ground-cover for dry site in full sun.

– *grandiflora* 'Superba' (syn. Betonica macrantha 'Superba')
Resembles a large, dark-pink nettle. 45 to 60 cm (18 to 24 in), July/August. Suitable for dry borders of heather garden. O: high meadows of Caucasus and Armenia. A: *Stachys niveus*, tall bellflowers, *Deschampsia cespitosa* and taller blue grasses.

– *lavandulifolia*
20 cm (8 in) high plant with grey leaves and in July dark red flowers with downy throats. Needs room in the garden to spread its creeping shoots. Suitable only for warm, gravelly sites in full sun. O: Caucasus, Asia Minor, Iran.

– *nivea*
Loose whorls of white flowers above wide, corrugated leaves. Over 20 cm (8 in), June/July. O: Caucasus and Syria.

Stratiotes, see Water plants p. 70

Synthyris · Figwort Family (Scrophulariaceae)
◐ ⊖ ≌ ⅄ ⏀ ⧧ H1

– *stellata* (syn. S. reniformis)
Round, glossy, bluntly toothed leaves with short spikes of mauve flowers from mid-March. A welcome addition to other early-flowering plants. O: western United States (Oregon, Washington). A: *Adonis amurensis*, *Primula juliae* hybrids, dwarf ferns.

Telekia · Ox-Eye · Daisy Family (Compositae)
○ to ○○○ ⊕ △ ‖ ⛁ ⬡ H1

– *speciosissima* (syn. Buphthalmum speciosissimum)

A rock plant for the sunniest, driest garden sites. Deep gold flowers on 30 cm (12 in) stems. Not a plant for the beginner. June/July. O: southern Alps.

Thalictrum · Meadow Rue · Buttercup Family (Ranunculaceae)
○ to ◑ ≅ ⊥ ⊔ ✕ ○ ♂ H1
– *aquilegifolium* · Great Meadow Rue
Highly decorative from mid-May to well into June with its feathery, white or pale mauve flowers. A good waterside plant for the formal rock garden or in a large natural rock garden. Excellent with *Iris sibirica* or white globe flowers. Avoid combining the mauve colour with yellow! O: watersides, woodedges, damp meadows, low moorland throughout Europe from sea-level to 2000 m (6500 ft), from southern Scandinavia to northern Mediterranean. Found wild with *Dentaria, Aruncus, Polygonatum, Pulmonaria, Aquilegia.* The great meadow rue has something of the look of rushing water about it.
The sulphur-yellow and blue-leaved meadow rues, which grow to head-height, are too tall to be included here.

Thymus · Thyme · Mint Family (Labiatae)
○ to ○○○ ⊕ ‖ ▭ ⋙ Υ ⑂ ○ ♔ ≢ F
Thyme has an important part to play in the rock garden and even more so in the larger wild garden.
– *praecox* var. *pseudolanguinosus* · Hairy Thyme
H1
The low-growing, evergreen hairy thyme rarely flowers, but is an excellent winter green plant, especially in an unpropitious, dry site—most effective where the ground undulates slightly. Ecxellent between heather and juniper, but welcome in any part of the rock garden. Tolerates more shade than the following type, but if my lengthy observa-

tions can be relied upon, not so well as *T. villosus.* O: western Europe.
– var. *arcticus* 'Coccineus' · Wild Thyme (often listed wrongly as *T. coccineus*)
An excellent deep red form of the familiar wild thyme. June/July. Excellent with *Campanula cochleariifolia*, which is in flower at the same time, planted within its carpets. In the shade the plant will eventually stop flowering. In a hot position it often looks after flowering as if the leaves have been burnt away by the sun, but they will reappear. O: *Thymus praecox* spreads its lemony scent throughout the countryside from alpine meadows up to the snowline, moorland, dunes, meadows, embankments, walls and wooded banks. All suit this little plant. It is extremely adaptable and very widespread. Grows wild with maiden pinks, *Antennaria dioica.*

– – 'Albus' has white flowers.
– – 'Pink Chintz' is salmon pink.
– *villosus (T. lanuginosus)*
H2

An excellent flat carpeter. Rarely flowers, but occasionally insignificant little mauve flower heads. Beautifully evergreen even in semi-shade. Excellent in either large or small expanses to divide different areas of the rock or wild garden. Easily kept in check. All it needs is a little patience until it begins to spread. O: south-west Spain, southern Portugal. A: smaller sedums, sempervivums, dwarf junipers.

Tiarella · Mitre-Wort · Saxifrage Family (Saxifragaceae)
☀ to ◑ ≅ ▭ Υ ♂ H1
– *cordifolia* · Foam Flower ⋙
Produces airy, fluffy spires of white flowers about 30 cm (1 ft) tall. Beautiful light-green foliage spreads by stolons and turns reddish-brown in autumn and, winter. Like the following species, needs moist, humus, shady position if it is to do well. O: North America (Nova Scotia and Ontario and south to Georgia).

– *wherryi*
A non-spreading species again producing its white, scented flower candles in May and June. Attractive foliage whose heart-shaped, matt-green leaves change colour with the seasons. Taller stems than *T. cordifolia* and needs less moisture. 30 cm (1 ft). O: south-east United States (Tennessee, North Carolina, Alabama).

Trapa, see Water plants, p. 70

Tricyrtis · Toad Lily · Lily Family (Liliaceae)
☀ to ◑ ≅ Υ H2
Plants from the forest edges of East Asia which flower from August to Cotober. 45 to 90cm (18 to 36 in). Curious plants whose leaves and pink, brown or ivory flowers are almost indescribable. Where to use them in the garden? In sheltered parts of the rock or wild garden in semi-shade with equally exotic neighbours!

Four European alpine plants which, with a little care, will thrive in the rock garden:
1. *Saxifraga oppositifolia*, the Purple Saxifrage (text p. 245), likes indirect sunlight.
2. *Veratrum album*, the White False Helleborine (text p. 274) – a giant among alpines.

3. *Soldanella carpatica* is related to the better-known *S. montana*, the Mountain Snowbell (text p. 255).
4. *Primula auricula*, the Auricula (text p. 223), played its part in the creation of the garden auricula, *P. X pubescens*, over 400 years ago.

Left-hand page:

1. *Sedum spectabile* (text p. 251), adds carmine-red to the summer garden. The flat flowers are a great attraction to butterflies.

2. *Sempervivum arachnoideum* ssp. *tomentosum*, the Cobweb Houseleek (text p. 253), shows here what it can achieve with natural planting in a crevice.

1. *Sedum* hybrid 'Immergrünchen' – one of the best evergreen, low-growing and always neat-looking carpet sedums.

2. The Bornim trial varieties of *Yucca filamentosa*, Adam's Needle (text p. 278–9), include 'BS Eisbär', 'Fontäne', 'Schellenbaum', 'Schneefichte' and 'Schneetanne'.

1. *Gentiana farreri* (text p. 176), needs a well-drained but moist soil in a shady position for successful cultivation. Accumulating winter wet leads to the death of this coveted gentian.

2. *Gentiana sino-ornata* 'Blauer Diamant' – a valuable new hybrid which has inherited all the good points of its parents *G. farreri* (text p. 176) and *G. sino-ornata* (text p. 193), and is easier to grow than either of them.

Crocus speciosus (text p. 114), brings forth its beautifully-shaped, finely-veined flower cups from early
September through to November. Once established it
will spread continuously.

1. *Clematis alpina*, the Alpine Clematis (text p. 122), with its blue or deep mauve flowers, is one of the best little climbing shrubs.

2. *Rhododendron impeditum* (text p. 127, 145), cannot be praised highly enough, and the 'Moerheim', 'Blue Tit' and 'Blue Wonder' varieties are particularly noteworthy. Completely hardy.

3. The ivy (text p. 122), has produced an astonishing number of dwarf varieties. *Hedera helix* 'Erecta' is one of the best for the rock garden.

4. *Kalmia latifolia*, the Calico Bush, with its rich flowers in May/June, grows to scarcely 2 m (6 ft) in Europe. Plant in an acid, humus-rich soil in semi-shade.

1. This natural-looking and effective combination of plants has the advantage of needing little care. Here shown are: *Clematis alpina* (text p. 122) (in flower), *Juniperus communis* ssp. *alpina*; in the crevice: *Soldanella montana* (text p. 255), *Saxifraga arendsii* hybrid 'Snow Carpet' and *Arabis procurrens* (text p. 156) (left).

2. *Cytisus X praecox*, an ivory broom, explodes into bloom from mid-April. Do not plant in an over-exposed situation. Any heather garden would be incomplete without this beautiful shrub.

Many gardeners are unaware that crocuses begin flowering in early autumn and with mild weather can last well into December.

1. *Crocus kotschyanus* (text p. 114) belongs to the robust autumn crocus varieties.

2. Anyone who has once planted *Crocus speciosus* (text p. 114) in their garden will have it for ever.

3. *Crocus byzantinus* (text p. 114), is long-flowering and increases well.

4. *Colchicum autumnale* (text p. 112), should be more widely-known. Only in a damp situation will it prosper for long and seed itself freely.

There are a number of types and hybrids of the autumn colchicum. Plant away from small neighbours so that in spring their strong leaf-shoots cannot harm other plants.

1. *Colchicum speciosum* (text p. 112) – the best-known species of all.

2. *Colchicum* hybrid 'The Giant', flowers late in October.

3. *Colchicum* hybrid 'Waterlily', is the largest and best-growing of all the double colchicums.

4. *Colchicum bornmuelleri* (text p. 112), flowers from the end of August with large, noble, cup-shaped blooms.

1. *Betula nana*, the Dwarf Birch (text p. 122) – a distinctive shrub of around 80 cm (32 in) in height.
2. *Salix retusa*, the Blunt-leaved Willow (text p. 123), is a dwarf shrub which would be excellent in any rock garden. It provides valuable protection for small plants.

3. *Daphne cneorum*, the Garland Flower (text p. 122), likes a sunny but not over-hot situation and slightly chalky, well-drained soil.
4. *Salix reticulata*, the Reticulated Willow (text p. 123), needs quite careful attention, preferring a damp, shady position and a gravelly soil.

1. *Globularia cordifolia*, the Matted Globularia (text p. 195), is pale mauve and looks beautiful with white- or pink-flowered plants. Experience shows it is best not planted over too wide an area.

2. *Arctostaphylos uva-ursi*. Apart from its medicinal properties this plant's beauty makes it a balm to the beholder. As good in the wild garden as in the rock garden.

3. *Moltkia petraea* (text p. 123) – a small, bright blue plant from the mountains of central Yugoslavia and central Greece. It is still a rarity in the rock garden.

1. Once again autumn fills the garden with colour. Striking effects can be created by combining plants in autumn colouring with berried shrubs. Here *Malus X purpurea* 'Aldenhamensis' is seen alongside *Miscanthus floridulus* (right). This giant grass can grow to 3 m (9 ft) and is thus only suitable for the border of a larger rock garden.

2. *Actaea rubra* (text p. 152), is already decked with shining red berries in August.

3. The bright red berry-heads of *Arum italicum*, the southern European arum (text p. 111), remind us that the new shoots of the green arrow-like leaves will soon be appearing.

1. The form 'Rubrifolia' of *Saxifraga cortusifolia* var. *fortunei* with its dark foliage is a great improvement on the species. It also flowers for about 14 days longer.

2. *Saxifraga cortusifolia* var. *fortunei* (text p. 248), bestows a wealth of flowers upon us in late autumn. This treasure of the garden will only thrive in a partly shady, damp situation and a humus-rich soil.

Right-hand page:
1. Hoar frost brings out the shape of dwarf shrubby conifers excellently, as seen here with *Picea abies* 'Nana'. A garden path in winter can often provide enchanting new effects.
2. *Juniperus horizontalis*, the Creeping Juniper (text p. 125), is just beginning to be well-known. It is one of the most luxuriant dwarf conifers, with several possible uses, serving as a low foil for taller neighbours or flowing like a waterfall down a steep slope.

1. *Colchicum bornmuelleri* (text p. 112), begins to flower from the end of August.
2. *Cyclamen purpurascens*, the scented Common Cyclamen (text p. 115), should only be planted in warm, draught-free, slightly shady situations. In the right conditions it is self-seeding.
3. *Cyclamen hederifolium*, the Sowbread (text p. 115), and *Polystichum setiferum* 'Plumosum Densum', a Fronded Fern, look magical together for weeks on end during August and September.

Berberis vernae – one of the richest-flowering and
richest-fruiting types. Green in summer, with yellow
flowers, producing clusters of berries which last well
into winter. Around 1.5 m (4¹/₂ ft) in height.

– *hirta* · Japanese Toad Lily
Whitish-mauve, purple-spotted
flowers, 75 cm (30 in). Late summer to autumn. O: Japan. A: use
this and the following type with
ferns and shade grasses.

– *macropoda*
Yellowish-white flowers with
light brownish or purple mar-
kins. Rather bell-shaped. 15 cm
(30 in), late summer to autumn.
O: Japan.

Trollius europaeus

Tricyrtis macropoda

Trollius · Globe Flower · Buttercup
Family (Ranunculaceae)
○ to ◑ ⚌ ⊥ ⊔ ✕ ○ Hi
The handsome globe flowers
make an excellent feature for any
natural or formal waterside garden. This is especially true of the
dwarf globe flower from the Himalayas and the equally attractive Chinese species and cultivars. These have a wilder look to
them than the more noble European species. They are included
at the end of the section since
they are later flowering. Globe
flowers are in bloom from the
end of April right through to August! They will tolerate a lot of
shade and with additional humus
and the occasional watering will
thrive even in a fairly dry site.
Globe flowers would be much
more common in the garden if
their long flowering time and
their ease of propagation by division in the spring were more
widely known.
I have listed the *Trollius* species
and cultivars by flowering time,
divided into three main groups. I
have not given a full description
of each separate form as they are

all very similar. The first and second flowering periods include
European plants, the third group
are from Japan and China. Home
of *Trollius europaeus* is meadows,
moorland, woodrows, limestone
valleys in mountains up to
3 000 m (9 750 ft). To the northern
tip of Scandinavia, much of central and western Europe,
throughout Carpathians to central south-east Europe and western Siberia. Also scattered
through the Apennines and
Pyrenees. Often grows wild with
*Ranunculus aconitifolius, Deschamp-
sia cespitosa, Potentilla aurea, Primula elatior, Crepis aurea, Orchis
maculata, Thalictrum aquilegifolium*.
Group three found in mountain
meadows of Asia. *Trollius pumilus*, the dwarf globe flower, is a
real treasure from the Himalayas.

1. Flowering time: end April

Trollius hybrid 'Earliest of All'
Small golden flowers, flowers
well a second time, 70 cm (2 ft
4 in).
– – 'Alabaster', a hybrid with pale
primrose flowers. Very distinctive. Lasts into summer.

*2. Flowering time:
end May, beginning June*

Trollius hybrid 'Goldquelle'
Beautifully rounded, orange-yellow flowers, another plant that
flowers a second time, 70 cm 2 ft
4 in).

– – 'Lemon Queen', beautiful,
closed, pale-lemon flowers; long-
flowering, 60 cm (2 ft).

*3. Flowering time:
from mid-June*

Trollius chinensis (syn. T. ledebouri)
Excellent, late-flowering wild
species, with open, orange flowers. Leaves appear well before
flowers and are extremely attractive. To almost 1 m (3 ft).
– – 'Golden Queen', cultivar of
T. chinensis. Leaves like golden
flames! Almost 100 cm (3 ft).

– *pumilus*
An excellent, rock-garden dwarf,
only 25 cm (10 in). Open yellow
flowers. Not immediately recog-
nisable as a globe flower at first
glance. O: Himalayas.

– *yunnanensis*
Latest flowering species, with
open, pale orange-yellow flowers. Leaves differ from *T. pumilus*
in being finely serrated. Up to
50 cm (20 in).

Typha, see Water plants p. 71

Uvularia · Bellwort, Merrybells ·
Lily Family (Liliaceae)
– *grandiflora*
◑ to ● ≈ Ƴ ♂ Hi
Looks like a large-flowered, yellow bellflower. This unusual
blue-green plant is extremely
hardy and will survive for tens of
years in a semi-shady position.
The full beauty of the plant
comes when it is well-esta-

blished. 30 to 60 cm (1 to 2 ft). End April/June. O: grows wild in woods of eastern Canada to Arkansas and Oklahoma. A: *Polemonium*, *Veronica armena*, *Iberis*, dwarf iris.

Veratrum · False Helleborine · Lily Family (Liliaceae)
○ to ☀ ≃ ⊥ ⊘ Hı
– *album* · White False Helleborine
A good substitute for the more attractive but difficult *V. californicum*. After seeding takes a few years to flower. Up to 2 m (6 ft). O: Finland, Norway, high European mountains (except for western Europe), Siberia, East Asia, also Alaska.
– *californicum*
A giant that grows to 180 cm (5½ to 6 ft). One of the best tall plants of the mountain valley. Must be allowed to establish itself thoroughly before it begins to flower. Too large for the small rock garden but in the larger garden individual plants make attractive eye-catchers. A curiously beautiful plant. This white *Veratrum* is the king of the false helleborines. For wild gardens use only with other mountain valley plants. Requires fairly rich soil. O: high meadows from Washington to California, New Mexico.
– *nigrum* · Black False Helleborine
Undoubtedly the best European false helleborine. Will survive for decades in a moderately good position, but produces its 1 to 1.5 m (3 to 4½ ft) flower spikes less freely. Curious shoots which have the appearance of palm leaves as they emerge from the soil. O: mountain meadows, woodland clearings, up to 1600 m (5400 ft). A rare plant but with quite a wide distribution. Central and southern Europe, East Asia.

Verbascum · Mullein · Figwort Family (Scrophulariaceae)
○ to ○○○ ⊕ ⊥ Υ ○ ⊘ Hı
There are perennial and biennial mulleins, beautiful and less beautiful, but none which are really unattractive in maturity. Perfect for the rock garden since they tolerate difficult, extremely dry positions, as do gorse or blue-green grasses. Great advances have been made with hybrids, derived usually from *V. nigrum* and *V. phoeniceum*.
All bloom from around mid-June until well into July, then again into autumn. In heat many types soon look tired but on a peaceful early morning mature bushes have an unbelievable beauty in the herbaceous bed, or better still in a rock or wild garden.

Verbascum hybrid 'Cotswold Queen'
An amber-coloured mullein with bronze markings and deep mauve anthers. A plant which takes several years to develop to its full beauty. Will tolerate replanting in full bud. 1.3 m (4 ft), June/July. A: delphinium, *Eryngium* species.
– – 'Hartleyi'
Biscuit to yellow mullein flushed with deep red which forms 1.3 m (4 ft) bushes.
– *densiflorum*
Indestructible species with pure yellow flowers with reddish anthers, like the cultivar above. Unfortunately only biennial. 60 cm (2 ft) tall. O: Europe from southern Sweden to European Soviet Union, Caucasus, northwest Africa.
– *olympicum*
This yellow mullein is most imposing and should feature in every rock or wild garden! By trimming flowers after fading I myself have kept a plant in a terrace wall for three years. In many gardens these plants seed themselves regularly, appearing in every spot imaginable. O: Asia Minor.
– *pyramidatum*
This truly hardy plant grows to 1.5 m (4 ft), beautifying half the summer with its bright yellow flowers before producing shorter flower stems again in September. The best of all hardy mulleins! For natural or wild gardens. O: Crimea.
– hybrid 'Letitia'.
The best of all for a rock garden, this dwarf mullein reaches only 25 cm (10 in). Its leaves are softly woolly and the flowers bright yellow.

Veronica · Speedwell · Figwort Family (Scrophulariaceae)
Decades ago, even before the introduction of the main garden varieties, the name Veronica had a magical sound. Now the speedwell, in blue or deep mauve, has become a real treasure of the early and late months of the year, a treasure whose best characteristic is to provide a blue element for dry positions.
Progress in cultivation has brought astonishing results. Wild species have been made to bring forth glowing blues which no one could have imagined. And there are still new blues to be achieved!
In my list I have omitted many less interesting or old-fashioned speedwells, to concentrate only on those best for the rock-garden.

1. Flowering time: mid April to May

Veronica armena
○○ ‖ ⊟ ○ Hı
An indestructible plant, semi-evergreen, with "mossy" foliage. Its gentian-blue flowers are delightful in the morning light,

when it catches every eye, before fading in the warm afternoon sun. This small plant (around 6 cm, 2½ in) will outlive its planter! O: mountains of Asia Minor and Armenia. This species is one which will go very satisfactorily with many other plants in the rock garden.

– – 'Rosea'
Pink form of the above.

2. Flowering time: early May to early June

– gentianoides
O to ☀ ≃ Υ ○ ⚲ Hı
This evergreen species flowers in May, or even by the end of April, with erect spikes of pale blue flowers to 40 cm (16 in). Needs slightly moist soil. O: Crimea, Caucasus, south-west Asia. A: in front of dark dwarf conifers.

– prostrata
O to OO ‖ ▭ ⋙ Υ ○ Hı
One is repeatedly surprised by the vitality and luxuriance of well established plants, which are as suitable for the garden as their cultivars. O of type: southern and central Europe, southeast Europe, Italy, Caucasus, western Siberia in dry, sunny heathland. Up to 1400 m (4200 ft). A: plant around bulbs.
– – 'Alba'
Forms a good, white-flowered carpet. Excellent with the similar carpeting varieties which follow. Allow time for carpets to develop.
– – 'Blue Sheen', clear blue.
– – 'Loddon Blue', deep blue.
– – 'Mrs Holt', pink.
– – 'Spode Blue', pale porcelain-blue.

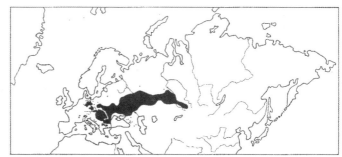

Veronica prostrata

3. Flowering time: end May and well into June

– austriaca ssp. teucrium · Large Speedwell
O to OO ⫾ Υ ○ Hı
20 to 40 cm (8 to 16 in) tall with flowers from light to deep blue. O: Spain, Alps, Balkans, central Europe, Caucasus, even to western Siberia.
– – – – 'Cratur Lake Blue', a longer flowering improvement on the next form, but must have sun. Sometimes requires support, but its colour is irresistible!
– – – – 'Sirley Blue', up to 40 cm (16 in) in maturity, an erect plant when fully established.
– – cinerea
A valuable carpeter with evergreen, silvery leaves. Spikes of pale-blue flowers to 15 cm (6 in).
– fruticans (syn. V. saxatilis) · Rock Speedwell
O to OO ≃ ▭ ⋙ ○ ≢ Hı

Veronica austriaca ssp. *teucrium*

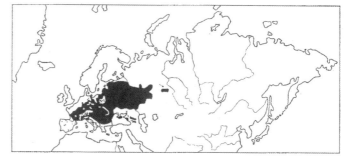

An extremely flat, evergreen carpeter which flowers in mid-May, ie two weeks ahead of the type below. The flowers are deep blue with reddish centres. Likes good soil. O: widespread in Europe, from northern Spain to north-west Soviet Union, also Corsica and central Yugoslavia.
– fruticulosa · Shrubby-Stalked Speedwell
O to OO ≃ ⌒ ○ ≢ Hı
A rather woody plant which forms cushions 20 cm (8 in) tall and produces pale blue flowers. This sturdy speedwell will, however, need replanting or an addition of fresh soil every few years if it is to continue to flower well. O: high mountains of western and southern Central Europe, from the Vosges and Sierra Nevada to north-west Yugoslavia. Mountain to alpine levels, ie up to 3000 m (10,000 ft). Poor grassland and rocks.

4. Flowering time:
end June to July and beyond

Veronica longifolia · Long-Leaved
Speedwell
H1
This summer-flowering speedwell is the largest of the European species which have been
developed for garden use. Lilac-
blue or white, 70 to 100 cm (2 ft
4 in to 3 ft). O: eastern and central
Europe, south-east to Bulgaria
and east to East Asia.
– – 'Alba'
A most luxuriant *V. longifolia*.
Same comments as for 'Foerster's
Blue'. Extremely beautiful as
flowers fade. The luxuriance and
form of the slender, graceful
flower stems is far superior to
the old *Veronica longifolia*. A: *Potentilla recta* 'Warrenii', *Veronica
longifolia* 'Foerster's Blue', grasses.
– – 'Foerster's Blue'
An improved dark blue colour,
rounded form, quick-growing to
around 1 m (3 ft). Free from virus
diseases and the familiar suscep-
tibility of the upper shoots to
greenfly. *Veronica spicata* looks
delightfully frail alongside this
plant.
– *spicata* ssp. *incana* · Silver Spiked
Speedwell
○ to ○○○ ☐ Υ ♂ H1
Deep blue flowers on stems
around a foot tall. I have border
plants that are still beautiful after
ten years. This speedwell is another sturdy little treasure,
whose true song has yet to be
sung. O: southern Soviet Union
to Mongolia and Japan. A: *Geum,
Sedum, Erodium*.
– – ssp. *spicata*
Another mauve summer speedwell, 30 to 40 cm (12 to 16 in) tall.
O: Europe, north to borders of
Scandinavia, east to East Asia,
west to England, also in Asia Minor and Caucasus.
– – – – 'Alba'
White variety.
– – – – 'Barcarolle'
Rose-pink, an extremely versatile colour which contrasts with
its very dark green leaves.

– – – – 'Red Fox'
The best *V. spicata* cultivar to
date. Foot-high, deep red speedwell which will flower again after
pruning. A: blue and white *Campanula carpatica*.
A word of warning against:
V. repens, unreliable and *V. filifor-
mis* dangerous.

Vinca · Periwinkle · Dogbane Family (Apocynaceae)
☀ to ● ⊕ ≃ ☐ ⋙ ∥ Υ ♂ H1
From 20 to 30 cm (8 to 12 in). End
April/May.
– *minor* · Lesser Periwinkle
Like the violet, the periwinkle
prefers shade, although both will
tolerate sun providing the periwinkle has moist soil. Will often
colonize quickly to form thickets, but in continued drought
will droop, even in shade, to take
on an almost menacing appearance. Will soon recover however
and can continue in the same
spot for thirty years forming ever
larger thickets. Remarkably many
small plants thrive in a bed of
periwinkle, *Epimedium* for one.
Ferns and grasses also look excellent with it. In a really cold
winter the plant loses its attractiveness and it is best cut back in
autumn in cold areas. Bluish-
mauve flowers in April/May. O:
fringes of woods, water-mea-
dows, heathland throughout central and western Europe, southern Europe to Asia Minor and
Caucasus. The same northerly
and easterly distribution as the
beech. A: sturdy *Epimedium* species, white and pink *Scilla hispanica*.

– – 'Alba'
An extremely attractive white

form, excellent with the above
and the variety below.
– – 'Atropurpurea'
Single, reddish-mauve flowers.
– – 'Bowles Variety'
Profuse, large, deep blue flowers.
– – 'Multiplex'
Extremely attractive erect, long-
stemmed, double flowers in red-
dish-mauve.

Viola · Violet · Violet Family (Viol-
aceae)
There are early-spring, spring
and even summer violets whose
flowers can continue well into
autumn, or violets which flower
again after a long intermission
and even everlasting violets—
many are scented, some have no
scent; colours from white, red,
yellow, mauve, purple, pink and
blue; single or double; short or
long-stemmed. The scented
spring violet likes sun and light;
the horned pansy and *Viola gracilis* in a sunny, continental climate should normally be given a
light position out of intense sunlight or with slight shade; if the
soil is kept extremely moist they
will also tolerate full sun. *Viola
gracilis* tolerates slightly more
sun and heat than *Viola cornuta* as
well as the occasional dry spell.
In cooler, damper climates both
should be in full sun. Do not
plant large groups of violets
close together, but in well-
spaced small groups, particularly
the scented spring violet! This
will tolerate heavy shade but
prefers full sun or slight shade.
The soil should not be too light
and barren if it is allowed to become dry. Nevertheless the
scented violet is extremely
adaptable. Large, close-planted
groups will stop flowering after
five years, whereas with correct
spacing they will flower for at
least twenty years before they
need replanting.
The more difficult forms have
obviously been omitted here.
Those listed both usefully extend the flowering time of the
scented violet, as well as being

excellent in their own right. Warm parts of the rock garden, such as south-facing walls help extend the flowering time, for they will flower here a good week and a half earlier—in shade much later. But in a warm climate cooler parts of the rock garden out of the sun are better for the horned pansy.

Again with horned pansies, they should not be planted too close together, nor too close to other smaller plants, for they produce a mass of shoots which spread over all around them.

The following list of violets is arranged by flowering time rather than alphabetically.

Viola odorata · Sweet Violet
○ to ◑ ⊕ ≃ □ ⋙ Ⴘ ✗ ○ ⴡ F Hı

The familiar scented violet of spring, which has unfortunately been rather neglected in recent years. It is time we remembered this treasure for the garden and especially for cut flowers. Violet-blue, March/April, usually reflowering in autumn. O: widespread throughout Europe, west to the Atlantic coast, north to Scotland, southern England, Scandinavia, south to northern Sicily. Also in North Africa (Atlas Mountains) and from Lebanon to the Caucasus.

– – 'Augusta'
Earliest-flowering cultivar, up to ten days before those below. Plant where it will catch the sun! While *Viola odorata* 'The Czar' or 'Triumph' are still in bud, the perfume of 'Augusta' greets us from many a warm corner.

– – 'The Czar'
Flowers March/April and September/October! In the argument over the relative merits of the 'Czar' and 'Triumph', 'The Czar' always came out on top for its superior flowers, quite apart from its second flowering period. If the argument had concerned the suitability of both for the garden, both would have had to be recognised as irreplaceable. The autumn flowers of 'The Czar' can be profuse enough to be visible from a good distance. In autumn its perfume has a slightly fruity overtone. Flowers are deep violet. Completely hardy.

– – 'Triumph'
A new treasure among the scented violets, the strongest of all the forms with darker, long-stemmed flowers.

All gardens would profit from lots of these scented violets. In the rock garden they will tolerate a dry position near shrubs, where weaker varieties would not long survive. In a wild garden they should be scattered over a carpet of grasses and ferns. Excellent with early and late crocuses in autumn.

When these three named cultivars have finished flowering, we have the even more beautiful perfume of the late scented violets to look forward to. These have large flowers, rounded like Parma violets, darker in colour and double. Their delightful perfume surpasses that of all other violets. To distinguish between these winter-hardy varieties I have given them the following names:

– – 'Tardiflora Plena'
Double violets have been known for 2000 years, and have been a garden plant for 300 years. A: long-stemmed primroses and auriculas.
Scented violets in red, white and yellow are little known.

– – 'Alba Grandiflora'
Large-blossomed, pure white, scented violet.

– – 'Coeur d'Alsace'
Red.

– – 'Sulphurea'
Apricot-yellow.

– *gracilis* · Olympian Violet
○ ≃ ‖ Ⴘ ✗ Hı

This early, velvet-lilac violet has been crossed with *V. cornuta* to produce two excellent garden hybrids which are markedly more resilient than the parent species and which make excellent rock-garden plants in a moist, not over-warm position. O: Balkans, Asia Minor. A: early-spring flowers, spring flowers, early-summer flowers, *Epimedium × youngianum* 'Niveum', *Saxifraga × elizabethae*, *Saxifraga haagii*, all mossy saxifrages which tolerate sun. Longest-flowering of all the violets!

Viola gracilis hybrids 'Major'
Deep purple flowers.

– – – 'Moonlight'
An unusual pale yellow form.

– *canina* · Heath Dog Violet
Blue flowers from end April to May, which continue the blue of the scented violets. Unfortunately this one is unscented. O: poor grassland, thickets, heath and moorland, light woods, on sand, loam or peat soil. Throughout Eurasia, in Greenland, Iceland, Britain, Siberia, Kashmir, Japan; south through Europe to northern Mediterranean.

– *biflora* · Yellow Wood Violet
☀ to ● ≘ ‖ Ⴘ ⊔ Hı

This yellow mountain violet is a great delight. Its charming little flowers above fresh green leaves tempt us to plant ever more of them. In the garden they require the same conditions as in the wild, ie a moist, shady site with porous humus soil. Under 15 cm (6 in), May/June. O: northern Europe, northern Asia, mountains of central and southern Europe, western United States.

– *cornuta* · Horned Pansy
○ ≃ ⸨ ‖ Ⴘ ✗ Hı

The wild form is inferior to the garden varieties in beauty, growth and resilience, being

taller and more rangy with smaller flowers.
The very long flowering time from May to October makes a little care over the choice of the right position worthwhile. O: Pyrenees and some parts of Europe. A: *Iris graminea, Eryngium alpinum,* small geraniums.

Garden varieties

Viola cornuta hybrid 'Alba'
A white form in flower from May/September. Although long flowering, its flowers are considerably smaller than those of the other hybrids.

– – – 'Boughton Blue'
Resembles a velvety blue garden pansy, moderate-sized flowers from April to November year after year in the same spot, but has yellow variegated leaves. Rather blotchy in appearance in spring but beautiful in summer with its covering of blue flowers. Propagation by division in spring.

– – – 'Minor'
Low variety of deep blue.

– – – 'W. H. Woodgate'
Large, mauve flowers, twice as tall as the previous variety.

– *labradorica.*
A completely prostrate plant to only 10 cm (4 in) tall with small, dark violet flowers. The form most commonly grown is 'Purpurea' with deep purple flushed leaves.

– *sororia* (syn. V. papilionacea)
☼ to ● ≃ ▭ Y ⤫ ⬡ H1
A charming, long-stemmed, scentless violet from North America, extremely long-living and undemanding even in an unpropitious site. The violet blue of its flowers is unlike any other violet. Tuberous root stock. O: North America. A: *Epimedium* species, small shade grasses and ferns.

– – 'Albiflora'
A profusely flowering, white variety, large flowers, self-seeding. Scentless like the type plant.

Vitaliana primuliflora (syn. Douglasia vitaliana) · Primrose Family (Primulaceae)
○ to ☼ ⊕ △ ‖ ⛁ ♁ ⋕ H1
A little jewel that forms thick, flat, golden mats from end April to May. 5 cm (2 in). Not a plant for beginners; requires additional soil from time to time. O: Alps, Abruzzi to Pyrenees, from 2000 to 3000 m (6000 to 9000 ft). Grows wild with: slow-growing sempervivum species and hybrids, encrusted saxifrages and *Androsace.*

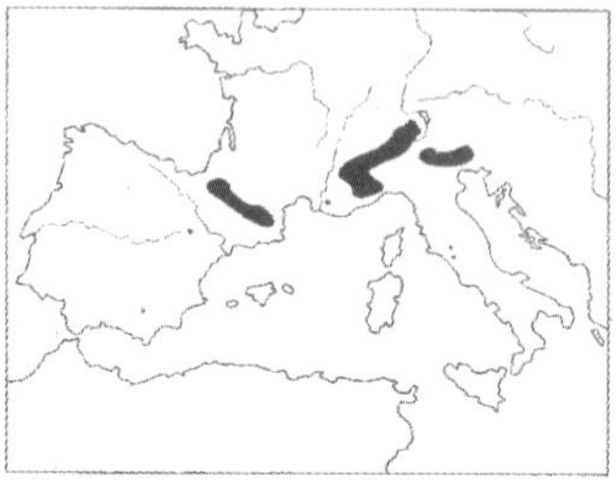

Waldsteinia · Barren Strawberry Rose Family (Rosaceae)
◐ to ● ▭ ‖ Y ♁ ⋕ H1

– *geoides*
An extremely robust green carpeter. Excellent for filling any gaps. Yellow, strawberry-like flowers in April/May. Thrives in shade and also resists incursion of roots, both of which make it good for beneath trees. 15 cm (6 in). O: Thickets from eastern Central Europe to southern Bulgaria and western Ukraine. A: *Hepatica, Adonis amurensis,* lungworts, *Brunnera macrophylla* and other early spring plants.

– *ternata* (syn. W. sibirica) Waldsteinia
After years in the garden this ground-coverer with its glossy, green, leathery leaves still looks beautiful. Unlike *W. geoides* it forms overground runners. Only 7.5 cm (3 in), April/May. O: from south-east Austria and north-west Yugoslavia to Siberia, Sakhalin and Japan. A: as for *W. geoides.*

Wulfenia · Figwort Family (Scrophulariaceae)
☼ to ◐ ≃ △ ‖ ⛁ H1

– *carinthiaca*
Flowering in July, the wulfenias continue the flowering time of ramonda, to which this plant is similar in appearance and in its preference for shade. Though similar in colour, the mauve flowers of wulfenia are different in form with spikes of small flowers on erect stems around 20 to 30 cm (8 to 12 in) tall. July/August. O: damp, shady places along the upper tree-line between 1000 and 2000 m (3000 and 6000 ft) in the eastern Alps and Montenegro. Grows wild with *Viola biflora* and alpine roses *(Rhododendron ferrugineum).*

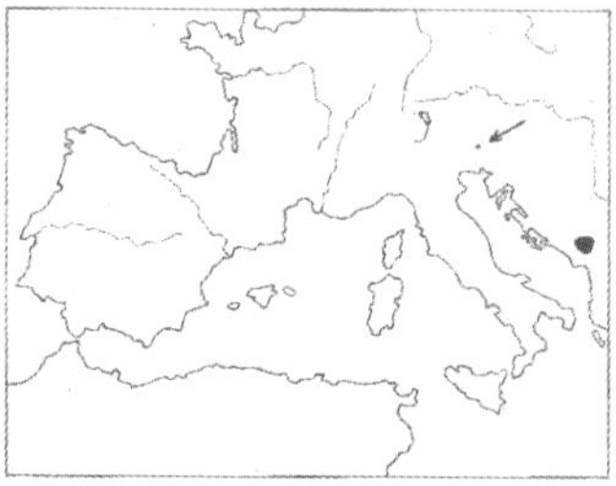

Yucca · Adam's Needle · Agave Family (Agavaceae)
○○ to ○○○ ⊕ ⊥ Y ⤫ ♁ ⋕ H2

– *filamentosa* · Thread Agave
The best plants grow to 1.6 to 2.0 m (5 to 6 ft) with their whitish-green, whitish-yellow or snow-white flowers. From a blue-green, 1 m (3 ft) high crown of thick, evergreen leaves rise branching stems supporting large, hanging bell-shaped flowers in June. It is amazing that this strange plant from the Florida area should be completely hardy in Europe. In cold areas the crown requires some protection in the first year after planting. In the course of thirty years I found that my plants suffered in only three winters, and even after the harsh Swiss winter of 1928/29 they blossomed successfully. But this plant is always quick to recover.

Even in the crown stage before flowering the plant is extremely decorative. The few difficult plants which are liable to suffer in a harsh winters have been excluded from my list. Suggestions for the uses of *Yucca*, and the plants with which they can be combined are included in the section on "Hardy succulents and other hardy exotic plants". But the formal rock garden also offers opportunities to use them to great decorative effect, to contrast with delphiniums, for example. Propagation is best carried out in pots, which eventually become so thickly enmeshed with roots, that they can be sold as green crowns of leaves firmly rooted in soil.

Only from a photograph can one fully appreciate the characteristics of this exotic plant. In maturity the crowns of leaves become more and more monumental and will tolerate excessive drought, as do all succulents, among which we can include many sedums and all the sempervivums.

– *flaccida*
Rather like *Y. filamentosa* but with softer leaves which have straight marginal threads. (They are curly in *Y. filamentosa*).

– *glauca*
Forms clumps of narrower leaves to 60 cm (2 ft) long. Flowers cream.

– *gloriosa* · Spanish Dagger · Palm lily
Very statuesque for a sunny spot, surprisingly effective in a group in a wild garden. Can reach 2 m (6½ ft) in height.

Zauschneria · Californian Fuchsia · Evening Primrose Family (Onagraceae)
H2
Brilliantly coloured late summer flowers make these valuable plants for any garden. Use in a well drained, sunny site and give some winter protection in cold areas.

– *californica*
Spikes of scarlet tubular flowers to 30 cm (1 ft) high from August onwards. They are enhanced by grey downy foliage. O: California.

– *cana*
Smaller and greyer in foliage. O: California.

Bibliography

Bailey, L. H.: Cyclopedia of Horticulture, New York, 1927

Bailey, L. H.: Manual of Cultivated Plants, New York 1954

Berg, J. und Krüssmann, G.: Freiland-Rhododendron, Stuttgart 1951

Boom, B. K. und Ruys, J. D.: Flora der Gekweekte, Kruidachtige Gewassen, Wageningen 1950

Carl, J.: Miniaturgärten in Trögen, Schalen und Balkonkästen, Stuttgart 1978

Correvon, H.: Rock Garden and Alpine Plants, New York 1930

Dieck, G.: Die Moor- und Alpenpflanzen des Alpengartens Zöschen bei Merseburg, Halle (Saale) 1899

Eiselt, G./Schröder, R.: Laubgehölze, Leipzig · Radebeul 1977

Eiselt, G./Schröder, R.: Nadelgehölze, Leipzig · Radebeul 1976

Encke, F./Buchheim, G. und Seybold, S.: Zander, Handwörterbuch der Pflanzennamen, Stuttgart 1979

Farrer, R.: The English Rock Garden, London 1919

Foerster, K.: Blauer Schatz der Gärten, Radebeul und Berlin 1953

Foerster, K.: Einzug der Gräser und Farne in die Gärten, Leipzig · Radebeul 1978

Foerster, K.: Lebende Gartentabellen, Berlin 1940

Foerster, K.: Neuer Glanz des Gartenjahres, Radebeul und Berlin 1970

Grunert, Ch.: Gartenblumen von A bis Z, Radebeul und Berlin 1964

Hansen, R.: Namen der Stauden, Stuttgart 1972

Hegi, G.: Illustrierte Flora von Mitteleuropa, München 1965

Jelitto, L./Schacht, W.: Die Freilandschmuckstauden, Band 1 und 2, Stuttgart 1963

Jelitto, C. R.: Schöne Steingärten für wenig Geld, Frankfurt (Oder) 1930

Köhlein, F.: Freilandsukkulenten, Stuttgart 1977

Krüssmann, G.: Rhododendron, andere immergrüne Laubgehölze und Koniferen, Hamburg und Berlin 1968

Mathew, B.: Dwarf Bulbs, London 1973

Müssel, H.: Bunte Welt der Gartenstauden, Stuttgart 1979

Müssel, H.: Sempervivum und Jovibarba, Freising 1977

Mütze, W.: Stauden, Nordhausen a. Harz 1936

Ohwi, Jisaburo: Flora of Japan, Washington, DC 1965

Pareys Blumengärtnerei, Band 1, Berlin und Hamburg 1953

Rothmaler, W.: Exkursionsflora (Kritischer Band), Berlin 1976

Schacht, W.: Blumen Europas, Hamburg und Berlin 1976

Schacht, W.: Der Steingarten, Stuttgart 1968

Schroeter, C.: Das Pflanzenleben der Alpen, Zürich 1926

Schubert, R./Wagner, G.: Pflanzennamen und botanische Fachwörter, Radebeul und Berlin 1975

Seyffert, W.: Stauden · Für Natur- und Steingärten, Berlin 1965

Seyffert, W.: Stauden · Vorkommen · Verwendung, Berlin 1964

Synge, Patrick M.: Gartenfreude durch Blumenzwiebeln, Radebeul und Berlin 1966

Wocke, E.: Die Kulturpraxis der Alpenpflanzen, Berlin 1940

Acknowledgements of photographs, distribution-maps and plant drawings

Colour photographs

Johannes Apel, Baden-Baden: S.137 96 (1); (3)

Michael Barthel, Sayda: S.45 (2)

Fritz Dölling, Berlin: S.225; 232 (1); 233 (1 to 3 and 5); 236

Bernhard Einert, Dresden: S.96 (2); 132 (4); 229 (2); 273 (1 to 4); 280 (4)

Axel Grambow, Berlin: S.33 (2); 37 (1); 40 (3); 41 (1); 44 (4); 46 (4); 96 (4)

Fritz Köhlein, Bindlach: S.45 (1); 88 (2); 89; 93 (1 to 4); 177 (1)

Fred-Walter Könecke, Stendal: S.38 (3); 144 (1); 180 (2); 181 (1)

Gerd Leuteritz, Radebeul: S.36 (4)

Dr. Hermann Manitz, Jena: S.84 (4)

Herbert Neumann, Potsdam-Rehbrücke: S. 33 (3); 46 (1); 277

Günter Pätzold, Wurzen: S.42 (4); 284 (1)

Johannes Prescher, Steina: S.42 (3 and 5); 44 (2); 281 (1 and 2); 284 (3)

Jürgen Röth, Halle: S.46 (3); 189 (2); 229 (1)

Karl Sauer, Marquardt: S.140 (1)

Dieter Schacht, München: S.39 (2); 133 (1); 184 (2 and 3)

Wilhelm Schacht, Frasdorf: S. 33 (1); 42 (1); 43 (1); 48 (1); 93 (5); 140 (3 and 4); 184 (1); 281 (3); 285 (1); 288

Erwin Schmidt, Wetzlar: S. 48 (2); 136 (3); 137 (2); 184 (4 and 5); 185 (1 and 2); 237 (1 to 3)

Arnold Schulze, Werder: S. 34 (4); 41 (2); 280 (2 and 3); 284 (2)

Christel Schwalbe, Neukieritzsch: S. 35 (3 to 5); 36 (1); 38 (2 and 4); 39 (3); 40 (1 and 2); 43 (2); 44 (1); 48 (5); 92 (1)

Hans Seibold, Hannover: S. 35 (1 and 2); 39 (1); 133 (3); 137 (1); 140 (2); 240; 285 (2)

Sebastian Seidl, München: S. 34 (3); 42 (2); 43 (4); 88 (1); 133 (2); 177 (2); 280 (1)

Wolfgang Sommer, Leipzig: S. 43 (3); 44 (3)

Sigrid Stiel, Erfurt: S. 92 (3 and 4); 129 (2); 132 (3); 136 (2); 192 (3)

Reinhard Suckow, Vitte: S.45 (4); 47; 48 (3 and 4); 233 (4)

VEB Erfurter Blumensamen, Erfurt: S.34 (2); 41 (3); 81; 84 (1 and 2); 129 (1); 188 (1 to 4); 189 (1); 192 (4); 228 (2); 232 (2 and 3)

Alfred Weinreich, Wolmirstedt: S.84 (3); 85 (2); 92 (2); 132 (2); 136 (1); 141 (1 and 2); 180 (1); 181 (2 to 4); 228 (1); 229 (3)

Kurt Zierold, Rodewisch: S. 34 (1); 36 (2 and 3); 37 (2 and 3); 38 (1); 45 (3); 46 (2); 85 (1 and 3); 96 (3); 132 (1); 144 (2 und 3); 192 (1 and 2); 276 (1 and 2); 281 (4)

Black-and-white photographs

Fritz Dölling, Berlin: S. 130 (2); 131 (1 and 2); 231; 234 (4); 239 (1); 274 (1); 275 (2)

Karl Foerster (Archiv), Potsdam-Bornim: S. 87 (1, 3 and 4); 90 (2 and 3); 94 (2 and 4); 95 (1, 2 and 4); 130 (1); 134 (2); 139 (2); 142 (1); 178 (1 and 3); 179 (1, 2 and 4); 183 (4); 186 (1 and 2); 187 (4); 226 (5); 230 (1 and 3); 239 (2 and 3); 274 (2); 278 (1 to 3); 279 (1 and 2); 283 (3); 286 (1); 287 (2)

Hermann Göritz, Potsdam-Bornim: S. 227

Kurt Herschel, Leipzig-Holzhausen: S. 82 (1); 83 (2 and 3); 86 (1 to 3); 87 (2); 130 (3); 131 (3 and 4); 134 (3); 135 (1); 138 (1 and 3); 139 (1); 182; 187 (2); 190 (1 to 4); 191 (1 to 3); 226 (1, 2, 3 and 4); 230 (2); 234 (1 to 3); 235; 238 (1 to 3); 282 (1 to 4); 286 (2)

C. R. Jelitto, Berlin-Dahlem: S. 82 (3); 83 (4); 91 (2); 95 (3); 134 (1); 142 (2); 143 (3); 183 (1); 283 (1 and 2)

Adelheid Müller, Berlin: S. 82 (2); 91 (1); 135 (2); 183 (2)

Karl Plomin, Hamburg: S. 287 (2)

Wilhelm Schacht, Frasdorf: S. 130 (4); 138 (2); 179 (3); 187 (1)

A. E. Sigl, Berlin: S. 94 (3); 143 (1 and 2); 178 (2); 183 (3); 187 (3); 275 (1); 278 (4); 286 (3)

Gretl Stölzle, Kempten: S. 94 (1)

C. G. van Tubergen, Haarlem: S. 90 (1)

Distribution-maps

We gratefully thank the publisher VEB Gustav Fischer Verlag Jena and the authors Dr. Hermann Meusel, Professor em. of botany, Martin-Luther-University, Halle – Wittenberg, Dr. Eckehart Jäger, Dr. Stephan Rauschert and Dr. Erich Weinert of the Sektion Biowissenschaften, Martin-Luther-Universität Halle – Wittenberg for permission to reproduce the distribution-maps of the title: "Vergleichende Chorologie der zentraleuropäischen Flora" for this book. The distribution-maps of *Acaena microphylla, Acanthus spinosus, Achillea umbellata, Arnebia pulchra, Asperula nitida, Campannula garganica, Campannula portenschlagiana, Ceratostigma plumbaginoides, Cimicifuga acerina, Dicentra eximia, Gentiana farreri, Gentiana sino-ornata, Haberlea rhodopensis, Iberis saxatilis, Jovibarba heuffeli var. reginae-amaliae, Leontopodium alpinum, Lewisia cotyledon, Mertensia virginica, Oenothera missouriensis, Petasites fragans, Platycodon grandiflorus, Polygonatum commutatum, Primula sieboldii, Ramonda myconi, Sedum selskianum, Sedum sieboldii, Stachys byzantina, Tiarella cordifolia, Tricyrtis macropoda, Uvularia grandiflora, Veronica armena, Yucca filamentosa* are taken from the sixth edition of "Der Steingarten der sieben Jahreszeiten" by Karl Foerster with some alterations by the editor.

Index of plants